船海書局
SHIPS AND OCEAN PRESS

国际豪华邮轮先进制造技术丛书

女王铸成之路：
"玛丽女王2号"建造实录

[英]史蒂芬·佩恩（Stephen Payne）著

陈大为 译 吕智勇 主审

主编单位

中船邮轮科技发展有限公司

参编单位

上海船舶工艺研究所

中国船级社上海规范研究所

中国船舶工业综合技术经济研究院

上海研途船舶海事技术有限公司

哈尔滨工程大学出版社
Harbin Engineering University Press

黑版贸审字08-2020-100号

Originally published in English by Haynes Publishing under the title:The RMS Queen Mary 2 Owners' Workshop manual written by Stephen Payne© Stephen Payne 2013.

图书在版编目 (CIP) 数据

女王铸成之路："玛丽女王 2 号"建造实录 / (英) 史蒂芬·佩恩著；陈大为译．
－－ 哈尔滨：哈尔滨工程大学出版社，2020.7
ISBN 978-7-5661-2524-8

Ⅰ．①女… Ⅱ．①史… ②陈… Ⅲ．①旅游船 – 船舶设计 – 概况 – 英国 Ⅳ．① U674.110.2

中国版本图书馆 CIP 数据核字 (2020) 第 124041 号

选题策划　王　露
责任编辑　史大伟
封面设计　高新锋

女王铸成之路："玛丽女王2号"建造实录

出版发行:哈尔滨工程大学出版社
邮政编码: 150001
传真: 0451-82519699
印刷:武汉精一佳印刷有限公司
印张: 24.75
版次: 2020 年 7 月第 1 版
定价: 248.00 元
电子邮箱: heupress@hrbeu.edu.cn

地址:哈尔滨市南岗区南通大街 145 号
电话: 0451-82519989
经销:全国新华书店
开本: 889 mm×1 194 mm　1/16
字数: 390 千字
印次: 2020 年 7 月第 1 次印刷
网址: http://www.hrbeupress.com

出品:船海书局
网址: www.ship-press.com
告读者：如发现本书有印装质量问题请与船海书局发行部联系。
服务热线: 4008670886

Foreword 序

by HRH The Prince Philip, Duke of Edinburgh
爱丁堡公爵菲利普亲王作序

白金汉宫

The age of the engine-powered ocean liner was relatively short, but its technical development was nothing short of phenomenal. The earliest engine-powered passenger ships were fairly primitive, but within little more than a hundred years their size and sophistication had developed dramatically.

Queen Mary 2 is the last in the line of the Atlantic Ocean passenger liners and,as this fascinating book makes clear, by far the most technically developed. It must be quite a challenge to design and build a skyscraper, but it cannot compare with the complication of creating such a monster ship capable of coping with the conditions on the North Atlantic in all weathers at speeds of up to 30 knots.

This splendid book tells the whole story in intriguing detail. Stephen Payne and his colleagues deserve the highest praise for their achievement, and Iam sure that everyone intersted in ships and the sea will welcome this magnificent publication.

由主机驱动的远洋班轮时代虽然相对短暂，但其技术发展过程却非同寻常。早期的机动客轮还相当粗糙落后，不过历经一百余年发展，远洋班轮在尺度和技术复杂性方面都取得了巨大的进步。

作为大西洋航线班轮的最新成员，如书中所言，"玛丽女王 2 号"更是一艘当今技术最先进的班轮。众所周知，设计和建造摩天大厦是一项巨大的挑战。但是，这些挑战都远远不能与创造一个无惧任何天气，可以以 30 kn 航速航行在北大西洋上的庞然大物的困难相比。

"玛丽女王 2 号"的众多精彩故事都将在本书中娓娓道来。史蒂芬·佩恩博士和他的同事们取得的伟大成就值得高度褒奖，而且我深信每位对船舶和海洋感兴趣的人士，定将对此书爱不释手。

Acknowledgements 致谢

In the preparation of this book, many people have been gracious in assisting with information, illustrations, advice and encouragement.

I owe a great debt to Jonathan Falconer, Senior Commissioning Editor at Haynes Publishing, for initially agreeing to my proposal for the book and latterly for his patience as I juggled various commitments and deadlines became somewhat extended.

At Cunard, my good friend Michael Gallagher, Cunard Line Public Relations Manager and Historian, has been an invaluable source of information and illustrations. Michael has been with Cunard for many years and he is probably the most knowledgeable person of the company's history. He is without doubt Queen Elizabeth 2's greatest fan, but nonetheless, he is very complimentary about Queen Mary 2.

Gordon Bauwens and Captain Stephen J. Card are two very talented marine artists whom I am fortunate to count among my friends. Both were commissioned to supply original artworks for the ship. Gordon is a native of Glasgow and regularly cycled the 30-mile round trip to Clydebank to watch Queen Elizabeth 2 take shape. Trained as a technical graphics designer, Gordon eventually decided to take up marine painting. He has produced many fine paintings, most of which are available as limited edition prints. Gordon was

在本书的编写过程中，众多热心的业界资深人士在信息、插图和建议等方面给了我很大的帮助和鼓励。

其中，特别感谢的是海恩斯出版社的资深编辑乔纳森·福尔克纳先生。他从一开始就极力支持我编写本书，并以极大的耐性容忍由于本人原因而造成的本书交稿时间一次次的拖期和延误。

我的挚交好友迈克尔·格拉赫——冠达邮轮公司的公共关系经理和历史学家，为我提供了宝贵的信息和插图。迈克尔在冠达邮轮公司服务多年，甚至可能是该公司历史上最博学的人。毫无疑问的是，他是"伊丽莎白女王 2 号"最忠诚的粉丝，同样的，他也非常喜欢"玛丽女王 2 号"。

戈登·博旺和史蒂芬·J.卡特船长是两位杰出的海事艺术家，我很荣幸他们能够出现在我的朋友名单之中。他们都被委托进行船舶的艺术设计创意。戈登是一位格拉斯哥人，经常骑行 30 英里①往返克莱德班克，去观摩"伊丽莎白女王 2 号"的建造过程。作为一名绘图设计师，戈登最终选择了海事类的绘图创作工作。他曾创作过很多优秀的作品，其中大部分都是限量版印刷品。受冠达邮轮公司

① 1 英里 =1.6 千米

commissioned by Cunard to produce the first public illustration of Queen Mary 2. After this painting was released it was decided to install two gas turbines into the ship, which required a large deckhouse at the base of the funnel that had the effect of rather foreshortening the funnel. Despite this, the painting was a very accurate representation of what the ship would eventually look like. A number of Gordon's paintings are displayed on board the ship including 'Cunard Queens' commemorating the first tandem crossing from New York to Southampton of Queen Mary 2 in company with Queen Elizabeth 2 in April 2004, and 'Queen Mary' (1936) arriving in New York. Gordon graciously agreed that a number of his paintings could be reproduced in this book.

Captain Stephen J. Card is a master mariner turned marine artist. A native of Bermuda, Stephen has had a varied maritime career and was at one time Queens Harbour Master of Bermuda. He is well known for his marine paintings and has many of his works on board the ships of Holland America Line and Cunard. Stephen produced many fine paintings for Queen Mary 2, which can mainly be found within the ship's numerous passenger stairways.

I owe a great debt of gratitude to many schoolteachers and university lecturers and mentors, particularly Patricia Boutle and Justin Johnson, teachers at Catford Boys' Comprehensive School in Lewisham, London, where I attended from 1971 to 1978. My father and three younger brothers were also pupils at this school, which sadly closed in 1991 and was demolished

委托，戈登为"玛丽女王2号"设计了第一版彩绘图。当这版彩绘图完成之后，人们又决定要在船上安装两台燃气涡轮机，这就需要在烟囱的底部增加一个大型甲板舱室，如此一来便大大缩短了烟囱的长度。尽管如此，这幅彩绘图仍然准确地展示了这艘船完工以后的全貌。戈登的许多绘画作品都陈列在冠达"女王"系列的船上，以纪念"玛丽女王2号"在"伊丽莎白女王2号"的陪伴下，于2004年4月完成了从纽约到南安普敦的处女航，并以此纪念1936年抵达纽约的"玛丽女王号"。在征得戈登先生本人同意后，本书将引用一些他的作品。

史蒂芬·J.卡特船长是一位精通航海技术的海事艺术家。作为一名土生土长的百慕大人，史蒂芬曾有一段丰富多彩的航海职业生涯，并且曾一度担任百慕大群岛女王港的管理者。他以海事类绘画而闻名，他的许多作品都被陈列在荷美邮轮和冠达邮轮的船上。史蒂芬为"玛丽女王2号"创作了许多精美的作品，这些作品大多在乘客区域的梯道内展示。

我非常感谢我的中小学的教师，大学讲师以及导师们，特别是帕特里夏·波特和贾斯汀·乔森。我在1971年到1978年间曾就读于伦敦路易斯汉姆的凯特福德男子综合学校，当时他们便在该校任教。我的父亲和三个弟弟也都是这所学校的毕业生。不幸的是，这所学校在

two years later. Patricia. Boutle was my English teacher for my first two years and she introduced me to public speaking and debating, as well as giving me a thorough grounding in spelling, grammar and skills such as writing letters. On leaving school I not unusually lost touch with Pat, but she recognised me on the television on Boxing Day 2003 as Queen Mary 2 approached Southampton on her delivery voyage and made contact. We have since become firm friends. Justin Johnson was my physics master from 1975 through to 1978 for both GCE O and A levels. After a succession of physics teachers, some not particularly well qualified to teach it, Justin arrived in time to rescue the class and ensure that the majority of us made it through O level with flying colours. The follow-on A level course was always made relevant and interesting, and Justin's philosophy in treating us as young adults rather than just pupils was much lauded. Both Pat and Justin added greatly to my education and I certainly believe that I would not have achieved many of the things I have done without their guidance in my formative years. Justin's particular contribution is further elucidated in this book.

I would like to thank Captain Kevin Oprey, master of Queen Mary 2, for his input in the section 'This is your captain speaking'. I first met Kevin while he was on board the ship with his wife Cheryl on a familiarisation trip before taking command. Kevin and I have become good friends despite his constant comment bemoaning the size of his cabin, which he asserts should have been significantly bigger!

1991 年关闭，并于两年后被拆除。我在该校就读的最初两年，帕特里夏·波特是我的英语老师，她教会了我如何进行公开演讲和辩论，同时还培养了我在拼写、语法和行文等方面的基础知识。离开学校之后，我并没有特意联系过帕特，但是在 2003 年的节礼日那天，当"玛丽女王 2 号"返航靠近南安普顿时，她在电视上认出了我并且联系上了我。从此我们成了关系亲密的朋友。贾斯汀·乔森在 1975 年到 1978 年间担任我的物理教师，负责教授我们 O 级和 A 级课程。当时，在连续更换了一系列不称职的物理老师后，贾斯汀总算是及时赶到，成功地拯救了我们班级的成绩，并且使得我们中大多数人通过了 O 级课程的考试。之后的 A 级课程变得简单而有趣，最值得赞扬的是，贾斯汀并没有像对待小学生一样对待我们，而是把我们当作年轻人一样看待。帕特和贾斯汀都使我受益良多，我相信，如果没有他们的教导，在我成长岁月里的很多事情都将是不可能完成的。本书后续内容还将进一步阐明贾斯汀的独特贡献。

我还要感谢"玛丽女王 2 号"的船长凯文·奥波雷先生在"船长之声"一章当中所做的贡献。我第一次见到凯文时，他正在和妻子谢丽尔在船上进行指挥工作开始前的家属观光游。凯文和我成了好朋友，尽管他总是抱怨他的房间

Hampton Dixon is a young American naval architect who recently graduated from Webb Institute at Glen Cove, New York, where I am a member of the Board of Trustees. In January 2013 Hampton sailed from New York to Southampton on board Queen Mary 2 and graciously took a number of photographs that he made available for publication in this book.

I certainly wish Hampton well in his chosen career and I will be following his progression with much interest.

Thanks are also due to Andy Brett of Rolls-Royce Marine and Carla Francis of Wärtsilä for assisting with illustrations from their organisations.

Many people play a large part in a project such as Queen Mary 2. No one person can take all the credit and to be successful, teamwork is paramount. I was very fortunate in having a tremendous team available to assist me, which is further detailed in the book. A key appointment was Gerry Ellis who acted as Cunard Line's project director. Gerry and I worked very closely together throughout the whole project and only disagreed on one small point (see below). Thank you also to interior architects Thomas and Robert Tillberg (Miami), Andy Collier of SMC Design, Fredrik Johansson of Tillberg Design of Sweden, Frank Seymou and Eric Mouzourides of Design Team-all worked as a marvellous collaborative team to provide Queen Mary 2 with some of the most iconic public spaces ever seen at sea. And a special mention of Maurizio Cergol, senior designer of Fincantieri, for assisting us in the early stages with staircase sizing

太小，并坚称船长的房间应该要比他现在的大得多！

汉普顿·迪克森是一位年轻的美国船舶设计师，他刚刚从纽约格伦科夫的韦伯学院毕业，我恰好是该学院董事会的成员。2013年1月，汉普顿乘坐"玛丽女王2号"从纽约前往南安普敦，途中拍摄了很多精美的照片，经他同意这些照片将在本书中出现。我由衷地希望汉普顿能在他所选择的职业生涯中取得好成绩，我会以极大的兴趣关注他的进步。

同样感谢罗尔斯－罗伊斯海事部的安迪·布雷特和瓦锡兰公司的卡拉·弗朗西斯，他们为我提供了他们公司产品的插图。

许多人在诸如"玛丽女王2号"这样的项目中扮演着重要的角色。没有一个人能独自赢得所有的荣誉和成功，团队合作才是最重要的。我很幸运地有一个支持我的庞大团队，在书中会有关于他们更详细的介绍。由格里·埃利斯担任冠达邮轮公司的项目总监，这是一个非常重要的任命。格里和我在整个项目中紧密合作，只在一个小问题上意见不一致（见下文）。同样要感谢室内设计师托马斯和罗伯特·蒂尔伯格（迈阿密），SMC设计公司的安迪·柯尔特，瑞典蒂尔伯格设计公司的弗雷德里克·约翰逊，设计团队中的弗兰克·塞莫和埃里克·穆佐里德斯，他们组成一个了不起的合作

and location.

I would particularly like to thank Ian Gaunt and John Hopkins, senior management of Carnival Corporate Shipbuilding at the time, for having the confidence and vision in allowing me at the age of 37 years to take 'Project Queen Mary' from inception through to delivery as Queen Mary 2. Ian and John gave me a complete free hand to deliver the project as I saw fit, but were always on hand if I needed help or advice.

As the designer of Queen Mary 2 I am the first to acknowledge quite rightly that the ship was the result of a huge collaborative effort of many talented and committed people. Several distinct teams were responsible both pre-contract and post-contract: the Carnival Corporate Shipbuilding team, the Cunard team, the shipyard Alstom Chantiers de l'Atlantique team, the Lloyd's Register team and the interior architects team.

Apart from my own team at Carnival Shipbuilding and the specific individuals who are detailed below, the ultimate success of the Queen Mary 2 project can be put down to the tremendous working relationship I had with my opposite number at Cunard Line, namely Gerry Ellis. Gerry joined the team early in the project and I think it fair to say we initially had a level of mutual wariness. Gerry was a seasoned bridge officer on Queen Elizabeth 2's transatlantic crossings and he was fully aware of the rigours of the North Atlantic and the challenges that it posed to a successful operation. He quite rightly doubted whether a young 37-year-old naval architect of cruise ships could have the necessary appreciation of the Atlantic. For

团队，为"玛丽女王2号"提供了一些海上最具标志性的公共空间。特别感谢芬坎蒂尼的资深设计师毛里齐奥·谢尔戈，他在早期阶段帮助我们确定了全船梯道的尺寸和位置。

我特别要感谢当时嘉年华新造船部的高级管理人员伊恩·盖特和约翰·霍普金斯，他们极富信心和远见，允许我在37岁时负责"玛丽女王2号"从立项到交付的整个项目。伊恩和约翰完全放手让我按自己认为合适的方案去执行项目，并且在我需要帮助或建议时，他们总是会助我一臂之力。

作为"玛丽女王2号"的设计师，我首先认识到，这艘船是许多有才华、有奉献精神的人们共同努力的结果。几个不同的团队负责合同签订前后的工作：嘉年华新造船部团队、冠达团队、阿尔斯通大西洋船厂团队、劳氏船级社团队和内装设计师团队。

除了我在嘉年华新造船部的团队和下文具体介绍的个人外，"玛丽女王2号"项目的最终完成可以归功于我和我在冠达邮轮公司的对口联系人格里·埃利斯间的极好的工作关系。格里在这个项目的早期加入了团队，必须承认，最初我们彼此都很谨慎。在"伊丽莎白女王2号"横跨大西洋的航行过程中，格里是一位经验丰富的操船官员，他充分意识到北大西洋环境的严酷，以及它对跨洋班轮

my part, having been with the project from inception, and having moulded the ship as I wanted, I resented Gerry being thrust upon the team at senior level. Thankfully, shortly thereafter Gerry and I had to visit the United States Coast Guard in Washington to gain approval for the relatively high placement of the ship's lifeboats. We were booked in the same hotel and we both arrived in the mid-afternoon, prior to the following day's meeting, where we gravitated to the business lounge. There we remained with gin and tonics in hand until the late evening when we both realised that we had struck up an amazing friendship and working relationship, which time and time again was pivotal to the project's success. The friendship remains strong to this day. Remarkably, we have only once had a difference of opinion. This related to the style of the 'Q' of Queen Mary 2 on the bow of the ship. Gerry initially thought that to promote a modern image, the 'Q' should be of modern stylised form with the tail looping under the ship's name. I did not particularly like this idea and we agreed to differ; Gerry later conceded that on reflection he was pleased that the traditional 'Q' had endured.

My first contact with the shipyard, Alstom Chantiers de l'Atlantique, was with the senior sales executive Didier Bourdin. Didier travelled to our London office from the shipyard and sat patiently while I outlined the project. Didier quickly grasped the concept of the ship, especially the fact that I had envisaged a true liner and not a cruise ship. He took the plans back to the shipyard and convinced the senior management that this was a project

的成功运作所带来的挑战。他很怀疑一个年仅 37 岁的邮轮设计师是否对大西洋有必要的了解。于我而言,从一开始就参与这个项目,并且已经按照我的意愿确定了该船的设计理念,我很不满格里被安排为高层。谢天谢地,此后不久,为了获得有关该船救生艇在高位布置方案的批准,格里和我不得不一起访问位于华盛顿的美国海岸警卫队。我们在同一家酒店预订了房间,于会议前一天的下午三点左右到达,并被接引到商务休息室。在那里,我们手里拿着杜松子酒和奎宁水直到深夜,我们俩都意识到我们已经建立起了极好的友谊和工作关系,这也是项目成功的关键。直到今天,我们的友谊依然牢固。值得注意的是,我们只有过一次意见分歧。这与"玛丽女王 2 号"在船首的字母"Q"的风格有关。格里最初认为,为了符合现代化的形象,"Q"应该设计成现代风格的形式,"Q"的尾巴应当环绕在船名的下方。我不是很喜欢这个想法,我们各自保留不同的意见。经过深思熟虑后,格里做出了让步,他很高兴传统风格的"Q"被保留了下来。

我与阿尔斯通大西洋船厂的第一次接触,是与高级销售经理迪迪尔·布尔丹一起。迪迪尔从船厂来到我们在伦敦的办事处,耐心地听我讲述这个项目。迪迪尔很快就理解了这艘船的设计理念,特别是我设想的是一艘真正的班轮而不

that the shipyard just had to secure. Didier introduced the shipyard's senior naval architect, Jean Jacques Gatepaille, to the project and personally took charge of all the specification and contract negotiations with us. Subsequently, Alain Crouzols and Jean-Remy Villageois had day-to-day responsibility for the project from the builder's side, both discharging this duty admirably.

The Carnival Shipbuilding team consisted of a small but very capable group of people. During the concept design stage I was aided by a junior assistant, Rick Moore. Rick worked tirelessly, translating ideas from sketches and discusssions into computer drawings that we used as part of the briefing to the five shipyards that were invited to tender for the project. Matt Suatt, a young marine engineer who had served time at sea on container ships, looked after the machinery definition for the ship. On the electrical side, seasoned veterans Mike Crawley and David Storer were entrusted with the concept design of the complex systems within this area. Post-contract, Jeff Frier joined the team as a naval architect with responsibility for the approval of structure and outfitting. Deck coverings, signage and crucially paint coverings were under the watchful eye of John Drew, an experienced professional from the marine paint industry. Tom Strang and Tuula Aer covered safety systems and Raoul Jack, recruited from within Cunard, took charge of electronic systems and bridge systems. Finally, Roger White looked after internal and external lighting, public address and entertainment systems. I mention here,

是一艘邮轮。他把设计计划带回了船厂，并说服高级管理层这是一个船厂必须拿下的项目。迪迪尔将船厂的高级船体设计师让·雅克·盖特佩尔介绍到这个项目中，并亲自负责所有规格书和合同的谈判。随后，阿拉因·克鲁佐斯和让·雷米·维拉卓以建造方的身份负责该项目的日常工作，他们都出色地履行了这一职责。

嘉年华新造船部由精干人员组成。在概念设计阶段，我得到了一位初级助理里克·摩尔的帮助。里克孜孜不倦地工作，把草图和讨论的想法转换成计算机图纸，这些图纸作为项目简介的一部分，发送给5个应邀投标的船厂。马特·苏亚特是一位年轻的海洋工程师，曾在集装箱船上工作，负责维护船上的轮机设备。在电气方面，经验丰富的迈克·克劳利和大卫·斯托尔被委托负责这个区域内复杂系统的概念设计。合同签订后，杰夫·弗埃尔以船舶设计师的身份加入了团队，负责结构和舾装的审批。甲板敷料、标志和至关重要的油漆涂料由约翰·德鲁监管，他是一个经验丰富的海洋涂料专家。汤姆·斯特朗和图拉·艾尔负责安全系统，从冠达内部招募的拉乌尔·杰克负责电子系统和桥楼系统。罗杰·怀特负责内部和外部照明、公共广播和娱乐系统。我在这里也提到许多朋友，如扎内·里奥、安德鲁·伯德、

also, numerous friends such as Zane Leo, Andrew Bird, Matt Suatt, Jeff Frier, Raoul Jack, Michael Drayton, Stephen Shaw, Brian Ansell and Jim McNeill, who have always been very supportive.

Finally, I must thank my family for their constant love and encouragement in all I do. My parents, Michael and Pauline, worked very hard to support me and ensure that I had the chance of attending university, even though this was well outside their own experiences. With my younger siblings, Alan, Victor and Richard, we were always given every opportunity and never went without. I am eternally grateful that my parents were able to witness my achievements with Queen Mary 2 before my father became burdened with dreadful Alzheimer's disease. I would also like to thank my good friend Jennifer for enjoying my company and being a willing traveller on Queen Mary 2.

马特·苏亚特、杰夫·弗埃尔、拉乌尔·杰克、迈克尔·安塞尔、吉姆·德雷顿、史蒂芬·肖、布莱恩·安塞尔和吉姆·麦克尼尔，他们一直非常支持我的工作。

最后，我必须感谢我的家人给予我始终如一的关爱和鼓励。我的父母迈克尔和保林，非常努力地支持我，使我有机会上大学，尽管这远远超出了他们自己的资历。还有我的弟弟们艾伦、维克托和理查德，他们总是给予我最大支持，永不抛弃。我永远感激我的父母，他们看到了我在"玛丽女王2号"上取得的成就，那时候我父亲还没有患上可怕的阿尔茨海默病。我还要感谢我的好朋友珍妮弗，感谢她陪伴我在"玛丽女王2号"度过的愉快时光。

Introduction 简介

There is no misunderstanding in that Queen Mary 2 is a very special ship. She is a true liner and not just some cruise ship marketed as one. She embodies all the traditional attributes of a liner such as strength, power/speed, deep draught, and fine hull lines without compromise. Specifically designed for the transatlantic run between Southampton and New York, with the ability to operate luxury holiday cruises, Queen Mary 2 is the very last ship of her type still

毫无疑问，"玛丽女王2号"作为一条船来说是非常特别的。作为一艘真正意义上的班轮，而不仅仅是普通的邮轮，她体现了班轮所有的传统特点：如强度、动力/速度、较深的吃水以及优美的船体线型。"玛丽女王2号"是同类型邮轮中最后一艘还处于运营状态的，她专为南安普敦和纽约之间的跨大西洋航线设计，同时具备奢华假日巡游

最后的相遇："伊丽莎白女王号"和"玛丽女王号"，1967年9月25日。接近午夜，两艘世界上最大的邮轮以超过每小时70英里的速度在大西洋中部相遇。"玛丽女王号"将前往南安普敦，她将于12月9日抵达长滩市。"伊丽莎白女王号"当时正前往纽约，在1968年11月退役前，她将继续为冠达邮轮航行最后一个航季。

in operation. After the delivery of Cunard Line's Queen Elizabeth 2 in 1969 there were many who doubted whether a ship of this type would ever be built again.

I am often asked, 'Where did the story of Queen Mary 2 actually begin?' For me, I like to think that it started on a cold September night, approaching midnight on 25 September 1967 to be exact, in mid-Atlantic. Passengers standing on the deck of a great liner bound for New York braved the cold to survey the dark horizon. In the distance a faint red glow was discerned and our passengers mused over whether the red glow could be the planet Mars or some other heavenly body. Within a few minutes the glow had become appreciably larger and shortly thereafter the passengers concluded that it could only be another ship on a parallel but opposite course to their own. Approaching each other at a combined speed of over 70mph, the once-distant ship was now almost abreast of our passengers' ship. As the two ships passed, each sounded its mighty steam whistles, sending forth a throaty blast that spread out across the expanse of ocean. It was now apparent that the red glow had been attributable to three enormous red and black funnels that were brightly illuminated by floodlights, set upon a vast hull and superstructure with thousands of lights burning brightly, twinkling like stars. Our passengers marvelled at the spectacle and glanced over their shoulders to look at their great ship. It too had red and black funnels that were similarly brightly illuminated, but in this case there were only two funnels, not three.

This event signalled what many

的能力。而在 1969 年"伊丽莎白女王 2 号"交付冠达航运时，许多人都还对是否继续建造该种邮轮而心存疑虑。

我时常会问："'玛丽女王 2 号'的故事应该从何说起？"从我个人角度来说，我更倾向于认为应始于 9 月的一个寒冷夜晚，准确地说是在 1967 年 9 月 25 日午夜的大西洋中部。在一艘驶往纽约的巨大班轮的甲板上，乘客们正顶着严寒，搜索着漆黑的地平线。一缕红色微光出现在远方，乘客们开始还以为这红光来自于火星抑或是什么其他天体。然而几分钟后，那道亮光明显更亮了。他们很快断定，那是另一艘船：与自己乘坐的船平行但朝着相反的方向航行的船。两艘船以超过每小时 70 英里的相对速度彼此接近，这艘曾经相距遥远的船现在几乎已驶到乘客们乘坐的船的旁边。当两艘船相遇时，她们鸣响汽笛，低沉的巨响在浩瀚的海洋中蔓延开来。现在能看到之前的红光是由于她那三个巨大的红黑相间的烟囱被强光灯照亮后映出的色彩。在其巨大的船体和上层建筑上，成千上万的灯火明亮地点燃着，像星星一样闪烁。乘客们对这一奇景感到惊奇，他们回头看了看自己乘坐的巨轮：她红黑相间的烟囱同样被明亮地照耀着，但是不同的是烟囱只有两个，而非三个。

这一次相遇被许多人认为是北大西洋班轮（一种横渡大西洋连接旧世界和新世界的客轮）时代谢幕的开端。人们

considered was the beginning of the end of the North Atlantic ferry: the transatlantic crossing by passenger ship linking the old world with the new. The westbound ship on which our passengers were sailing was Cunard Line's mighty flagship, RMS Queen Elizabeth (1940), the largest passenger ship the world had ever seen. The other ship was her consort, RMS Queen Mary (1936) and this was to be the last time that they would cross in mid-Atlantic.

Queen Mary was on her last transatlantic crossing and had already been sold to the city of Long Beach in California to become a museum, hotel and convention centre after a farewell cruise and delivery voyage. Queen Elizabeth was also scheduled for withdrawal during the following year and her fate was as yet undecided. All hopes

当时乘坐这艘向西航行的船舶是当时冠达公司的旗舰："伊丽莎白女王号"（1940年），它是当时世界上最大的客轮。另一艘是她的姐妹船"玛丽女王号"（1936年），这是她们最后一次在大西洋中部相遇。

这是"玛丽女王号"最后一次横渡大西洋，这之后在经过一次告别巡航和游历之旅后，她将被卖给加利福尼亚州的长滩市，改造成为一座博物馆、酒店和会议中心。而"伊丽莎白女王号"也计划在次年退役，但她的命运还尚未决定。现在所有的希望都寄托在冠达最新的班轮上，即"伊丽莎白女王2号"，它刚在几天前的9月20日在位于克莱

2007年1月10日，佛罗里达州劳德代尔堡的"玛丽女王2号"和"伊丽莎白女王2号"。（冠达邮轮提供）

now rested on the new Cunard liner, Queen Elizabeth 2, which had been launched only a few days earlier on 20 September from the John Brown Shipyard on the Clyde (the same yard that built the earlier Queens, and in fact the same slipway). Hold-ups in construction and faulty propulsion turbines would conspire to delay the entry into service of Queen Elizabeth 2 until May 1969, several months after Queen Elizabeth's withdrawal in November 1968. Everybody – the media, pundits, enthusiasts and shipping professionals – all anticipated that once Queen Elizabeth 2 had seen out her lifespan, the Atlantic ferry would be finished and would cease to exist. In recalling the story of Queen Mary 2 to schoolchildren and others, I always remark that the story of the ship is an outstanding collaborative effort and that my former colleagues at Carnival Corporation, Cunard Line, my own shipbuilding team and our friends at Chantiers de l'Atlantique where the ship was built, have collectively rewritten history. And that is a very powerful story to tell.

Genesis

My own interest in passenger ships began as a young boy. I lived in south-east London in the borough of Lewisham not far from Greenwich. A favourite aunt and uncle lived at Greenwich so there were frequent trips to see them, which often included visiting the preserved tea clipper sailing ship Cutty Sark and the nearby National Maritime Museum. Although my uncle had been in the Royal Navy he was now a security guard and there were no other nautical links in

德的约翰·布朗船厂（John Brown 船厂）下水（实际上该船厂使用同一个船台建造了之前的几艘"女王号"）。在"伊丽莎白女王号"于1968年11月从英国退役几个月后，由于建造的推迟和推进涡轮机故障导致"伊丽莎白女王2号"的服役日期推迟到了1969年5月。所有人——包括媒体、专家、航海爱好者和航运专业人士都预计，一旦"伊丽莎白女王2号"完成了她的使命，大西洋班轮会就此终结并将不复存在。每当我向学生们或其他人讲述"玛丽女王2号"的故事时，我总是说，这是一个杰出的有关努力合作的故事，我在嘉年华集团的前同事、冠达邮轮、我自己的造船团队以及我在大西洋造船厂（Chantiers de l'Atlantique，"玛丽女王2号"的建造船厂）的朋友们一起共同改写了历史。这是一个激动人心的故事。

起源

我对客船的兴趣始于孩提时代。那时我住在伦敦东南部的刘易斯沙姆区，离格林尼治不远。由于我最喜欢的叔叔和婶婶住在格林尼治，所以我时常去看望他们，同时也常去参观运茶帆船"卡蒂萨克号"和附近的国家海事博物馆。虽然我叔叔曾在皇家海军服役，但他现在是一名保安，家里也没有其他与航海有关的人。我父亲是一位品茶师，母亲

the family. My father was a tea taster and my mother was an administrative officer at a local school. Coming home from primary school I remember switching on the television and watching the iconic BBC television children's news and magazine programme Blue Peter, which aired twice a week. First broadcast in 1958, it is the world's longest-running children's television programme, still showing to this day.

On that memorable day on 24 May 1965 the programme featured the presenters Valerie Singleton and Christopher Trace sailing on board Queen Elizabeth on the last leg of one of her eastbound transatlantic crossings from Cherbourg to Southampton. The presenters visited the bridge, engine room and many of the grand public spaces, which all appeared magnificent despite the grainy black and white television picture of the day. Valerie watched the radio officer send a Morse code message and she saw the skilful chefs preparing sugar decorations for buffets. It occurred to me even then that it would be fun to grow up and either work on such a ship, or to have something to do with the building of one. In modern parlance, I suppose it would be said to be 'cool'. I remember the day that I watched that programme as if it was yesterday and for many years thought that it was broadcast during 1967. However, researching this book I searched the BBC Blue Peter archive and I was amazed that it was two years earlier, in 1965. I was five years old at the time.

Four years later, in June 1969, my parents and my then two younger brothers (now three) went on summer holiday to the south coast resort of Bascombe near

是当地一所学校的行政官员。记得小学回到家后，我打开电视去看当时有名的BBC儿童新闻和杂志节目《蓝彼得》，这节目每周播出两次。它于1958年首次播出，是世界上播放时间最长的儿童电视节目，至今仍在播放。

1965年5月24日，在那个值得纪念的日子里，节目主持人瓦莱丽·辛格尔顿和克里斯托弗·崔丝登上了"伊丽莎白女王号"，参加了她从瑟堡到南安普顿东行横渡大西洋的最后一段航程。主持人参观了桥楼、机舱和许多大型公共区域，尽管当时的电视画面是黑白的，但这些地方仍看上去十分壮观。瓦莱丽看到电台工作人员发送了一条摩尔斯电码，她也看到技术娴熟的厨师正在为自助餐准备糖衣装饰。那时我就在想，长大后在这样一艘船上工作，或是建造这么一艘船一定是一件很有趣的事情。用现代的说法，我想它会很"酷"。我仍记得那天我看的那个节目，就好像在昨天一样，许多年来我一直以为它是在1967年播出的。然而，为了这本书，我搜索了BBC蓝彼得档案馆，惊讶地发现它的播放时间是两年前的1965年，而当时我还只有5岁。

四年后的1969年6月，我和父母以及两个弟弟（现在是三个）前往伯恩茅斯附近的南海岸度假胜地巴斯科姆度假。在那的两周时间里，我们乘坐长途汽车去了南安普敦的码头，在那里，全新的"伊丽莎白女王2号"停靠在她大西洋上航

史蒂芬·佩恩和蓝彼得的照片在冠达邮轮的"维多利亚女王号"上展出,这表明了BBC具有悠久的历史。过去,"玛丽女王号"和"伊丽莎白女王号"提供每周一次的跨大西洋航行,照片中,七岁的作者与他的弟弟艾伦坐在祖父母家花园的椅子上。展览中最显眼的是两份1973年的《蓝彼得年鉴》,一份是封面,另一份是描述 RMS "伊丽莎白女王号"的历史和消亡的页面。这篇文章的最后一段宣称,"伊丽莎白女王号"是一艘超级班轮,但像它这样的船以后再也不会建造了。作者在13岁时,就有了不一般的想法——伟大的想法……(作者提供)

Bournemouth. During our two weeks there we took a coach excursion to Southampton Docks where the brand new Queen Elizabeth 2 lay at the Ocean Terminal between Atlantic crossings, just one month into her illustrious career. In those far-off days before the onset of heightened security, Cunard, in common with other passenger lines, allowed visitors to their ships. Queen Elizabeth 2 was a huge magnet and attracted many coach parties as well as our own. On that heady day we walked around the great ship, still fresh in her new paint, while my father took Super 8 cine movies to record our visit.

We strolled through all the main public rooms and I clearly remember the

程中段的码头上,她的辉煌生涯当时才刚刚开始一个月。在那个还未加强安保措施的遥远的日子里,冠达公司和其他客运公司一样,允许参观者进入他们的船只。"伊丽莎白女王2号"就像一块巨大的磁石,吸引了包括我们在内的许多团队来访。在那个令人兴奋的日子里,我们绕着"巨轮"转了一圈,船上的油漆焕然一新,而我父亲则用超8摄影机记录了我们的旅程。

我们漫步在所有的主要公共舱室中,我清楚地记得那间巨大的游客级"布列塔尼亚"餐厅,入口有 "布列塔尼亚"

vast tourist-class Britannia restaurant with a sailing-ship-style figurehead of Britannia herself at the entrance. The first-class Queens Room with its distinctive fluted columns was notable, as was the great double-room lounge. Standing on the top deck the pencil-slim funnel appeared very tall, with only its attendant wind scoop painted in Cunard's traditional red funnel colour. Suddenly in the distance, swathed in bright sunshine and appearing sleek and resplendent, came United States Line's SS United States (1952) steaming in on one of her last season crossings. Nearby in an adjacent dock lay Royal Mail Line's venerable Andes (1939), gleaming white with her buff funnel, no doubt preparing for another cruise departure to distant lands. What a grand day that was! Memories of it are still very strong and it only added to my fascination of great passenger ships and an ambition to design and build such ships for a living.

On 9 January 1972, I was again watching Blue Peter when Valerie Singleton announced that they were linking up by satellite to Hong Kong Harbour. There on fire from end to end was SS Seawise University, formerly none other than the Queen Elizabeth. Once sold by Cunard the ship had had a chequered history as

史蒂芬·佩恩 2004 年获得的蓝彼得（Blue Peter）金色徽章（作者提供）

女神的帆船船首雕像。头等舱的"女王"厅以其独特的雕花柱让人印象深刻，"垂拔"厅也是如此。笔直的烟囱位于顶层甲板上，看起来非常高，它的导风穴是冠达传统烟囱的红色。这时候，沐浴在明媚阳光下的美国邮轮公司的"美国号"（1952 年）从远处驶来，看起来辉煌灿烂，然而这将是她的最后一个航季。在邻近的码头停靠着皇家邮政公司庄严的"安第斯山号"（1939 年），它的浅褐色烟囱闪闪发光，正准备再次远航。这是多么盛大的一天啊！这段记忆深深地印在了我的脑海中，让我更加迷恋这些伟大的客轮，投身设计和建造这类船的意愿也更加强烈。

1972 年 1 月 9 日，我在看蓝彼得节目时，电视中瓦莱丽·辛格尔顿宣布他们正通过卫星连线到香港港口。电视画面中，"海上学府号"着起了熊熊大火，该船即是原来的"伊丽莎白女王号"。这艘船被冠达公司出售后，曾作为佛罗

an attraction based at Fort Lauderdale in Florida before being sold to the Chinese shipping magnate CY Tung. After a tortuous voyage to Hong Kong, the ship was being refitted to become the jewel in CY Tung's shipping empire and was destined to sail as a combined university campus and first-class cruise ship. It was during the complex refitting process, where much of the ship's systems were being upgraded or renewed, that the fatal conflagration occurred, undoubtedly a case of deliberate arson. In the final moments of the BBC programme the great ship gently rolled over on to her side, as if to give up on the struggle for survival and die.

One of the Christmas presents I received that year was the 1973 *Blue Peter annual* - a book published each year to commemorate noteworthy features from the programme over the past year. On pages 34 to 37 there was a feature all about the Queen Elizabeth. Two pages of text were accompanied by a two-page sectional view showing the interior of the ship, drawn by the well-known graphic artist Geoffrey Wheeler. Comparisons with Queen Elizabeth 2 and Cunard Adventurer and a facts and figures section, made for a very interesting article, but the last paragraph of text caused me much consternation. It read, 'It was a sad moment for everybody that loves great ships. The Queen Elizabeth was the last of a great age - a Superliner, and nothing like her will ever be built again.' For someone who believed that everything Blue Peter said was gospel, this was a hard statement to take. I had by this time set my sights on designing and building a new superliner that would

里达州劳德代尔堡的一处景点，在那里有过一段曲折的历史，之后被出售给中国航运巨头董浩云。该船经过一段曲折的航行后到达香港，成为董浩云航运帝国的一颗明珠，并随即被改装，未来她将成为一艘结合大学和头等舱特征的邮轮。这艘船的大部分系统都将升级或更新，正是在这复杂的改装过程中，致命的大火发生了，这无疑是有人蓄意纵火。在电视节目的最后一刻，这艘巨轮慢慢地向一侧倒去，仿佛放弃了求生的挣扎。

那一年，我收到的圣诞礼物之一是1973年的《蓝彼得年鉴》，这本书每年出版一本，以纪念该节目在过去一年曾经播放过的那些值得关注的内容。在第34至37页，都是关于"伊丽莎白女王2号"的内容。文字旁还附有两页由知名艺术家杰弗里·惠勒绘制的剖面图，展示了船舶内部的情景。文章将"伊丽莎白女王2号"和"冠达冒险者号"联系在一起，并列举了一些事实和数据，是一篇非常有趣的文章，但最后一段文字却让我非常惊愕。它写道，对于每个热爱船的人来说，这是一个悲伤的时刻。"伊丽莎白女王号"是这个伟大时代的最后一艘超级班轮，像这样的船以后再也不会建造了。对于那些相信蓝彼得所说的一切都是真理的人来说，这句话简直难以接受。因为那时我的目标是设计和建造一艘比"伊丽莎白女王号"更大更好的新超级班轮。

1973年初，我在凯特福德男子学校，

indeed be bigger and better than Queen Elizabeth.

At Catford Boys' School early in 1973 my English class was learning how to write letters. The English teacher, Miss Patricia Boutle, advised that the most important type of letter to master was the letter of complaint. To be able to effectively complain and influence an outcome was deemed a very desirable social skill and the class was charged with writing a letter of complaint for homework. I decided to write to Blue Peter informing them of the exception that I took to that last paragraph of the Queen Elizabeth article. In due course I received a letter back from the programme, signed by the editor, Biddy Baxter. In essence the letter advised that the presenters were fascinated by my ideas for a new superliner but it stressed that I shouldn't be too disappointed if it never came to fruition. Blue Peter awarded a number of badges, ranging from blue to gold according to the relevance or importance of the subject matter, to those writing in. My letter was accompanied by a blue Blue Peter badge and not the gold one that I had been hoping for! When talking of my experiences to school groups, I always remark that this was one of the first occasions that I had to deal with disappointment, and that it was an object lesson in dealing with such situations!

Catford Boys' School was a secondary comprehensive institution that offered a good general education up to the age of 16 at CSE and GCE O level, and to 18 with GCE A level.In choosing subjects for my A levels I opted for pure mathematics, physics and chemistry, which I thought would be a good grounding for later studies

我们的英语课程内容是学习如何写信。我的英语老师帕特里夏·波特小姐，告诉我们要掌握的最重要的信函是投诉信。因为它能够有效地表达不满并对结果产生影响，是一种非常有用的社交方式，并要求我们班级将它作为家庭作业来完成。而我决定写信给蓝彼得，告诉他们我对"伊丽莎白女王号"文章的最后一段不同的看法。过了一段时间，我收到了节目组的回信，上面有编辑毕蒂·巴克斯特的签名。回信上讲，主持人被我的关于新超级客船的想法吸引了，但他强调，如果它将来无法实现，我也不要太失望。蓝彼得编辑部会根据主题的相关性或重要性，给写信的人颁发徽章，从蓝色到金色。我的信中附有蓝色的徽章，而不是我一直希望的金色徽章！在谈及学生时代时，我总是说这是我第一次不得不面对失望的时候，并且为今后再处理类似环境提供了借鉴！

凯特福德男子学校是一所二级综合性学校，为16岁以下的学生提供中等教育CSE和普通教育GCE O级的课程，为16到18岁的学生提供普通教育GCE A级课程。在选择A级课程时，我选择了理论数学、物理和化学，我认为这将为日后在大学学习船舶专业打下良好的基础。我的家人中没有人上过大学，所以我很依赖职业服务中心和资深教师的建议来指导我选择大学课程。他们明确建议说："不要选择船舶专业或工程专业，因为这些行业在英国正在衰退，如果你

of naval architecture at university. Nobody from my family had ever been to university so I was particularly dependent on the advice from the careers service and senior teachers to guide me through the process of selecting a university course. Their advice was unequivocal: 'Don't choose naval architecture or engineering as this is in terminal decline in the UK and if you do you'll never find a job once qualified.' Faced with this I reluctantly decided to study just chemistry at university. One year into the course I met my former physics teacher, Justin Johnson, who expressed his severe displeasure at the fact that I had been persuaded to abandon the notion of becoming a naval architect. Justin convinced me that I had made the wrong decision and with his help I obtained a further grant and I was able to join the Ship Science course at the University of Southampton - ship science being another term for naval architecture. Three years later I qualified with a Bachelor of Science in Engineering - Ship Science.

After a short stint at Marconi Radar in Chelmsford, I joined Technical Marine Planning Ltd (TMP) in London. TMP was a company of marine technical consultants that had been engaged by Carnival Cruise Lines since its formation in 1972, initially to act as technical operators and latterly as new-building project managers. Eventually the majority of TMP's personnel would become fully integrated into Carnival under the initial guise of Carnival Corporation Technical Services and more recently as Carnival Corporate Shipbuilding. My first project at TMP was assessing the stability of the new cruise ship MS Holiday in January

选择这类专业，你永远也找不到一份好的工作。"考虑到这一点，我被迫决定在大学学习化学。课程开始一年后，我遇到了物理老师贾斯汀·乔森，对于我被说服并放弃成为一名造船师的想法，他觉得很生气。贾斯汀让我相信我做了一个错误的决定，在他的帮助下，我获得了很多资助，并且参加了南安普敦大学的船舶科学课程——船舶科学（船舶工程的另一个名称）。三年后，我获得了船舶科学的工学学士学位。

在切姆斯福德的马可尼雷达公司短暂停留后，我加入了伦敦的海洋规划技术有限公司（TMP）。TMP是一家海洋技术顾问公司，自1972年成立以来一直为嘉年华邮轮服务，最初其是技术运营商，后来成为新建项目的管理方。最终，TMP的大部分员工将以嘉年华公司技术服务的名义完全融入嘉年华，并在最近成为了嘉年华造船部。我在TMP的第一个项目是在1985年1月为新邮轮"MS假日号"评估稳性。在完成了和嘉年华相关项目之后，我被任命为荷美邮轮新旗舰"MS鹿特丹号"（1997年）的项目经理，该船在位于威尼斯玛格拉的芬坎蒂尼船厂建造。这是一项令人心酸的任务，因为"MS鹿特丹号"将取代的船是我最喜欢的班轮"SS鹿特丹号"（1959年）。随着"MS鹿特丹号"的交付，我被任命为歌诗达"大西洋号"的项目经理，该船建造于赫尔辛基玛莎船厂。虽然这些都是伟大的客船，但他们都是典型的

"女王号"的起源：史蒂芬·佩恩向纽约韦伯学院介绍"玛丽女王2号"。韦伯学院是美国最负盛名的船舶工程和海洋工程学校之一，并且作者被提名为名誉董事。在董事会会议后，当日程安排允许时，作者向学生和员工讲解客船设计和航海历史（这些讲座可在互联网上查看）。（纽约州韦伯学院提供）

1985.After a succession of Carnival and Carnival- affiliated projects, I was made project manager for the construction of the new Holland America Line flagship MS Rotterdam (1997) at the Fincantieri shipyard, Marghera, Venice. This was a particularly poignant assignment, as the ship MS Rotterdam would replace was the venerable SS Rotterdam (1959), my favourite passenger liner. With MS Rotterdam delivered, I was assigned to be project manager for the Costa Atlantica building at Masa Yards, Helsinki. Although these were great ships, they were firmly in the cruise ship mould and I resigned myself to the fact that I would probably never get the chance of designing and building my dream boat.

In May 1998 I decided to take a transatlantic crossing on Queen Elizabeth 2, New York to Southampton. The engineering

邮轮，那时我一度以为自己可能永远都不会有机会设计和建造梦想的船了。

在 1998 年 5 月，我决定搭乘"伊丽莎白女王2号"横跨大西洋，从纽约到南安普敦（英国港口）。当时冠达为卡瓦纳工程集团所有，这是 1996 年他们收购特拉法尔加豪斯集团获得的。我作为客座讲师参与航行，对跨大西洋航线的历史进行演讲。在航程中途，嘉年华邮轮集团和一组挪威投资公司收购了冠达邮轮公司的新闻公布。之前我没有收到任何暗示，甚至我从未想过会发生收购，因此我对此事十分震惊；之前坊间曾经疯传，宝城保险很可能会收购该公司。在几个小时后，伦敦办公室通过卫星电话通知我，要求我尽快返回并作为"伊丽莎白女王2号"的接替者开始工作。该项目被称作"玛丽女王项目"。

嘉年华公司副董事长兼首席运营官

group of Kvaemer owned Cunard at this time, a throwback from their acquisition of the Trafalgar House group in 1996. I sailed as a guest lecturer giving talks about the history of transatlantic liners. Midway through the voyage it was announced that Carnival and a group of Norwegian investors had purchased Cunard Line. This came as a complete shock as I had no inkling that the purchase was even being considered; press rumours had suggested that the Prudential Assurance was likely to acquire the company. Within a few hours the London office called the ship by satellite telephone to advise me that I was required back as soon as possible to start work on a successor to Queen Elizabeth 2, which would be given the code name 'Project Queen Mary'.

Howard Frank, Vice Chairman and Chief Operating Officer of Carnival Corporation told me that as negotiations with Kvaerner regarding the purchase of Cunard neared a conclusion, Howard saw a large sterling silver model of the Queen Elizabeth 2 in Kvaerner's offices that Trafalgar House had commissioned in the 1970s. Insisting the model came with the company, Kvaerner declined, and the meeting broke up with Howard advising that the deal was off without the silver model and that once he boarded his plane back to Miami there would be no second chance. Howard received a call accepting his terms before he reached the airport. The model was initially displayed in the midships lobby of Queen Elizabeth 2 and now resides within the Hemispheres night club on the new Queen Elizabeth.

On 6 November 2000 after the formal signing of the contract in Paris, I was fortunate to be invited to lunch with the

霍华德·弗兰克告诉我，当时与卡瓦纳公司关于收购冠达的谈判已接近达成，霍华德在卡瓦纳公司的办公室看到了一个由特拉法尔加豪斯于1970年制作的"伊丽莎白女王2号"大型纯银模型。由于坚持在收购中将该模型与公司打包，卡瓦纳公司拒绝了，会议终止。霍华德通告对方，因不包含那个大型纯银模型该笔交易取消，并且一旦他登上飞机回到迈阿密，就没有第二次机会了。霍华德在到达机场之前接到一个电话，对方表示接受他之前的条件。该模型最初被放置在"伊丽莎白女王2号"的中央大厅中，现在被放置在新"伊丽莎白女王号"的半球夜总会中。

2000年11月6日，在巴黎正式签署合同后，我有幸应邀与嘉年华公司的董事长兼首席执行官米奇·阿里森一起共进午餐。午餐时米奇说，在我的一生中，我只求有机会设计和建造一艘船像"玛丽女王2号"的项目，而且最好是一次就将它做好。我觉得在这一点上我们已经达成了共识。午餐后，米奇问我"玛丽女王2号"交付后可能做些什么，我厚着脸皮回答道，"兴登堡2号？"他回答道"你知不知道你相当相当疯狂！"

在2004年1月12日，开启处女航程的当天，蓝彼得节目组派了一个影片摄制小组上船。主持人康妮·胡克在布列塔尼亚餐厅找到了我，并针对邮轮的建造方面对我进行了采访。在镜头前，我被授予了一枚金色蓝彼得徽章——这个节目

Chairman and CEO of Carnival Corporation, Micky Arison. During lunch Micky remarked that in all probability I would only get the chance to design and build a ship like Queen Mary 2 once in my lifetime and that had therefore better get it right the first time. I hope that the general consensus is that this was achieved. After lunch Micky asked me what could possibly do to follow on from Queen Mary 2 once she was delivered. I cheekily replied, 'Hindenburg 2?', to which the reply was, 'You know that you're quite, quite mad!'

On the day of departure of the maiden voyage on 12 January 2004, Blue Peter sent a film crew on board. The presenter, Konnie Huq, caught up with me in the Britannia restaurant and interviewed me about the building of the ship. On film I was presented with a gold Blue Peter badge the programme's highest accolade. It remains one of my most prized possessions and I have great delight in taking it to the many schools where I give talks about striving for achievement; it never fails to raise gasps of amazement and admiration.

In the autumn of 2004 I had the great honour of being awarded the OBE by Her Majesty the Queen for 'Services to Shipping'. This was subsequently followed by the Merchant Navy Medal and a three-year stint as the President of the Royal Institution of Naval Architects, 2007-10. In 2006 the Royal Academy of Engineering presented me with the first 'Special Achievement Award' for the design and construction of Queen Mary 2.

的最高荣誉。它是我最珍贵的财富之一，并且我非常乐于把它带到许多学校，在那里我为我靠奋斗而取得的成就进行演讲。它总是能带来惊讶和赞美的声音。

在 2004 年秋天，我因"献身航运"有幸被女王陛下授予大英帝国"官佐勋章"*。随后是商船舰队奖章和三年皇家造船师协会的主席的任期（2007—2010 年）。在 2006 年，皇家工程学院将第一个"特别成就奖"授予了我，以表彰我对"玛丽女王 2 号"在设计及建造方面的贡献。

围绕在作者身边的"玛丽女王 2 号"同事（后排左起：大卫·斯托尔和马特·苏亚特，前排拉乌尔·杰克，史蒂芬·佩恩和船厂的"玛丽女王号"项目经理让·雷米·维拉卓）庆祝史蒂芬·佩恩被授予皇家学院工程的"特别成就奖"。该引文写道，"感谢他的成就对工程学产生深远影响"，2006 年 1 月 19 日。（英国皇家工程学院提供）

*：大英帝国勋章中的第 4 级——官佐勋章（Officer），简称"OBE"。官佐勋章人数虽不设限额，但每年授勋的人数不可多于 858 位。——译者注

全面解析世界现役最大远洋班轮设计、建造和运营故事

目 录

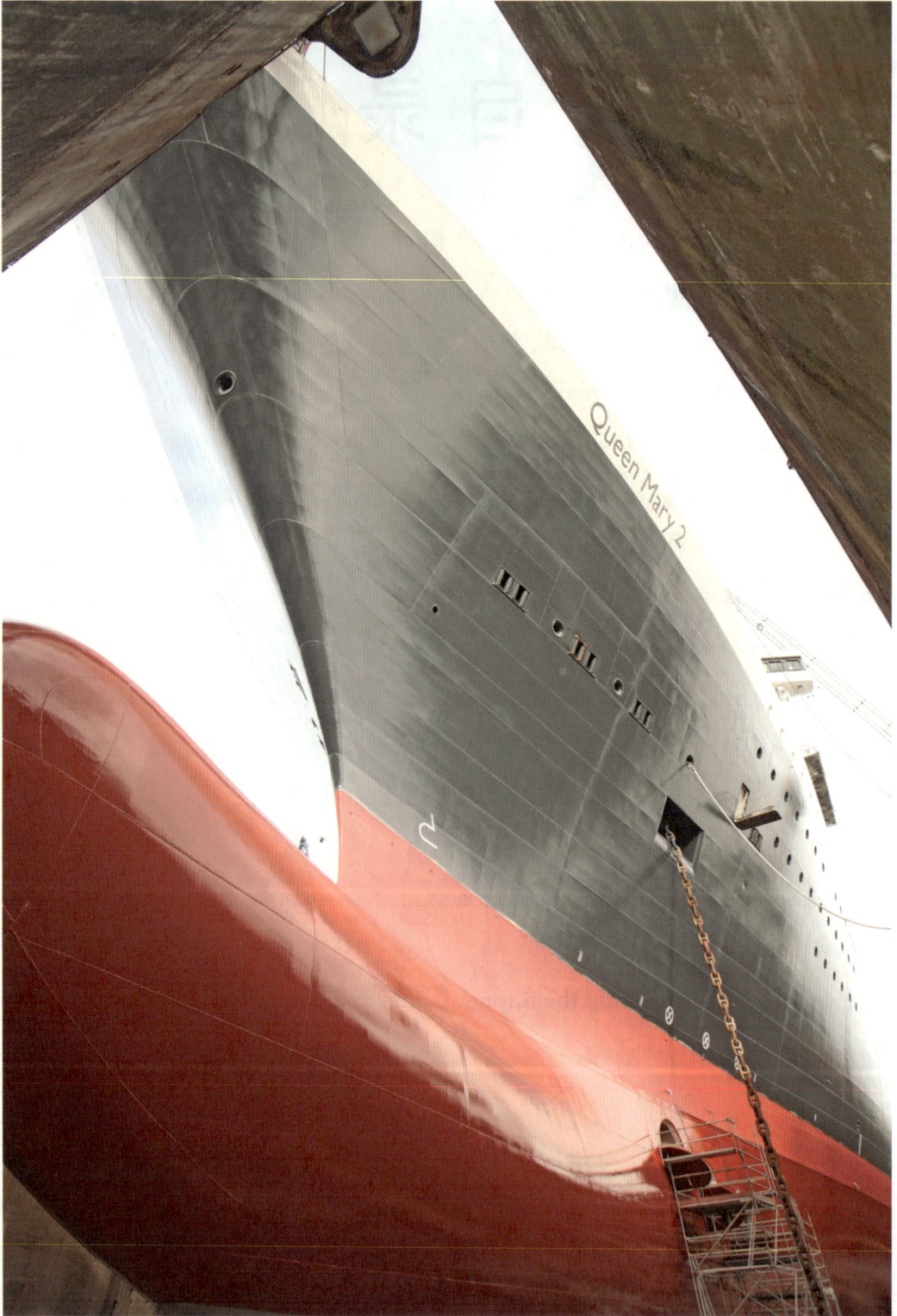

第一章 冠达和北大西洋上的"女王"们
Chapter One:Cunard and the North Atlantic Queens

Cunard has been synonymous with transatlantic travel since 4 July 1840 when the diminutive paddle steamer Britannia left the port of Liverpool bound for Boston; later voyages would use New York. At the resumption of services following the Second World War, it was Cunard's superlative Queens that dominated the Atlantic trade - Queen Mary 2 is the heiress to that glorious legacy.

1840年7月4日，一艘小型蒸汽明轮船"布列塔尼亚号"从利物浦港驶往波士顿（之后的目的地改为纽约），从此时开始，"冠达"就一直是跨大西洋旅行的代名词。第二次世界大战后，北大西洋恢复通航，冠达旗下最顶级的班轮主宰着大西洋上的贸易——"玛丽女王2号"就是这一光荣遗产的继承者。

　　"毛里塔尼亚号"在一次跨大西洋航行中最后到达利物浦，背景是著名的皇家利物浦大厦，而她的姊妹船"卢西塔尼亚号"准备前往新大陆。这两艘船从投入运营之日起就是大西洋上的速度女王，她们拥有4个由汽轮机驱动的螺旋桨，在性能上相较从前有了极大的飞跃。旅客住宿也达到了新的豪华程度，促使白星航运公司推出了"奥林匹克"级邮轮。（本图为冠达旗下的"玛丽女王2号"A座梯道内的作品，由艺术家高登·鲍文斯绘制）

　　"毛里塔尼亚号"在1906年11月3日至7日期间进行了航速测试，平均航速达到了26.04节①。按照这一航速，每天消耗的煤炭超过1 000吨；需要312名炉前工为锅炉服务。"毛里塔尼亚号"的辉煌一直持续到1934年。22年来，它是世界上最快的商船，也是传说中大西洋蓝丝带奖的保持者。

During 1920s Cunard line's express transatlantic service was operated by a trio of ships. The venerable Mauretania which entered service in 1907, was the smallest at 31,000grt, but she held the distinction of being the world's fastest liner for 22 years (25 knots) during which time she was acknowledged as the holder of the Blue Riband of the Atlantic. The second ship was the 45,000grt Aquitania of 1914, which had been originally designed as Cunard's reply to White Star Line's 'Olympic' class. She was a much more

在20世纪20年代，冠达旗下有3艘姊妹船服务于跨大西洋运输业务。在1907年服役的"毛里塔尼亚号"是最小的，为31 000总吨，但她是22年来世界上航速最快的班轮（25节），在此期间，她被公认为大西洋蓝丝带奖的保持者。第二艘是1914年投入运营的45 000总吨的"阿奎塔尼亚号"，最初的设计是作为冠达对"白星航运"的"奥林匹克"级的回应。与"毛里

① 1节 =1海里/小时，1海里 =1.852千米。

economical ship to operate compared to Mauretania, with a service speed of 23.5 knots. The final member of the trio was Berengaria, a ship of 52, 117grt that had started life as the Hamburg America Line's lmperator in 1913 before she was ceded to Great Britain from Germany under the terms of the Versailles Peace Treaty. Although the three ships were well regarded, they were not particularly well matched, offering different facilities and speed potential.When Mauretania lost the Blue Riband to the North German Lloyd liner Bremen in 1929 she lost part of her appeal. By the mid-1920s advances in naval architecture and marine engineering reached the position where it was theoretically possible to design ships to operate a weekly transatlantic service with a departure in each direction using two, instead of three, ships. This was the genesis of the idea that ultimately led to the construction of the revered Queen Mary and Queen Elizabeth.

In order to maintain a weekly service with two ships it was necessary to increase the average continuous sea speed from the hitherto 23.5 knots up to 28.5 knots in all but heavy seas. To provide this speed and give a reasonable return on investment it was determined that the smallest ships that would be able to reliably operate under these conditions would need to be in the order of 80,000grt, some 30,000grt larger than the current ships.

Before the first of the new ships

塔尼亚号"相比,她是一艘相对经济很多的船,服务速度为23.5节。3艘中最后一艘是"贝伦格里亚号",为52 117总吨。1913年,她作为汉堡美国航线的领头羊开始了运营,后来根据《凡尔赛和约》的条款从德国割让给英国。虽然这3艘船广受好评,但她们并不是特别相配,因为她们的配置和航速各不相同。1929年,随着"毛里塔尼亚号"把大西洋蓝丝带输给了北德劳埃德航运的"不莱梅号",她开始逐渐丧失了吸引力。到20世纪20年代中期,造船学和海洋工程的发展到达新的高度,从理论上能够使用两艘船而不是三艘船对向航行,来执行每周一次的跨大西洋航行服务。源于这种设计理念,最终促使了令世人敬仰的"玛丽女王号"和"伊丽莎白女王号"的建造。

为了通过两艘船维持每周的服务,必须将平均航速从23.5节提高到28.5节。为了保证在这一航速下得到合理的投资收益,可靠运行的船舶最小需要维持在80 000总吨左右,比目前最大的船舶大出约30 000总吨。

在订购第一批新船之前,必须考虑满足三个重要因素。第一个问题涉

could be ordered, three important considerations had to be met. The first related to the provision of a graving dock of suitable dimensions at Southampton to service the ships during overhaul. Since 1919 Cunard had been operating its express transatlantic service from the port after moving operations from Liverpool. At that time Southampton Docks were owned by Southern Railway, and it was representations to that company that resulted in the construction of the King George V dry dock at the end of Southampton's Western Docks. Upon completion in 1934 this was the largest dry dock in Great Britain. The second consideration was the provision of suitable berthing arrangements at Southampton and New York. Southampton was not a problem as the existing Ocean Dock(originally named White Star Dock when that line's ships exclusively used the facility before Cunard relocated operations to Southampton) was adequate, but New York was more of a problem. Moorings at New York took the form of piers that jutted out into the fast-streaming Hudson River. It was essential therefore that the piers were of sufficient length to adequately secure the ships, but none of the existing piers were long enough to accommodate the planned new ships. Once the port authorities agreed to build extended piers there remained only one further obstacle and this was not so easily solved. Cunard's new ships would be significantly bigger, at around

及在南安普敦配置一个适当尺寸的干船坞，以便在船舶大修期间提供维修服务。自 1919 年冠达从利物浦搬离以来，一直在南安普敦运营其跨大西洋航运业务。当时南安普敦的船坞属于南方铁路公司所有，正是该公司在南安普敦西部码头的尽头建造了乔治五世干船坞。直到 1934 年完工时，它一直是英国最大的干船坞。第二个考虑是在南安普敦和纽约具有适合的停泊条件。南安普敦并不是问题，因为现有的远洋码头足够使用（最初被命名为"白星码头"。在冠达将业务迁往南安普敦之前，该码头专供白星航运公司的船只使用），但在纽约则有大的问题。 在纽约，系泊的码头延伸到水流湍急的哈德逊河中间。因此，这些码头必须有足够的长度来确保船舶的安全，但现有的码头都不具有足够的长度来停靠计划建造的新船。如果港口当局同意扩建码头，就只剩下一个障碍，而这一障碍并不容易解决。冠达的新船将比当时最大为 50 000 总吨的船（当时最大的船是汉堡—美国航运公司旗下的 3 条姊妹船，分别是"贝伦格里亚号""利维坦号"和"威严号"）大得多，约 80 000 总吨，没

80,000grt, than the then largest liners of 50,000grt, and no single entity was prepared to offer insurance for such a high risk. (The largest liners at the time were the former Hamburg America Line trio then sailing as Berengaria, Leviathan and Majestic.)It took some time before a syndicate was established to spread the risk, but once in place Cunard could finally go ahead with arranging the building of its new ships.

Cunard decided to order the first ship from John Brown & Company, Clydebank. This shipyard had a strong heritage of building express ships for

有任何一个机构准备为如此高的风险提供保险。直至其后可以分摊风险的联合企业成立，冠达终于可以继续安排新船的建造。

冠达公司决定从位于克莱德班克的约翰布朗公司订购第一艘船。这座船厂有着为冠达公司建造快船的优良传统，最著名的是1906年的"卢西塔尼亚号"（"毛里塔尼亚号"的姊妹船，1915年被德国U20号潜艇击沉）和"阿基塔尼亚号"。594号造船订单

"玛丽女王号"停靠在南安普敦前远洋码头。这个内含火车站并具有极高艺术装饰水平的码头在1950年建造完成，但在1983年惨遭拆除。2009年以后一个新的远洋码头矗立在原码头对岸。（乔纳森·福尔克纳收集）

"贝伦格里亚号"，即前汉堡—美国航线公司的"统治者号"，与肖特公司 S.23 型帝国飞行艇"库伦加塔号"和梅奥综合型水上飞机"玛雅号"（最前者）一起停在南安普敦。

Cunard, with most notably the Lusitania in 1906(Mauretania's sister ship that was sunk by the German submarine U20 in 1915), and Aquitania. Order number 594 was signed on 1 December 1930 and the keel laying commenced on 31 January 1931. Across the English Channel the shipping company French line were planning a similar-sized ship of their own and the ships looked set to become keen rivals for transatlantic traffic.

After just a year of manufacture, on 11 December 1931 work was suspended on 594 when the ravages

于 1930 年 12 月 1 日签署，龙骨铺设开始于 1931 年 1 月 31 日。而在英吉利海峡的对岸，法国邮轮公司正计划建造他们自己的、具有相似尺寸的船只，这两艘船似乎将成为横渡大西洋的竞争对手。

仅仅在建造了一年之后，在 1931 年 12 月 11 日，大萧条摧毁了冠达公司的资金链，594 号订单的工作被迫暂停，这致使公司宣布无法再继续完成该船舶的建造。船体在船台上闲置了

of the Depression devastated Cunard's revenues, leading the company to announce that it could not afford to continue with the construction of ship. For more than two years the hull remained idle on the slipway. Following representations by David Kirkwood, the Clydebank MP to the government, a government loan was offered to Cunard to allow completion of the ship and the construction of a running mate. Strings

两年多。在克莱德班克议员戴维·柯克伍德向政府提出交涉后，政府向冠达公司提供了一笔政府贷款，以便完成这艘船的建造以及再建造一艘运兵船。在附加条件中，最引人注目的是，冠达公司必须与它的劲敌白星邮轮公司合并。至此，在1933年12月，这两家公司合并，形成了冠达·白星邮

1936年5月27日，"玛丽女王号"离开英格兰，开始她的处女航，途径瑟堡（法国西北部港市），于当年6月1日到达纽约。尽管从各方面来看，她都是一艘优秀的船，但她并不像她的法国对手"诺曼底号"那样放荡不羁，她被认为是一艘改进型的船而非革命性的船。（乔纳森·福尔克纳收集）

1940年3月8日，纽约哈德逊河沿岸。世界上最大的三条班轮并排在一起，从左到右分别是：英国的“伊丽莎白女王号”“玛丽女王号”和法国的“诺曼底号”。“女王号”们将作为超级运兵船离开，而“诺曼底号”注定要在港口结束她的生涯，她在改成运兵船的过程中被一场大火摧毁。（乔纳森·福尔克纳收集）

were attached, most notably that Cunard would have to unite with its arch but ailing rival, the White Star line. Thus in December 1933 the two concerns merged, forming the Cunard White Star Line with Cunard being the senior partner. Drastic rationalization soon followed, with most of the White Star Line fleet being sold off scrap. Work now resumed on hull 594, the first task

轮公司，而冠达是该公司的高级合伙人。随之而来的是公司内部激烈的合理化改革，大部分白星航运公司的船都被廉价卖掉了。然后在594号订单的船体上的工作重新开始，第一个任务就是清除船上累积的130吨铁绣。这艘船很快就做好了下水的准备，并被授予与她同名的“玛丽女王殿下号”。

being to remove 130 tons of accumulated rust. The ship was soon readied for launching and she was set afloat by her namesake, Her Royal Highness Queen Mary.

The delay in construction allowed the French Line Normandie (80,000grt) to enter service ahead of the Cunarder. Normandie was a superlative vessel in every sense of the world, a true rival to Queen Mary, and could be described as revolutionary rather than evolutionary

英国那边施工的延迟使得法国邮轮公司的"诺曼底号"（80 000 总注册吨位）先于冠达公司的船投入运营。在各种意义上"诺曼底号"都是世界上最高级的船，是"玛丽女王号"真正的竞争对手，由于其采用创新的涡轮电力推进装置和折衷主义装饰风格的乘客舱，她被认为是一艘革命性的船而非改进型的船。相比之下，"玛

在纽约的一个灿烂的日子里，"玛丽女王号"在随行拖船的帮助下，停靠在曼哈顿的冠达公司 90 号码头。（本图摆放在"玛丽女王 2 号"2 层甲板的大厅内，由冠达邮轮提供，戈登·鲍文斯作品）

due to her innovative turbo-electric propulsion plant and eclectic passenger accommodation. By comparison Queen Mary (81,000grt) was rather staid, if still spectacular. She entered service, sailing on her maiden voyage on 27 May 1936, and soon built up a loyal following. Paradoxically the Queen Mary was by far the more successful of the two ships from a commercial standpoint and she was in fact the only 'ship of state' (ie national flagship) of the period to operate at a profit. This was largely attributable to the quality of her second-

丽女王号"（81 000 总注册吨位）虽然仍很壮观，却显得相当古板。她于 1936 年 5 月 27 日开始了她的处女航并投入运营，而且很快获得了忠实的粉丝群。矛盾的是，从商业角度来看，"玛丽女王号"是目前为止两艘船中更为成功的一艘，事实上，她是当时唯一一艘盈利的"国家之船"（即国家旗舰）。这在很大程度上要归功于其二等舱和三等舱的住宿质量优于"诺曼底号"，因此她吸引了相当多的顾客。

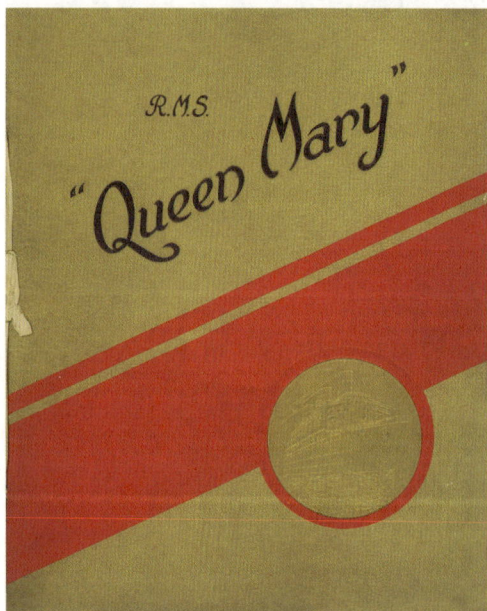

一个无价的艺术品：1936 年 5 月"玛丽女王号"首航时给乘客的纪念手册。这张全彩的跨页画展现了查尔斯·E·特纳对"玛丽女王号"的美好印象，那时位于克莱德班克的约翰·布朗公司刚刚将其引入到克莱德河完成下水。（约翰·奥斯汀提供）

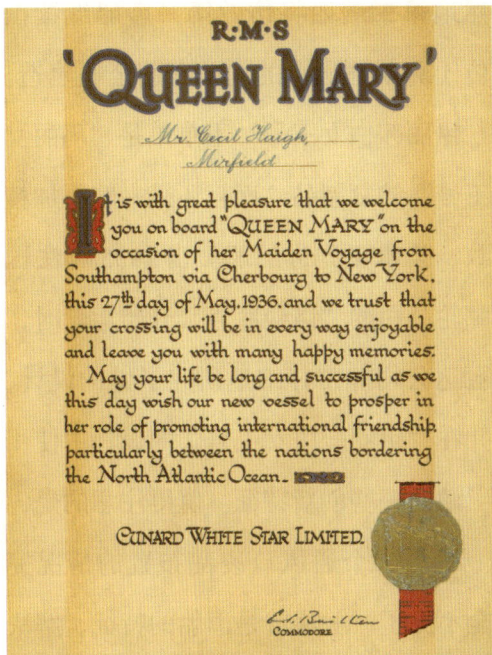

在"玛丽女王号"首航时向乘客颁发的奢华的"欢迎登船"证书。（约翰·奥斯汀提供）

and third-class accommodations that were in many ways superior to those on Normandie, thereby attracting considerable patronage. There were only two major issues with the ship. The first was vibration, which was particularly heavy in the part of the ship when she was running at her service speed of 28.5 knots. Nothing could really be done to improve this situation, which mainly affected the aft crew accommodation. The second was a rather glaring omission. Cunard had anticipated that the size of Queen Mary would render her immune to the ravages of the Atlantic weather and that she would be a stable platform. Internal handrails were largely excluded in corridors in order to provide a clean vista. In reality she had the

这艘船仅有两个主要问题：第一个就是振动，当以她的28.5节的服务航速运行时，部分船体的振动特别大。这种情况直接影响船尾机组人员的起居，而且没有切实有效的办法改善这种情况；第二个就是一个相当明显的纰漏。冠达公司曾预计，"玛丽女王号"的体型将会使她免受大西洋恶劣天气的破坏，她将成为一个稳定的平台。为了提供一个更宽敞的空间，走廊内的扶手被大量取消。而在实际航行中她有严重的横倾，每舷的倾斜角有时竟高达40°。

"玛丽女王号"一投入运营，面

propensity to roll heavily, sometimes up to 40 each side of the vertical.

As soon as Queen Mary entered service, work started on her running mate. It was only natural that the second ship should follow the first in being built at John Brown & Company, Clydebank. The Elizabeth was not merely a copy of the Mary but a much more refined and technically advanced ship. When the French Line Normandie entered service in 1935, Cunard had studied her design very carefully and a number of her innovative features were used in the design of Queen Elizabeth. Notably the upper deck was free from the clutter of numerous ventilation intakes that were a feature of the older ship, these being dealt with by grouping them at the base of the funnels within a housing on which the funnels sat. Significantly Queen Elizabeth required only two funnels, whereas Queen Mary needed three, since the number of boilers was halved from 24 to 12; the much larger boiler on the Elizabeth were more efficient, leading to economies in operation. The funnels themselves would be self-supporting without the need for external guy wires through the internal structure, the whistles being cocooned within their tops. Forward, the well-deck of the Mary was dispensed with since it was prone to flooding in heavy weather, causing momentary instability until the water dispersed overboard-instead the forecastle was flush decked. The rake of the stem was also marginally increased

向她的姊妹船的工作也开始了。顺其自然地第二艘船将仿效第一艘船继续由位于克莱德班克的约翰布朗公司建造。"伊丽莎白女王号"不单单是"玛丽女王号"的复制品，而且还是一艘更加精致、技术更先进的船。当 1935 年法国邮轮公司的"诺曼底号"开始运营时，冠达公司非常仔细地研究了她的设计，并在"伊丽莎白女王号"的设计中使用了她的一些创新特征。值得注意的是，上甲板多个通风口凌乱布置的情况完全不见了——这曾是旧船的特征，解决方法是将这些烟囱底部的通风进口都聚集到烟囱下面的一个房间内。另一个值得注意的地方是，"伊丽莎白女王号"只需要两个烟囱，而"玛丽女王号"需要 3 个，这是因为锅炉数量从 24 个减半到 12 个；"伊丽莎白女王号"上这些更大的锅炉更加高效，使得整个运营非常的经济。烟囱本身的结构很强，不需要外部的支撑缆绳穿过其内部结构，汽笛设置在它们的顶部。在船首，"玛丽女王号"采用下沉式甲板而不是平直甲板，这使其在恶劣的天气下会被水淹没，在水排除之前会造成船体暂时的失稳。船首的前倾也略有增加，以便可以容纳第三个船首锚，增加的前倾可以允

so that a third bow anchor could be accommodated, set within itself, the increased rake allowing the anchor to be deployed without the risk of fouling on the low stem.

The new ship launched on 27 September 1938 and took the name of her sponsor, Queen Elizabeth. To name the ship the Queen had travelled to Clydebank without the King, who had elected to remain in London at the height of the Munich crisis. The ship was due to enter service and join Queen Mary during 1940, but before this could happen Europe was plunged into war. Realizing that Queen Elizabeth (83,000

许锚部署在其船体内部，而不会有弄脏船首底部的风险。

新船于1938年9月27日下水，并以她的资助人伊丽莎白女王的名义命名。为了命名这艘船，女王在没有国王陪同的情况下只身前往克莱德班克，而国王在慕尼黑危机最严重的时候选择留在伦敦。这艘船计划于1940年投入运营并加入"玛丽女王号"系列，但在此之前，欧洲就已经陷入了战争。由于"伊丽莎白女王号"（83 000总吨）的目标和资产巨大，造船厂迫切希望

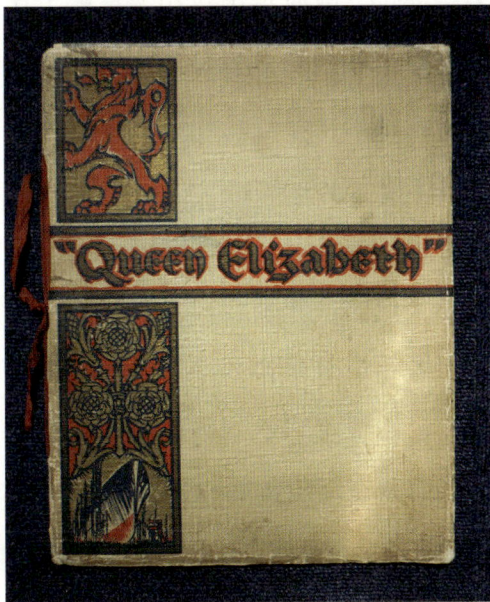

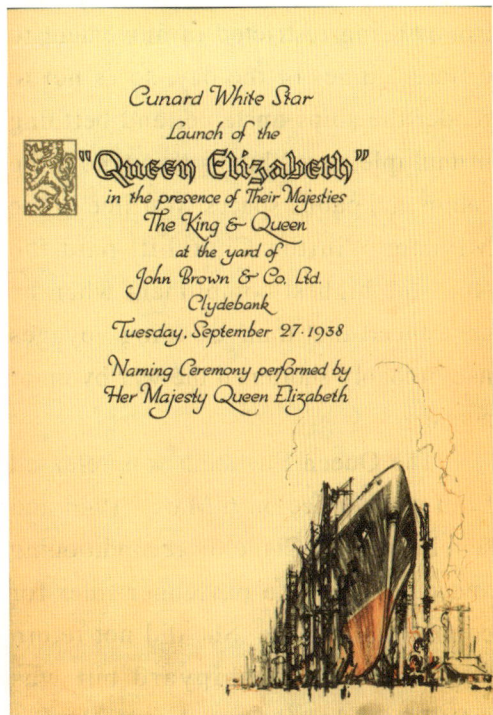

1938年9月27日，在克莱德班克，"伊丽莎白女王号"下水仪式上发给来宾们的纪念册。（作者收集）

grt) was a considerable target and asset, the shipyard rushed to get the ship ready to sea. On leaving the shipyard early in March 1940, it was widely leaked that the ship would be proceeding to Southampton, but in reality she was destined for New York where she arrived unannounced on 7 March 1940. Queen Mary was already in lay-up at the port, as was Normandie, and for a few short months the three largest liners in the world were docked together in the port. Subsequently both Queen Mary and Queen Elizabeth were requisitioned by the government and refitted as troop transports, each having a troop capacity of up to 16,000 per trip. The organisation for these voyages was colossal, with troops being restricted in movement to different times of the day, so as not to render the ships unstable, and berthing in multiple tiered bunks throughout the cabins and public spaces. Wartime Prime Minister Winston Churchill paid the ships the highest compliment when he announced that their trooping voyages had probably shortened the war by up to a year.

The Queen Elizabeth was released from war service on 6 March 1946 and sent back to the Clyde for reconditioning and outfitting as a passenger liner for commercial service. She did not return to John Brown's shipyard but was refitted while afloat and at anchor in the river, as it would have been very difficult for her to navigate back up the river due to her draught. The Queen

这艘船尽快出海。在 1940 年 3 月初该船出厂时，人们普遍猜测她将前往南安普敦，但实际上她在未对外宣布的情况于 1940 年 3 月 7 日已抵达了纽约港。此时"玛丽女王号"已经停靠在港口内，"诺曼底号"也是如此，短短几个月，世界上三艘最大的班轮同时停靠在此港口。随后，"玛丽女王号"和"伊丽莎白女王号"被政府征用，并被改装为运兵船，每航次的运输能力达 16 000 人。这些航行的组织工作是艰巨的，部队被要求在一天的不同时间分批登船，以防止船舶稳性出现问题，并在所有船舱和公共场所搭设多层铺位。战时英国首相温斯顿·丘吉尔对这两艘船致以最崇高的敬意，他郑重地说，通过这些船进行转运兵员可能使战争缩短了近一年的时间。

1946 年 3 月 6 日，"伊丽莎白女王号"退役，并被送回克莱德，作为商用客轮进行整修和舾装。由于吃水过深，她很难回航到约翰·布朗造船厂，而是在河上漂浮锚泊的情况下重新装修的。随后，"伊丽莎白女王号"于 1946 年 10 月 16 日开始她作为客轮的处女航行。

而"玛丽女王号"直到 1946 年 9

Elizabeth subsequently sailed on her maiden voyage as a passenger ship on 16 October 1946.

The Queen Mary was not released from war service until September 1946 and she was subsequently reconditioned at Southampton, a special temporary tent village being built near Winchester for the workforce. She resumed commercial service on 31 July 1947 when the two Queens were able to provide the two-ship weekly transatlantic service that Cunard had first envisaged way back in 1927. The two ships were eminently successful and for the next decade they were the true stars on the Atlantic, the only real competition coming from United States Lines from 1952 when the heavily subsidized super-liner-cum-troop-carrier, SS United States, entered service in 1952.

In 1957, non-stop transatlantic jet air travel between North America and Europe was made possible with the introduction of the Boeing 707 airliner. Cunard did not see this move as a threat to their services and, if anything, actually dismissed it as a fad. During the late 1950 s studies began into a replacement for Queen Mary and these became known as the Q3 Project (i.e. the third Queen ship). This ship was to be somewhat smaller than the existing Queens at 75,000 grt but she was to have been a thoroughbred transatlantic liner with no provision or even consideration for off-season cruising. However, Cunard's fortunes were now very much

月才从战争服役中解脱出来，随后在温彻斯特附近一个特别为工人临时搭建的帐篷村庄——南安普敦，进行了重新装修。她于1947年7月31日恢复商业运营。就如冠达邮轮早在1927年设想的那样，两艘女王号能够提供双船每周一航次的跨大西洋服务。这两艘船非常成功，在接下来的十年里，她们是大西洋上真正的明星，仅在1952年才有来自美国航线真正的竞争，即重金资助下建造的超级班轮兼运兵舰——"合众国号"，其在1952年开始投入运营。

1957年，随着波音707客机的引入，在北美和欧洲之间实现了跨洋直飞的喷气式飞机。冠达邮轮没有把这一举动看作是对他们服务市场的威胁，如果有，实际上也是把它当作一时的热潮。在20世纪50年代后期，冠达开始研究"玛丽女王号"的替代船，即后来被称为Q3的项目（即第三艘"女王号"船）。这艘船原本要比现存的女王号稍小一些，75 000总吨，计划仅是跨大西洋班轮，不准备甚至不考虑淡季巡航。然而，随着货运部门也开始出现赤字，客运业务的损失越来越大，冠达邮轮的资产现在正在快速

被漆成深灰色、高速迂回前行的"玛丽女王号"。在第二次世界大战的恶劣环境下，她由一艘护卫舰陪同执行跨大西洋快速运兵任务。（乔纳森·福尔克纳收集）

仍涂装战时单调的灰色伪装的"玛丽女王号"，驶过她的姐姐船"伊丽莎白女王号"。她作为班轮刚完成了开创纪录的航程——从新斯科舍州的哈利法克斯出发，于1946年9月27日到达南安普敦，2 531英里的旅程历时3天15小时48分钟。"伊丽莎白女王号"在和平时代早期已招收了服务人员，但直到1946年10月16日，她才为她的民用处女航做好准备。（乔纳森·福尔克纳收集）

in decline, with mounting losses on passenger operations made worse when the cargo division also started to show a deficit. Shareholders revolted and forced the board to reconsider the folly that was Q3. The design of the ship was subsequently recast as an even smaller 65,000 grt ship that was heralded as the first vessel that would be dual purpose and f for cruising and transatlantic service, even though Cunard's own Caronia (34,000 grt, 1949) had been successfully operating as such since her introduction.

The new ship, designated Q4, was ultimately ordered from John Brown & Company and was built on the same slipway as the previous Queens, Aquitania, Lusitania and HMS Hood. Meanwhile, losses continued to mount and drastic measures were required if Cunard was to survive. Early in 1967 it was announced that Queen Mary would be withdrawn that autumn, while Queen Elizabeth would follow in 1968, seven years earlier than planned-it had been envisaged that the Elizabeth would operate in conjunction with the new liner under construction, but the company decided that the future lay only with the new ship. The Caronia, Carinthia and Sylvania were also deemed uneconomic and were sold to raise finance to complete the new ship. The Queen Mary became a hotel, museum and convention centre at Long Beach in California, but success eluded Queen Elizabeth in a

缩水。股东的反对迫使董事会重新考虑启动 Q3 这一被认为是愚蠢的项目。因此，该船的设计后来被修改成一艘甚至更小的 65 000 总吨船，并被宣布为第一艘两用船，既可用于邮轮巡航，又可用于班轮跨洋航行。冠达邮轮自己的"卡罗尼亚号"（34 000 总吨，1949）自从运营以来一直也成功地采用这种运作方式。

这艘名为 Q4 的新船，最终订单是被约翰·布朗公司获得，与之前的"女王号"们、"阿基塔尼亚号""卢西塔尼亚号"和海军"胡德号"在同一船台上建造。与此同时，亏损持续增加，如果冠达邮轮要生存下去，必须采取强硬措施。1967 年初冠达宣布"玛丽女王号"将于秋季停止运营，而"伊丽莎白女王号"紧随其后将于 1968 年停运，比计划提前 7 年——根据设想，"伊丽莎白女王号"将与正在建设中的新班轮一起运营，但公司决定未来只运营新船。同时"卡罗尼亚号""卡林西亚号"和"西尔韦尼亚号"也被视为亏损，并被出售以筹集资金完成新船的建造。"玛丽女王号"后来成为加利福尼亚州长滩的一家酒店、博物馆兼会议中心，而在佛

1952年6月停泊在纽约北河码头上的3条船，是三个国家的海上骄傲，分别代表英国、法国和美国。从前到后："玛丽女王号""自由号"和"合众国号"。"自由号"之前是北德劳埃德的"欧罗巴号"，她的历史可追溯到1930年。"合众国号"于1952年7月3日首航，并以平均35.59节的航速成为历史上最快的班轮，从"玛丽女王号"手中夺走蓝丝带。（乔纳森·福尔克纳收集）

similar capacity at Fort Lauderdale in Florida. Subsequently sold to the Chinese shipping magnate CY Tung for conversion into a seagoing campus and called Seawise University, the ship was

罗里达州的劳德代尔堡，"伊丽莎白女王号"以同样的方式顺利运营。随后卖给中国航运巨头董浩云，并被改造成一个海上大学，称为"海上学府

由女王陛下新命名的"伊丽莎白女王 2 号"，于 1967 年 9 月 20 日在克莱德班克的约翰·布朗船厂下水。冠达邮轮新建的 Q4 班轮的船名在发布之前一直保密。该船被见证从建造过"卢西塔尼亚号""阿基塔尼亚号"和以前的"女王号"们的船台上滑下。这艘船现在看似不起眼的球鼻艏，随着人们对这种船体构件所带来的水动力优势的理解的不断深入，在她的航行生涯后期被加大了尺寸。

destroyed by what was almost certainly a coordinated arson attack while refitting before re-entering service on 9 January 1972.

In 1971, two years after the introduction of Queen Elizabeth 2, the Cunard Board recommended to shareholders acceptance of a buy-out proposal from the engineering and Construction conglomerate' Trafalgar House plc. The new management quickly moved to improve the profitability of Cunard and this included withdrawing Carmania and Franconia and purchasing two small cruise ships that were under construction, which they named Cunard Adventurer and Cunard Ambassador. Queen Elizabeth 2 was also reconfigured to increase revenue with the addition of further cabins, the substitution of a library with a casino, relocating the shops to the upper level of one of the lounges and operating the ship on a more intensive schedule. The latter measure turned out to be ill-advised as the ship had been designed for operation on four boilers, but she was only fitted with three as an economy measure. The heightened schedule did not allow sufficient maintenance to be carried out, as all three boilers were invariably required to be in steam - the deleted fourth boiler would have allowed a rotating maintenance schedule to be performed.In consequence, the ship's boilers soon began to show serious defects including leaking tubes, which would result in a number of high-profile

号"，后来该船因蓄意纵火而损毁，经修缮，该船于1972年1月9日重新投入使用。

1971年，在"伊丽莎白女王2号"投入运营两年后，冠达邮轮董事会建议股东接受工程和建筑集团旗下特拉法尔加豪斯公司的收购建议。新管理层迅速提升了冠达邮轮的盈利能力，其中包括撤出"卡曼尼亚号"和"法兰克尼亚号"以及购买两艘正在建造的小型邮轮，他们将其命名为"冠达冒险者号"和"冠达大使号"。"伊丽莎白女王2号"也进行了重新配置以增加收入：增加了更多的客舱，用赌场代替图书馆，将商店搬迁到其中一个休息室的上层，并以更密集的时间表来运营。后一种措施的结果显示是不明智的，因为这艘船最初的设计是用4台锅炉运行，但出于经济因素考虑她只配备了3台。由于所有3台锅炉总是需要处于工作状态，而紧张的时间表无法让锅炉进行充分的维护——减掉的第四台锅炉原本允许船舶在航行状态下进行维护。因此，该船的锅炉很快就开始出现严重的问题，包括管道泄露，这将导致一些明显的故障出现。到1985年，冠达邮轮意识到若不能重新为"伊丽莎白女王2号"装设引擎，则

breakdowns. By 1985 Cunard realised that they would either have to re-engine Queen Elizabeth 2 or withdraw her, and they eventually chose to do the former by replacing the original steam turbine machinery with a state of the art diesel electric plant.The huge £100 million refit was undertaken over the winter of 1986/87 at Lloyd-Werft in Bremerhaven, and the rejuvenated ship was redelivered to Cunard on 27 April 1987.

必须撤回她。他们最终选择通过用最先进的柴油发电机取代原来的汽轮机来完成这一方案。1986 年至 1987 年冬天，"伊丽莎白女王 2 号"在位于德国不来梅哈芬市的劳埃德威夫特船厂接受了价值 1 亿英镑的巨型改装工程，1987 年 4 月 27 日，这艘重新焕发活力的船再次交付冠达邮轮。

"伊丽莎白女王 2 号"沿南安普敦水域开往南大西洋，并于 1982 年 5 月 12 日担任福克兰群岛特遣部队的运兵船。事实上，由于"伊丽莎白女王 2 号"患有慢性锅炉病，这次出航只是假装恐吓阿根廷军政府。在只有 3 个大型锅炉中的一个可以使用的情况下，这艘船跟趾地驶向一个僻静的锚地，在那里，她一直停留到第二天。一旦第二台锅炉开始运转，她就以 24 节的航速驶往福克兰群岛，当最后一台锅炉维修完，其航速可达 27 节。

"伊丽莎白女王 2 号"于 2008 年 10 月 5 日对克莱德的最后一次访问。

华丽的化身：2008 年 11 月 11 日，"伊丽莎白女王 2 号"准备最后一次离开南普敦。（作者提供）

Through constant upgrades and refits, the ship kept abreast of the competition. One popular change was the introduction of a heritage trail, which tapped into the increasing nostalgia market. In 1996 Trafalgar House was itself acquired by the Anglo-Norwegian Kvaerner group and Cunard was one of the assets that was subsequently deemed as disposable because it wasn't within the core activities of the company. In 1998 Carnival Corporation, in conjunction with a group of Norwegian investors, purchased the Cunard Line. However, within a short period Carnival bought out its Norwegian partners and Cunard passed completely into Carnival's ownership. In June 1998 Carnival announced that consideration was being given to a new transatlantic liner, code named 'Project Queen Mary'. Initially slated as merely a paper project to investigate the economic viability of building and operating a new-generation transatlantic liner, it would ultimately lead to the placement of an order with Alstom Chantiers de I'Atlantique at St Nazaire on 6 November 2000 and delivery of Queen Mary 2 on 23 December 2003.

With the introduction of Queen Mary 2, Queen Elizabeth 2 lost her designation as flagship and was relegated to see out her remaining years as a cruise ship. Her final Cunard voyage was in November 2008 when she arrived in Dubai for conversion into a floating hotel and museum. The

通过不断的升级和改装，这艘船在竞争中与对手并驾齐驱。其引进的一条古迹观光航线令人耳目一新，这条航线挖掘了日益增长的怀旧市场。1996年，特拉法尔加豪斯公司被盎格鲁-诺唯真·卡瓦纳集团收购，因为不属于公司的核心业务范围，所以作为其资产之一的冠达邮轮被忽视。1998年，嘉年华集团与一群挪威投资者一起收购了冠达邮轮。然而，在短期内，嘉年华集团又收购了其挪威合作伙伴，至此冠达邮轮完全归嘉年华集团所有。1998年6月，嘉年华集团宣布考虑建造一艘新的跨大西洋班轮，代号为"玛丽女王号项目"。最初，该项目被指责仅仅是一个纸上项目，旨在调查建造和运营新一代跨大西洋邮轮的经济可行性。最终，2000年11月6日，嘉年华集团与位于法国圣纳泽尔的阿尔斯通大西洋船厂签订订单，计划于2003年12月23日交付"玛丽女王2号"。

随着"玛丽女王2号"的诞生，"伊丽莎白女王2号"失去了旗舰称号，降级为普通邮轮度过余生。她的最后一次航行是在2008年11月，抵达迪拜后准备被建成一座海上酒店和博物馆。但随后的全球经济衰退导致该项目被取消。与此同时，两艘新船"维多利亚女王号"和"伊丽莎白女王号"

subsequent general economic downturn led to the project being cancelled. Meanwhile, two new ships have entered service with Cunard: Queen Victoria and Queen Elizabeth. These two ships are stretched versions of Holland America Line's successful Vista-class cruise ships (Zuiderdam et al.), the additional length being used for the incorporation of a ballroom (Queens Room).

Queen Mary 2 remains the consummate transatlantic liner, offering a mix of crossings and other voyages. She is eminently successful in this role and immensely popular. Feted wherever she sails, there is simply no other passenger ship in the world to match her iconic style and presence. She is truly a Queen in being.

加入冠达邮轮开始运营。这两艘船是荷美邮轮公司成功的 Vista 级邮轮（如"宅德丹号"等）的加长版，增加的长度用来合并成一个舞厅（"女王"厅）。

"玛丽女王 2 号"一直是最完美的跨大西洋班轮，她提供一系列跨洋和其他类型的航行。她非常成功，也非常受欢迎。无论她在哪里航行，世界上没有任何一艘客轮可以与她标志性的风格和存在相媲美。她是真正的"女王"。

（译者：王露、丁悦、贺明鸣）

壮丽的"玛丽女王 2 号"和"伊丽莎白女王 2 号"（由戈登·鲍文斯提供的原创油画）

3 艘"女王号","玛丽女王 2号""伊丽莎白女王 2 号"和"维多利亚女王号"在南安普敦相遇。

2009 年 2 月在迪拜拉希德港的"伊丽莎白女王 2 号"。(维基百科提供)

在壮丽的景色中,"玛丽女王 2 号"气势磅礴地向右转弯。这艘船轻松地穿过平静的海面,展示了一艘旗舰班轮的优良特征。(冠达邮轮提供)

第二章 "玛丽女王2号"的故事
Chapter Two:The Queen Mary 2 story

The realisation of Queen Mary 2 was not a foregone conclusion _ Project Queen Mary, a comprehensive design and economic review, had to prove conclusively that a new Atlantic liner would deliver a commensurate level of return on investment before the project could proceed. A five-year timeline between May 1998 and December 2003 would ensue before Queen Mary 2 was ready for service.

"玛丽女王2号"的建成并非一帆风顺——"玛丽女王号"项目在进行之前,一项综合了设计和经济性的评估最终证明,一艘新的大西洋班轮将带来等量的投资回报。从1998年5月到2003年12月,历时5年,"玛丽女王2号"已经完全准备好投入运营。

"玛丽女王2号"在旧金山湾,刚刚穿过金门大桥。（冠达邮轮提供）

Queen Mary 2 timeline
"玛丽女王 2 号"时间表

1998 8 June

'Project Queen Mary', is announced just one week after Carnival Corporation completes its purchase of the Cunard Line. Plans to undertake the design and development of a new class of transatlantic liner are unveiled.

1998 年 6 月 8 日

"玛丽女王号项目"，是在嘉年华集团完成对冠达邮轮公司的收购后仅仅一周时宣布的。设计和开发新型跨大西洋班轮的计划公之于众。

CUNARD ANNOUNCES 'PROJECT QUEEN MARY'

New concept to evoke the spirit of a bygone era of elegance

冠达宣布"玛丽女王号项目"

全新的概念唤醒旧时优雅的时光

OSLO, 8 June 1998

The new Cunard Line Limited today unveiled plans for 'Project Queen Mary', the undertaking of the design and development for a new class of stately superliner that will invoke the spirit of a bygone era of seagoing luxury. The announcement was made here to Cunard's Norwegian shareholders by Larry Pimentel, the line's President, who said 'The project will lead to the development of the grandest and

1998 年 6 月 8 日，奥斯陆

冠达邮轮公司今天宣布了"玛丽女王号项目"的计划，设计和开发新级别的宏大的超级班轮，去唤醒昔日的海上胜景。该计划由冠达·诺唯珍邮轮公司总裁、董事拉里·皮门特尔宣布，并说明："这一项目将引领有史以来最宏伟、最大的班轮的开发，也将会是优美、时尚、雅致的典范。"

"我们的目标是建造新一代的远

largest liner ever built — the epitome of elegance, style and grace.

'It is our objective to build a new generation of ocean liner that will be the very pinnacle of the shipbuilder's art; the realisation of a dream of another time. Our goal is nothing less than to create a new Golden Age of sea travel for those who missed the first,' he said. Pimentel also advised the shareholders group that the recent acquisition by Carnival Corporation and the subsequent merger of Cunard and Seabourn Cruise Line will lead to stability and growth.

'Stability of management and cost containment are high priority goals of our new organisation. We will be a highly cost efficient operation while at the same time developing ourselves into the world's strongest, most profitable cruise operation in the luxury segment of the industry, he said. 'Cunard Line is the world's only truly global cruise brand,' he stated. 'Nearly 50 per cent of its business comes from outside North America, from Europe including the UK, with significant business from Australia and the Far East. We also intend to consolidate shoreside operations for greater efficiency and cost savings, and will scrutinise our budgeted marketing funds carefully and allocate them between the Cunard and Seabourn brands in a highly targeted and efficient manner 'he told the shareholders group. He concluded by saying 'We will operate two, and only two, five star luxury brands, Cunard and Seabourn. Finally, we have already begun an accelerated

洋班轮,使之成为造船艺术的巅峰,实现一个时代的梦想。"他说:"我们的目标就是为那些错过第一次环球航行的人创造一个新的海上旅行的黄金时代。"皮门特尔还向股东们表示,嘉年华集团最近的收购,以及随后与冠达邮轮和世邦邮轮公司的合并,将给集团带来稳定及利润的增长。"

"稳定的成本管理和控制是我们新公司的首要目标。我们将成为一个高效运作,同时发展成为世界上邮轮运营行业中最强大的、最赚钱的豪华邮轮运营商,"他说,"冠达邮轮公司是世界上唯一真正意义上的全球邮轮品牌,"他同时声明,"公司近50%的业务来自北美以外,包括英国在内的欧洲、澳大利亚和远东。我们也打算规范岸上的操作以提高效率,节约成本。我们还将仔细审查营销预算资金,从而以高度的针对性和有效的方式分配给冠达和世邦品牌,"他最后说:"我们将运营两家(也只有两家)五星级豪华品牌——冠达和世邦。最后,我们已经开始了一项加速计划,以持续改进我们岸上的客户服务标准,并进一步完善我们整个舰队的客户服务标准。"

在皮门特尔的演讲之后,一个新组建的"玛丽女王号项目"团队将召开第一次会议,该团队将定期就这一概念举行会议,以研发并最终确定布

programme to continue and improve our customer service standards ashore, and to refine further the guest service standards throughout our fleet.'

Pimentel's presentation here is to be followed by the first meeting of a new 'Project Queen Mary' planning team which will meet regularly on the concept to develop and finalise plans and design features. Although details of the size, guest capacity and deployment have yet to be determined, the concept is expected to develop into the next evolution of a true ocean liner and not a substitute for Cunard's elegant top liner, Queen Elizabeth 2.

局和设计特性。虽然具体的尺寸、载客量和航线部署还有待确定，但这一概念预计将发展为下一代真正的远洋班轮，而不是冠达公司优雅的顶级班轮"伊丽莎白女王2号"的替代品。

在嘉年华集团和挪威投资集团收购了冠达之后，于上月组建了新的冠达航运公司。冠达和世邦将合并成一个新的实体。

冠达邮轮公司备受期待的、新经

1999

8 November

Cunard announces that the general arrangement plans for the liner is completed. 'Project Queen Mary', is to be the largest passenger ship ever built First image is released.

1999 年

11 月 8 日

冠达公司宣布，该邮轮的总布置图已经完成。"玛丽女王号项目"将是有史以来建造的最大客轮。

CUNARD ANNOUNCES LARGEST PASSENGER SHIP EVER BUILT

General arrangement plans are complete; details and shipyard to be announced at turn of the year

冠达宣布建造有史以来最大的客轮

总布置图已完成，该船的细节和建造船厂将在年初公布

The new Cunard Line was organised last month following the acquisition of Cunard by Carnival Corporation and the group of Norwegian investors. Cunard and Seabourn are merging into the new entity.

Plans for Cunard Line's much anticipated, classic new ocean liner, a grand and glamorous link to the golden age of sea travel, have now been finished and the company will name the vessel and builder by the year's end. She is expected to be the largest passenger ship ever built. This news was revealed by Larry Pimentel, President & CEO of Cunard Line Limited, who said he was prompted to comment on progress to date because of increasingly high interest in the new ocean liner.

'Of the many ships being built, this Cunard ocean liner is perhaps the most intriguing. She will be the most famous ship in the world even before she takes to the seas. The level of interest is beyond our wildest imagination.' He added that based on Cunard's timetable, the vessel is expected to be introduced in 2003.

The silhouette of Project Queen Mary will be unmistakable. She will be sleek and majestic with a dramatic raked prow, similar to QE2, reflecting the grandeur of the great Cunard liners of the past. At more than 1,100 feet long, her hull will be longer than three football fields and painted a matt black, a Cunard tradition dating back nearly 160 years. Her giant single stack, painted in the historic Cunard Red with black bands,

① 1 英尺 =0.3048 米

典远洋班轮的布置图现已完成,该公司将在今年年底前确定这艘船的名称和建造船厂。新型远洋班轮将会唤起旧时海上航行的黄金岁月。预计她将成为有史以来建造的最大客轮。冠达邮轮公司总裁兼首席执行官拉里·皮门特尔透露了这一消息。他说,由于人们对这艘新远洋班轮的兴趣日益浓厚,所以他公布了项目截止目前的进展。

"在众多正在建造的船只中,这艘冠达远洋班轮可能是最吸引人的。在她出海之前,她就已经是世界上最著名的船。受关注程度超出了我们的想象。"他补充道,根据冠达的时间表,这艘船预计将于2003年投入使用。

"玛丽女王项目"从外观来说,是不可能会被认错的。她有一个圆润、雄伟的、引人注目的倾斜船首,类似于"伊丽莎白女王2号",体现了曾经的冠达班轮的荣光。她的船身将超过1 100英尺①长,超过3个足球场,船身涂上了哑光黑漆,这一传统可以追溯到近160年前。她那巨大的单体烟囱,漆上具有历史意义的冠达红,再配上黑色的条纹,巨大而醒目。在其龙骨之上,建筑体量超过20多层。前方,她的引人注目的白色上层建筑将从破浪犁开始逐层累加,到船尾又逐层下降,与经典班轮的侧面轮廓相呼应。她的发电装置发出的电力足以点亮和

海洋艺术家 Gordon Bauwens 受冠达公司委托为"玛丽女王2号"新邮轮绘制了一幅草图。这幅画是在决定在烟囱底部的房子里将两个燃气轮融入设计之前准备的。

will tower more than 20 storeys above her keel. Forward, her eye-catching white superstructure will be stepped far back from her raked prow, and stepped aft as well, in the classic liner profile. Her power plant will produce sufficient electricity to light a city the size of Southampton. And her engines will produce 140,000 horsepower - the equivalent of 1,400 family cars. Her great whistle will be audible from a distance of ten miles. The unique Cunard liner will carry 2,500 guests in dramatic palatial interior spaces, reminiscent of the White Star liner Titanic. Considering that smaller ships sailing today carry many

南安普敦大小差不多的城市。她的发动机将产生14万匹马力①的动力——相当于1 400辆家用汽车。她巨大的汽笛声从十英里外就能听到。独特的冠达班轮将容纳2 500名客人，其引人注目的宫殿般的室内空间，让人回忆起白星邮轮的"泰坦尼克号"。考虑到如今更小的船只可以承载更多的客人，这2 500名幸运的乘客将享受到可谓奢侈的人均空间，船上每两个客人就配有近一名工作人员提供贴心服务，从而确保了其他任何大型船只都无法比拟的服务标准。

① 1 马力 =735 瓦

more guests, those 2,500 fortunate will enjoy an extravagant amount of space per guest, and the skilled attention of nearly one staff member per couple of guests on board, assuring a service standard unmatched on any other large vessel.

The ship's ambience will reflect a high style and grace, with classic Cunard hallmarks such as grand staircases, expansive promenades elegant grand restaurants and gracious public rooms of an imposing scale. Some of the features already revealed include a Heritage Trail highlighted by mementos and artefacts from Cunard's 160-year history and an onboard Maritime Museum of liner history; a pub with its own onboard microbrewery; an advanced Computer Learning Centre and an extravagant spa and health centre. Other unique design concepts will be revealed as the final yard selection is made.

While Project Queen Mary is expected to be the largest passenger vessel ever built, Pimentel said she will nevertheless maintain a feeling of intimacy with smaller, comfortable spaces ideal for contemplation and privacy. Three-quarters of all suites, staterooms and apartments will have large private balconies.

Larry Pimentel continued: 'Ever since we announced we would build a giant classic liner, our mail has been flooded with requests for information and wherever I go I am besieged by questions about her. Guests have even sent in deposits without knowing the specifics of the product or the

船上的环境将体现出高贵和优雅，这与经典的冠达公司的特征保持一致。如宏伟的楼梯间、宽阔的过道、优雅的大餐厅和亲和的公共景观区域。船上的海洋历史博物馆中已经揭示了冠达公司的特色，其中包括一段展示冠达邮轮公司 160 年历史的纪念品和人工制品的历史遗迹长廊；一个有自己专属小啤酒厂的酒吧；一个先进的电脑学习中心和一个奢侈的水疗和健康中心。其他别具匠心的设计理念将会在选定船厂后再展现出来。

据皮门特尔介绍，"玛丽女王号"预计将成为史上建造的最大客轮，但她仍将保持一种亲密感，拥有更小、更舒适的空间，是沉思和私人活动的理想场所。四分之三的套房、贵宾室和公寓将配有大型私人阳台。

拉里·皮门特尔继续说道："自从我们宣布要建造一个巨大的经典班轮以来，我们的邮件系统就被大量的咨询信息所淹没，无论我走到哪里，我都被关于她的问题所包围。客人甚至在尚不知道产品细节或部署的情况下就预付定金。坦率地说，他们想成为 30 年来首次建造的远洋客轮上的第一批客人。这个项目是如此的万众瞩目，我们必将谨慎而小心地执行。项目规模巨大，成本高昂。我们将在新千年的关键时刻公布'玛丽女王号'

deployment. Candidly, they want to be the first guests on the first ocean liner to be built in thirty years. While we realise that details of this wonderful project are eagerly awaited, we are proceeding prudently and deliberately. The grand scope and cost of the project dictates this approach. We will unveil complete plans for Project Queen Mary on the cusp of the new millennium. We will build a unique liner that fosters the tradition and legacy of British seagoing excellence. We can't be, and we won't be, rushed. Maritime architects, marine historians and interior designers have been hard at work developing the form and style of the ship and completing detailed plans and drawings for her creation.'

General arrangement plans have been completed. However, it is expected that the shipyard ultimately selected may well suggest minor modifications and improvements. Three shipyards have already quoted on her building and two others will provide quotes within a month.

Pimentel was careful to distinguish between Cunard's planned ocean liner and today's large modern cruise ships. 'The true nature of an ocean liner is that of a majestic thoroughbred roaming the oceans of the world. They are conceived with a long, streamlined hull, a proportionally long bow section and a stepped stern, giving them a sleek profile that is distinctive and pleasing to the eye. They are capable of very high speeds. The speed of Project Queen Mary will probably not exceed that of Queen Elizabeth 2, Cunard's current

项目的完整计划。我们将打造一艘独特的班轮，以此来弘扬英国优秀的航海传统和伟大遗产。我们不能，也不会仓促行事。船舶设计师、海洋历史学家和室内设计师一直在努力工作，设计船舶的形式和风格，完成详细的规划和图纸。"

总布置图已经设计完成。然而，可以预见的是，船厂最终会提出一些较小的修改和改进的建议。三家船厂已经给出了建造成本的报价，另外两家将在一个月内给出报价。

皮门特尔详细地分析了冠达拟建造的远洋班轮和现代化的大型豪华邮轮之间的区别。"远洋班轮的实质是漫长而纯粹地航行在世界各地的海洋上。设想中，她们具有修长的流线船壳，修长的船首和阶梯状的船尾，使她们圆滑的侧面轮廓变得特点鲜明和赏心悦目。她们具有较高的航速。'玛丽女王项目'的航速将可能难以超过冠达的现役旗舰'伊丽莎白2号'。然而，她的建造方案将保证她也能达到30节的航速。因此，她必须具有较高的强度和稳性，以便在远洋高速航行。同时，为了提高舒适性和稳定性，需采用较深的吃水和较小的水线面。现代豪华邮轮的航线大多靠近她们几乎每天需要到访的停靠港。海乘体验完全不同。当然，很多人都有在邮轮上的海乘体

flagship, which is the fastest deep sea passenger ship in the world. However, she will certainly be built to operate at speeds in the vicinity of 30 knots. She must therefore possess an inherent strength and stability necessary for high-speed passage through open ocean conditions, and a deep, narrow draft to cut the water for a comfortable and stable ride.Modern cruise ships stick more closely to ports of call which they visit on an almost daily basis. The seagoing experiences are different. Certainly, there is a vast public for the cruise experience.We believe, similarly, there is an eager and growing audience for the drama, elegance and shipboard ambience exemplified by sailing aboard a true Atlantic ocean liner.We know that details of our liner are eagerly awaited but no one has built a true ocean liner in more than 30 years. It is nearly a lost art. Shipbuilders can't simply go into their plan files and pull out a convenient blueprint. We are recreating history.

Pimentel stated emphatically that Project Queen Mary would not only extend Cunard's global brand position and popularity among discerning guests, but would undoubtedly be the most profitable liner ever built.

Concluding, Pimentel stated, 'The extraordinary interest we have experienced in this magnificent ocean liner tells us there is yearning for a return to the golden age of sea travel. It's a bygone era and an exciting concept for a new audience and a new time, and that time is now.'

验。我们相信,与此相类似,人们渴望通过登乘一艘真正的跨洋班轮,获得一种戏剧性、优雅和完全生活在船上的体验。我们知道大家都在热切期待着了解班轮的具体细节,但是已经有30多年没有建造过真正意义上的远洋班轮了,这几乎是一门失传的技艺。工程师不是简单地列出计划,设计出可行的蓝图就可以的,我们是在重新创造历史。"

皮门特尔着重强调道,"玛丽女王项目"不仅将扩大冠达品牌的全球地位和口碑,而且会毫无疑问地成为有史以来最赚钱的班轮。

总而言之,皮门特尔坚信,"我们对这艘壮观的远洋班轮所表现出的极大兴趣,说明人们渴望重返航海的黄金时代。对现在的人来讲,那曾经是一个激动人心的时代,是时候重现辉煌了。"

2000

10 March

Letter of intent signed with Chantiers de I'Atlantique shipyard in France for the £550 million Queen Mary 2.

2000 年

3 月 10 日

法国大西洋船厂签署 5.5 亿英镑的"玛丽女王 2 号"的意向书。

CUNARD SIGNS LETTER OF INTENT FOR QUEEN MARY 2

$700 million liner will be the world's longest,

largest ever – and the fastest cruise liner since QE2

冠达签署"玛丽女王 2 号"意向书

7 亿美元的班轮将成为世界上自"伊丽莎白女王 2 号"以来最长、

最大、最快的班轮

Cunard Line announced today that the company has signed a letter of intent to build its superliner Queen Mary 2 at the Alstom Chantiers de I'Atlantique shipyard in St-Nazaire, France. The liner is expected to be launched in the last quarter of 2003. Once launched, Queen Mary 2 is intended to fly the British flag with her homeport being Southampton.

Micky Arison, Chairman and CEO of Carnival Corporation, Cunard's parent company, said:

'The signing of this letter of intent is a significant milestone in the birth of this unique vessel. Over the last months,

冠达公司今天宣布,他们与位于法国圣纳泽尔的阿尔斯通大西洋船厂签订了建造"玛丽女王 2 号"超级班轮的意向书。班轮预计将于 2003 年的最后一个季度投入运营。运营后,"玛丽女王 2 号"拟挂英国国旗,母港为南安普敦。

冠达的母公司嘉年华集团的董事长兼首席执行官米奇·阿里森说:"这份意向书的签署对于这艘独一无二的船的诞生具有里程碑性的意义。在过去的几个月里,我们建造新一代首艘

our vision of the first true ocean liner to be built in a generation has evolved from a dream to a detailed plan on paper. We are satisfied that the shipyard that created Normandie, France and other legendary liners has the capability to make that dream a reality.'

Alstom Chantiers de I'Atlantique, which employs over 4,000 workers in its facility, has a continuing record of delivering ships of unusual size and style. Recent projects at the yard resulted in large ships for the coastal cruising trade. However, it is entirely another matter to construct a purpose-built transatlantic liner.From the architect's plans to the nature of the steel plating that forms the skin of the hull, a liner differs in most details from the sorts of ships that have been built in the last three decades. Nonetheless, Alstom's officers are confident that their company represents the best choice for Cunard.

真正远洋班轮的设想已经落实为详细的设计图纸。我们对曾经建造过'诺曼底号''法国号'和其他传奇班轮的造船厂非常满意,他们有能力将我们的梦想变为现实。"

阿尔斯通大西洋船厂雇佣了4 000名工人,是业界建造特殊船型的翘楚。其最近交付的大船项目用于沿海贸易。然而,建造一艘特制的跨大西洋班轮完全是另一回事。由于班轮船型的不同,导致从设计师的方案到形成船舶外壳的钢板都和过去30年间建造的船有很大的差异。尽管如此,阿尔斯通公司的高层仍然坚信他们是冠达公司的最佳选择。

北大西洋上的归家之路。在波涛汹涌的北大西洋上,"玛丽女王2号"从容地保持着航向和速度,完成经典的跨洋航行。"玛丽女王2号"具有20世纪30年代的"国之旗舰"的优雅,是唯一仍然提供定期往返航行的客船。(该画为尊敬的戈登·鲍文斯所作)

Alstom Chantiers de I'Atlantique Chairman and CEO Patrick Boissier: 'We want to build this magnificent ship because of our history and because of our future. We understand the character of the ship they want to build, and we know how to build that kind of ship.'

Cunard Line President and CEO Larry Pimentel: 'The level of excitement and interest in this project is beyond anything we could have imagined. Queen Mary 2 seems to embody the public's renewed fascination with the romance of a bygone era of sea travel. Now that excitement and interest is being transformed into a tangible project, with dollars and cents attached to it. From the start, we believed that this project could be realized. Now we have agreed to the fundamentals of how we are going to make Queen Mary 2 not merely a reality, but a sound investment and a resounding success. QM2 will measure over 1,130 feet in length-that's just 117 feet shorter than the Empire State Building is tall. She'll tower nearly 21 stories in height from keel to masthead, with a gross registered tonnage of nearly 150,000 tons.'

Pimentel stated that QM2 is expected to carry just 2,800 guests, which is a very small complement for a ship of this size, and a guest-to-crew ratio of about 2-to-1 will enable a superb service standard.

Pimentel: 'But aside from her sheer size, she is a marvel of innovative features, specifically designed for her.

阿尔斯通大西洋船厂的董事长兼首席执行官帕特里克·布瓦西耶说:"建造这艘壮观的班轮,是由于我们悠久的造船历史和丰富的造船经验,更是为我们自己创造未来。我们不但了解要建造的这艘班轮的特性,而且知道如何建造。"

冠达邮轮公司的总裁兼首席执行官拉里·皮门特尔说:"这个项目的吸引力超乎我们的想象。'玛丽女王2号'反映了人们希望重温往日海上航行的浪漫体验的愿望。现在所有的期待都寄托在这个即将实行的项目上,资金已经启动。从一开始,我们就坚信这个项目会得到落实。现在我们已经达成共识,即开展'玛丽女王2号'项目的基础,不仅仅在于该船的成功建造,同时也要实现投资的成功回报。'玛丽女王2号'的长度将超过1 130英尺——只比帝国大厦短117英尺。他从龙骨到桅杆的高度将达21层楼,注册总吨近150 000吨。"

皮门特尔称"玛丽女王2号"预计载客只有2 800人,这个数字对于这种尺度的船来说非常小。为实现超高的服务标准,乘客船员的比例达到约2∶1。

皮门特尔说:"但是除了巨大尺寸之外,她还是一项具有个性化的创新设计的奇迹。例如,她采用世界首个四吊舱的推进系统,其中两个为固

For instance, she will be propelled by the world's first four-pod ship propulsion system, utilizing two fixed and two rotating propulsion pods that will enable her to cruise at nearly 30 knots. Inside, she'll have all the dramatic features and grand scale that marked the great liners of the past, enhanced by the latest technology for comfort and convenience. The combination of all of these elements will produce the most luxurious ocean liner ever built.'

The final building agreement is subject to several conditions including the finalization of definitive contracts and financing.

定式,另两个为可回转式,它们为船提舶提供了近30节的巡航速度。内装方面,她将具有昔日伟大班轮所有的显著特征——大尺寸,并通过现代科技提高舒适度和便利性。所有这些元素的整合将产生有史以来最豪华的远洋班轮。"

加利福尼亚长滩最近与运营"玛丽女王"海上酒店的附属公司签订了协议,这为冠达邮轮将"玛丽女王2号"用作新造班轮的船名扫清了障碍。

最终的建造协议的签署受制于确定性合同的定稿和融资等几个方面的影响。

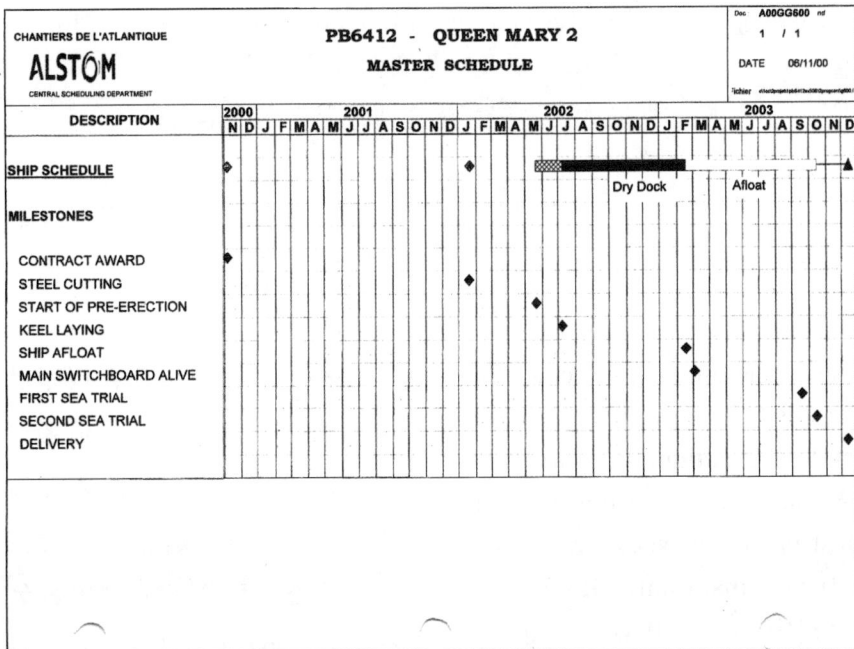

初步的总进度表(作者提供)

6 November

Formal contract signed in Paris by Micky Arison (Chairman and CEO of Carnival Corporation) and Patrick Boissier (President of Alstom Marine and Chairman and CEO of Chantiers de l'Atlantique). At the same time in London the interior design for QM2 is unveiled.

QM2 will be the largest, longest, tallest, widest and most expensive passenger ship ever.

11月6日

正式合同由米奇·阿里森（嘉年华公司董事长兼首席执行官）和帕特里克·布瓦希尔（阿尔斯通海事总裁以及大西洋船厂董事长兼总裁）于巴黎签署。同时，"玛丽女王2号"的内装设计于伦敦揭开序幕。

"玛丽女王2号"将成为有史以来最大、最长、最宽和最昂贵的客船。

CONTRACT SIGNED FOR QUEEN MARY 2
Alstom Chantiers de l'Atlantique will build the world's largest liner
"玛丽女王2号"建造合同的签订
阿尔斯通大西洋船厂将建造世界上最大的班轮

Cunard Line announced today that a contract has been signed with Alstom Chantiers de l'Atlantique shipyard in St-Nazaire, France, to build the grandest and largest passenger vessel liner ever, and the first transatlantic liner to be constructed in over 30 years. Queen Mary 2 is scheduled to enter service in late 2003 and will be built at a cost of approximately 538 million (at the

冠达邮轮公司今天宣布已与位于法国圣纳泽尔的大西洋造船厂签订合同，将建造有史以来最宏伟和最巨大的班轮，同时也是近30多年来建造的第一艘跨大西洋班轮。"玛丽女王2号"计划在2003年底投入运营，建造花费预计近5.38亿英镑（按目前汇率）。合同由冠达邮轮母公司嘉年华集团董

建造中的船首部分（法国 STX 提供）

current rate of exchange). The contract was signed by Micky Arison, Chairman and CEO of Cunard's parent, Carnival Corporation and Patrick Boissier, Chairman and CEO of Alstom Chantiers de I'Atlantique.

Like millions of other immigrants in the 19th and 20th centuries, Mr. Arison first arrived in the United States aboard a Cunard liner, Mauretania, as a child with his family. According to Mr. Arison: 'From the moment we first discussed purchasing Cunard Line, our plans included building a new liner. Cunard's tremendous global brand equity was built by many famous liners and now it will be carried on by this beautiful new addition.'

事长兼首席执行官米奇·阿里森及阿尔斯通大西洋造船厂董事长兼首席执行官帕特里克·布瓦希尔共同签订。

与 19 和 20 世纪上百万移民一样，童年时期的阿里森先生与全家乘坐冠达邮轮的"毛里塔尼亚号"首次登陆美国。阿里森先生表示："当我们第一次讨论收购冠达邮轮公司时，我们就已经计划建造一艘新的班轮。冠达巨大的全球品牌资产是建立在以往许多著名班轮基础上的，现在也将通过这艘美好新船的加入得以延续。"

通过近两年的策划，"玛丽女王 2 号"将成为海上最豪华的班轮，并将

Nearly two years in the planning stages, Queen Mary 2 will be the most luxurious liner afloat and will set new standards in seagoing holidays, with dramatic public spaces designed to evoke the style and elegance of the grand transatlantic era of ocean travel.

Commenting on the new ship's place in the history of his company, Larry Pimentel, President and CEO of Cunard Line said: 'Cunard Line has been carrying people between Europe and America and around the world for more than 160 years. For the last six decades, there has always been a Cunard Queen on the sea. Queen Mary 2 will be the heir to all that has gone before, and also she will be a showcase of the art of shipbuilding in its most refined and masterful form. Queen Mary 2 will carry the grace and elegance of a bygone era into the future.'

Speaking for his company, Mr Boissier said: 'We are extremely pleased to have been selected for one of the most sought-after and highly anticipated shipbuilding contracts in modern-day cruising. Queen Mary 2 will be a piece of history and a work of art.'

Because the ship is a prototype of unique design, negotiations were unusually detailed and extensive research was required. Everything from the overall shape and architectural skeleton to the thickness of the steel plates that make up the liner's hull had to be designed from scratch. Teams of architects, engineers, designers and maritime experts in the UK have been at

通过梦幻般的公共空间设计唤起伟大跨大西洋海上旅行时代的优雅风潮，从而设定海上度假的新标准。

提起这艘新船在其公司历史上的地位，冠达邮轮总裁兼首席执行官拉里·皮门特尔说："冠达邮轮公司运载乘客来往欧洲、美国及全球各地已经超过 160 年。近 60 年来，海上永远有冠达的"女王号"船只。'玛丽女王 2 号'将成为所有既往的延续，并且在她身上也将展现出细致和精湛的造船艺术。'玛丽女王 2 号'将旧时岁月的优美和雅致带向未来。"

布瓦希尔先生代表其公司发言时说："我们非常高兴获得这一份现代邮轮业最受追捧和高度期待的船舶建造合同。'玛丽女王 2 号'注定将成为一段历史和一件艺术品。"

由于这艘船独特的原型设计，所有有关的探讨都异乎寻常地细致并需要深入地研究。从总体形状和建筑骨架到船体的钢板厚度都必须从头开始设计。英国的建筑师、工程师、设计师和海事专家团队工作了两年多，才使得该船舶的设计达到现在的阶段。现在船厂将开始统计规格和材料订货等进程，这意味着在焊工开始组装第一个船体分段之前还有数月的细致工作要做。

阿里森先生总结道："冠达是豪

work for over two years to bring the liner to this point. Now the yard will begin the process of calculating specifications and ordering materials, meaning that there are still months of intensive work left to do before the welders begin fabricating the first pieces of the ship.

Mr Arison concluded: 'Cunard is synonymous with luxury cruising and Queen Mary 2 with its elegant public areas, modem amenities and spacious, well-appointed accommodation will usher in a new era in ocean travel while providing Carnival Corporation a unique opportunity to build upon the line's rich tradition.'

华邮轮的代名词。'玛丽女王 2 号'有着优雅的公共场所、现代化的设施和宽敞、设施完善的住舱,她将带来一个全新的海洋旅行时代,同时也提供给嘉年华集团一个契机来延续这条航线的丰富传承。"

2001

January

'Patron's Preview' programme launched, granting passengers who sail on board QE2 and Caronia in 2001 an exclusive month–long preview of QM2's maiden season.

2001

1 月

"赞助人预览"计划启动，授予 2001 年搭乘"伊丽莎白女王 2 号"和"卡罗尼亚号"的乘客为期一个月的"玛丽女王 2 号"首次航行季独家预览机会。

February

Tank tests of QM2 model successfully completed.

2 月

"玛丽女王 2 号"船模水池试验圆满成功。

TANK TESTS COMPLETED FOR QUEEN MARY 2

QM2 model proves hull and propulsion design is perfect for transatlantic crossings

"玛丽女王 2 号"水池试验完成

"玛丽女王 2 号"的船模试验证实其船体型线和推进系统设计完美适合跨大西洋航行的要求

Tank tests conducted on a scale model of Cunard's new flagship Queen Mary 2 resulted in a triumph for the new hull and propulsion design. The 15-foot, self-propelled model weathered

针对冠达的新旗舰"玛丽女王2号"的缩尺比船模开展的水池试验验证了新船体型线和推进系统设计的成功。15 英尺的自航船模通过了模拟飓风条

推进试验（作者提供）

simulated hurricane conditions with her raked prow splitting the waves perfectly and her wake straight astern. Designers, engineers and executives are all extremely pleased with the results of the testing, which were recently undertaken at facilities of the Dutch firm MARIN.

QM2 will be the largest, longest, tallest, widest and most expensive passenger ship ever when she is delivered at the end of 2003 and the fastest liner built since QE2 in 1969.

Pamela Conover, Cunard's President and Chief Operating Officer, says: 'We are delighted that the design performed as well as we had hoped it would. It's always a big step to actually put a model in the water and see the design become real. Transatlantic service calls for speed, safety, reliability

件下的气象考验，其倾斜船首完美地劈开了波浪和其船尾后的尾波。对在荷兰的 MARIN 水池实验室里进行的测试结果，设计师、工程师和高管们都感到非常满意。

在 2003 年年底交船时，"玛丽女王 2 号"将是有史以来最大、最长、最高、最宽和最昂贵的客船，同时也是自 1969 年"伊丽莎白女王 2 号"建造以来最快的班轮。

冠达邮轮公司总裁及首席运营官帕米拉·科诺弗说到："我们很高兴设计结果和我们所希望的一样。在水里放入船模并看到设计成为现实，这是很大的一步跨越。跨大西洋服务要

and comfort. We designed a hybrid vessel, with classic lines above the water and very modern and innovative features below, and the design met or exceeded all our expectations.'

The design for QM2 is the first vessel to be propelled by four podded propellers extending beneath the hull. The two forward pods are fixed and the two aft pods are steerable. Utilising this steering system, the model performed manoeuvres in compliance with standards for similar vessels using different propulsion and steering systems. Two sets of stabilizers likewise performed perfectly, smoothing the model's motion to create an enviable standard of comfort on board.

求速度、安全、可靠和舒适。我们设计的船舶混合了水面上经典的型线和水面下非常现代和创新的船型特点，这种设计满足或者说超出了我们所有的期望。"

"玛丽女王2号"是第一艘设计了4台伸出船体下部的吊舱式螺旋桨推进的船舶。靠前的2台吊舱推进器为固定式，而靠后的2台吊舱推进器则为可转向式。采用这套转向系统，模型试验证实其操纵性和采用舵桨系统的船舶相当。2对减摇鳍同样表现完美，减缓了船模的摇摆运动，达到了船上令人羡慕的舒适性标准。

"玛丽女王2号"风洞试验模型（作者提供）

After the manoeuvring tests, a series of 'sea- keeping' tests were performed, to discern the hull's performance in different sea conditions. Once again, the model performed as hoped as it breasted a simulated 12 metre swell at a forward speed of 18 knots with almost no water over the bow.

Gerry Ellis, Manager of Newbuildings and Special Projects for Cunard Line, reported: 'That's a hurricane condition. She parted the sea perfectly. Absolutely brilliant!'

Serge Toxopeus, Consultant Manoeuvring at MARIN, was no less enthusiastic, though perhaps a bit more clinical in his analysis: 'Overall, it can be concluded that after completion of the hydrodynamic studies a reliable and feasible design was obtained.'

在操纵性试验后进行了一系列的适航性试验来判断船体在不同海况下的表现。船模试验表现再一次符合预期，在12米涌浪，18节前进航速下，船首几乎不上浪。

冠达邮轮公司新造船及特别项目经理格里·埃利斯报告到："这是在飓风的海况下。她完美地破浪前行，相当精彩！"

荷兰水池的操纵性能顾问瑟日·托克索普同样也很激动，尽管在其分析报告中他比较冷静地说到："总的来说，在完成所有水动力研究后可以得出结论，我们得到了一个可靠和可行的设计。"

November
Cunard announces that Canyon Ranch will operate the health spa.

11月
冠达宣布将由峡谷牧场公司运营健康水疗中心。

2002
16 January
Pamela Conover, Cunard's President and Chief Operating Officer, presses the button to cut the first sheet of steel for QM2.

2002

1 月 16 日

冠达邮轮公司总裁及首席运营官帕梅拉·康诺弗按下按钮，为"玛丽女王 2 号"切割第一块钢板。

March update

73% of steel material ordered;

2 panels (out of 580) completed;

6% of the steel cut.

3 月

73% 的钢板材料已订货；

两个小分段（共 580 个）已完工；

6% 的钢板已切割。

April update

82% of steel material ordered;

6 panels (out of 580) completed;

11% of the steel cut.

4 月

82% 的钢板材料已订货；

6 个小分段（共 580 个）已完工；

11% 的钢板已切割。

May update

90% of steel material ordered;

7 panels (out of 580) completed;

15% of the steel cut (5,200 tons).

5 月

90% 的钢板材料已订货；

7 个小分段（共 580 个）已完工；

15% 的钢板已切割（5 200 吨）。

11 June update

Cunard announces date for maiden voyage (12 January 2004) and 2004 schedule for new flagship.

6 月 11 号

冠达邮轮宣布这艘最新旗舰船只的首航日期（2004 年 1 月 12 日）及 2004 年度航行计划。

MAIDEN VOYAGE FOR QUEENMARY2

Cunard announces maiden voyage date and 2004

schedule for new flagship

"玛丽女王 2 号"的处女航

冠达邮轮宣布处女航日期和新旗舰 2004 年的航行计划

Monday 12 January 2004 will be an historic day for Cunard Line and Great Britain because Queen Mary 2-the largest, longest, tallest, widest and most expensive passenger ship in history - will leave from Cunard's homeport, Southampton, on her

对冠达邮轮和英国来说，2004 年 1 月 12 日的星期一，是个历史性的日子。历史上最大、最长、最高的"玛丽女王 2 号"将离开母港南安普敦，开始她的处女航。14 天后，这艘冠达邮轮公司的新旗舰和英国商船队伍将

maiden voyage. Fourteen days later, the new flagship of Cunard and the British merchant fleet will arrive to an expected tumultuous welcome in Fort Lauderdale. 'Sailaway Fares' for the maiden crossing start from £2,099 per person.

QM2's first year will see the ship sail 17 transatlantic crossings as she takes over the role currently operated by her sister QE2 as Cunard's carrier. OM2's maiden westbound crossing of the Atlantic from Southampton to New York will depart on 16 April. Her maiden eastbound crossing will be similarly historic for Cunard as both OM2 and QE2 will depart New York on 25 April for a sixday crossing of the Atlantic together. The day in New York will also be the first time that two Cunard Queens have been berthed in the port together since March 1940. QM2 transatlantic 'Sailaway Fares' start from £999 per person.

The year will also see OM2 offer nine Caribbean cruises, a voyage to Rio and back,five European cruises and two taking in Canada and the East Coast of America. These cruises range from four to fourteen days with 'Sailaway Fares' starting from £449 per person.

Bookings will be open to the general public on 1 August 2002. 'Sailaway Fares' offer savings of 20% on selected categories.

Pamela Conover, Cunard's President and Chief Operating Officer, says: 'Ever since we announced our

在热烈的欢迎声中抵达劳德代尔堡。处女航票价从 2 099 英镑 / 人起售。

"玛丽女王 2 号"第一年将运营 17 个航次，取代其姊妹船"伊丽莎白女王 2 号"正在运营的跨大西洋航线。"玛丽女王 2 号"将在 4 月 16 号离开南安普敦，开始驶向纽约的横跨大西洋西行首次航程。此后"玛丽女王 2 号"将和同属冠达邮轮公司的"伊丽莎白女王 2 号"于 4 月 25 号同时离开纽约，开始其具有历史意义的为期 6 天的横跨大西洋东行首次航程，这一天也是自 1940 年 3 月以来第一次有两条冠达"女王号"邮轮同时停靠在纽约港。"玛丽女王 2 号"跨大西洋东行航线船票从 999 英镑 / 人起售。

2004 这一年"玛丽女王 2 号"也将运营 9 次加勒比海航次，包括 1 次里约热内卢往返巡游，5 次欧洲巡游，两次加拿大巡游和一次美国东海岸巡游。这些航程涵盖了 4 天到 14 天的行程，票价从 449 英镑 / 人起售。

预订将从 2002 年 8 月 1 日起向公众开放，其中特定的航线有 20% 的折扣。

冠达邮轮公司总裁兼首席运营官帕米拉·科诺弗说："当我们对外宣布有意建造'玛丽女王 2 号'的时候，立即有成千上万的游客迫切地想知道处女航日期和第一年的巡游路线。现在我怀着无比激动的心情，自豪地公

intention to build Queen Mary 2, we have been inundated with requests from thousands of people wanting to know where and when the new liner would sail in her maiden year. I am delighted to be able to reveal her first year's itineraries with the release of the first OM2 brochure. I would advise all those wanting to sail on OM2 in what will be a truly historic year to book early to avoid disappointment!'

布'玛丽女王2号'的第一份巡游计划。同时我会对所有想在极具纪念意义的年份就体验'玛丽女王2号'的游客说，赶快提前订票吧！以免后悔莫及！"

QUEEN MARY 2 OVERVIEW OF MAIDEN PROGRAM

DATES	FROM/TO	CRUISE AREA	DAYS
12 JAN–26 Jan	SOU–FLL	Maiden voyage	14
31 Jan–11 Feb	FLL–FLL	Inaugural Caribbean	11
11 Feb–23 Feb	FLL–RIO	South America	12
23 Feb–06 Mar	RIO–FLL	South America	12
06 Mar–16 Mar	FLL–FLL	Caribbean	10
16 Mar–26 Mar	FLL–FLL	Caribbean	10
26 Mar–12 Apr	FLL–SOU	Transatlantic	17
12 Apr– 16 Apr	SOU–SOU	Cruise Break	4
16 Apr–22 Apr	SOU–NYC	Inaugural transatlantic (westbound}	6
25 Apr–01 May	NYC–SOU	Inaugural transatlantic (eastbound / with QE2)	6
01 May–-07 May	SOU–NYC	Transatlantic westbound	6
07 May–10 May	NYC–NYC	Cruise break	3
10 May–18 May	NYC–NYC	Caribbean	8
18 May–24 May	NYC– SOU	Transatlantic eastbound	6

（续表）

DATES	FROM/TO	CRUISE AREA	DAYS
24 May– 05 Jun	SOU–SOU	Mediterranean	12
05 Jun– 11 Jun	SOU–NYC	Transatlantic westbound	6
11 Jun– 19 Jun	NYC–NYC	Caribbean	8
19 Jun–25 Jun	NYC– SOU	Transatlantic eastbound	6
25 Jun– 01 Jul	SOU–NYC	Transatlantic westbound	6
01 Jul– 05 Jul	NYC–NYC	US east coast	4
05 Jul– 11 Jul	NYC– SOU	Transatlantic eastbound	6
11 Jul–25 Jul	SOU–SOU	Norwegian fjords	14
25 Jul–31 Jul	SOU–NYC	Transatlantic westbound	6
31 Jul––06 Aug	NYC–SOU	Transatlantic eastbound	6
06 Aug–18 Aug	SOU–SOU	Mediterranean	12
18 Aug–24 Aug	SOU–NYC	Transatlantic westbound	6
24 Aug–30 Aug	NYC–SOU	Transatlantic eastbound	6
30 Aug–11 Sep	SOU–SOU	Mediterranean	12
11 Sep–17 Sep	SOU– NYC	Transatlantic westbound	6
17 Sep– 29 Sep	NYC–NYC	US/Canada	12
29 Sep–11 Oct	NYC–NYC	US/Canada	12
11 Oct– 17 Oct	NYC–SOU	Transatlantic eastbound	6
17 Oct–31 Oct	SOU–SOU	Mediterranean	14
31 Oct– 06 Nov	SOU– NYC	Transatlantic westbound	6
06 Nov–16 Nov	NYC–NYC	Caribbean	10
16 Nov–26 Nov	NYC–NYC	Caribbean	10
26 Nov– 06 Dec	NYC–NYC	Caribbean	10
06 Dec–19 Dec	NYC–FLL	Caribbean	13
19 Dec–02 Jan 05	FLL–FLL	Caribbean Christmas	14

SOU Southampton   NYC New York   FLL Fort Lauderdale   RIO Rio de Janeiro

"玛丽女王 2 号"处女航年巡游计划

日期	始发 / 到达	巡游线路	天数
1.12 ~ 1.26	南安普敦—劳德代尔堡	处女航	14
1.31 ~ 2.11	劳德代尔堡—劳德代尔堡	加勒比首航	11
2.11 ~ 2.23	劳德代尔堡—里约热内卢	南美	12
2.23 ~ 3.6	里约热内卢—劳德代尔堡	南美	12
3.6 ~ 3.16	劳德代尔堡—劳德代尔堡	加勒比海	10
3.16 ~ 3.26	劳德代尔堡—劳德代尔堡	加勒比海	10
3.26 ~ 4.12	劳德代尔堡—南安普敦	大西洋	17
4.12 ~ 4.16	南安普敦—南安普敦	停泊休整	4
4.16 ~ 4.22	南安普敦—纽约	跨大西洋首航—西行	6
4.25 ~ 5.1	纽约—南安普敦	跨大西洋首航－东行 / "伊丽莎白女王 2 号"同行	6
5.1 ~ 5.7	南安普敦—纽约	跨大西洋航线—西行	6
5.7 ~ 5.10	纽约—纽约	停泊休整	3
5.10 ~ 5.18	纽约—纽约	加勒比海	8
5.18 ~ 5.24	纽约—南安普敦	跨大西洋航线—东行	6
5.24 ~ 6.5	南安普敦—南安普敦	地中海	12
6.5 ~ 6.11	南安普敦—纽约	跨大西洋航线—西行	6
6.11 ~ 6.19	纽约—纽约	加勒比海	8
6.19 ~ 6.25	纽约—南安普敦	跨大西洋航线—东行	6
6.25 ~ 7.1	南安普敦—纽约	跨大西洋航线—西行	6
7.1 ~ 7.5	纽约—纽约	美国东海岸	4
7.5 ~ 7.11	纽约—南安普敦	跨大西洋航线—东行	6
7.11 ~ 7.25	南安普敦—南安普敦	挪威峡湾	14

（续表）

日期	始发 / 到达	巡游线路	天数
7.25 ~ 7.31	南安普敦—纽约	跨大西洋航线—西行	6
7.31 ~ 8.6	纽约—南安普敦	跨大西洋航线—东行	6
8.6 ~ 8.18	南安普敦—南安普敦	地中海	12
8.18 ~ 8.24	南安普敦—纽约	跨大西洋航线—西行	6
8.24 ~ 8.30	纽约—南安普敦	跨大西洋航线—东行	6
8.30 ~ 9.11	南安普敦—南安普敦	地中海	12
9.11 ~ 9.17	南安普敦—纽约	跨大西洋航线—西行	6
9.17 ~ 9.29	纽约—纽约	美国 / 加拿大	12
9.29 ~ 10.11	纽约—纽约	美国 / 加拿大	12
10.11 ~ 10.17	纽约—南安普敦	跨大西洋航线—东行	6
10.17 ~ 10.31	南安普敦—南安普敦	地中海	14
10.31 ~ 11.6	南安普敦—纽约	跨大西洋航线—西行	6
11.6 ~ 11.16	纽约—纽约	加勒比海	10
11.16 ~ 11.26	纽约—纽约	加勒比海	10
11.26 ~ 12.6	纽约—纽约	加勒比海	10
12.6 ~ 12.19	纽约—劳德代尔堡	加勒比海	13
12.19 ~ 2005.1.2	劳德代尔堡—劳德代尔堡	加勒比海圣诞旅程	14

注：SOU–南安普敦 / 英国、NYC – 纽约 / 美国、FLL – 劳德代尔堡 / 佛罗里达州 / 美国、RIO – 里约热内卢 / 巴西。

船厂工人正在焊接烟囱（法国STX船厂提供）

June update

94% of steel material ordered; 62 panels (out of 580) completed; 28% of the steel cut (9 700 tons).

6月

钢材订货率94%，小型分段组立62个（共计580个）已完工，钢材切割率28%（共计9 700吨）。

4 July 2002

Keel-laying ceremony takes place.

2002年7月4日

铺龙骨仪式。

July update

98% of steel material ordered; 120 panels (out of 580) completed; 35% of the steel cut (11 800 tons).

7月

钢材订货率98%；小型分段组立120个（共计580个）已完工；钢材切割率35%（共计11 800吨）。

2003 年 7 月，"玛丽女王 2 号"（法国 STX 船厂提供）

8—11 August

First block of QM2 floats for the first time and moves into the second position of the building dock.

8 月 8 日至 11 日

"玛丽女王 2 号"第一个大型分段转运到船坞内新位置进行搭载。

September update

273 panels (out of 580) completed; 70% of the steel cut (23 500 tons); 14 blocks (out of 97) are on board.

9 月

小型分段组立 273 个（共计 580 个）已完工；钢材切割率达到 70%（共计 23 500 吨）；大型分段搭载 14 个（共计 97 个）。

October update

430 panels (out of 580) completed; 93% of the steel cut (31 300 tons); 44 blocks (out of 97) are on board.

10 月

小型分段组立 430 个（共计 580 个）已完工；钢材切割率达到 93%（共计 31 300 吨）；大型分段搭载 44 个（共计 97 个）。

Nov update

516 panels (out of 620) completed; 99% of the steel cut (33 400 tons); 49 blocks (out of 98) are on board.

11 月

小型分段组立 516 个（共计 620 个）已完工；钢材切割率达到 99%（共计 33 400 吨）；大型分段搭载 49 个（共计 98 个）。

1 December

QM2 floats down to the deeper end of the dry dock.

12 月 1 日

"玛丽女王 2 号"起浮到干船坞端部深水处。

2003 January update

620 panels (out of 620) completed; 100% of the steel cut (33, 700 tons); 94 blocks (out of 100) are on board.

2003 年 1 月

小型分段组立 620 个（共计 620 个）已完工；钢材切割率达到 100%（共计 33 700 吨）；大型分段搭载 94 个（共计 100 个）。

5 February

450 crew cabins and 8 balcony cabins have been loaded by this date. About 87% of cabin windows and portholes are installed.

2月5日

450个船员舱室和8个带阳台舱室已完成安装。窗户和舷窗安装大约完成87%。

16 March

Mast-stepping ceremony takes place.

3月16日

立桅仪式。

21 March

QM2 leaves the building dock for the first time and is moved to the fitting-out basin.

3月21日

"玛丽女王2号"首次漂浮离开建造船坞，移位到舾装码头。

May update

Approximately 1,000 of the 2,017 passenger and crew cabins have been installed. Installation of funnel and mast completed.

5月

大约1 000个（共计2 017个房间）乘客和船员舱室安装完成，烟囱和主桅杆安装完成。

June

The painting of QM2's exterior begins. Installation of the four 'pods' completed.

6月

"玛丽女王2号"船体外部涂装开始。4个吊舱安装完成。

2003 年 7 月，"玛丽女王 2 号"（法国 STX 船厂提供）

25—29 September

QM2 takes to the open sea for the first time and undergoes her first sea trials.

9 月 25 日至 29 日

"玛丽女王 2 号"首次前往开阔海域并进行她的首次试航。

7—11 November

QM2 undertakes owners' trials.

11 月 7 日至 11 日

"玛丽女王 2 号"进行船东试航。

22 December

QM2 is handed over to Cunard.

12 月 22 日

"玛丽女王 2 号"移交给冠达邮轮公司。

2004

8 January

QM2 is officially named in Southampton by Her Majesty Queen Elizabeth Ⅱ.

2004 年 1 月 8 日

伊丽莎白女王二世为"玛丽女王 2 号"命名。

12 January

QM2 departs on her 14-day maiden voyage from Southampton to Fort Lauderdale.

1 月 12 日

"玛丽女王 2 号"开始为期 14 天的从母港南安普敦到劳德代尔堡的处女航。

（译者：王露、高金军、鲁鼎）

试航（冠达邮轮提供）

2013 年 7 月 6 日，曼哈顿对面的布鲁克林邮轮码头，"玛丽女王 2 号"准备开始第 200 次横跨大西洋航程。（作者提供）

第三章 设计一艘远洋班轮

Chapter Three:Designing an ocean liner

Designing any ship is a compromise between numerous conflicting demands; prioritising these, particularly with a passenger ship, is a prerequisite. When the passenger ship is a liner rather than a cruise ship, the task becomes even more onerous. Queen Mary 2 was the ultimate challenge.

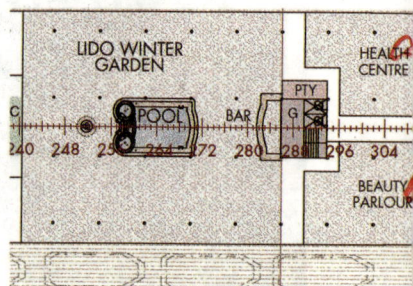

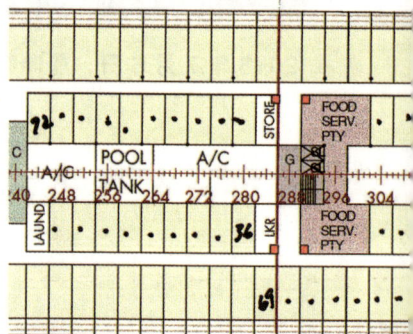

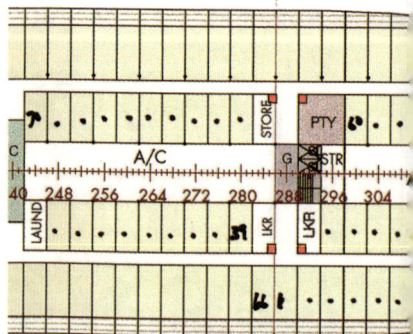

任何一艘船舶的设计，都是在许多矛盾的要求间寻求妥协的过程；对这些要求进行优先级排序，这是开展客船设计的一个先决条件。班轮和邮轮都是客船的一种，但班轮比邮轮的设计任务更加繁重。"玛丽女王 2 号"是一项终极挑战。

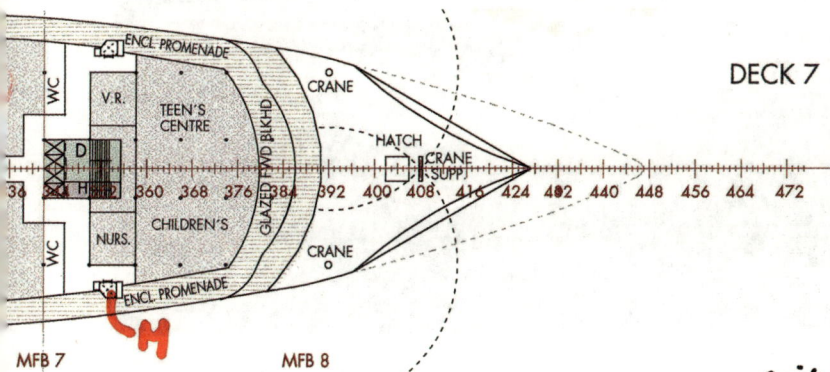

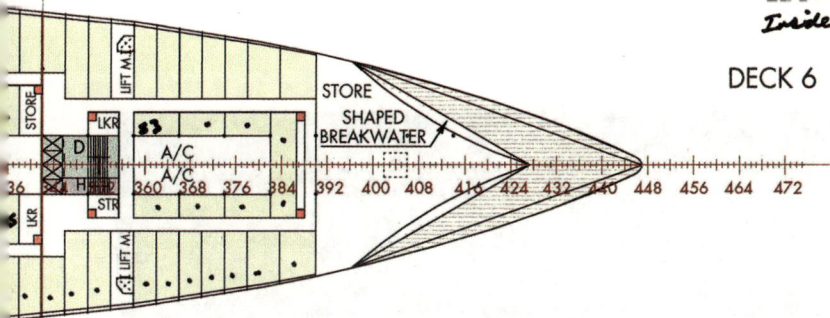

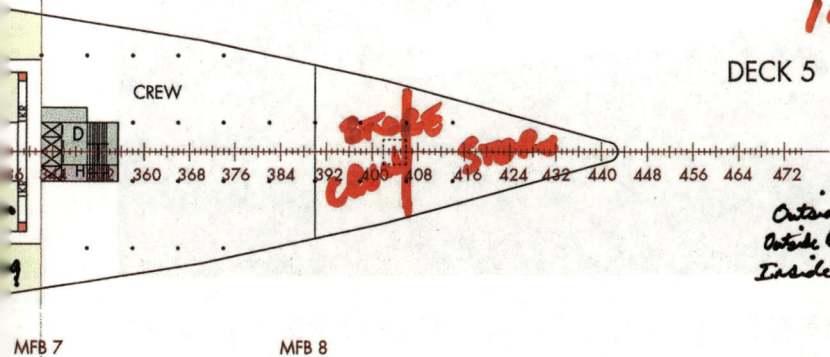

工作图："玛丽女王号"项目初期总布置图的局部，1999年6月。（作者提供）

这艘重达 101 509 吨的“嘉年华凯旋号”定期从德克萨斯州加尔维斯顿的母港驶向加勒比海。（作者提供）

尽管与以往的每艘客船都有很大不同，但毫无疑问，“伊丽莎白女王 2 号”是一艘真正的班轮。（冠达邮轮提供）

The brief was simple. To design a passenger ship that would supersede Queen Elizabeth 2 and operate as a dual purpose transatlantic liner and cruise ship. The design of the ship had to be such that when marketed she would attract the level of cabin and on-board revenue that would provide as near as possible the same return on investment as if her construction and operational costs had been directed to building cruise ships for any one of Carnival Corporation's cruise ship brands. The execution was somewhat more difficult. I was given a free hand in the design of the ship but I would have to convince Carnival Corporation's senior management and Cunard that my proposal was the optimal solution. There was no question in my mind that the ship would have to be a fully fledged liner, rather than just a cruise ship in disguise. I had estimated that a liner would cost something in the order of 40% more than the equivalent-sized cruise ship. On announcing this fact I was immediately put on the defensive as I strove to convince Carnival that this was the only way to go. The trouble was that Carnival had no experience whatsoever of what the differences were between a liner and a cruise ship and their respective capabilities. Although Carnival had started operations with a second hand transatlantic liner in 1972, there had been so many cruise ship deliveries since their first newbuild MS Tropicale in 1981, that the distinction had become very blurred. The senior management team of Cunard were also very much in the dark, as they had been parachuted in by Carnival from Seaborn Cruise

设计要求很简单——设计一艘取代"伊丽莎白女王2号"的客轮，并用作跨大西洋班轮和邮轮的双重用途。该船的设计必须要能做到：当推向市场时，该船与相同投资的任何一艘嘉年华集团的豪华邮轮相比，其获得的船票收入和船上消费收入水平应达到尽可能相近的投资回报率。然而，真正执行起来却有点难。我可以自由地设计这艘船，但我必须说服嘉年华集团的高级管理层和冠达邮轮公司，让他们相信我所提供的是最佳方案。毫无疑问，我认为这艘船必须是一艘真正意义上的远洋班轮，而不是一艘经过伪装的邮轮。我估计，一艘班轮的成本大约比同等大小的邮轮高出40%。当我宣布这个事实后，我立刻处于被动境地，因为我必须试图说服嘉年华集团，把她设计成一艘班轮。麻烦的是，嘉年华集团没有任何经验去分辨班轮和邮轮之间的区别以及它们各自的功能。尽管嘉年华在1972年就开始运营一艘二手的跨大西洋班轮，但自1981年第一艘新造邮轮MS"热带号"建造以来，已经有很多艘邮轮交付，班轮和邮轮的区别已经变得非常模糊。冠达邮轮公司的高级管理团队也很不了解情况，因为他们是1998年冠达公司被收购时，从世邦邮轮公司空降过来的。在嘉年华集团的所有

Line when Cunard had been acquired in 1998. Of all Carnival's brands, Seabourn was by far the most removed from liner aspirations as their ships were more like sedate large yachts than liners or even cruise ships.

For the record, a liner generally has the following superior attributes compared to a cruise ship:

• A deeper draught for good sea-keeping and dead-weight capacity.

• A finer hull form to enable the ship to slice through high waves in bad weather rather than ride over them. This is good for sea keeping and powering efficiency.

• High propulsion power with sizeable reserves to produce a high sustained speed for ocean transits even in inclement weather.

• Increased structural strength to allow the ship to be driven hard in bad weather without the fear of damage that would force lesser ships to slow down or even alter course.

品牌中，世邦邮轮公司旗下的船是迄今为止最不像班轮的，因为他们的船更像稳重的大型游艇，而不是班轮，甚至也不是邮轮。

需要指出的是，班轮相较于邮轮往往拥有以下几点优势：

• 拥有更深的吃水，因而有更好的耐波性和载重量裕度。

• 拥有更好的船体线型，使其在恶劣海况下能够冲破巨浪而非骑浪而行。这对耐波性和能源消耗效率都有好处。

• 拥有较高的推进功率，具有相当大的功率储备使其即使在恶劣的天气下也能持续以较高的速度完成运输任务。

• 增加了结构强度，使船在恶劣的天气下不受损害且不必担心船体破损，而这往往会迫使较小的船只减速或改变航向。

"玛丽女王号"优美的船首（1936年）。"伊丽莎白女王号"的船首进行了进一步的改进，引入了更大的倾角，这样一来就可以把船首锚固定起来。可以看到在"玛丽女王号"的船名后面取消了下沉甲板。下沉甲板有时会没入海中，这会影响稳性，使船发生惊人的横摇从而变得很不舒适。（乔纳森·福尔克纳收集）

These characteristics are particularly important when the voyage profile of a transatlantic liner sailing between Europe and New York is compared to, say, the voyage profile of a Caribbean cruise ship. On a seven-day Caribbean cruise from a Florida port, there can be three or four port stops with three or four days at sea. If the weather becomes too adverse due

当将航行在欧洲和纽约之间的跨洋班轮的航迹与航行在加勒比海的邮轮的航迹进行比较时，这些特性尤为重要。一个历时7天的加勒比海邮轮航程，从佛罗里达（美国）港口出发，沿途可以有三到四个港口可以停靠，三到四天在海上航行。如果遇到像热带风暴

"伊丽莎白女王2号"利落的船首，与以往女王号的船首完全不同，她拥有一个气势恢宏的飞剪型船首。（冠达邮轮提供）

"玛丽女王2号"的船首设计主要基于"伊丽莎白女王2号"的船首设计，但后者明显更大，这反映了两艘船的尺寸差异。（冠达邮轮提供）

"伊丽莎白女王2号"的船首划过一片平静的海面；经验表明它在穿越恶劣海况时特别有效。（冠达邮轮提供）

to, for example, a tropical storm, the ship can easily divert and can even miss out a port of call. Slowing a ship down in bad weather greatly enhances the comfort on board by limiting the ship's motions and in addition the stress and strain imposed on the vessel is minimised, thus reducing the risk of structural damage. In short, the ship can be operated in a very flexible manner and can usually make it back to her terminal port without undue delay to the schedule.

For a ship engaged in the transatlantic trade, on a back-to-back voyage schedule, things are very different. Since the turn-arounds at each terminal are only ten hours (sometimes less), it is imperative that the ship arrives and departs on time. Failure to do so can jeopardise the whole schedule for a year, causing thousands of travellers to reschedule hotel and airline bookings, with massive inconvenience and expense. This situation is not tolerable for a scheduled service. The problem is that there is very little flexibility with a transatlantic transit. There are no intermediate ports that can be dropped. If speed is reduced, involuntarily or voluntarily, distance has to be made up later in the voyage by speeding up - impossible it sufficient margins and reserves haven't been incorporated. A slight change of course may be deemed prudent to minimise ship motions and route away from the worst weather but this increases the distance required to run to port, necessitating a later increase in speed as before.Invariably, cruise ships don't

这样的不利天气，邮轮可以很容易地改变航程，甚至可以跳过其中一个停靠港。在遭遇恶劣天气时，通过减慢船速以限制船的摇晃，这样可以大幅提高邮轮上的舒适度，还可以使施加在船体上的应力最小化，从而降低了结构损伤的风险。简而言之，邮轮可以通过非常灵活的方式进行操控，从而无延误地按计划返港。

而对于一艘按照往返式的航程计划跨洋航行的船舶，情况就变得截然不同。由于在每个港口逗留的时间只有 10 小时（有时更少），所以到达和出发的准时性就变得尤为重要。如果出问题可能会影响一整年的计划，导致数以千计的旅客重新预订酒店和机票，这将带来巨大的麻烦和经济损失。对于一个定期航班而言，这种情况是不可容忍的。难点在于，跨大西洋航运的灵活性很小，航行途中没有可供船舶停靠的港口。如果航速减慢，不论是主观原因还是客观原因，都必须在后面的航程中加快速度把时间弥补回来——所以必须在制订航线计划时考虑足够的余量和储备。当然，为了减轻班轮的摇晃和躲避恶劣天气而对航线进行适当地调整是明智的，但这会增加班轮到港的距离，同样会迫使班轮在后期提速。毫无疑问，邮轮无法做到这一点，而且

have such reserves to enable them to do this and their fuller hull forms and lighter construction dictates that they would be foolhardy to do so in bad weather for fear of structural damage. The axiom is, if you want to offer regular express transatlantic voyages on a passenger ship, you really do need a liner; a cruise ship simply won't do.

Faced with such an expensive proposition, Carnival's management suggested that I take a look at the new Disney Magic, Disney Cruise Line's first ship. This vessel delivered in 1998 and has a long bow, black hull, white superstructure and two prominent red and black funnels. To the casual observer, to

它们丰满的船型和轻量化的结构决定了它们无法在恶劣的天气像班轮一样航行，因为担心船体结构方面的损伤。众所周知，如果想要开展准时的跨洋快运业务，你需要一艘真正的班轮，而不是邮轮。

面对如此重要的项目，嘉年华集团的管理层建议我去看看迪斯尼邮轮公司的第一艘船"迪斯尼魔法号"。这艘船于 1998 年交付，拥有长长的船首，黑色的船体，白色的上层建筑和两个显著的红色和黑色烟囱。在漫不

2008 年 1 月，"伊丽莎白女王 2 号"在前往纽约的途中，该照片是从与该船一起航行的新"维多利亚女王号"上拍摄的。可以看到"伊丽莎白女王 2 号"船身虽然倾斜，但是外飘的艏部型式有效地防止了艏部上浪。（作者提供）

all intents and purposes, she is a liner. And of course this is the deception that her designers and operators want to convey. However, she does not embody any of the true liner attributes and her flirtation with one runs only skin deep. She is an illusion of a liner and is merely a cruise ship in disguise.

I decided that I needed to employ a shock tactic to convince everyone that we had to build a liner despite the cost. At an early senior management meeting with both Carnival and Cunard executives attending, I presented a report outlining the differences between liners and cruise ships and described two incidents where even well-found liners had had a mauling from the ferocity of the North Atlantic. The first incident involved the Italian Line flagship Michelangelo in April 1966 when the ship was struck by an enormous wave while approaching New York. The forward face of the superstructure below the bridge was ripped open and two passengers were swept from their cabins and thrown overboard. In all 3 people died and over 50 were injured. A similar event occurred with Queen Elizabeth 2 on 11 September 1995 when the ship was struck by a succession of 30-metre-hiah waves. One wave dumped what was estimated to be 7,000 tonnes of water on the forecastle, causing it to partially set down towards the deck below. Although there were no fatalities there was extensive damage and flooding in the forward part of the ship, but her liner pedigree ensured her survival and she reached New York without further incident where she was repaired. Photographs of these episodes really

经心的观察者看来,她确实是一艘班轮。当然,这正是她的设计师和营运商想要营造的假象。然而,她并没有体现任何真正班轮的特质,仅仅是表面上相似而已。虽然伪装出班轮的错觉,但她只是一艘邮轮。

我决定采用冲击策略来说服每个人——我们就是要建造一艘班轮,不考虑成本。在嘉年华集团和冠达邮轮公司高管参加的早期高层会议上,我递交了一份报告,概述了班轮和邮轮之间的区别,并描述了两起事故,以此说明即使是一些性能优越的班轮也难以经受北大西洋恶劣海况的威胁。第一起事故发生在1966年4月,意大利邮轮公司的旗舰"米开朗基罗号"在接近纽约时遭遇巨浪袭击。位于驾驶室下方的上层建筑前部结构被巨浪撕裂,两名乘客从他们的客舱中被拖出到船外。事故造成3人死亡,超过50人受伤。1995年9月11日,"伊丽莎白女王2号"也发生了类似的事故,当时船遭遇到一连串30米高的巨浪袭击。一股估计约7 000吨重的巨浪拍击艏楼,导致部分结构向下层的甲板沉降。这次事故虽然没有人员伤亡,但船的前部有大量的损坏和进水,她的班轮血统确保了她的生存,在没有发生衍生事故的情况下抵达纽约,并在

1966 年 4 月 10 日上午 10 点，意大利邮轮公司的"米开朗基罗号"在前往纽约的途中，在猛烈的大西洋风暴中被巨浪击中。

估计超过甲板 18 米高的巨浪沿艏部甲板向后扫过。巨浪严重损坏了"米开朗基罗号"的前部铝质上层建筑。因为客舱被冲击力撕裂，造成 3 人死亡。

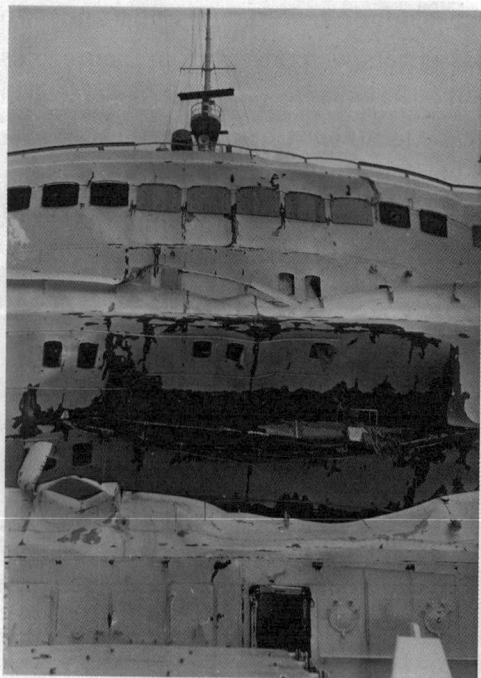

focused the Carnival/Cunard audience and thereafter there was no question that if we were to maintain the tradition of transatlantic crossings, it was agreed that it had to be by liner and not cruise ship.

The stages in the design of a passenger ship may be defined as:

1.Determine the ship service requirements such as route, speed, deadweight (weight of fuel, stores, passengers and so on) etc.

2.Determine the hotel service requirements such as class disposition, cabin types and distribution.

3.Estimate the spatial requirements for the hotel and technical requirements according to the service requirements listed above.

4.Estimate length, breadth and number of decks required.

5.Draft first general arrangement of passenger decks, placing main fire zones and staircases as a priority and main structural elements such as main bulkheads and pillars.

6.Draft first machinery arrangement.

7.Estimate the lightship weight of the vessel (the weight of the ship without stores, fuel, water, etc) and the final displacement with the deadweight.

8.Determine the hull shape required to provide the requisite buoyancy to support the lightship and deadweight.

9.Check stability and powering requirements.

10.Adjust all above as required to produce a viable design.

11.Proceed to final full design, making small adjustments as necessary.

A passenger ship is composed of

那里进行修复。这些事故的照片吸引了嘉年华及冠达邮轮公司听众的关注。此后大家一致认同,如果我们要保持跨大西洋航运传统,就必须要建造班轮而不是邮轮。

设计一艘客船流程总结如下:

1. 确定船舶的运营功能需求,例如航线、航速、载重量(燃料、仓储、乘客)等。

2. 确定酒店服务需求,例如客舱等级设置、房间类型和分布。

3. 根据服务功能需求来评估以上列出的居住和工艺空间需求。

4. 预估所需要的甲板长度、宽度和数量。

5. 首先绘制游客甲板的总布置草图,优先设置主防火分隔区域、梯道和主要结构件(如竖区壁和支柱)。

6. 绘制初版机舱布置草图。

7. 估算空船重量(不包括仓储、燃料、水等)和考虑载重量后的最终排水量。

8. 确定需要的船体形状以提供足够的浮力,来平衡空船重量和载重量。

9. 校核稳性和动力需求。

10. 按需求调整以上参数,形成可行性设计方案。

11. 进行最终全局设计,进行必要的小调整。

a number of spatial groups, which are discrete but nonetheless interconnected. Obviously, by her very nature, a passenger ship requires space for her passenger accommodation- cabins, public rooms and open decks. To serve the passengers and operate the machinery of the ship, a crew must be provided of the requisite size to enable the level of service to be delivered. Like passengers, the crew will need cabins and public areas. Room for stores and consumables, with ease of access for loading and means of distribution throughout the ship, is a necessity. Similarly so for galleys, pantries, steward lockers and laundries. The comprehensive technical plant for propulsion and hotel services requires considerable space and in some instances must be placed strategically adjacent to certain hotel areas. Finally, command facilities such as the bridge and engine control room are needed, as well as capacity for lifesaving and safety systems. The space required for many of these areas varies in relation to the others, more passengers require more crew, more stores etc, so varying one has a domino effect on the others. With these considerations in mind, the layout of the ship deck by deck, collectively called the 'general arrangement', can be started, not forgetting the placement of passenger and crew stairs and lifts. The positioning of these is of fundamental importance since they impact on the arrangements throughout the ship, deck by deck.

Queen Elizabeth 2 had been conceived as a five-day transatlantic ship with a sustained speed requirement of 28.5 knots. Propulsion was originally

一艘客船由许多空间组构成，它们分散在各处但却是互相连通的。显然，一艘客船本该就为乘客的起居提供必要的空间，包括客舱、公共场所和开敞甲板。为了服务乘客和操纵船上机械，船员必须拥有必要的空间来保证提供一定水准的服务。像乘客一样，船员也需要住舱和公共活动区域。同时，配有方便装卸货物以及可在全船运送的通道，这些都是不可或缺的。对于厨房、配餐间、酒店库房和洗衣房，其要求也是同样的。复杂的推进设备和酒店服务需要相当大的空间，而且在有些情况下，这些空间必须有针对性地靠近某些特定的舱室区域。最后，还需要提供空间给控制设施（如驾驶室和集控室）和救生安全系统。这艘船每层甲板的设计工作开始之前，必须将这些要点铭记于心，这些统称为"总体布置"，其中还包括客梯、船员梯和电梯的布置。由于这些场所的位置会影响到全船每层甲板的布置，所以它们的位置至关重要。

"伊丽莎白女王2号"被设定为一艘可以凭借28.5节的持续航速在5天内完成跨洋航行的船。推进系统最初设定为由蒸汽轮机发出110 000匹轴马力来驱动两台螺旋桨。基于可靠性的考虑，冠达邮轮公司决定分别在

　　和"伊丽莎白女王2号"一样，"玛丽女王2号"的后方甲板也设计成阶梯状以减少艉部过多的重量。

　　从"玛丽女王2号"的"海图室"酒吧明显可以看出，该船的公共区域在设计时额外加入了二层甲板的高度。

灯光下的"伊丽莎白女王 2 号"桥楼区域，在最后一次航行出发前拍摄于南安普敦。"玛丽女王 2 号"则是将桥楼区域扩大并且完全封闭起来。

任何大型客船上的厨房都很宽敞，"玛丽女王 2 号"也不例外。

affected by 110,000 shaft horsepower steam turbines through two propellers. Due to reliability issues Cunard decided to completely re-engine Queen Elizabeth 2 over the winter of 1986/87 with a diesel-electric plant. Fuel consumption was reduced from approximately 500 tons per day to around 370 tons for the same speed, with greatly enhanced reliability. In 1997 transatlantics were rescheduled to a longer six-day crossing with a speed requirement of about 24 knots.

Queen Elizabeth 2 had been conceived and ordered from John Brown & Company, Clydebank, as a three-class ship: First, Cabin and Tourist. Late in the construction it was decided to merge the Cabin and Third classes into one, Tourist, which was later given the new name of 'Transatlantic class'. This transformation was largely driven by the consideration that it would be easier to reconfigure a two-class transatlantic ship into a seasonal single-class cruise ship than amalgamate three classes into one for cruises. The resulting arrangements had much merit and the ship was an icon for modernity and style. Over the years a number of changes and additions were made but Queen Elizabeth 2 continued to operate two-class transatlantics and one-class cruises. The transatlantic season began in mid-April afnd continued through to mid-December. Several cruises punctuated the season, with departures being offered from both Southampton and New York. After a Caribbean Christmas and New Year cruise from New York the ship undertook an extensive world cruise, departing from New York in early January and arriving

1986年和1987年的冬季将她的动力系统完全替换为柴－电机组。在同等航速下，燃料消耗从之前的每天500吨减少到每天370吨，并且大大增加了可靠性。在1997年，跨洋航程被调整为更长的6天，航速调整为24节。

"伊丽莎白女王2号"的订单被下发给克莱德班克的约翰·布朗公司船厂，并确定为一艘具有三个等级的船：头等舱级、二等舱级和经济舱级。在施工后期，决定把二等舱级和经济舱级合并成一个等级，"经济舱级"后来又有了一个新名字"跨大西洋级"。这种转变在很大程度上是出于这样一种考虑，即将一艘二级设定的跨大西洋船改装成季节性的单级邮轮比将三级合并为一级要容易得多。采用此种方式布置会产生很多优点，这艘船是现代和时尚的象征。多年来，"伊丽莎白女王2号"改变和增加了许多东西，但其始终以两级设定作为跨洋班轮，单级设定作为邮轮的模式运营。横跨大西洋航行季始于四月中旬，一直持续到十二月中旬。其几次作为邮轮的巡航填补了南安普敦和纽约间的跨洋航行季空白。在加勒比海的圣诞节主题航行和纽约的新年主题航行之后，这艘船会进行一次全球巡航，一月初从纽约出发，四月中旬返回。这样的

back in mid-April. The sequence repeated year after year.

First-class passengers dined in the single-sitting 500-seat Columbia restaurant, while Transatlantic class dined in the 800-seat Britannia restaurant on a two-sitting basis. As on the previous Queens Mary and Elizabeth, there was also a Grill Room, an extra-tariff a la carte restaurant seating just 100. The ship sailed in this configuration for three years before major changes were instigated as a result of Cunard Line being taken over by Trafalgar House plc during 1971 the new management aggressively seeking to maximise revenue potential. Additional cabins were added to the ship and the Britannia restaurant was reconfigured with the adjacent Lookout lounge being converted into a dedicated galley to serve it. More significantly, the 736 Club (First-class nightclub) was converted into an up-scale restaurant called the Queens Grill and the existing Grill Room was renamed the Princess Grill. Thus the Queens Grill would serve the most deluxe and expensive cabins on the ship, with the next grades dining in the Princess Grill-both single-sitting a la carte. The remaining First-class passengers continued to eat in the Columbia restaurant, while Transatlantic class dined in the two-sitting Britannia. These manoeuvrings allowed accommodations assigned to the two Grills to be marketed atpremium fares well above normal First-class rates. In 1995, the two-class designation was dropped and thereafter Queen Elizabeth 2 sailed as a one-class ship, although the accommodation pairings with the

安排年复一年地重复。

头等舱级的乘客在500座（单人座椅）的"哥伦比亚"餐厅用餐，而跨大西洋级的乘客在800座（双人座椅）的"布列塔尼亚"餐厅用餐。与前面的"玛丽女王号"和"伊丽莎白女王号"一样，船上还有一个烧烤厅，它其实是一个需要额外征税的100座的点菜餐厅。由于在1971年冠达邮轮公司被特拉法尔加豪斯公司收购从而发生了重大的改变。在此之前，这艘船在保持这种配置下航行了三年。新的管理层积极寻求收入最大化的可能性。额外的舱室被添加到船上，"布列塔尼亚餐厅"被重新整改，与之相邻的"瞭望"厅也被改为服务于它的厨房。更重要的是，"736"俱乐部（头等舱级夜总会）被改造成一家名为"女王"的高级餐厅，而现有的烧烤厅被改名为"公主"餐厅。因此"女王"餐厅为船上顶级的乘客提供用餐服务，下一个等级的乘客在"公主"餐厅用餐，这两个餐厅都采用的是单人座席。其余的头等舱级的乘客继续在"哥伦比亚"餐厅用餐，而跨大西洋级的乘客则在双人座席的"布列塔尼亚"餐厅用餐。这些改装使得匹配有两家餐厅的头等舱房的售价可以远高于市面上普通头等舱的价格。随后在1995年，

restaurants remained as before.

To parallel Queen Elizabeth 2 the basic operating profile of 'Project Queen Mary' would therefore be:

• Single class.

• Queens Grill, Princess Grill, main restaurant-all paired to specific cabin grades.

• Speed/endurance optimised for a six-day transatlantic crossing.

This was sufficient to begin work on designing the new ship. The first task was to prepare a list of facilities that space would have to be provided on board. I decided that the best approach would to study in detail the layout of Queen Elizabeth 2; She was after all designed for this service and has successfully operated in dual transatlantic and cruising mode for nearly 30 years. My aim was to identify the characteristics that were quintessential to maintaining the dual role at service levels required. I would question every aspect to determine whether the present QE2 arrangements and working were optimal, or if we could take aspects from modern cruise ships where advantageous. In 1998 the operation and disposition of Queen Elizabeth 2 had evolved since 1969 through the series of major refits, rebuilding and shifts in tastes and markets. Although many and profound, I had to judge whether the changes since had been limited by the being 'An existing ship'; Would they have been more extensive starting from scratch? Were alternations constrained by budget considerations, which are always greater for an existing ship compared to a new build? I set one important rule, that we would not adopt

这种双等级的标准被废除，此后尽管居住区以及与之相配的餐厅还保持原样，但"伊丽莎白女王2号"以单级模式运营。

向"伊丽莎白女王2号"看齐，"玛丽女王项目"的基本运营定位将是：

• 单一等级。

• "女王"餐厅，"公主"餐厅，主餐厅——以上皆对应于特定级别的舱室。

• 航速、续航力针对6天跨大西洋航行进行了优化。

以上这些内容足以开始进行新船的设计是足够的，其后的首要任务是确定安装在"玛丽女土2号"的设备清单，最后我选择了研究借鉴"伊丽莎白女王2号"总体布置的方案，因为她们不仅设计出发点相同，而且"伊丽莎白女王2号"有在跨洋班轮和邮轮双模式下近30年成功运营的经验。为了找出"伊丽莎白女王2号"在不同运营模式下保持服务水准的诀窍，我孜孜以求，不断求证"伊丽莎白女王2号"的布置和经营是否都是最优化的，或当代邮轮上是否存在一些先进之处可以借鉴？从1969年开始，"伊丽莎白女王2号"在历经一系列重大整修、改造和风格及市场的转变后，到1998年她已完全改变了。即使这些

any new practice or arrangement that would dilute the 'transatlantic experience'. I argued that this was after all, the raison d'être of the ship.

One major point of consideration was the number of large entertainment venues required. Queen Elizabeth 2 had been originally built with a First-class lounge (the Queens Room), a Tourist-class lounge (the Double Room on two levels with a large open well, which under the envisaged three-class configuration would have been the separate cabin – and third-class lounges) and a 530-seat theatre. All three spaces were devoid of an open bar and the lounges were primarily sitting areas, although they each had a large dance floor. In much the same way as on the previous Queens Mary and Elizabeth, entertainment would be limited. In her latter one-class configuration, the Queens Room was primarily in use as ballroom, a venue for afternoon tea and "welcome aboard" cocktail parties, while the Double Room had evolved into and entertainment venue, with the theatre being used for cinema films and an extensive passenger lecture programme. Modern-day cruise ships at the time usually had a very large main show lounge without a bar, a smaller secondary entertainment venue with a bar and no theatre/cinema. This was of course all very well for a cruise ship with limited days at sea, punctuated by port visits. On a transatlantic crossing where there were many days at sea, often with limited access to the open decks at sea due to wind, rain and fog, passengers had to be kept amused inside the ship. A matrix of two venue options was considered., foregoing one of

演变众多而且深奥，我也必须评估这些修改是不是受限于对"既有船舶"的改造限制？或者假如从零开始，他们会不会做得更彻底？或者是不是因为受到经费预算的限制？因为同新建船舶相比，旧船改造面临的预算问题更大。一直以来，我始终坚持"跨大西洋航行经验"是"伊丽莎白女王 2 号"存在的根本，任何有悖于此的方法和布置都是不能采用的，这也是我为本船制定的一条基本原则。

另一个主要考虑方面是船上大型娱乐场所的数量。"伊丽莎白女王 2 号"最开始的配置是一个头等舱级的休息厅（"女王"厅），一个经济舱级的休息厅（带开放式天井的跨层空间，符合既定的三级舱室配置设定中的第三级标准）以及一个拥有 530 个座位的剧场。上述处所都设巨型舞台和座位区，但没有设置开放式吧台。以往的"玛丽女王"和"伊丽莎白女王"系列班轮都存在类似问题，船上的娱乐活动有限。因此在后续系列中，"女王"厅被用于跳舞、喝下午茶和举行登船鸡尾酒会，"垂拔"厅成为娱乐会所，剧院演变成电影院和演播大厅。在当代邮轮上，通常会设一个无吧台的巨大演艺大厅，一个小一些但带吧台的副演艺厅，但是没有影院 / 剧院。当然

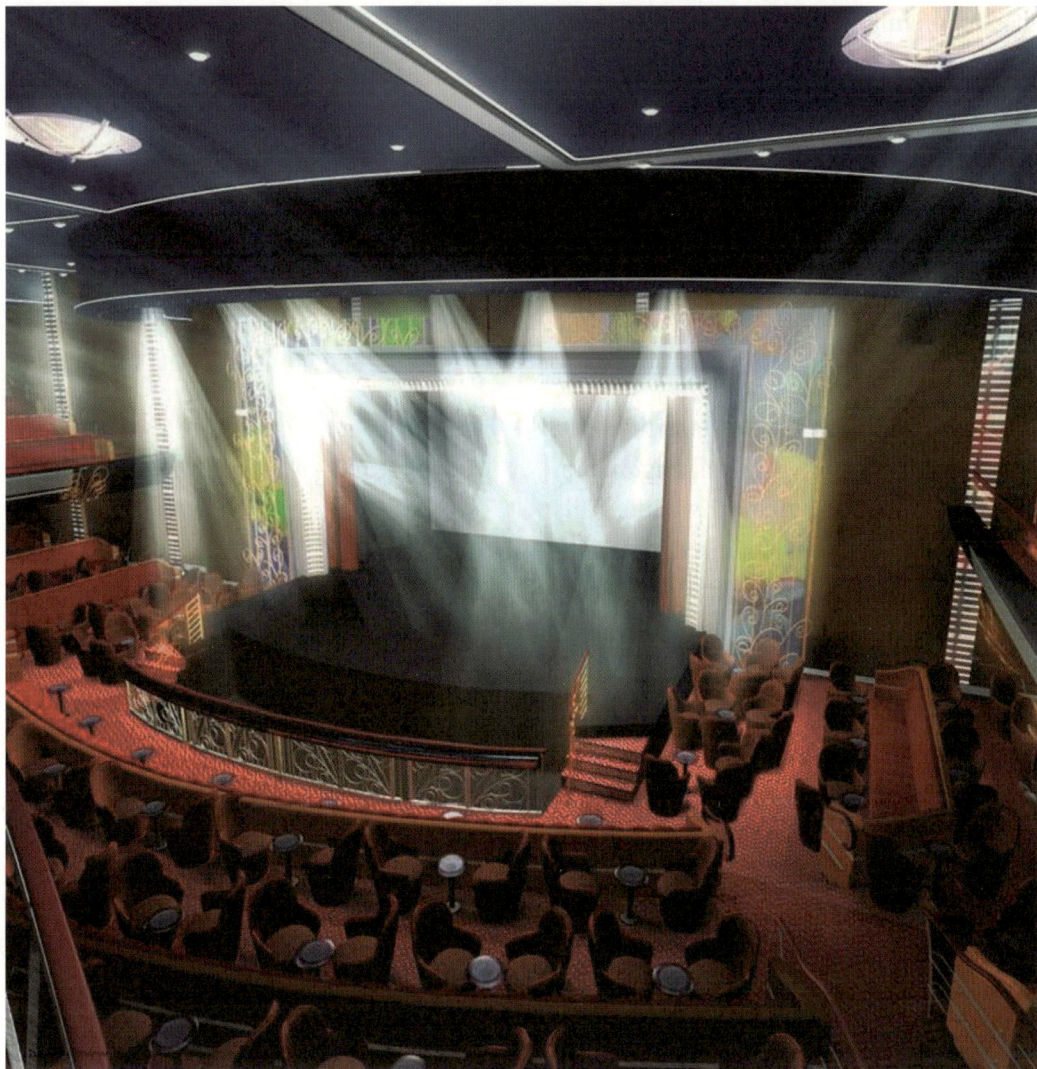

效果预览：艺术家眼中"玛丽女王2号""宫廷"剧院的艺术概念图（冠达邮轮提供）

the venues in turn and assessing as a paper exercise what services and features could be provided.

Timetables showing the availability of each space for the required functions were drawn up and all gaps in service noted. After much consideration and deliberation it was decided to retain a separate show lounge, ballroom and

这样的设计对于短途航行、间断靠港的邮轮而言也是相当不错的。然而在跨大西洋航行中，室外活动易受雨雪等气候的限制，这将导致室内娱乐成为了乘客们的唯一选择。我们也考虑了设置两个娱乐场所的可能性，采用纸上轮番推演评估的方法，来测试在

theatre, mainly on the basis of the special requirements of the transatlantic run.Each room would be designed for multi-purpose use with as little down time as possible to maximize utilisation. This philosophy led to a planetarium being incorporated into the theatre and the show lounge being used during the day for amateur dramatics in association with the Royal Academy of Dramatic Arts (RADA).

On-board revenue constitutes an important income on any passenger ship, greatly augmenting ticket revenue. This can be generated from a number of sources such as bars, shops, casino, spa and beauty salon. Space would have to be arranged for all these areas. In a similar way to the large lounge analysis, the number and disposition of bars was carefully assessed. On board ships, bars predominantly get busy immediately before lunch and dinner. It is therefore desirable to place bars as close to the dining venues as possible. Bars in the vicinity of the main dining room are particularly important due to the large number of passengers that use this room, compounded further by virtue that it operates on a two-sitting basis. The observation lounge would also require an extensive bar and in the final analysis 14 bars were deemed necessary, spread around the ship.

Shopping is a very popular on-board activity. Duty-free alcohol, perfume and tobacco are traditionally sold towards the end of a voyage from one shop. Cruise line and ship-specific branded goods are always in demand, with clothing high in the popularity stakes. This requires significant space located within a high-

取消一个娱乐场所之后，还可以提供哪些特色服务。

我们制定了显示每个功能空间的使用时间的时间表，并标注了服务之间的空档。经过深思熟虑，我们决定保留一个独立的演艺厅、舞厅和剧院，这主要是为了满足跨大西洋航线的特殊要求。每个房间都被设计成多用途的，以尽可能地减少闲置时间来提高其利用率。这种理念导致天文馆被并入剧院。在白天，演艺厅被用于表演与皇家戏剧艺术学院（RADA）联合创作的业余戏剧。

乘客在船上的消费是客船重要的收益来源，其极大地补贴了船票收入，如在酒吧、商店、赌场、SPA和美容沙龙的消费。必须为这些区域安排空间。以类似于大型休息厅的分析方式，对酒吧的数量和配置进行了仔细的评估。在午餐和晚餐之前，船上酒吧是很忙碌的。因此，酒吧宜尽量靠近餐厅。主餐厅附近的酒吧特别重要，因为这里的顾客非常多，而且将来很有可能采用两班用餐制以分流用餐乘客。"瞭望"厅里也要有一个宽敞的酒吧。归根结底，整艘船共需要14个酒吧。

购物是一种非常流行的船上活动。传统上，免税的酒、香水和烟草在船上可以一直出售直到航程结束。邮轮

位于二甲板的"布列塔尼亚"厨房的布置图。（作者提供）

traffic easily accessible area. A sundries shop is also necessary to cater for the inevitable forgotten essentials such as toothbrushes, sun cream and limited pharmaceuticals. On a high-class ship the potential sale of luxury goods such as expensive jewellery, artworks and so on is greatly enhanced if a recognised branded shop is involved. As with Queen Elizabeth 2, it was therefore decided to provide space for an extensive array of specialist branded shops that would be offered on a concession basis.

In 1911 the White Star Line introduced their new liner Olympic on the transatlantic run. One of the features that the owners hoped would entice First-class passengers to sail with them rather than rival Cunard

公司和船上特定品牌的商品总是供不应求，名牌服饰也会有很高的人气。这要求将商店布置在人流量高且显眼的地方。杂货店也是必要的，因为乘客难免会遗忘一些必需品，如牙刷、防晒霜和受控的药品。如果在船上引入知名的品牌店，那么诸如贵重珠宝、艺术品等奢侈品的销售量将大增。因此，与"伊丽莎白女王2号"一样，我们也决定引入大量特许经营的专业品牌商店。

1911年，白星邮轮公司在大西洋航线上引入了他们的新班轮"奥林匹

Line was the incorporation of a Turkish bath and a swimming pool; innovations such as these were also always important for publicity purposes. In keeping with her two-class demarcation, Queen Elizabeth 2 entered service with an outdoor and indoor swimming pool for each class. In 1982 the former First-class indoor swimming pool area was rebuilt as an oceangoing spa comprising pool, jacuzzi baths, treatment rooms and an exercise area all operated by the Californian Golden Door Spa. This was the first fully fledged spa of its type at sea and was the forerunner of the considerable facilities found on board most modern cruise ships. Cunard were keen to ensure that the new liner offered the most extensive spa at sea, so I was asked to ensure sufficient space was made available to enable the largest facility of its kind at sea to be incorporated. The spa would need a hydrotherapy pool, various hot-steam rooms, relaxation area and an array of treatment rooms.

Finally, space had to be allocated for various ancillary, but nonetheless important, areas, such as the passenger reception (called the Front Desk), numerous offices and public toilets. A similar spatial planning exercise was performed for the hotel services: galleys, pantries, stewards' stores, provision and consumable stores, passenger launderettes and the main laundry.

On a passenger ship, most of the technical outfit such as the propulsion plant can be located below the waterline where it is undesirable to place passenger or crew accommodation. However, one type of technical outfit that has to be distributed throughout the ship is the air-

克号"。船东在这条船上增加了一些特色项目，希望能吸引头等舱的乘客与他们同行，从而避免与冠达航运公司的同质化竞争。这些项目就是增加了一个蒸汽浴室（土耳其浴室）和一个游泳池。出于公关目的，诸如此类的创新总是很重要的。为了保持其二级设定的模式，"伊丽莎白女王2号"为每个等级都配备了室外和室内游泳池各一个。1982年，原头等舱级的室内游泳池被重建为一个海洋水疗中心，包括游泳池、按摩浴缸、理疗室和一个由加利福尼亚金门水疗中心运营的健身区。这是海上第一个完全成熟的水疗中心，也是大多数现代邮轮上类似设施的先驱者。冠达邮轮公司非常希望新班轮能够提供最大程度的海上水疗服务，因此要求确保有足够的空间以容纳海上最大的水疗设施。水疗中心将需要一个水疗池、各种热蒸汽房、放松区和一系列的理疗室。

最后，必须为各种作为附属但依然重要的功能区域分配空间，例如旅客接待处（前台）、众多办公室和公共厕所。在酒店服务方面也进行了类似的空间规划工作：厨房、配餐间、酒店库房、供应品和消耗品库房、旅客自助洗衣房和主洗衣房。

在客轮上，大多数技术设备，如

conditioning plant. For fire safety, the ship is divided from top to bottom into a number of fire zones, each separated from the adjacent one with fireproof bulkheads. Each zone requires its own air-conditioning handling units and distribution system. On modern ships these can usually be placed within the superstructure on the centerline, inboard of the passenger cabins.

Once the spatial requirements of the ship are determined, attention can focus on performing the initial weight calculation so that the hull design and requisite buoyancy can be provided. The weight calculation can be problematic. Most new passenger ships are variants of extant ships since it is much easier and cheaper to recycle earlier designs than to start afresh. Where data survives from previous designs it can be used as a starting point for the new one, with compensations made where the new plan differs from the existing one.

For Queen Mary 2 there was no immediate comparable ship. Nonetheless, a weight calculation had to be undertaken, so I chose the most logical step and used Queen Elizabeth 2 as the starting point. This ship was less than half the size of the new vessel on a gross tonnage basis and had an aluminium superstructure, rather than being of all steel construction, which was preferred for the new ship.Weight calculations are broken down into discrete groups called 'group weights', and these are usually defined as hull weight, machinery, accommodation and hull outfit. As far as practicable, the weights for these items were either identified from published data for Queen Elizabeth 2,

推进装置可以位于水线以下，因为在那里设置乘客或船员住宿是不合适的。然而，空调设备必须广泛分布于全船空间。为了防火，船舶从上到下分成若干防火主竖区，各相邻的防火主竖区采用防火舱壁隔开。每个区域都配有自己独立的空调器和布风系统。在现代船舶上，这些设备通常可以放置在上层建筑的中线附近，位于乘客舱区域的内侧。

一旦确定了船舶的空间要求，就可以集中精力进行初始重量计算，以便估算船体设计必需的浮力。重量计算很复杂。大多数新的客轮都是现有船只的衍生体，因为利用母型设计比重新设计要容易得多，也便宜得多。如果设计数据从以前的设计中延续下来，它可以作为新船设计的起点，并可在新设计与母型设计不同的地方进行修正。

对于"玛丽女王2号"来说，暂无可以用作比对的母型船。尽管如此，还是要进行重量计算，所以我选择了最符合逻辑的步骤，并以"伊丽莎白女王2号"为起点。按总吨位计算，"伊丽莎白女王2号"还不到新船的一半，并具有铝制上部结构，而不是全钢结构——上层建筑采用全钢结构是新船的首选方案。重量计算被分解成各重

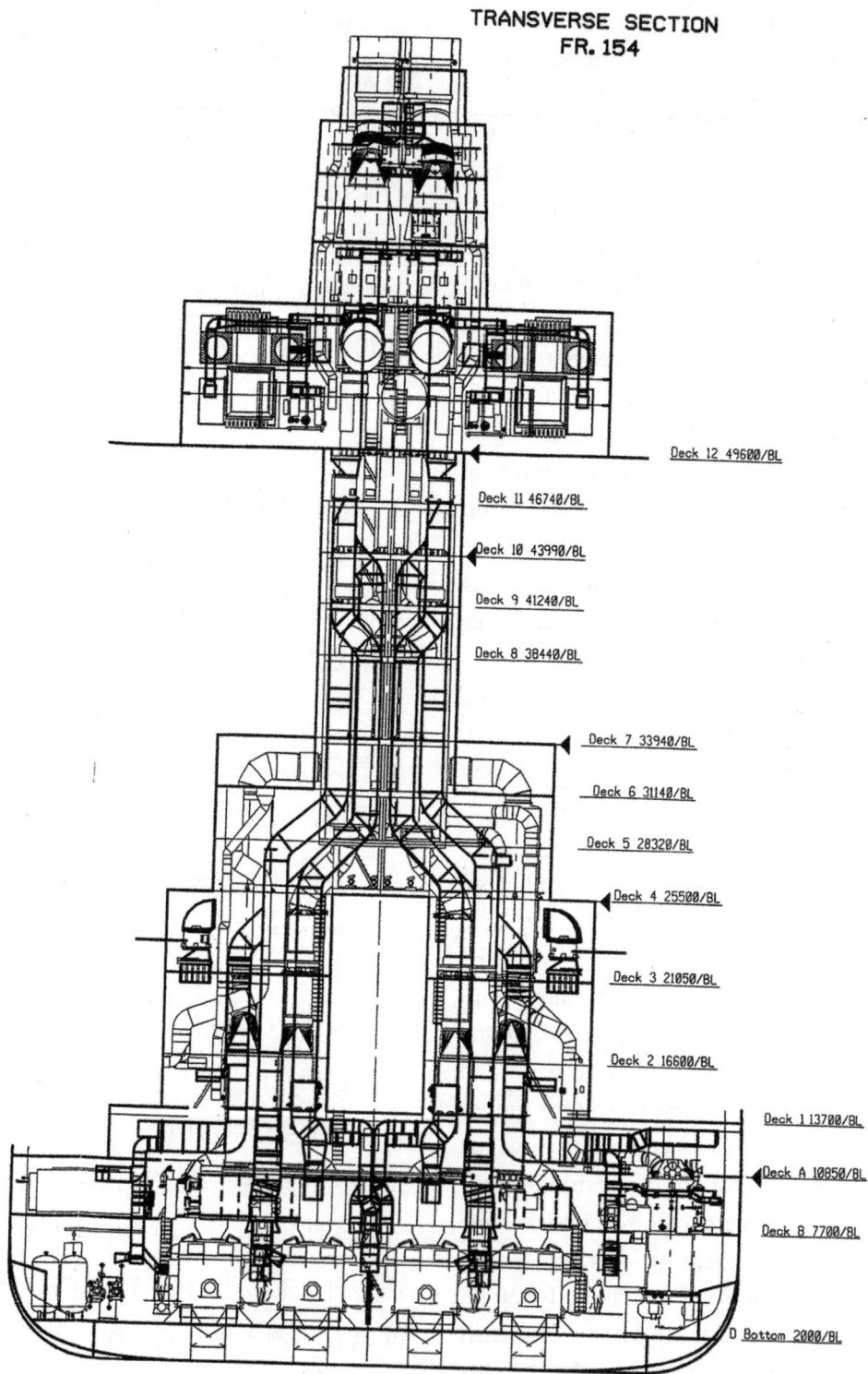

TRANSVERSE SECTION
FR. 154

Deck 12 49600/BL

Deck 11 46740/BL

Deck 10 43990/BL

Deck 9 41240/BL

Deck 8 38440/BL

Deck 7 33940/BL

Deck 6 31140/BL

Deck 5 28320/BL

Deck 4 25500/BL

Deck 3 21050/BL

Deck 2 16600/BL

Deck 1 13700/BL

Deck A 10850/BL

Deck B 7700/BL

D Bottom 2000/BL

"玛丽女王2号"154号肋位横剖面（作者提供）

史蒂芬·佩恩博士正在观赏船厂的第一个"玛丽女王2号"船模。这是"玛丽女王2号"的外观首次以三维立体化的方式呈现出来。（作者提供）

or estimated using established formulae based on trend analysis. Once the figures for QE2 were established, these were modified for the new ship using a series of scaling factors to take into consideration the increased size of the craft and material differences such as a change in propulsion system, the superstructure being all steel and not aluminium etc. The individual group weights were then combined to produce the 'lightship weight'. This is the weight of the ship without fuel, water, ballast, stores, passengers, crew, luggage etc, and with a 3% margin was estimated to be 62,000 tonnes.

量分项，通常包含船体结构重量、机械设备重量、内装和船体舾装重量。在切实可行的范围内，这些分项重量要么是从"伊丽莎白女王2号"已有的数据中确定，要么是根据公式进行预估。一旦确定了"伊丽莎白女王2号"的各个参数，就用一系列比例因子对新船参数进行修改，需要充分考虑船体尺寸的增加和材料差异，例如推进系统的变化、上层结构全部为钢制而非铝制等。然后将各分项重量组合成

The next figure to be estimated was the 'deadweight' which is the weight of fuel (6,500 tonnes), water(3 870 tonnes), stores, passengers and luggage (320 tonnes), crew and effects (130 tonnes) and so on. This was estimated to be 14,000 tonnes using established weights for each passenger, baggage, crew etc.

Adding the lightship and deadweight together produces the total weight of the ship, and this is the weight that the underwater hull must support through providing the equivalent buoyancy and is known as the 'displacement'. In the calculations for our new ship this was 76,000 tonnes.

Considering that salt water is denser

"空船重量"。这是船舶没有携带燃料、水、压载、仓储、乘客、船员、行李等的重量，并保留 3% 的冗余，预估为 62 000 吨。

下一个预估的参数是"载重量"，即燃料（6 500 吨）、水（3 870 吨）、仓储、乘客及行李（320 吨）、船员及相关物品（130 吨）等的重量。按每名乘客、每件行李、每名船员的既定重量计算，预估为 14 000 吨。

空船重量和载重量加在一起构成船舶的总重量，这是水下船体通过提供同等浮力支持的重量，称为"排水量"。

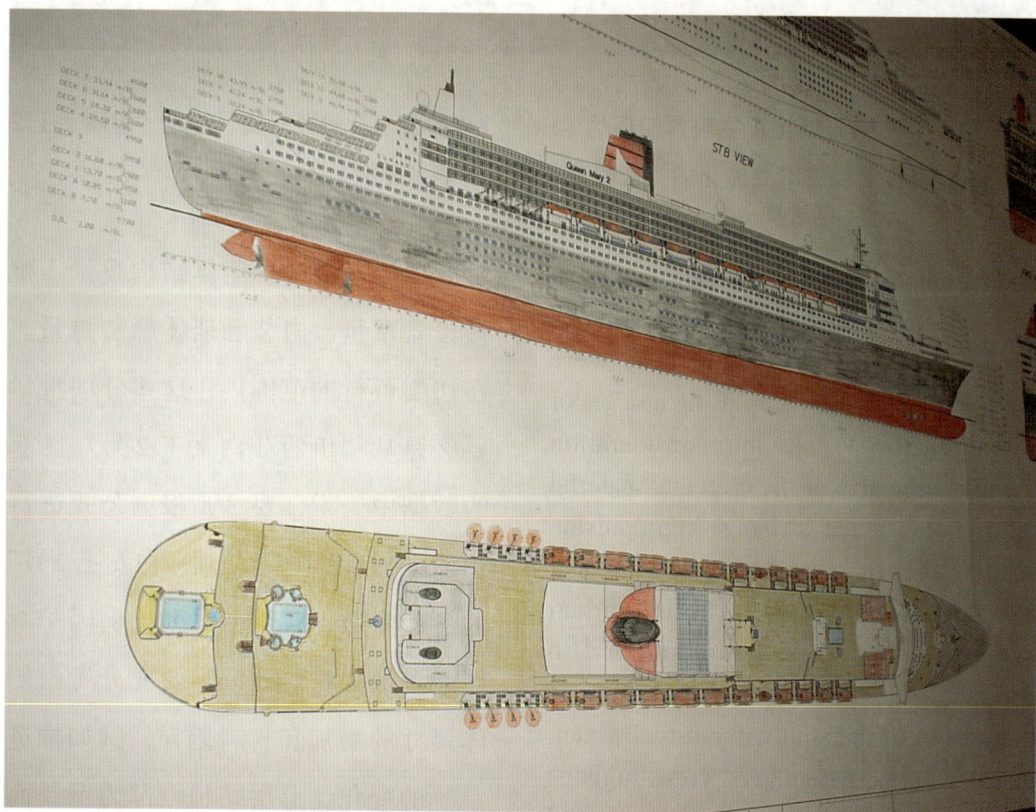

史蒂芬·佩恩博士彩涂的玛丽女王2号的外形图。（作者提供）

than fresh water, using a density of salt water at 1.025kg/m^3, the volume that the hull would need to displace was calculated at 76,000/1.025 = 74,150 m^3.

Considering the length of the ship underwater (just over 300 metres), the ship's beam (set at 41 metres to provide adequate stability) and the ship' draught (limited to 10 metres for port accessibility) the hull shape could be approximated to provide the necessary volume of 74,150 m3. This would later be refined during optimization through the model test tank programme.

The design of the ship evolved over the period of 18 months. There

新船的计算结果为 76 000 吨。

考虑到海水比淡水密度高，以 1.025 kg/m^3 的海水密度计算，船体需要排开水的体积为 76 000/1.025=74 150 m^3。

考虑到船在水面以下的长度（刚刚超过 300 米）、船的宽度（设定为 41 米以提供足够的稳定性）和吃水（港口通行限制为 10 米），船体可以达到的体积大约为 74 150 立方米。船体体积还可通过水池模型试验优化后得到精确值。

在超过 18 个月的设计优化过程中，

"玛丽女王 2 号"船上"布列塔尼亚"餐厅的艺术概念图。（冠达邮轮提供）

"玛丽女王 2 号"船上"凉亭"泳池的艺术概念图。（冠达邮轮提供）

were numerous setbacks and twice the project was put on hold for re-evaluation. Everything centred on maximizing the revenue potention of the ship to offset the huge contract price – the liner premium. This meant marking the best use of the number of cabins and ensuring that as many as possible were high-revenue balcony types. A historic milestone was reached on 29 May 1999 when Carnival's senior management indicated that the project could proceed to the next phase and an outline specification should be prepared for distribution to selected shipyards. By this stage the general arrangement phase was shaping up nicely and a meeting was convened in Miami between Tillberg

我们遇到了许多困难，该项目曾两次被推迟以进行重新评估。所有这一切都集中在如何使船舶的收益最大化——即班轮的溢价，以抵消高昂的建造成本。这意味着要充分利用客舱的数量，以确保提供尽可能多的带阳台的客舱来增加收入。1999 年 5 月 29 日注定是历史性的里程碑日，当天嘉年华集团的高层管理人员表示，该项目可继续进行下一阶段的工程，并将为选定的船厂提供技术规格书。在这个阶段，总体布置进行得很顺利，蒂尔伯格（内装设计公司）、芬

从"瞭望"甲板上往船尾看救生艇设备。（作者提供）

正在通过韦拉札诺海峡大桥的"玛丽女王2号"，2013年7月6日开始其第200次跨大西洋航行。（作者提供）

从"伊丽莎白女王 2 号"上拍摄到"玛丽女王 2 号"驶近韦拉札诺海峡大桥。（作者提供）

(interior architects), Fincantieri's tead naval architect Maurizo Cergol (acting as a consultant and assisting with the sizing of the escape staircases) and me. We finalized the stairs and many other details, At this stage we estimated that the cabin count would be 1,251, but with further refinements this figure reached 1,310. Changes were constantly made and the effects carefully considered and accordingly compensated. This process is known as the design spiral – every change has a knock-on effect but gradually the design gets tighter and tighter unitl it reaches an optimum point.

坎蒂尼的首席船舶设计师毛里佐·切尔格（担任顾问并协助调整逃生楼梯的尺寸）和我在迈阿密召开的会议上把楼梯和许多其他细节问题都定了下来。在这一阶段，我们估计客舱数量将是 1 251 个，但是经过进一步细化后，这个数字达到 1 310 个。经常会有新的调整出现，其效果会被仔细考虑，并做出相应的补偿。这个过程被称为设计迭代——每一次变化都会产生连锁反应，但设计会逐渐变得越来越紧密，直到达到最佳状态。

其他设计考虑
Other design considerations

Another crucial factor in the design of Queen Mary 2 was the height of the lifeboats above the waterline. Normal arrangements would have limited the height of the lifeboat davit head to 15 metres above the waterline, but Queen Mary 2 was given dispensation by the UK and USA regulatory authorities - on the grounds that she would be operating in liner service - to raise this to 28 metres. This was particularly important as it was roughly the height at which the boats and davits on Queen Elizabeth 2 had been set and operational experience on the Atlantic decisively showed that it wouldn't be prudent to lower them.

In setting out the initial parameters of the ship, the length, draught and height were determined by the constrictions imposed by her main terminal ports of Southampton and New York. Maximum height was limited to 62 metres (the maximum air draught) due to the available height below the Verrazano Narrows Bridge at the entrance to New York Harbour. With an air draught of 62 metres, Queen Mary 2 has less than three metres' clearance at the high point of mid-span at high tide. The length of the ship at 345 metres was determined

"玛丽女王2号"在设计上的另一关键因素是救生艇距离水面的高度。常规布置要求救生艇架端部离水面高度限制在15米以内，但"玛丽女王2号"因班轮化营运而得到了英国和美国监管当局的豁免，允许将此高度提升到了28米。这非常重要，因为这与"伊丽莎白女王2号"上救生艇和艇架的高度基本一致。大西洋上的运营经验表明，降低此高度是不明智的。

在确定船舶基本参数时，南安普敦和纽约母港码头的限制决定了她的长度、吃水和高度。依据纽约港入口处韦拉扎诺海峡大桥下方可用高度，船舶最大高度限制在62米（最大净空高度）。62米船高的"玛丽女王2号"在高潮位时与桥跨中点最高处的间隙距离不足3米。南安普敦码头可供回转空间和纽约哈德森河上手指状码头的长度决定了船舶长度最大为345米。再长一点，船就不易在码头上靠泊了，同时在南安普敦港口转向也会存在问题。"玛丽女王2号"10米的吃水深

by the available turning space at Southampton Docks and the length of the New York finger piers on the Hudson River. Any longer and it was considered that the ship would be difficult to tie up at the piers, as well as proving problematic in turning at Southampton. The draught of 10 metres was set to be the same as Queen Elizabeth 2 so that the ship would have unrestricted access to Southampton and New York, without the need to wait for high tides, as Queens Mary and Elizabeth had to.

The initial design of Queen Mary 2 foresaw an eight-diesel installation, split within two watertight compartments, four engines in each. This presented a considerable challenge as the exhaust casings took up a disproportionate amount of space within the public rooms and cabin decks. On Chantiers de l'Atlantique's advice, it was decided to replace the aft engine room with two gas turbines. As these were relatively compact and light, they didn't need to be fitted at the bottom of the ship but could be placed up top immediately behind the funnel. This eliminated the aft engine room casings and freed up space for larger public rooms and additional cabins.

The structural arrangements of the ship were very carefully determined from the outset. In consultation with Lloyd's Register, the structural design of the vessel was evaluated to produce arrangements that would fulfil the liner pedigree and provide a 40-year fatigue design life. Pillars were carefully

度与"伊丽莎白女王 2 号"相同，这样船舶就能像"玛丽女王号"和"伊丽莎白女王号"一样不必等待涨潮，可以不受限制地进出南安普敦港和纽约港。

"玛丽女王 2 号"最初的设计考虑安装 8 台柴油机，分别布置在 2 个水密机舱中，每个舱内布置 4 台。这样就产生了一个相当大的挑战，容纳排气管的机舱棚占据了公共处所和舱室区域大量的空间。在大西洋船厂的建议下，我们决定用 2 台燃气轮机来取代艉部机舱内的动力机组。燃气轮机相对更紧凑，也更轻，因此它们不用必须安装在船舶的底部，而可以布置在烟囱正后方。这样取消了在机舱后的机舱棚，就可以腾出空间给公共处所和布置更多的住舱。

我们一开始就对船体的结构设计进行了认真的研究，并且在英国劳氏船级社的咨询帮助下，对船体结构设计进行了评估，结果显示其完全满足线型要求并且疲劳寿命达到 40 年。从船底延伸到船顶的支柱布置合理，上部舱壁甲板结合两道位于船内，几乎形成连续的纵舱壁，以上这些为主船体提供足够的整体强度。由于采取了相比其他任何邮轮都要厚的外板，同时进行了船体线型优化，这艘船被成功设计为可以横跨大西洋航行的邮轮，

positioned to be continuous from the bottom to the top of the ship and the superstructure cabin decks were provided with two inboard near-continuous longitudinal bulkheads that would provide great integral strength. With hull plating considerably thicker than employed on any cruise ship, and refined hull lines, the craft was well placed to operate express transatlantic crossings. This has been amply demonstrated throughout the ship's service to date. During the detailed design phase finite element analyses were performed to identify high stress points so that these areas could be additionally strengthened as required. Similar techniques were employed to investigate and minimise vibration and noise.

The beam of 41 metres was assessed from earlier designs to provide the margin of stability necessary for a stable ship and to meet all the regulatory requirements. The positioning of watertight bulkheads and other aspects of the subdivision were finalised early in the detailed design process. Similarly, the disposition of fire bulkheads and levels of insulation were carefully considered with reference to earlier ships.

并且到目前为止的成功运营已经充分地证明了这一点！在船舶详细设计阶段，通过有限元计算分析出高应力点，并对这些区域进行局部额外加强以减小应力集中。与此同时，类似的先进技术也被用来研究降低振动噪音对船体的影响。

为了满足和船舶稳性相关法规的要求，在早期设计阶段，经评估采用41米的船宽来提供足够的必需稳性裕度。在详细设计初期阶段完成了水密舱壁和其他舱壁的划分。与此同时，参考早期母型船的资料确定了舱壁防火分隔和绝缘等级。

（译者：王露、谢旭晨、杨勇）

"玛丽女王 2 号"停靠在利物浦港。（冠达邮轮提供）

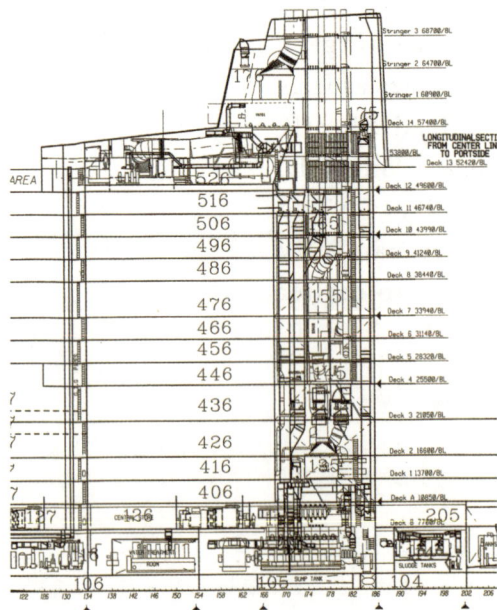

"玛丽女王 2 号"烟囱剖面截图（作者提供）

"玛丽女王 2 号" 艏部中纵剖面图（作者提供）

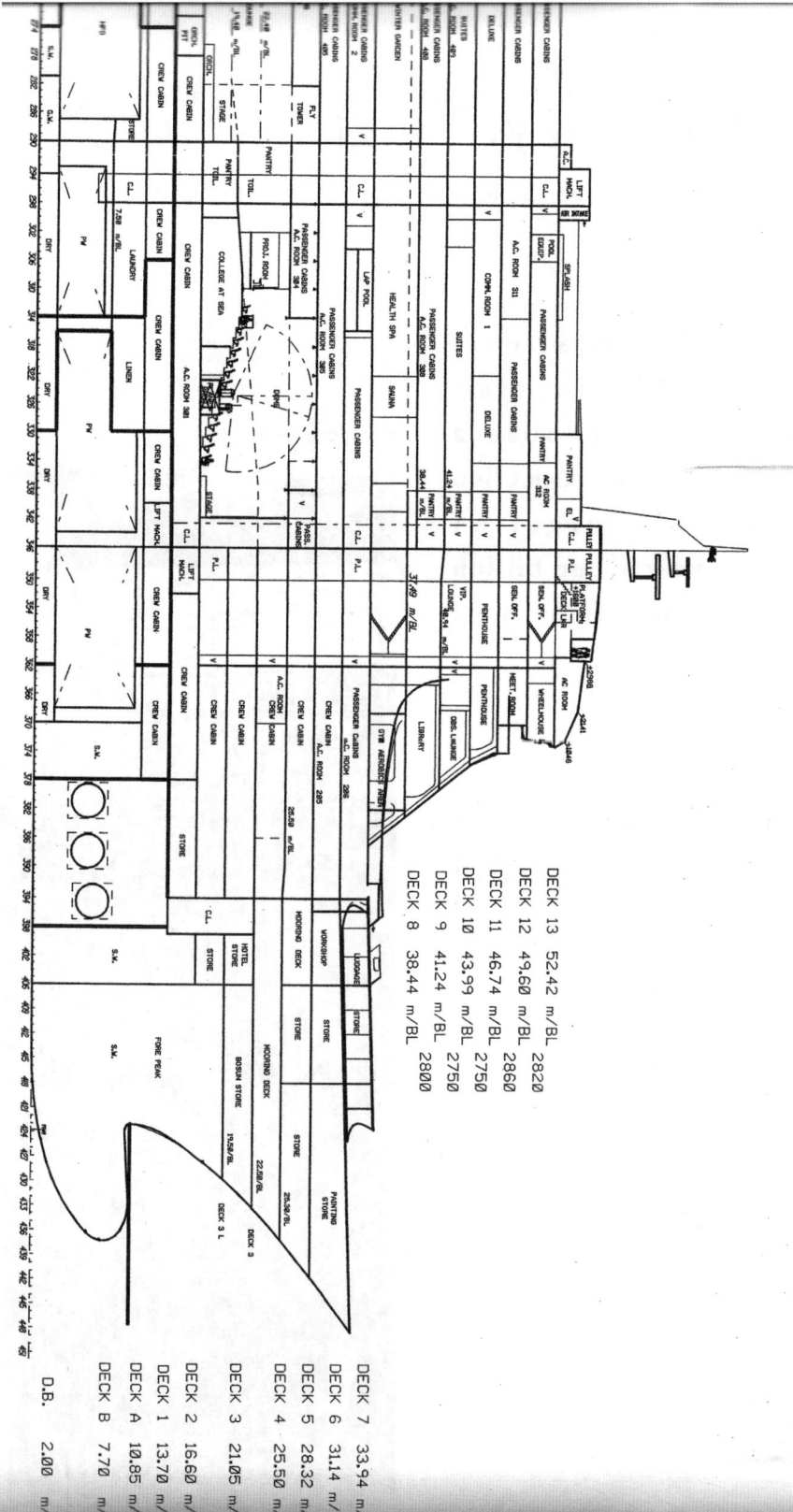

DECK 13	52.42 m/BL
DECK 12	49.60 m/BL 2820
DECK 11	46.74 m/BL 2860
DECK 10	43.99 m/BL 2750
DECK 9	41.24 m/BL 2750
DECK 8	38.44 m/BL 2800
DECK 7	33.94 m/
DECK 6	31.14 m/
DECK 5	28.32 m/
DECK 4	25.50 m/
DECK 3	21.05 m/
DECK 2	16.60 m/
DECK 1	13.70 m/
DECK A	10.85 m/
DECK B	7.70 m/
D.B.	2.00 m/

第四章 建造"玛丽女王2号"

Chapter Four:Building Queen Mary 2

You start with a plan; next draw up a specification; draft a contract; then choose a shipbuilder; involve an inspection team-and don't forget an investment of nearly one billion dollars. Thirty-five months later: Queen Mary 2!

从一张图纸开始，到制定一份规格书，起草一份合同，再到选择造船厂和监造小组，加上近10亿美元的投资。35个月后："玛丽女王2号"诞生了！

　　从船首向船尾望去，"玛丽女王 2 号"有着非常好的结构完整性，无数的梁、柱子和舱壁都清晰可见。在船的底部，双层底延伸到整个船长，可通过前方舱壁来看出其高度。一台伸长吊臂的吊车用于向船上吊运材料。天文馆的穹顶结构暂时停放在天井开口之下。

The shipbuilders

Late in 1999 the preliminary outline specification and general arrangement plan were distributed to five leading European shipyards:

m Fincantieri, the Italian state-owned shipbuilder, with several yards well versed in passenger ship construction, including Marghera, Monfalcone and Genoa.
• HDW, Kiel, Germany, a private shipyard with some passenger ship experience.
• MASA Yards, Helsinki and Turku, formerly Wartsila Marine industries, with a strong passenger ship pedigree.
• Chantiers de I'Atlantique, St-Nazaire, France, owned by the engineering group Alstom and with a rich history of passenger ship building, especially transatlantic liners for the French line.
• Harland & Wolff, Belfast, Northern Ireland, owned by Fred Olsen and with a long history of building passenger ships.

We deemed that these shipyards might have the potential to fulfill the contract to deliver the ship. Initial discussions led to the Finns, Italians and Germans bowing out of the negotiations due to lack of spare capacity or size of project issues. This left Harland & Wolff and Chantiers de I'Atlantique to develop the project and offer final tenders for it. Chantiers were regarded as strong contenders right from the start as they

造船厂

在1999年底，初步的技术规格书和总布置图已发给欧洲五大主流船厂：

• 芬坎蒂尼，意大利国有造船集团，拥有几家精通客船建造的船厂，包括马尔盖拉，蒙法尔科内和热那亚。

• 位于德国基尔的霍瓦特·德意志船厂是一家有着丰富客船建造经验的私有船厂。

• 位于赫尔辛基和图尔库的玛莎船厂，其前身为瓦锡兰海洋工业公司，拥有强大的客船建造传统。

• 位于法国圣纳泽尔的大西洋船厂，该公司归阿尔斯通工程集团所有，有着丰富的客船建造历史，尤其是为法国班轮公司建造的跨大西洋班轮。

• 位于北爱尔兰贝尔法斯特的哈兰德·沃尔夫船厂，由弗雷德·奥尔森所有，同样有着建造客船的悠久历史。

我们认为这些船厂都能够履行合同并交付船舶。最初的时候，由于缺乏闲置产能或项目规模过于巨大，导致芬兰人、意大利人和德国人退出了谈判。只剩下哈兰德·沃尔夫船厂和大西洋船厂参与这个项目并对其进行最终投标。大西洋船厂从一开始就被认为是强有力的竞争者，因为他们得

received full backing and support from their parent group Alstom. Harland & Wolff, however, was in a much weaker position as it had nor built a fully fledged passenger ship since the P&O Canberra of 1961. The yard decided to form a consortium comprising LIoyd Werft, based at Bremerhaven in Germany and specialists in passenger ship outfitting, Gammell Laird, based at Birkenhead in the UK and specialists in project management, and themselves. Although Harland & Wolff was very enthusiastic at the prospect of the order, the company was unable to match the financial guarantees offered by the much larger Alstom group and eventually withdrew from the tendering process.

On 10 March 2000 at the Miami Cruise Shipping Seatrade conference exhibition it was announced that a letter of intent had been signed between Chantiers de I'Atlantique and Cunard's parent company, Carnival Corporation, indicating that the two companies would work together to formalize a full contract for the construction of the first true liner since the delivery of Queen Elizabeth 2 in 1969. After an intense period of negotiations, the order was formally placed on 6 November 2000, with delivery set December 2003.

Founded in 1861 by Compagnie Generale Transatlantique, the Chantiers shipyard is located at St-Nazaire where the River Loire meets the Bay of Biscay. The original concept behind the formation of the yard was promote

到了其母公司阿尔斯通集团的全力支持。而哈兰德·沃尔夫船厂的处境就要艰难得多，因为自 1961 年 P&O 邮轮公司的"堪培拉号"下水以来，该公司还没有造过一条成熟的客船。该船厂决定组成一个联盟，其成员包括总部位于德国不来梅港的劳埃德尔造船厂及一批客船舾装专家，英国别根海特的项目管理专家甘梅尔·莱尔德及一批专家。尽管哈兰德·沃尔夫船厂对这一订单的前景非常乐观，但该公司无法匹敌比其规模大得多的阿尔斯通集团提供的财务担保，最终也退出了此次投标程序。

2000 年 3 月 10 日在迈阿密邮轮航运海事展上，大西洋船厂与冠达邮轮公司的母公司——嘉年华集团宣布签订意向书，这标志着两家公司将共同努力，正式签订一份自 1969 年"伊丽莎白女王 2 号"交付以来的第一个真正意义上完整的班轮建造合同。经过一轮激烈的谈判，该订单于 2000 年 11 月 6 日正式生效，交货日期定于 2003 年 12 月。

大西洋船厂由大西洋班轮总公司于 1861 年创立，该船厂位于卢瓦尔河与比斯开湾交汇处的圣·纳泽尔。最初创立船厂的目的是提高法国建造第一批钢制班轮的能力。这一切都是由苏格兰工程师约翰·斯科特实现的，

the capability to build the first steel-hull liners in France. This was all made possible by a Scottish engineer, John Scott, who organized and achieved the necessary transfer of technology from Britain to France for this purpose. The first ship, Imperatrice Eugenie, was launched in 1865. About 80 other liners were to follow between 1865 and 1962, as well as naval vessels, oil tankers and methane carriers.

The French line and Chantiers enjoyed a very close relationship, just as John Brown Shipyard on the Clyde did with Cunard. French Line and Cunard were the greatest of rivals throughout most of the last century.

Chantiers de I'Atlantique built some of the finest liners of the 20th century, including the first France (1912), lle de France (1927), Normandie (1935) and France (1962). The Normandie is considered by many to be the finest transatlantic liner ever constructed, although QM2 is now a serious contender for that claim! All four ships were renowned for their external and internal designs.

One of the greatest rivalries of the mid-1930s was that between the great so-called 'ship of state': Normandie and Cunard's Queen Mary (1936). Both ships vied with each other for the greater size and speed, with Queen Mary ultimately winning on speed and her sister, Queen Elizabeth (1940), winning the size accolade. It is interesting to note that whereas Queen Mary was a

他为此专门组织并实现了从英国到法国的必要技术转让。自从第一艘船"尤金号"在 1865 年下水以来，在 1865 年到 1962 年之间，大约有 80 艘除此之外的班轮、海军舰艇、油轮和甲烷运输船相继建成。

法国班轮公司和大西洋船厂有着非常密切的关系，就像克莱德的约翰·布朗船厂和冠达公司一样。在 20 世纪的大部分时间里，法国班轮公司是冠达公司最大的竞争对手。

圣·纳泽尔船厂建造了一批 20 世纪最精美的邮轮，其中包括第一艘"法国号"（1912 年）、"大巴黎号"（1927 年）、"诺曼底号"（1935 年）和"法国号"（1962 年）。"诺曼底号"被许多人认为是有史以来建造的最优秀的跨大西洋班轮，而"玛丽女王 2 号"现在是这一说法的有力竞争者！这四艘船都以内外装设计而著称。

20 世纪 30 年代中期所谓的"国家旗舰"称号的最大竞争者是"诺曼底号"和冠达的"玛丽女王号"（1936 年）。两艘船都在比拼更大的尺寸和更快的速度，"玛丽女王号"最终以速度取胜，而她的姊妹船"伊丽莎白女王号"（1940 年）摘得了尺寸的桂冠。有趣的是，"玛丽女王号"在财政上取得了成功，而"诺曼底号"却需要国家补贴才能维持运

financial success, Normandie required a generous state subsidy to remain in operation. In the late 1960s and early 1970s a similar rivalry existed between France and Queen Elizabeth 2.

At the time of building Queen Mary 2, Alstom Chantiers de I'Atlantique had about 4,500 employees in St-Nazaire, with some 7,500 subcontracting companies'employees working with them inside the shipyard, bringing the total workforce involved in building ships in St-Nazaire to 12,000.

In the 1980s and 1990s, Chantiers was responsible for the construction of many of the current generation of now older cruise ships, and since the delivery of Queen Mary 2 the shipyard has continued to delivery high-class cruise ships to several owners, particularly MSC Cruises.

营。在20世纪60年代末和70年代初,"法国号"和"伊丽莎白女王2号"之间也存在类似的竞争。

在建造"玛丽女王2号"时,阿尔斯通旗下的圣·纳泽尔船厂有4 500名雇员,另外还有约7 500名分包公司的雇员在船厂工作,这使得在圣·纳泽尔造船的工人总数达到12 000人。

在20世纪80年代和90年代,圣·纳泽尔船厂负责建造了许多当时是主流,但现在过时了的邮轮,自从"玛丽女王2号"交付后,该船厂相继向几家船东公司尤其是地中海邮轮公司(MSC)交付多条高级邮轮。

Specification, contract, model tests and construction

规格书、合同、模型试验以及建造

Specification

The first specification for 'Project Queen Mary' was compiled by Carnival Corporation's shipbuilding team with chapters outlining the salient features of the design and the general standards to which the owners expected the ship to be built. This first specification was termed the 'Outline Specification' and its purpose was

规格书

"玛丽女王项目"的第一版规格书由嘉年华集团的建造团队编写,概述了邮轮的特点和船东对这条邮轮的设想。第一版规格书被称为"简要规格书",其给出造价、交付日期等信息。各船厂可以根据这些信息,评估是否参加正式的招标流程。

　　"SS 法国号"，体现了 20 世纪 60 年代法国建筑设计的时尚和风格，是法国班轮"诺曼底号"的继承者。她在圣·纳泽尔建造并于 1962 年开始运营，在政府撤销维持其运营的补贴后，她在法国班轮公司仅运营了 12 年。从外表上看，这艘船是有史以来建造的最漂亮的班轮之一。但与她的前辈相比，这艘船还是有许多差强人意的地方。后来，她成为了挪威·加勒比邮轮公司的邮轮，并运营了很长一段时间。

to provide potential shipyards with sufficient information to enable them to assess whether they wanted to be included in the formal tendering process and to enable them to provide an indicative price and delivery date for the project.

Following the selection of Chantiers de I'Atlantique as the shipyard to build the ship, the months between March and November were taken to develop the full

　　大西洋船厂拿到建造合同后，在 3 月到 11 月的时间里完成了详细规格书的编写，共分为十节，内容如下：

　　1. 总则；

　　2. 安全；

　　3. 船体；

　　4. 舱室和公共区域；

　　5. 环境；

　　6. 轮机；

specification. This was arranged in ten sections:

1. General Information.
2. Safety.
3. Hull.
4. Accommodation and Public Spaces.
5. Environmental.
6. Machinery.
7. Accessories for Machinery.
8. General Outfit and Ship's Systems.
9. Electricity, Automation, Navigation and Communication.
10. Painting.

These sections were contained in one volume entitled simply, 'Chapter 1 Technical Specification'. Each section carefully detailed what had to be incorporated into the ship, with performance criteria where appropriate. A second volume entitled 'Chapter 2 Exhibits', contained numerous sample plans and arrangements that had been agreed up to that time within 18 sections. Specific documents included an agreed list of suppliers and makers from which the owners had agreed the shipyard could approach for equipment supply; a list of supplies that the owners would deliver to the ship, such as flags, mattresses, bedding etc; passenger and crew cabin layouts; and equipment lists such as that for catering.

The principal particulars as given in the specification were as follows:

7. 轮机相关系统；

8. 外舾装和船舶系统；

9. 电气、自动化、导航和通信；

10. 涂装。

以上十节的内容被合成为一章，称为"第一章技术规格"，每节都详细地描述了设计和建造内容以及可行的性能指标。第二章是"样例"，用18节的篇幅，将当时已经被船东认可的许多设计和布置的样本进行了阐述。具体文件包括船东和船厂商定的供货商清单，船东提供的物品如旗帜、床垫、床上用品等，乘客和船员的舱室布置以及似餐饮设备清单那样的全船设备清单。

规格书中给出的主要船型参数如下：

Length overall	345.00 metres	总长	345.00 米
Length of waterline	314.25 metres	水线长	314.25 米
Length between perpendiculars	301.35 metres	垂线间长	301.35 米
Beam,moulded	41.00 metres	型宽	41.00 米
Design draught	10.00 metres	设计吃水	10.00 米
Maximum air draught	62.00 metres	最大净空高度	62.00 米
Lightship	61,500 tonnes	空船重量	61 500 吨
Deadweight at design draught	14,300 tonnes	载重量（设计吃水）	14 300 吨
Displacement at design draught	76,500 tonnes	排水量（设计吃水）	76 500 吨
Speed,maximum	29.62 knots	最大航速	29.62 节
Passenger cabins	1,310	乘客住舱	1 310 间
Passengers	2,800	乘客数	2 800 名
Crew cabins	703	船员住舱	703 间
Crew	1,253	船员数	1 253 名
Gross tonnage	150,000 approximately	总吨	150 000 吨
Classification	Lloyd's Register	入级	英国劳氏船级社
Flag	Originally UK,now Bermuda	挂旗	最初挂英国旗，现在挂百慕大旗
Port of registry	Originally Southampton,now Hamilton	港籍	最初为南安普敦，现为汉密尔顿

It is always difficult defining the standard of construction, especially passenger and crew accommodation areas, both cabins and public rooms. Invariably the method used is to specify items as fully as possible and to reference items to a known standard, ie that of an existing ship. The highest quality/standard that had been applied within the Carnival Corporation to date was for the new Holland America Line flagship Rotterdam, which was delivered in October 1997. To this end, the passenger accommodation was referenced to specific public spaces on Rotterdam. This would eventually require those shipyards wishing to tender for the project to visit the Dutch ship with their public room assessors in order to gauge the quality level and cost accordingly.

International standards for design, construction and operation of ships are defined within a set of regulations called 'Safety of Life at Sea' (SOLAS) and are laid down by the United Nations' agency, International Maritime Organisation, which is based in London. Representatives from maritime nations meet and debate maritime issues and formulate the SOLAS and other maritime regulations. Queen Mary 2 was designed to meet fully, and in many cases exceed, the requirements, as provided by SOLAS.

Queen Mary 2 is classed with Lloyd's Register. This 'Lloyd's' must not be confused with the Lloyd's of London insurance underwriters, but is an assurance organization which acts

建造标准总是很难确定,特别是乘客和船员的居住区域,包括舱室和公共区域。采取的措施是建立尽可能完善的指标体系和引用参考相关船的标准。截至目前,荷美邮轮公司的新旗舰"鹿特丹号"采用了嘉年华集团的最高标准,这条船是在 1997 年 10 月交付的。因此,乘客的起居处所可以参考"鹿特丹号"上划定的公共区域。这要求参加竞标的船厂派遣公共区域工程师考察"鹿特丹号",以便明确相应的质量水平和成本。

《国际海上人命安全公约》(SOLAS)规定了船舶设计、建造和运营的国际标准,该公约由联合国的分支机构——国际海事组织(IMO,总部位于伦敦)制定。成员国的代表定期举行会议讨论海事问题,制定或修订 SOLAS 和其他海事法规。"玛丽女王 2号"的设计方案完全符合 SOLAS 的要求,有些方面甚至超过 SOLAS 的要求标准。

"玛丽女王 2 号"入级英国劳氏船级社。此处提到的英国劳氏船级社不是下文提到的伦敦劳氏保险公司,而是一家对船舶、结构、铁路等项目进行质量担保的机构。除了所有的相关法规外,英国劳氏船级社自己还有

under charitable status to survey and monitor ships, structures, railways and many other facets of daily life. Lloyd's Register has its own set of standards for design and construction, in addition to all the statutory rules, and ships are surveyed by qualified inspectors during construction and throughout their service life to ensure the highest standards are being maintained. Lloyd's Register's top classification is given the notation +100 Al and Queen Mary 2 carries this designation in combination with several enhancements.

Additionally, by operating under the British flag with British regulation (from December 2003-October 2011) the ship had to comply with the specific interpretations and requirements of the UK Maritime Coastguard Agency (MCA). Reflagging to Bermuda has not materially affected this situation as the MCA regulations are adopted there. Surveys by the MCA and the flag authority are regularly undertaken in addition to those of Lloyd's Register. As with Lloyd's, all identified deficiencies have to be made good within specified conditions, and where safety may be compromised, the ship can be prevented from sailing until the shortcomings are rectified.

一套关于设计和建造的标准。为了确保建造质量高标准地落实，经过认证的验船师会在建造和运营期间对船舶进行检验。英国劳氏船级社的顶级船级符号是"+100 A1"，"玛丽女王2号"取得了这个入级符号以及其他的一些附加入级符号。

此外，按照英国的规定（2003年12月到2011年10月），挂英国旗的船舶必须符合英国海事海岸警卫署（MCA）的法规和要求。同时悬挂百慕大旗的船只也要满足MCA的要求。除了英国劳氏船级社，MCA和挂旗国也会对船舶进行检验。和英国劳氏船级社一样，MCA和挂旗国也要求被检验的船只必须改正发现的缺陷，特别是涉及到安全的，船只甚至会被勒令停航直到问题解决。

Contract

The contract document for Queen Mary 2 was primarily written by Carnival Shipbuilding, mostly by Ian Gaunt and myself. The document outlined all the contractual clauses that had to be satisfied, procedures for plan approvals, inspections and change orders, financing arrangements and penalties for non-compliance of specified items.

The contract was laid out within the following 31 sections:

1. Subject of the Contract.
2. Vessel's Classification - Rules and Regulations - Certificates.
3. Vessel Characteristics.
4. Builder's Supply - Owners' Supply.
5. Required Information - Drawings - Supplies by Third Parties - Architectural Drawings.
6. Hull Number - Construction Progress - Schedules.
7. Inspection of Construction.
8. Delivery - Risk of Loss.
9. Price.
10. Payment Conditions.
11. Interest Rates - Affiliate - Maximum Liquidated Damages.
12. Trials.
13. Speeds - Liquidated Damages.
14. Deadweight - Liquidated Damages.
15. Stability, Vibrations and Noise - Liquidated Damages.
16. Passenger Accommodation Capacity - Liquidated Damages.
17. Fuel Consumption - Liquidated

合同

"玛丽女王2号"的合同文件主要由嘉年华集团造船部的伊恩·刚特和我共同编写。该文件概述了所有必须满足的合同条款、计划批准程序、检查和变更程序、融资方案和对不符合规定的项目的处罚。

合同包括以下31个章节：

1. 合同正文；
2. 船舶入级—法律法规—证书；
3. 船舶特性；
4. 建造方供应商—船东方供应商；
5. 所需信息—第三方图纸—设计师图纸；
6. 船号—施工节点—进度表；
7. 施工检验；
8. 交货—灭失风险；
9. 造价；
10. 付款方式；
11. 利率—附属公司—最大的违约赔偿金；
12. 试航；
13. 航速—赔偿金；
14. 空船质量—赔偿金；
15. 稳性、振动和噪声—赔偿金；
16. 载客量—赔偿金；
17. 能耗—赔偿金；
18. 船东违约—合同终止；
19. 船厂—合同终止；
20. 产权；

Damages.

18. Default by Owners - Termination of the Contract.

19. Default by Builder - Termination of the Contract.

20. Property Rights.

21. Expenses.

22. Insurance.

23. Change Orders.

24. Guarantee.

25. Events of Force Majeure; Permissible Delays.

26. Patents.

27. Integration of Agreements - Waiver.

28. Assignment of Contract.

29. Law of the Contract - Disputes - Language.

30. Address for Notices; Correspondence.

31. Effectiveness.

As can be seen, there are numerous references to liquidated damages for defaulting in an area that would significantly impair the operational effectiveness and profitability of the ship for the owners. Chantiers de I'Atlantique, in line with every responsible shipyard, jealously guarded their reputation and strove to ensure that the ship met every stipulated criterion so that no liquidated damages were applicable.

21. 费用；

22. 保险；

23. 更改订单；

24. 保障；

25. 不可抗逆的事件、允许的延误；

26. 专利；

27. 协议的整合—弃权；

28. 合同转让；

29. 法律条款—争端—用语；

30. 信件的地址、通信；

31. 有效性。

由此可见，一旦削弱了船舶的运营效率，降低盈利能力，是要支付赔偿金给船东的。为了不支付赔偿金，大西洋船厂会尽力维护自己的声誉，并确保船舶满足所有规定。

Model tests

An extensive array of model tests was outlined within the specification, based on our experience with the various cruise ship contracts. The range of tests was the most extensive that we had undertaken to date and the £1 million-plus cost was met by the shipyard as part of the contract.

Maritime Institute (MARIN), Wageningen, the Netherlands

Not far from Arnhem of 'a bridge too far' fame, lies the Dutch town of Wageningen, which is noted for being

模型试验

根据之前在多条邮轮项目上的经验,我们在规格书中列出了一系列模型试验。这是迄今为止我们做过的范围最广的试验,作为合同的一部分,它将花费造船厂 100 万英镑以上的费用。

荷兰海事研究所(MARIN),瓦赫宁根,荷兰

瓦赫宁根镇位于荷兰,距离"遥远的桥"的故事发生地阿纳姆不远,

"玛丽女王 2 号"风洞模型安装在"林白"风洞的转盘上。该模型将按照系统设定进行旋转,并在多个"攻角"下对迎面而来的风进行风洞测试,以评估在所有可能性下的表现。(作者提供)

the base of the country's agricultural university and home to its maritime institute. The Maritime Institute of the Netherlands, known simply as MARIN, is one of the most respected hydrodynamic institutes in the world. Successive classes of Carnival and Carnival-brand ships were model tested here to optimise hydrodynamic efficiency, sea-keeping and manoeuvrability. My own experience of working with MARIN began in the late 1980s with the model testing of Carnival Cruise Line's Fantasy class; this began as a two-ship contract with Wartsila Marine Industries at Helsinki, but was extended to eight ships when Wartsila was reformed after bankruptcy into MASA

它既是荷兰农业大学的所在地，也是荷兰海事机构的所在地。荷兰海事研究所，简称MARIN，是世界上最有名的水动力研究所之一。嘉年华品牌下的系列船舶在这里通过模型试验进行了推进效率、耐波性以及操纵性等相关方面的优化。我与MARIN的合作始于20世纪80年代嘉年华"幻想级"邮轮的模型试验，起初是和位于赫尔辛基的瓦锡兰海洋工业公司签订了两艘船的建造合同，但在瓦锡兰破产后改为在马萨船厂建造，且将合同标的

接近完工的"玛丽女王2号"在舾装船坞中矗立。(作者提供)

Yards.

The optimisation of the hull for hydrodynamic efficiency took several steps and began with measuring the basic hull form resistance. A large wooden model was constructed and towed up MARIN's propulsion tank fixed to a dynamometer at successively higher speeds to measure the frictional and wave-making drag.

A bulbous bow is a forward appendage attached to the stem of a ship below the waterline. As a vessel moves forward through water, the water being dense and viscous finds it difficult to get out of the ship's way and builds up, forming the characteristic bow wave. A basic law of physics states that you can't get something for nothing, and in this instance it equates that the energy needed to lift up the water into the bow wave and form the wave system around the ship must come from the ship itself. This manifests itself as wave-making drag and is one of two main drag components, the other being the hull frictional drag. At slow speeds the frictional drag predominates, while at higher speeds the wave making drag becomes the more significant. A bulb modifies the flow of water around the region of the stem accelerating it downwards, and if correctly designed this can completely cancel out the upward trend, resulting in no bow wave. This simple expedient can save around 6% in the required propulsion power. The main difficulty is that a bulb can only be optimised for one speed/ draught and trim combination. Any deviation from any of these design

数量增加至 8 艘。

船体水动力效率优化始于船体线型阻力测量，一般包含数个步骤。将制作的大型木制模型固定在 MARIN 水池的测力计上并依次以多个速度在推进水池内进行拖曳以测得摩擦和兴波阻力数值。

球鼻艏是一种在船舶水线以下依附于船首前方的附体。当船在水中向前移动时，由于水自身的密度和黏性而难以与船身分离，进而形成典型的艏波。能量守恒是物理学中的一个基本定律，也就是说，将水抬起形成艏波进而形成围绕着船体的艏波系所需要的能量必然来自于船体本身。这就是兴波阻力的由来，它是船体阻力的两大组成部分之一，另一个是船体摩擦阻力。在船舶低速航行时，摩擦阻力是船体阻力的主要组成成分，但在更高的速度航行时，兴波阻力则变得更为重要。球鼻艏可以改变船体首部周围的水流，使水流向下方加速，如果设计得当，向下的水流可以完全抵消水流抬起的趋势，使艏波消失。这个简单的方法可以节省 6% 左右所需的推进动力。但主要的问题是，一种既定形式的球鼻艏只能针对一个速度/吃水和纵倾载况组合进行优化。任何偏离这些设计点的情况都会降低球鼻艏

points renders the bulb less efficient; too much deviation can even make the bulb deleterious! Using computer flow techniques the initial design of the bulbous bow for the Queen Mary 2 was determined and tested on the model, with subtle incremental modifications being incorporated using plasticine.

Once the form of the bulb was considered as optimal as possible, other areas of the hull were examined and perfected, the bilge keels being the next appendage to be inspected. Bilge keels run along the midships part of the underwater hull on each side of the ship for about 40% of its length. They are formed by a flat plate projecting perpendicularly from the ship's hull and their function is to dampen roll motions. They work by offering resistance as well as shedding eddies and can be particularly effective for a passive device. The main concern with bilge keels is to align them with the flow around the hull; if not aligned properly they induce additional drag. Two methods can be employed to determine the correct orientation. Tufts of coloured wool can be fixed in rows along the hull model, which when towed at the scale service speed causes the wool tufts to align with the flow. Using underwater cameras the orientation can be assessed and the bilge keels ranged accordingly. The other method is to use a bead of viscous paint, applied in rows like the wool tufts. Running the model at scale speed causes the paint to run in streaks aligned with the flow, which can be used to adjust the bilge keels.

的效率；过大的偏差甚至会使球鼻艏造成负面影响！借助计算机流体仿真技术，“玛丽女王2号”球鼻艏的最初设计是在数字模型上进行确定和测试的，而细微的增量修改则是用工业黏土来实现的。

一旦确定球鼻艏的形状已足够理想，且船体的其他区域也优化完成，舭龙骨是下一个需要确认的附体。舭龙骨位于船舶中部水下部分两侧，沿船长方向延伸，约占船长40%的长度。它们是由一个垂直于船体的平板构成，其作用是抑制横摇。它们通过产生阻力和涡流来达到效果，对于被动装置尤其有效。舭龙骨的主要问题是必须使其与船体周围的水流方向保持一致；如果没有准确对齐，它会产生额外的阻力。有两种方法可以确定准确的水流流向。一种方法是使用彩色绒线沿着船体模型一排排固定，当按模型尺度下的服务航速进行拖曳时，绒线会与水流保持一致。再用水下摄像机观测水流在船身上的走向，舭龙骨就可以依此进行布置。另一种方法是使用黏性涂料，像羊绒一样排成数排。以模型尺度下的服务航速拖曳模型，会使涂料沿着水流流动，形成与水流方向一致的条纹，同样可以用来定位舭龙骨。

The initial design of the ship called for four propulsion pods, two fixed just for propulsion and two azimuthing, providing steering as well as propulsion. Steering of pods up to that time had been based on hydraulic actuation like most modern cruise ship rudders. The problem with hydraulics was that although adequate, some 'wiggle' or 'hunting'occurred, something akin to a flutter. This was not such a problem for rudders but we had concerns that it would not be good for the pods as even a fraction of a degree of hunting would produce large manoeuvring forces. The solution was to lock the azimuthing pods at zero and to steer at sea with a relatively small auxiliary rudder. However, results from the towing tests surprisingly revealed that even a small rudder introduced considerable additional drag. A solution soon presented itself when Mermaid,the pod manufacturer, offered us the option of electric, rather than hydraulic, pod azimuthing. This would be a prototype system but we seized upon the advantages, which significantly meant that there would be no chance of the hunting phenomenon. Thus we were able to dispense With the auxiliary rudder, realising a credit from the shipyard for the cost of the rudder, the steering gear and associated system as well as eliminating the related rudder drag.

The orientation of the propulsion pods was also carefully examined to ensure that they offered the least drag and maximum efficiency. The 'toe-in' angle (offset from the centreline)

初始设计时在船上设有 4 个推进吊舱，两个固定吊舱用于推进，两个全回转吊舱不仅用于推进，还用于控制转向。就像大多数现代邮轮的舵一样，吊舱转向是基于液压驱动的。液压技术尽管非常适用，但吊舱偶尔会发生一些类似于震颤的"抽动"或"摇摆"。对于普通的舵来说，这并不是什么大的问题，但我们发现，对于吊舱来说这就非常不利了，因为哪怕是很小的一个角度的摇摆都会产生巨大的机动力。其解决方案是将转向吊舱固定在零位，在航行时使用相对较小的辅助舵来完成操舵。然而，拖曳试验的结果出人意料地显示，即使是一个小舵也会带来相当大的额外阻力。当吊舱制造商美人鱼公司为我们提供了电动（而非液压）吊舱选择时，一个解决方案很快就出现了。这是一个原型系统，但我们抓住了它的最大优点，这意味着将不会出现摇摆现象。因此，我们能够免除辅助舵，为船厂节约舵、舵机和相关系统的费用，同时消除了舵的阻力。

推进吊舱的布置也需要仔细考虑以确保他们能够产生最小的阻力和提供最大的效率。将吊舱设置成内束角（相对于中心线的偏移）是通过将吊舱角度依次递增布置并测量阻力来确定的——绘制"角度－阻力"曲线时，

在罗尔斯·罗伊斯公司（罗罗）位于克里斯蒂娜港的工厂中，一台"美人鱼"推进吊舱上用于转向功能的电动执行机构正在接受测试。这是电动马达首次用于这一功能，由于它的成功应用，"玛丽女王2号"将没有传统的方向舵。（作者提供）

was determined by setting the pods at incremental angles and measuring the resistance - when plotted, the angle where the least drag occurred was identified as optimum. The orientation of the pod shaft lines and motor housing was set according to the flow lines around the stern.

The stern of Queen Mary 2 is unconventional in being a cruiser/transom hybrid. All previous transatlantic liners had been provided with either a counter stern like the Mauretania/Titanic, or a cruiser stern

出现最小阻力的角度被确定为最佳角度。吊舱轴线的方向和电机壳体根据船尾周围的水流场来设置。

"玛丽女王2号"的船尾是一种非常规的巡洋舰/方艉的混合型船尾。以前所有横渡大西洋的班轮都配备了像"毛里塔尼亚号"或"泰坦尼克号"这样船型的船尾，或像之前的3艘冠达"女王号"一样的船尾。现代邮轮总是使用方艉，因为它提高了水动力

like the three previous Cunard Queens. Modern-day cruise ships invariably utilise a transom squared-off stern as it provides an increase in hydrodynamic efficiency and an expansion in revenue-earning volume.

Having sailed transatlantic on board Queen Elizabeth 2 on several occasions I had experienced first hand her pitching motion in the Atlantic swells, which at times was quite severe. Despite the motion the ship did not appear to suffer from any aft slamming as the hull rose and then plunged back into the ocean, no doubt a consequence of her nicely rounded cruiser stern. I was aware that the squared-off transom sterns fitted to some cruise ships gave rise to slamming even when the ships were in port, the wash from other passing vessels or waves racing into the flat underside generating considerable forces, with consequential bangs and vibrations. My concern was that if the new ship was fitted with such a transom her pitching motion might induce a tremendous, annoying, slamming cacophony. The golden adage previously mentioned led me to examine the sterns fitted to two Italian liners built in the mid- 1960s, namely Home Line's Oceanic and Costa Armatori's Eugenio C. Both these ships had a hybrid stern: modest transoms at the waterline with a cruiser stern attached as if an above water appendage, designed by Nicolo Costanzi, the naval architect entrusted with the ships'designs. I convinced the shipyard to test such a stern on Queen Mary 2 and it was found to be a good compromise and so was adopted.

效率以及增加船体体积进而增加营收。

我曾多次乘坐"伊丽莎白女王2号"横渡大西洋,亲身体验过她在大西洋汹涌的波涛中的摇摆,有时会相当剧烈。尽管船体运动很剧烈,但当船体在海浪中上下颠簸时,这艘船的船尾似乎并没有受到任何的海浪拍击。毫无疑问,这是由于她那漂亮的圆形船尾。我意识到,一些邮轮上安装的方尾即便是在港口内也会受到很强的拍击作用,其他驶过的船只或海浪冲进平坦底面时产生的水波会产生相当大的力道,并造成相应的拍击和振动。我担心的是,如果新船安装了这样的船尾,当她发生纵摇时可能会引起巨大的、恼人的、刺耳的噪音。之前提到的金科玉律让我注意到两条建于20世纪60年代中期的意大利班轮的船尾,即家园邮轮公司旗下的"大洋号"和歌诗达邮轮公司的"尤金号"。这些船都拥有一种混合型船尾:在水线附近是一种适度的方艉,而水线以上则为巡洋舰式的圆艉,这种船尾由尼可洛·康斯坦奇设计,他是一名海军船舶设计师。我说服造船厂在"玛丽女王2号"上测试这样的船尾,结果发现这是一个很好的折中方案,所以就被采纳了。

Gulliver simulation

Although the specification defined the speed and power characteristics the ship had to meet under trial conditions, it was not until the hydrodynamic model tests were completed that there was sufficient data available to accurately predict what the performance of the ship would be in service.It was crucial

"格利佛"软件模拟

虽然规格书规定了船舶在试验条件下必须满足的航速和功率特性，但直到水动力模型试验完成后，才有足够的数据可以准确预测船舶在运营时的性能。船舶能够准时到达每个跨大西洋的港口是至关重要的，因为在有

"玛丽女王2号"的模型在荷兰海事研究所的耐波性水池内接受到大规模飓风模拟测试。模型表现出了卓越的性能，且之后被实船验证。船首突出部分的形状和挡浪型的形状在应对特别严重的海况时特别有效。（作者收集）

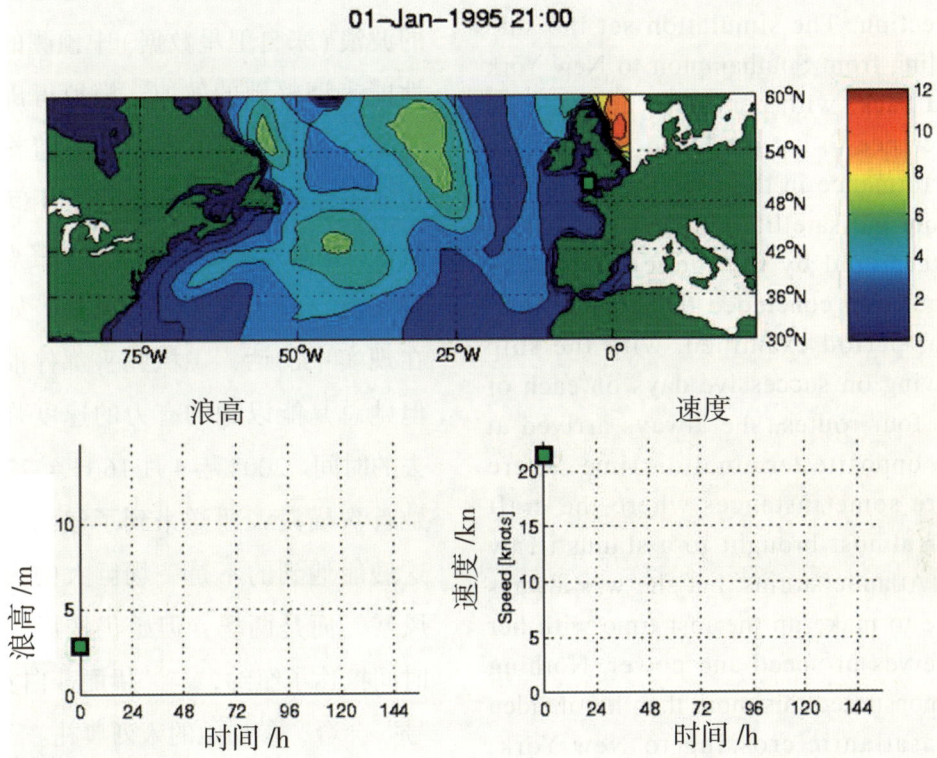

在 MARIN 的"格列佛"模拟实验中，"玛丽女王 2 号"的电脑模型在实际测量的环境条件下穿越北大西洋。这张图显示了横越大西洋时的海浪高度和相应的船速，显示了 1995 年 1 月 1 日 21 时 00 分的情况——注意北海 12 米高的风暴！（作者收集）

for the vessel to arrive on schedule at each of the transatlantic terminal ports, as with a limited ten-hour turnaround any delays would have a serious impact on the ship's subsequent scheduling. To assess transatlantic performance, MARIN Maritime Institute of the Netherlands utilised a new simulation programme that it had just developed called 'Gulliver'.Satellite weather data for a five-year period was extracted for the transatlantic route, giving the wave height and direction. Four transatlantic

限的 10 小时逗留期内，任何延误都将严重影响船舶的后续调度。为了评估跨大西洋航行船舶的性能，荷兰海事研究所利用一种刚刚开发的新的模拟程序，称为"格列佛"。为了模拟跨大西洋航行，实验提取了大西洋 5 年的卫星气象数据，给出了海浪的高度和方向。实验评估了 4 条跨大西洋航线，每条方向各有两条。模拟设定了这艘船从南安普敦航行到纽约，然后返回，

routes were evaluated, two in each direction. The simulation set the ship sailing from Southampton to New York and back, with her speed adjusted by reference to her predicted sea-keeping performance in the encountered waves (from the satellite data) as previously determined by the model tests. The simulation concluded that for the five-year period examined, with the ship leaving on successive days on each of the four routes, she always arrived at the opposite terminal on time. There were some instances where the craft was almost brought to a standstill by the Atlantic storms, but she was always able to make up the lost time with her reserves of speed and power. Nothing demonstrated this more than her maiden transatlantic crossing to New York, between 16 and 22 April 2004. The ship encountered not one huge Atlantic storm but two, yet she still arrived on schedule in New York to meet up with the Queen Elizabeth 2 for her inaugural celebrations.

并根据之前的模型测试给定她在遇到的波浪（来自卫星数据）中预测的航海性能来调整她的航速。模拟得出的结论是，在5年的考察期间，随着船舶在4条路线中的每条路线上不间断地航行，她总是准时到达下一个终点站。有几次，由于大西洋的风暴，如果是在现实中的话，飞机几乎都停航了，但她总是能以她的有力的速度弥补失去的时间。2004年4月16日至22日，她首次横渡大西洋来到了纽约。途中这艘船遇到的不是一场巨大的大西洋风暴，而是两场，但她仍按原定计划时间抵达了纽约，与"伊丽莎白女王2号"会合，参加她的入列典礼。

Force Technology, Lyngby, Denmark

Wind-tunnel tests were performed at Force Technology based in Lyngby, a suburb of Denmark's capital, Copenhagen. The establishment is well equipped with five wind tunnels and other facilities and is respected as a leader in the field of ship aerodynamics. Wind-tunnel tests are used to perfect funnel designs to limit smoke and smut nuisance as far as possible, to optimise

空气动力技术公司，林白，丹麦

风洞试验在位于丹麦首都哥本哈根郊区的空气动力技术公司进行。该公司拥有5条风洞以及其他设施，在船舶空气动力学领域处于领先地位。风洞试验是为了完善烟囱设计，尽可能地减少烟灰的污染；优化挡风玻璃的位置，以限制甲板上的风；确定港口操纵和推进需要克服的风阻力。最

在丹麦的空气动力技术公司的风洞里，放置着一个"玛丽女王2号"的测试模型。模型处于一个定量的风速环境下，烟流从烟囱和船尾厨房／焚烧炉排气管以相应的速度排出。试验对烟流进行跟踪，观察它们是否会侵扰后方。早期的测试显示，理论上烟囱需要更高一些，但在纽约港入口处的韦拉札诺海峡大桥下的净空间隙不允许这样。风洞试验导致了烟囱设置导风穴的开发，它提供了足够的上升气流，在最不利的条件下，使船舶免受烟灰的侵扰。（作者提供）

the position of windscreens to restrict windage over the decks, and to determine the wind drag and forces for harbour manoeuvring and propulsion. The most crucial wind-tunnel tests involved evaluating the funnel. The height that a ship projects above the water is called the 'air draught'. This dimension is used to assess whether a ship can pass under bridges or, in some instances, hanging cables. At the entrance to New York Harbour a bridge spans the Hudson River between the New York boroughs of Staten Island and Brooklyn. The Verrazano Narrows Bridge is a double-decked bridge. Ships passing beneath

重要的风洞测试是对烟囱造型进行评估。船在水面上方的高度称为"水上净高"。这个高度用于评估一艘船是否能通过桥下，或者在某些情况下是否能通过悬挂的电缆。在纽约港的入口处，一座横跨哈德逊河的大桥横跨纽约史坦顿岛和布鲁克林之间。韦拉札诺海峡大桥是一座双层桥。在船的中心跨度下通过的船只，为了留有大约3米的高度间隙，必须有不超过62米的水上净高。"伊丽莎白女王2号"

its central span must not have an air draught exceeding 62 metres in order to have a clearance of approximately 3 metres. The Queen Elizabeth 2, with an air draught of 52.5 metres, including the funnel height of 21.2 metres, has an ample margin. However, Queen Mary 2's greater bulk and structural height sadly necessitated a much reduced funnel. Accommodating four diesel exhausts, two gas turbine exhausts and a number of auxiliary exhausts, meant that the funnel on Queen Mary 2 had to be of significant size, if not height. The problem with such a squat funnel was that the smoke plumes were sucked downwards by the differential pressure effects caused by the slipstream moving around the funnel.

The funnel tests were performed using a 1:150-scale model of the ship with all the main exhausts precisely simulated to reflect a particular service condition. To accurately represent the air flow around the model, the intakes and exhausts for the air-conditioning and engine room ventilation were also carefully imitated. The only way to force the plumes further upwards was to deploy a wind scoop, as used on board Queen Elizabeth 2. A modest scoop was first tried in the wind tunnel but with only little improvement. The scoop was successively increased in height until it was shown to be effective, the top reaching almost to the height of the funnel cowling. In order to make the funnel appear taller, Gerry Ellis came up with idea of projecting the forward section further forward so that the funnel house, where the funnel sat, could be incorporated within the funnel itself, the flat forward face being painted Cunard red to match the scoop and cowling, with the curved

的净空高度为 52.5 米，包括烟囱高度 21.2 米，其有充足的相对余量空间。然而，“玛丽女王2号”更大的体积和结构高度需要大大减少烟囱的高度。“玛丽女王2号”的烟囱可容纳4个柴油机排气管、2个燃气轮机排气管和一些辅助排气管，这意味着烟囱如果不是很高的话，直径就必须是相当大的。这种矮胖型的烟囱问题在于：由于在烟囱周围的气流活动所造成的差压效应，烟流会被向下吸走。

烟囱试验使用的是 1:150 的比例模型，所有的主要排气口都被精确模拟，以反映特定的使用条件。为了准确展现模型周围的气流，我们对空调和机舱通风的进排气也进行了细致的模拟。迫使烟流进一步上升的唯一方法是部署一个导风穴，就像使用在“伊丽莎白女王2号”上的一样。我们首先在风洞中尝试了一个初版的导风穴。随着实验深入进行，导风穴的高度不断被增加，直到其产生效果，此时导风穴的顶部几乎达到烟囱罩顶的高度。为了使烟囱看起来更加高大，格里·埃利斯想出一个办法，把前部进一步向前扩展，这样烟囱底部的舱室就可以合并到烟囱本体，扁平的前脸被涂成了冠达红，以匹配导风穴和顶部，烟囱弯曲的部分涂装成黑色。这个简单的方法

main part of the funnel being black. This simple expedient dramatically improved the visual look of the funnel. Another important device that helped to prevent the smoke plume from being sucked down behind the funnel was the railing at the aft end of the gas turbine house. The railing modified the air flow behind the funnel in such a way that it aided in reducing the suction effect.

The model was also used to measure the windage over the decks and assist with the placement of the windscreens.

极大地改善了烟囱的视觉效果。另一个重要的装置是燃气轮机机房后部的挡风幕墙，它改变了烟囱后面的气流，使其有助于减少吸入效应，从而防止烟流被卷入烟囱后方。

该模型还被用于测量甲板上的风压，并评估挡风幕墙的布置。

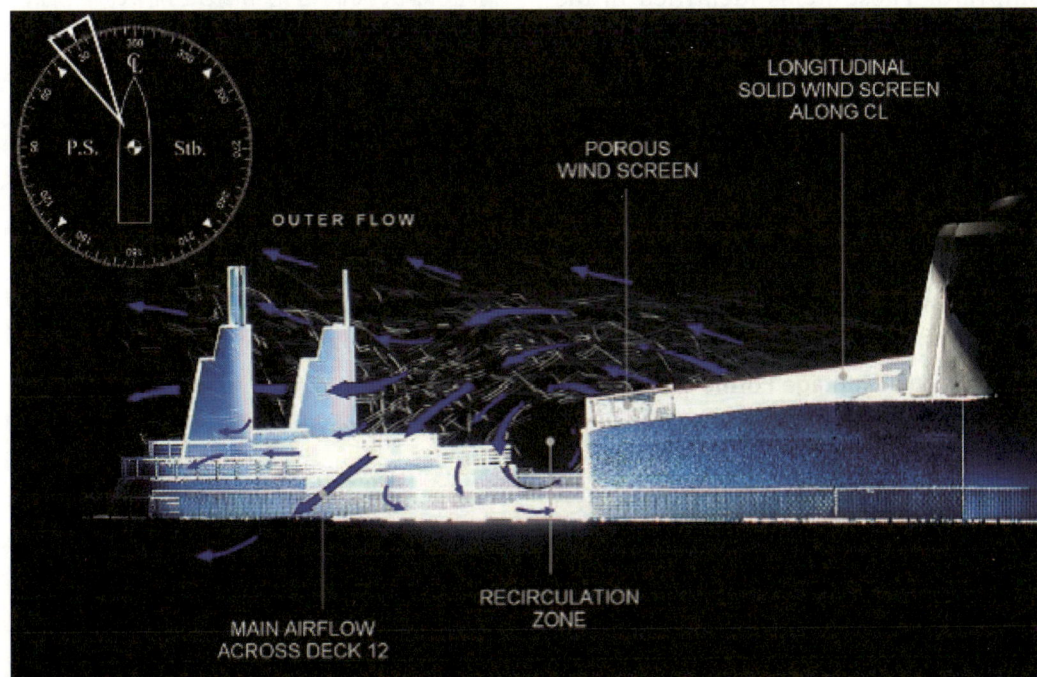

空气动力技术公司关于"玛丽女王 2 号"烟囱性能报告的一条详细信息表明，燃气轮机机房后部的挡风幕墙是非常重要的。挡风幕墙会提供上升气流，有助于烟气污染物远离船尾部甲板。（作者收集）

Construction

Immediately the contract for Queen Mary2 was signed on 6 November 2000 the shipyard mobilised a huge workforce to start work on the detailed planning of the ship. It was crucial for the aforementioned model tests to be completed as soon as possible so that the hull design could be finalised and the construction drawings prepared. The shipyard's purchasing department promptly dispatched numerous purchasing enquiries for components, equipment, and technical items large and small. When the quotations were received they were compared and checked against the purchase specification before preselection by the shipyard. Those items identified in the specification for the owners' approval were then sent to Carnival Shipbuilding for our consideration and ultimate sanction. The approved components were then integrated into the detailed design, each successive issue of plans

建造

2000年11月6日，"玛丽女王2号"的合同一签订，造船厂就动员了大批工程人员开始详细地规划这艘船。尽快完成上述模型试验的先决条件是船体设计和施工图纸绘制。造船厂的采购部门迅速发出大量采购询价，对大大小小的零件、设备和技术项目着手采购。在收到报价进行预选之前，船厂会根据采购规格对报价进行比较和核对。在规格书中需要船东认可的那些采购项随后被送到嘉年华集团造船事业部供我们考虑和最终确认。然后，经批准的部件被集成到详细设计中，每份关联的设备图纸变得更加详细和精确，直到最终施工图纸编制完成和发布。这一过程一直持续到建造过程

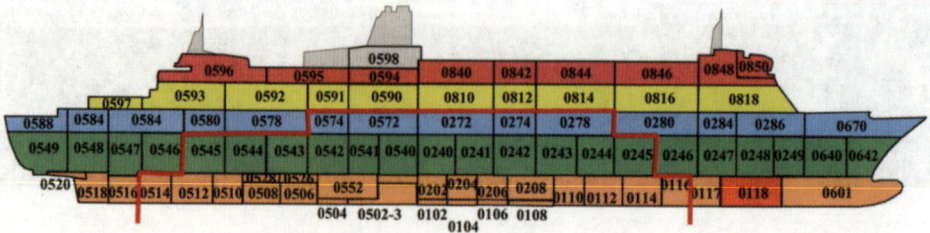

"玛丽女王2号"的分段搭载网络图显示，共有98个大分段最终会组成这艘巨轮。（作者收集）

becoming more detailed and refined until the final construction drawings were prepared and issued. This process continued up to the last few months of construction.

Just after one year of planning and approvals, the shipyard was ready to begin construction. On 12 January 2002, Pamela Conover, President of the Cunard Line (who had superseded Larry Pimentel the previous year), started the construction process by pressing the button of a computerised cutting machine that began carving out steel profiles. Throughout the shipyard steel plates destined for Queen Mary 2 were usually identifiable because they were so much thicker than those appropriated for other ships. In fact we were advised by the yard that steel plates of that thickness had not been used since the shipyard built the French Line France of 1962 and that it was necessary for the welders to undergo specific training to ensure that the material was fused properly.

The cut profiles were welded together into 580 separate panel sections. These in turn would be bound by welding into 98 blocks, each one weighing up to 600 tonnes. This work was performed under cover within huge sheds and the blocks eventually emerged to be transported by huge multi-wheel loaders to an area beside the construction dock. Two huge gantry cranes manoeuvred the blocks into the dock in a carefully controlled sequence. The first two blocks were joined together on 4 July 2002 - a happy coincidence as

的最后几个月。

经过一年的规划和认证,船厂已经做好建造前的准备。2002年1月12日,冠达邮轮公司的总裁帕米拉·科诺弗(他在前一年接替了拉里·皮门特尔)按下了数控切割机的按钮,完成了开工仪式。在整个船厂中,运往"玛丽女王2号"的钢板通常是可以很容易被辨别出来的,因为它们比其他船只所用的钢板要厚得多。事实上,工厂告诉我们,自从1962年造船厂建造法国班轮公司的"法国号"以来,这些钢板就再未被使用过。焊工必须接受特殊培训,以确保正确焊接这些钢板。

切割好的钢板被焊接到一起,成为580个独立的小分段。这些小分段将依次焊接成98块大分段,每一块重达600吨。这项工作是在巨大的遮蔽空间下完成的,这些分段最终由大型的多轮运输车运送到建造船坞旁边的一个区域。两个巨大的龙门起重机依靠精确控制的程序将分段吊入船坞。前两个分段于2002年7月4日搭载拼接完成,这是一个令人兴奋的巧合,因为这一天是美国独立日,也是冠达邮轮公司的"布列塔尼亚号"明轮汽船在1840年从利物浦开往波士顿的首

it was American Independence Day, and also the 162nd anniversary of the maiden departure of Cunard's first sailing with the paddle steamer Britannia in 1840, from Liverpool bound for Boston. These first sections incorporated the main engine foundations and within a short time the four large diesel engines were being placed on board, being entombed as other blocks were positioned around them.

航 162 周年纪念日。第一部分安装包括柴油主机的基座。在短时间内，4 个大型柴油主机被预装在船上，然后周围的其他船体分段被吊装定位。

一块龙骨分段被安放和就位在建造船坞里的坞墩上。从图中可以清晰地看出双层底的高度，舱顶的轮机设备也已经安装就位。可以看到有一段舭龙骨突出在船体外，它可以起到被动减摇的作用。（法国 STX 船厂／伯纳德比格提供）

冠达邮轮公司的总裁帕米拉·科诺弗和大西洋船厂的管理总监帕特里克·波希尔于 2002 年 1 月 12 日在圣纳泽尔主持了第一块钢板的切割仪式。众多媒体嘉宾见证了这一仪式。（法国 STX 船厂 / 伯纳德比格提供）

一块前期用于构建船底的龙骨分段显示出钢结构的复杂程度。（法国 STX 船厂 / 伯纳德比格提供）

在大西洋船厂的遮蔽工棚内正在建造的一个船体小分段。（法国 STX 船厂 / 伯纳德比格提供）

第一批 4 台瓦锡兰 16 缸 46 C 型柴油主机被吊装上船。船底舱顶板上的主机基座清晰可见，它们可以将主机的重量和作用力散布到周边的结构上去。（法国 STX 船厂 / 伯纳德比格提供）

从龙门起重机的顶部俯瞰，船坞空置着，为"玛丽女王2号"的建造做好了准备。预先建造好的分段整齐排列在船坞旁，像孩子们巨大的麦卡诺玩具一样等待着最终在船坞内合拢。（法国 STX 船厂 / 伯纳德比格提供）

结构分段等待着依次吊装上船。在上面相对渺小的施工人员凸显了分段尺寸的巨大。（法国STX船厂／伯纳德比格提供）

下一条搭载线：船首底部分段由龙门起重机吊起，从临时存放区运向船坞，在那里分段将被吊装到位。可以注意到，大部分分段在沿船长的方向上已经安装了舭龙骨板。（法国STX船厂／伯纳德比格提供）

建造采用塔式搭建的方式进行，从船中开始沿船长方向搭建分段。这张图的视角为从船尾部向前看。艉部分段正在被吊至指定位置。与此同时，通过阳台的开孔可见船中的第一个客舱分段已经就位。（法国STX船厂／伯纳德比格提供）

龙门起重机正吊运一个包含第4、第5和第6层甲板结构的客舱分段，舷侧外板上的阳台开孔清晰可见。最终，由结构舱壁包围形成的中间核心区域将布置为空调机间和其他船舶服务处所。舱壁沿船长方向沿伸，形成"玛丽女王2号"的主体结构。（法国STX船厂／伯纳德比格提供）

该图视角为从船尾向前看，船舶建造进展顺利。船的首部和尾部已建至第3层甲板，船中较长范围内已完成第4、第5和第6层甲板结构建造。位于龙门起重机后方的"布列塔尼亚"餐厅和美术馆的窗户清楚可见。3个临时帐篷竖立在露天甲板上，以保护设备和材料免受天气影响，随着后续分段吊装至船上进行合拢，这些帐篷将被拆除。（法国STX船厂／伯纳德比格提供）

在其中一个客舱甲板上，空调风管安装在上层甲板的反底结构与舱室天花板的空隙内。几段预制的风管结构放置在甲板上，每段预制的风管结构都将按照严格的顺序进行定位安装。大部分风管采用包覆铝箔的材料进行绝缘处理。（法国STX船厂／伯纳德比格提供）

在林立的船厂建造设备包围下，在合拢形成船首大分段前，部分船首结构部件（船首最前部）被搁置在临时的支撑上。（法国 STX 船厂／伯纳德比格提供）

该图视角为从"布列塔尼亚"餐厅附近的位置向船首看，船体的左舷延伸到远处。包含第7、第8和第9层甲板结构的第一个上层建筑分段已经在船中部就位。与此同时，位于第4、第5和第6层甲板的矩形大开口非常明显，预制的舱室模块将通过该开孔被引导进船内，并运送至船上指定位置进行固定。（作者提供）

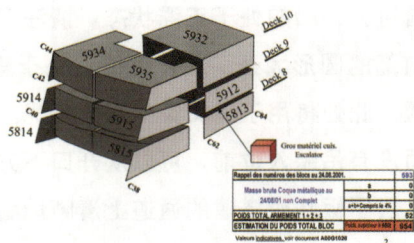

该图表显示593号大分段由10个已编号的小分段组成。如图所示该分段包含第8、第9和第10层甲板结构，并最终将在其中布置第7、第8和第9层甲板的居住设施。（作者收集）

593 号分段包含公司——"冠达"的焊接钢板结构，顶部的字母"C"清晰可见。一张全船侧视图设置在该分段上方，图中采用红色标记其位置，显示与其他分段的关系，并标明该分段重达 613 吨，将于 2003 年 1 月 17 日吊装至船上进行合拢。（作者提供）

位于上层建筑艉部的 593 号分段等待吊装至船上，该分段包含第 7、第 8 和第 9 层甲板结构。分段内设有"女王"餐厅和"公主"餐厅（位于 7 层甲板）以及复式套房（位于第 8 和第 9 层甲板）。拼写在焊接板上的公司——"冠达"清晰明显，其最终将被漆成冠达红色，置于上层建筑的纯白色之上。分段上向后倾斜的开口将最终安装挡风玻璃。（作者提供）

2002 年 12 月初，施工进展顺利，"玛丽女王 2 号"第一次在船坞内起浮，并移位到坞内最终建造泊位。图中从艏部向艉部看过去，船舶处于正浮状态。请注意甲板前部的圆形大开口，开口位置处于第 4 甲板，此处将用于天文馆的穹顶采光。在穹顶没有吊装入位前，可以从开口下方的第 2 层甲板临时搭建的通道上清晰地看见其圆屋顶的结构骨架。（作者提供）

By 1 December 2002 construction had advanced to the point where 49 blocks had been sited in the dock. The lower blocks were made watertight and the dock flcc;ded to enable the ship as it was to be floated and moved down to a location nearer the dock exit gates. Once pumped dry and with the ship firmly grounded and supported by dock blocks, construction recommenced. By 16 March 2003 the vessel was structurally complete and a ceremony was arranged to step the mast, attended by various dignitaries, the press and the travel trade. Coins were welded below the mast for good luck, as traditionally undertaken in the days of great sailing ships and before. In just over 14 months 33,700 tonnes of steel had been cut, formed, welded and fashioned into the largest ocean liner the world had ever seen. By this stage prefabricated passenger and crew cabins were being embarked and manoeuvred into position on board and non-structural partition bulkheads erected. Ducting, piping and cabling was subsequently installed and tested as appropriate. Insulation for fire and noise suppression was placed throughout in carefully considered schemes, protected where necessary with fibre glass cloth where it would be prone to damage.

Throughout the build process, equipment such as anchor capstans, thrusters, lifts et al. were situated and tested. On 24 March 2003 the ship was floated and moved out of the construction dock to be subsequently

截至 2002 年 12 月 1 日，已有 49 个大型分段吊装到位，实际建造进度已领先于计划节点。底部分段已焊接完成并且水密性实验全部结束，这使船舶可以在船坞内起浮并移位到靠近坞门的新泊位。待船坞内海水全部泵出，且船舶准确落位在坞楞上后，施工将继续进行。到 2003 年 3 月 16 日，分段搭载即船体建造部分基本完成。在各界政要、新闻媒体朋友及业内人士的见证下，为求好运永久眷顾，遵循传统的航海仪式，在这一天举行隆重的立桅仪式，将硬币焊接固定在主桅杆筒体底部。在短短的 14 个多月时间里，由 33 700 吨钢材通过切割、整型、焊接成形的历史上最大的远洋班轮已初显其美丽的轮廓。到了舾装阶段，首先将预制的乘客和船员舱室单元吊运并转移到船内的指定位置，安装好非结构性壁板；接下来按照工序合理地进行通风管路及船舶管系的安装和电缆的敷设，并在安装完成后进行调试检验。之后再按照工艺要求严格完成防火降噪绝缘的敷设，并且需要对有可能被破坏的区域用玻璃纤维布进行必要的保护。

在整个坞内建造过程中，锚绞盘、侧推、电梯等设备都已安装上船并调试结束。2003 年 3 月 24 日，"玛丽女王 2 号"起浮并在拖轮的帮助下移位到舾装码头。在船体结构搭载完成后，码头

manoeuvred to the outfitting quay. Construction continued at a cracking pace and outfitting within the steel hull was ramped up. By May 2003 1,000 out of 2,017 passenger and crew cabins had been embarked. Installation of the four Mermaid propulsion pods commenced in June 2003 and outfitting of the public spaces was in full swing. Carpeting was being laid, decks sheathed with teak and galley equipment fitted. Dock trials with the diesels and gas turbines under test were being performed. Safety systems were being commissioned and everything that could be tested alongside the quay was being put through its paces and scrutinised. Between 25 and 29 September the ship undertook her first (shipyard) trials. On successful completion of these she returned to the shipyard and was immediately dry-docked for underwater hull cleaning and final painting. Queen Mary 2 subsequently sailed on her second (owners') sea trials from 7 to 11 November. As with the first trials, these were successfully completed and the ship returned to the shipyard for the last time for final completion.

舾装工程的建造继续快速推进。截止到2003年5月，总共2 017个乘客和船员舱室中的1 000个已经安装到位。四台艉部吊舱推进器已于2003年6月开始安装。与此同时，公共空间的舾装工程也在如火如荼地进行当中，地毯铺设，甲板上的柚木和厨房设备都已安装完成，柴油主机和燃气轮机的码头实验工作正在进行当中，安全系统也正在紧张地调试当中，所有的码头实验项目都在按照建造计划忙碌而有序地进行严苛的调试检验。2003年9月25日至29日，"玛丽女王2号"进行了第一次试航（船厂主导）。试航取得了圆满成功，"玛丽女王2号"返回船厂后立即进入干船坞内，进行水下船体结构的清洗和最后的涂装工作。"玛丽女王2号"随后于当年的11月7日至11日进行了第二次试航（船东主导）。同第一次试航一样，第二次试航也取得了圆满成功，同时船舶也最后一次返回船厂进行收尾完工工作。

船体的尾部,图中的船名和港籍名(南安普敦)由钢板切割出来的字母焊接而成。可以看到两个应急发电机的排气口从两个船体临时开口中穿出,这两个临时开口最终也将同图中预切割线所示的区域一起,被切割成腰圆形大开口。(作者提供)

"CUNARD"标志(全船共四个,装点在上层建筑的侧板)中的"ARD"三个字母。同船名和港籍名一样,其名字也由钢板切割并焊接在船体外板上。这些字母突出于外板之上,从而方便对其进行单独涂装,避免对周边已经完成的涂装产生破坏。(作者提供)

一个前部上层建筑正在分段制造车间内建造。图中可以看出,为了便于施工,分段相比搭载位置呈90°搁置。图中的复杂圆弧线形结构由弯板拼接而成,并用筋板加强,而且可以看出窗户开孔还没有切割。图中竖立着的部分是由钢板和分布在上面的错综复杂的结构桁材及筋板拼接而成的一段甲板。(法国STX船厂/伯纳德比格提供)

位于干船坞内一侧的优美的艏部上部分段正在搭载当中。由于线形收缩导致分段底部的落脚面积小,采用很多临时支撑为其加固,并且在分段周围都搭起了脚手架以用于加快焊接进度。外板上的圆形标记是为了满足复杂的线形要求而进行热加工留下的痕迹。(作者提供)

含有三个艏侧推的下部分段正在向船首部位置吊装。艏侧推管隧的开口可以由其附带的钢质门关闭。这些门用类似于蝶阀的设计通过轴向的铰链来实现开闭，当门开启时，一半的门在隧道里面，一半突出船体外部。在船体两侧的管隧开口都安装了这种门以保证船体线形的完整性，从而减少船舶航行时侧推管隧开口处形成的涡流，进而降低对船舶性能的影响。（法国 STX 船厂 / 伯纳德比格提供）

在夜晚从龙门吊上看船舶尾部。船坞内的黄色支撑架被用来临时支撑还未完全焊接完成的艉部分段，同时艉部的游泳池清晰可见。（法国 STX 船厂 / 伯纳德比格提供）

建造泊位上的"玛丽女王2号"。图中可以看出艉部上方的分段还没有吊装到位，但是球鼻艏已吊装入位；游步甲板（第7甲板）的施工正在稳步推进，救生艇艇架已吊装到位；上层建筑部分也在紧张地施工当中，但是其标志性的艏部弧形结构还没有就位。用于方便分段对接施工而临时搭建的脚手架清晰可见，右下角的船坞边上存放着一个还没被吊装上船的分段。（法国 STX 船厂 / 伯纳德比格提供）

艏部上层建筑分段正在等待吊运合拢。这个分段前面的曲面结构是船上最复杂的地方;无论对于设计还是制造都极具挑战性。设计必须兼顾伴随着复杂线型的加强结构,以及长廊、图书馆和"海军司令"俱乐部诸多窗口的开口。对于建造过程,曲面结构必须是光滑的,不能有影响美观的扭曲。它必须是完美的数学曲线。由此而来的外观是"玛丽女王2号"最具标志性的外部特征之一,独一无二、与众不同。(法国 STX 船厂 / 伯纳德比格提供)

在投光灯的辅助下,艏部上层建筑分段在夜间被吊到船上合拢。艏部复杂的曲面形状显而易见。(法国 STX 船厂 / 伯纳德比格提供)

虽然驾驶室分段已经吊到艏部上层建筑分段的上面,但后者并没有完全地与其下方分段焊接到位。可以清楚地看到组成艏部上层建筑钢板间的焊缝,经过预涂处理,以防止生锈,确保完美的光洁度。(法国 STX 船厂 / 伯纳德比格提供)

船首的顶部分段区域悬挂在船的上方。图中所示的三角形区域就是"雪犁"防浪犁的前部,并将和后面较大的主体部分对齐安装。穿着蓝色工作服的一群人已经就位,准备引导分段进入最后的合拢位置。(法国 STX 船厂 / 伯纳德比格提供)

桥楼分段在被吊到船上合拢之前已接近完工。桥楼上方的隆起构成了一个空调机间；尽管桥楼窗开口用胶合板临时覆盖着，但艉部套房和靠近乘客观景台的大西洋厅的窗户开口尚未施工。（法国 STX 船厂 / 伯纳德比格提供）

桥楼分段向最终在船上合拢的地方靠近。（法国 STX 船厂 / 伯纳德比格提供）

桥楼在船上合拢前的阶段。现在所有的窗户开口都已完成并且可以见到艉部套房的天花板结构也全部显露出来。艉部的船员楼梯明显地从梯道内伸出并且可以看到横向结构舱壁。（法国 STX 船厂 / 伯纳德比格提供）

快到了！桥楼分段被放进合拢区域，与此同时在船头的尖端，一个造船厂的工人正在旁观并提供了体量的对比。（法国 STX 船厂 / 伯纳德比格提供）

"玛丽女王2号"结构部分基本完工。在这个由船首向船尾看的视图中,巨大的防浪犁已经整装待发去挑战任何敢于靠近他的大西洋巨浪;对于主体建造完工只剩下桅杆和烟囱的安装工作。(法国STX船厂/伯纳德比格提供)

"玛丽女王2号"停靠在舾装船坞,同时船坞内的水已被排空,以便在船尾安装4个"美人鱼"推进吊舱。目前这艘船结构已经完工,桅杆和烟囱已安装到位。部分船体的灰色底漆上面已经喷涂了第一层接近黑色的"联邦灰"油漆。(法国STX船厂/伯纳德比格提供)

一个"美人鱼"推进器吊舱及其所带的不锈钢螺旋桨已从码头的支架上吊起,并悬挂在已排空水的舾装船坞内,以便在船尾下方进行安装。(法国STX船厂/伯纳德比格提供)

尚未安装推进吊舱的船尾在干坞中。正在进行涂装工作,尤其是红色的水下防污涂料。这艘船巨大的尺寸使得周围的一切看起来都很渺小,包括高空车和卡车。(法国STX船厂/伯纳德比格提供)

在船尾的4个"美人鱼"推进器吊舱。靠前的一对是固定式的，并且只提供纵向的推力。靠后的一对可以旋转并在提供推力的同时提供舵效，因此"玛丽女王2号"不需要装配传统的舵叶。（法国STX船厂/伯纳德比格提供）

烟囱的内核正在内场建造，周围环绕着脚手架。两个大型燃气轮机的排气管清晰可见。烟囱的下部最终会安装一个大围护罩，两边各装有一个导风穴用以帮助烟雾散去。（法国STX船厂/伯纳德比格提供）

烟囱的下半部被吊到船上，冠达红和黑色条纹使其熠熠生辉。（法国STX船厂/伯纳德比格提供）

重要的一天：2002年3月24日清晨，"玛丽女王2号"首次移位，她的结构几近完成，只有烟囱顶部尚未安装。为了表示这一时刻的重要性，船厂安装了临时照明装置，营造出一种船已经投入运营的假象，拖船们小心地将船从建造船坞拖到舾装码头。（法国STX船厂/伯纳德比格提供）

在灯光的照射下，天文馆穹顶的结构框架已经起吊至指定位置上。在表面覆盖一层可反射的白膜后，穹顶将可用作天文馆的投影屏幕。不使用时，穹顶被安置在座位上方的天井内；使用时，穹顶会下降 3.5 米并展开。（法国 STX 船厂 / 伯纳德比格提供）

"布列塔尼亚"餐厅初露端倪：主餐厅正在建设中，顶部发光的穹顶已经就位，照明灯具正在安装过程中。入口处的宏伟楼梯还是未经装饰的钢结构，但很快就会被打扫干净，安装栏杆，铺好地毯。完工后，这里将成为最美丽的海上用餐场所之一。（法国 STX 船厂 / 伯纳德比格提供）

皇家宫廷剧院的结构已经完成，正处于早期的舾装阶段。在舞台上，可以清楚地看到转台中央的升降架以及其"X"形举升机构。也可以清楚地看到伸缩式乐池处于略低于其正常高度的位置上。这里还没有装饰性的壁板和地毯，很难辨认出这将是一座宏伟的娱乐中心。（法国 STX 船厂 / 伯纳德比格提供）

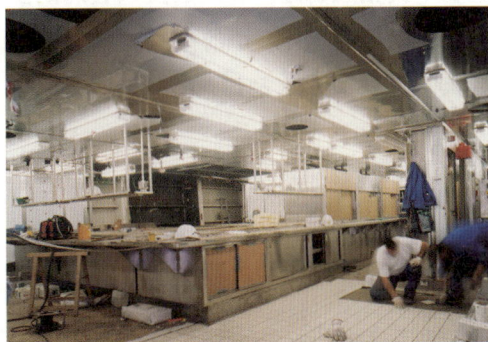

防滑瓷砖正被铺装到船上的一个厨房里。按照最严格的公共卫生要求，所有餐饮区域都用不锈钢包覆，甲板和柜台也由相同的材料制成。这有助于清洁，确保始终保持最高的卫生标准。（法国 STX 船厂 / 伯纳德比格提供）

位于第 10 层甲板首部的皇家套房正在舾装。可以看到艏部结构加强筋间的窗斗结构，而被铝箔包裹的绝缘材料已经安装在曝露的钢结构和甲板上。空调布风系统的圆形螺旋风管构件排布在结构减轻孔内。电缆还悬挂着等待最终安装。一旦所有的服务系统就位，将为套间安装壁板以及所有用于奢侈生活的物品。（法国 STX 船厂／伯纳德比格提供）

未安装柚木地板的第 8 层甲板尾部的泳池区域。斜靠在桑德林厄姆复式套间阳台上的爬入梯以及下方尚未安装的位于露天甲板的特勒斯酒吧。这层甲板的中心是托德·英格兰餐厅。在双层复式套房的上方，一对厨房／焚烧炉的排气管掩盖在脚手架下。（法国 STX 船厂／伯纳德比格提供）

在舾装的最后阶段，艉部泳池区域接近完工。游泳池已经铺了瓷砖，但是还没有在圆形开口内安装照明，而泳池四周正在准备贴瓷砖。在其他地方，舾装工作仍在继续进行，钢结构很快就会被喷上第一层白漆。（法国 STX 船厂／伯纳德比格提供）

　　出坞后停泊在舾装码头的"玛丽女王 2 号"全景。如同缝缀彩锦一般，她的初始面貌会在系统性打磨和漆装后彻底改观。由于干坞内龙门吊的施工高度限制而尚未实施的烟囱顶部安装作业也会很快完成，从而为整个建造进程画上圆满的句号。（法国 STX 船厂 / 伯纳德比格提供）

　　迎接伟大：完成艏部上层建筑第一层白色涂装（黑色油漆分界线尚未绘制）的"玛丽女王 2 号"。此刻的船内是一片繁忙景象，成百上千的工程和承包方们正在为项目完工奋力拼搏着。（法国 STX 船厂 / 伯纳德比格提供）

　　停泊舾装船坞内接近完工状态的"玛丽女王2号"。艉部上层建筑和驾驶室外表面的黑色油漆分界线涂装还未开始，艉部的吊舱单元已经成功安装，而顶部甲板导风穴的舾装收尾工作仍在进行。（法国STX船厂／伯纳德比格提供）

　　成功进行第一次试航后，返回舾装码头开展后续舾装和完工作业的"玛丽女王2号"。此刻的"玛丽女王2号"在交付给冠达邮轮公司之前，还有大量工作有待完成，诸如第二次的航行验收试验等。（法国STX船厂／伯纳德比格提供）

史蒂芬·佩恩为一名在"玛丽女王2号"建造过程中有突出表现的船厂员工颁发"血腥玛丽"奖章,一枚印有冠达邮轮公司旗帜的领针。这些奖章受到了高度追捧、广受欢迎,当这些事迹在船厂传播开以后,颁奖成为了一个定期仪式。(作者提供)

The crew began moving on board several weeks before delivery and busied themselves by storing and cleaning the ship. Training was intense and many safety drills were undertaken. Some of them with regulatory authorities in attendance. The ship was 'inclined' by carefully shifting water ballast in a pre-prescribed manner and the angle of the heel measured using long pendulums temporarily erected within two lift shafts. This experiment is used to calculate the ship's vertical center of gravity so that the stability can be accurately assessed. All the tests were satisfactorily completed and the ship was cleared for delivery.

During the construction of the ship I was keen for everyone to feel they had the ownership of the project, right down to every member of the shipyard workforce. I decided to invent the 'Ancient Order of the Bloody Mary' and the badge of office was a small Cunard lapel pin badge that was commercially available. I bought a job lot of the badges and at each visit to yard, mostly on the advice of the yard management team, chose a number of recipients

船员们在交船前几周开始登船,然后忙碌于货物存储和船舶清洁等作业。与此同时,热火朝天的培训、大量安全演练工作也陆续展开,其中部分活动还有监管机构出席。船舶的倾斜试验是根据预先规定好的方法调节压载水使船倾斜,然后采用长摆锤来测量船舶的横倾角。该试验用于测量船舶垂向重心高度,以便准确评估船舶的稳性。所有的试验都圆满完成,而且交船前的清洁工作也全部结束。

建造期间,我热衷于让每个项目参与者都持有主人翁心态,并致力于把这一理念传达给船厂的所有成员。我决定推行"血腥玛丽时代的古代勋章制度",官制奖章是一枚小型的冠达领针,这个方案从经济性来说完全可行。为此我购入大量奖章,并在每次拜访船厂期间颁发给获奖者们,人

for them. The presentation of badges rapidly became known throughout the shipyard and I had to reserve time on each shipyard visit to meet with the workers who keen to show me what they were doing, often working late to finish items. Many of those who had received badges were seen proudly wear them, giving me the thumbs up to indicate how pleased they were, as I walk round the yard and ship. As a consequence, the yard management advised that the productivity had improved. The air of bonhomie prevailed throughout the building of the ship.

The final Bloody Mary badge was presented at the last progress meeting with the shipyard immediately prior to the ship's delivery. The individual chosen was by unanimous decision – one of the French shipyard's senior electrical engineers. A typically Gallic man, he had formerly been with French military before joining the shipyard, and although always polite, had a direct manner when dealing with us. Over the life of the project we had a number of hard negotiating sessions with him, but over time he had mellowed. On several occasions the cancelling of specified items improved his budgetary position, and invariably I would receive something of greater value for the ship by return, such as a fibre-optic illuminated name, of which more later. On the day of presentation, the shipyard's project team ensured that this man attend the last meeting so that we would honour him for 'Services to Queen'. When his name was announced he was completely overcome with emotion and burst into tears. Along with the badge we presented his with a bottle of malt whisky, which

选主要由船厂管理团队推荐。很快颁奖这个事变得全厂皆知，以致于我在后来去船厂访问时都不得不预留一些时间，去见一见那些渴望向我展示他们工作成果的工人们，为此我经常工作到很晚。

在交船前最后一次的进度会议上，我颁发了最后一枚奖章。这枚奖章是经决议授予一名厂内高级电气工程师。他是一个典型的法国人，在进入船厂以前一直服役于法国军队，虽然他平时彬彬有礼，但和我们打起交道来却是直来直往。项目合作期间，我们双方展开过一系列艰难谈判，然而随着时间推移，他成长迅速而且更加成熟。他遇到的预算困境经我们取消了几个指定项目而有所改善，但最后我们从船厂的回报中获得更多，比如采用光纤照明的船名牌，这件事后面会加以描述。颁奖当天，船厂项目组承诺会让他出席会议，以便我们表彰他"为女王的服务"。当他的名字被宣布以后，他激动不已，热泪盈眶，非常感激能被授予这枚奖章和一瓶威士忌。这个故事只是成百上千个感人事迹中的个例，这使我们和法国人在项目工作中一直相处愉快。项目结束后，双方都给予了对方极大的尊重。更重要的是，

he greatly appreciated. It was only one instance among hundreds where human story touched an individual and it made working with the French a delightful throughout the building of the ship. By the end of the project there was considerable mutual regard between the two teams. It is significant that many members of the owner's team have revisited the shipyard to maintain contact with their former colleagues.

At an earlier monthly meeting another presentation was made. The safety expert on my team who has responsible for all the safety system and lifeboats etc lived on the Isle of Wight a short distance from Southampton. A keen sailor, he regularly participated in the island's annual circumnavigation race. Just before monthly meeting he was in the race when contrary to all the rules and regulations he fell overboard without wearing a lifejacket and subsequently had to be rescued. On telling the shipyard the story they presented my colleague with a lifebuoy ring at the meeting, to considerable amusement to all!

船东项目组的很多成员都会回访船厂，以保持和这些前同事的联系。

在较早的月度会议上还进行了另一项颁奖。我团队中有一位负责所有安全系统和救生艇等设备的安全专家，定居在南安普敦附近的怀特岛。这是一名热情的水手，一直定期参加每次的年度环岛航行赛事。正好在月度会议前，他在参赛时违规没有穿救生衣，结果从船上落水后不得不被救援人员捞起来。当这个故事被讲述给船厂后，他们特意在会议时向我同事颁发了一个救生圈，所有人都被逗乐了。

（译者：王露、高茜、陈熙）

2013 年 10 月 7 号 星期五，"玛丽女王2号"和她的守护拖轮驶离圣·纳泽尔，准备第二次试航。她的设计和性能极限会通过一系列全面试验来进行验证。这些试验的成功与否是船舶按时交付的关键，而令人高兴的是，所有试验都圆满通过。

第五章 试航和交船
Chapter Five:Sea Trials and delivery

Sea trials are always exciting affair. The ship moves under her own power for the first time and is put through her paces to ensure that the conditions of specification and contract are duly met. Only then can the vessel proceed to delivery as the latest expression of the ship builders' art.

　　试航总是让人兴奋。这条船首次依靠自身力量起航，用她的表现来验证规格书和合同中的条款是否都得到了充分满足。只有此刻，这条船才会作为船舶建造者精湛技艺的终极表达，被交付给船东。

"玛丽女王 2 号"在既定的回转性测试中，执行向左舷急转的动作。（法国 STX 船厂提供）

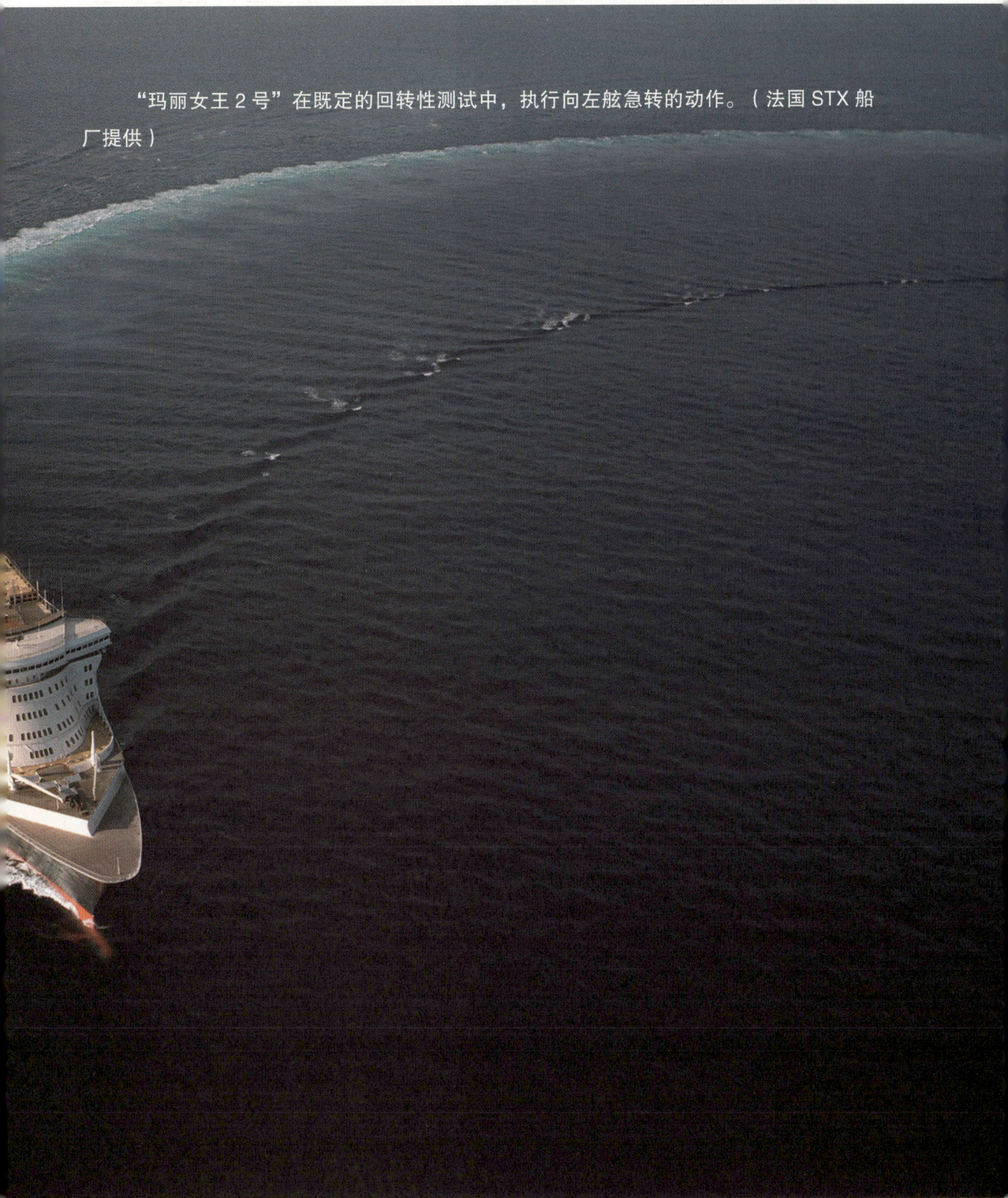

Sea trials

Testing and trials are an important aspect of quality control in many engineering and manufacturing processes. In shipbuilding, the requirements of tests and how they are conducted are outlined within the provisions of the contract and specification. Individual items of equipment may be scrutinised several times during the ship's construction phase; initially at the manufacturing facility, on board the vessel immediately after installation with the ship alongside the outfitting quay, and finally during sea trials. In many instances the latter test may be the first time that the equipment has been able to work fully as intended, as it might, for instance, be dependent on a number of other items or systems that also require commissioning and assessing. On a large passenger ship there will be hundreds of items of equipment that require rigorous testing and acceptance before the ship can be formally delivered and commissioned into service.

Equipment manufacturers are bound by their contract of supply with the shipyard, which stipulates what is expected of the item to be provided. At the appropriate time the manufacturers advise the shipyard when and where they intend to factory test the equipment. In turn the shipyard notifies the owners' shipbuilding team and a meeting is arranged so that the shipyard and owners' team can agree on a test protocol

海试

在许多工程和生产过程中，测试和试验是质量控制的重要环节。在造船行业，测试的要求以及如何进行测试是由合同和规格书规定的。在船舶建造阶段，个别设备可能会被检查多次；首次测试在制造工厂进行，第二次在舾装码头，设备安装完毕后立即随船测试；最后一次测试是在海上试航时。在许多情况下，最后这种测试可能是设备第一次完全按照预期效能运行，例如，它可能依赖于一些其他设备或系统，而这些设备或系统本身也需要进行调试和评测。在一艘大型客轮上，在正式交付并投入使用之前，将有数百项设备需要经过严格的测试和验收。

设备制造商受其与船厂的供货合同约束，该合同规定了需要提供的设备和服务内容。在适当的时候，设备商会通知船厂他们打算在何时何地进行设备的工厂测试。反过来，船厂会通知船东造船组，并安排一次会议，以便船厂和船东在参加实际测试前就测试方案达成一致。在某些情况下，如果该系统或设备是重要安全系统或其他关键系统的组成部分，船级社和船旗国的代表也可受邀参加。在工厂测试的当天，设备商通常会在开始的

prior to attending the actual test. In some instances, where a system or piece of equipment forms part of a strategic safety system or other key system, members from the classification society and the flag state may also be invited to attend. On the day of the assessment the manufacturer usually begins by offering a short presentation about the equipment, highlighting its purpose and the tests to be undertaken. These tests are then performed according to the previously agreed protocol and if successful all the parties sign a memorandum detailing all the aspects of the tests. Any comments from any party are duly recorded and noted. If the equipment has failed in any respect, the manufacturer is invited to make any adjustments as may be necessary before a retest is ordered.

Occasionally, where time is short and where the equipment is required urgently at the shipyard in order to meet the production schedule, the items may be provisionally accepted pending final testing on board. There are usually strict financial penalties laid out within the shipbuilding contract between the shipyard and its suppliers dealing with late deliveries or non-performance. In turn, the owners can hold the shipyard similarly to account under the provisions of the shipbuilding contract and specification. It is rare for equipment to completely fail the acceptance tests. Shipyards and ship owners are crucially aware that delays can be very costly and only equipment and systems with a proven track record are usually chosen for installation. Where a new design or

时候对设备进行简单的介绍,并强调拟实现的功能和将要进行的测试。然后,这些测试将按照先前商定的计划进行,如果测试成功,所有各方将签署一份备忘录,详细记录测试的所有方面。任何一方的意见都会被记录下来并注明。如果设备在任何方面出现故障,设备商应在重新测试之前进行必要的调整。

有时,工期较紧,在船厂急需该设备以满足生产计划的情况下,这些设备可以暂时先被接受,上船后再进行最后测试。在造船合同中,船厂与供应商之间通常会有严格的罚款条款约定,以处理交货延迟或功能缺陷的问题。反过来,船东也可以根据造船合同和规格书的要求,以类似的方式控制船厂。设备完全不能通过验收测试的现象是很少见的。船厂和船东都非常清楚,延期的代价会非常高,因此通常只会选择有可靠业绩的设备和系统进行安装。如果是新设计或创新布置的情况,应安排额外的时间用于增加的测试和必要的补救措施。多次失败可能会导致设备商的声誉严重受损,从而导致失去以后的项目。因此,大多数信誉良好的设备商都会小心翼翼地维护自己的声誉,并尽可能确保他们的设备满足合同的所有要求。

对于"玛丽女王2号",总部位

novel arrangement is considered, extra time is allocated to provide for additional testing and any remedial action as may be necessary. Persistent failures could lead to the reputation of a manufacturer being severely compromised, with the consequence that they are not chosen for future projects. Accordingly, most reputable manufacturers jealously guard their reputations and ensure as far as they are able that their equipment satisfies all the contractual obligations.

For Queen Mary 2, major factory tests were regularly attended by the owners' shipbuilding management team based in London. However, as the owners' site team based in the shipyard became established, more and more of the factory checks were handled by this group. Once the ship had floated and moved from the building dock to the outfitting quay, the rate of testing and inspections dramatically increased. The advance guard of ship's crew was ramping up at this time and they too began undertaking examinations to relieve the pressure on the site team.

Passenger ships invariably undertake two sets of sea trials. The first outing is usually termed 'builder's trials' and is to allow the shipyard to fine tune the ship in preparation for the all-important second set of tests, which are referred to as the 'owners' sea trials'. During these latter assessments the shipyard is responsible for demonstrating every aspect of the ship's performance against the specification requirements. Since the vessel is still technically owned by the shipyard,

于伦敦的船东造船管理团队会按期参加主要的工厂测试。随着船东现场监造组的成立，越来越多的工厂试验由这个团队来监督完成。一旦新船下水了，从建造码头移到舾装码头，测试和检查的数量就会大大增加。当接船船员开始陆续到达，他们也开始承担检查任务，以减轻监造组的压力。

所有客船都必须进行海试。第一次出海通常被称为"船厂试航"，其目的是让船厂为第二次至关重要的试航做好准备，即"船东试航"。在第二次海试中，船厂应根据规格书要求展示船舶性能的各个方面。由于该船在名义上仍为船厂所有，船厂应联合船东项目组和供应商代表，并全权负责管理船舶和进行试验。如果有任何不足之处，应仔细记录，并可用三种方法来处理：船厂可以在船舶交付前修整缺陷；或与船东约定凭信用证付款，船厂可以免除对该项目的责任；或者与船东约定有轻微缺陷的，可以不予修改。如果缺陷的处理方案的性质足够严重，可能需要进行再次海试，该项费用由船厂承担。经过成功的海试和适当修整，并就所有缺陷达成一致后，该船完成了交船准备。

"玛丽女王2号"于2003年9月25日进行了她的第一次海上试航，于4天后的29日返回。当这艘船离开大西

the yard takes full responsibility for manning the ship and conducting the trials in association with the owners' team and representatives from the equipment suppliers. If there are any deficiencies these are carefully noted and may be dealt with in one of three ways. The shipyard may elect to remedy the shortcomings before ship delivery; or in agreement with the owners against a credit, the shipyard may obviate its responsibility for the item; or in minor cases of infringement in agreement with the owners, the item may be ignored. If the deficiencies are of a serious enough nature, further sea trials at the builder's expense may be necessary. Following successful sea testing and rectification and agreement on all faults, the ship is prepared for delivery to the owners.

Queen Mary 2 embarked on her first sea trials on 25 September 2003 and returned after four days on the 29th. As the ship left the fitting-out dock at the St-Nazaire shipyard, many of the workers from around the yard massed at the quayside to see the ship under way for the first time. Such was the spectacle of the largest passenger ship in the world leaving for sea trials that traffic on the St-Nazaire bridge straddling the Loire in sight of the shipyard came to a halt, with drivers leaving their cars to watch the stately progress of the ship as she headed out to sea. It was a gloriously sunny day and although the ship was not yet fully painted she presented a wondrous sight and a foretaste of what she would look like once she was completed. Up on the ship's bridge and

洋船厂的舾装码头时，船厂的许多工人聚集在码头边，第一次看到了这艘船航行的样子。世界上最大的客船前往海上试航，这样的场面盛况空前，横跨卢瓦尔河的圣纳泽尔大桥的交通都停滞了，司机们从车里出来目睹这个庄严的景象，并目送她驶向大海。这是一个阳光灿烂的日子，尽管这艘船的油漆还没全部完成，但它却呈现出一幅奇妙的景象，并且可以预见一旦完工，它会是什么样子。在驾驶室和集控室里，仔细地记录了船舶的航行情况，所有的推进系统都被小心地监控着。几名船厂工人还流下了眼泪：他们对这艘伟大的船感到非常自豪，这是这代人建造的第一艘真正的远洋班轮，他们甚至感到自己正在创造历史。

一出海，船厂就花了几个小时对船舶的系统进行各种调试，特别是推进装置。在这段时间里，当这艘船在圣·纳泽尔海域的贝拉小岛附近航行时，对船上的罗经进行了校正。当船厂确信推进装置工作正常后，在不同的功率下进行了一系列的测速试验，以便绘制航速－功率曲线图。在100%（86 MW）功率工况下，进行4次单程测速，每个方向各2次（顺流和逆流），70%（58 MW）和45%（38 MW）功率工况下，均进行2次单程测试（每个方向1次）。先在顺流航向进行测速，

in the machinery control room careful note was made of the ship's progress, with all the propulsion systems being judiciously monitored. Several of the shipyard workers shed tears: so much was their pride in this enormous ship, the first true ocean liner in a generation, that even they sensed that this was history in the making.

Once at sea the shipyard spent the first few hours making various modifications to the ship's systems, especially the propulsion plant. During this time the compasses were adjusted as the ship tracked up and down the coast off St-Nazaire near the small island of Belle He. Once the shipyard was confident that the propulsion plant was working correctly a series of speed runs was undertaken at different power settings so that a speed-power curve could be plotted. Four runs, two in each direction (base course and its reciprocal), were performed for the 100% (86MW) power setting, and two runs, one in each direction, were conducted for 70% (58MW) and 45% (38MW). Performing speed tests on a base course and again on the opposite reciprocal course, and taking the average of the two cancelled out to some extent the effects of wind and current to give a more accurate result. Corrections were then applied to the calculated speeds to account for deviations from the contractual draught, trim and environmental conditions. With the underwater hull as yet unclear of the weed fouling that had accumulated during the outfitting period, the ship achieved a very creditable 29.21 knots;

然后再在相反的航向上进行测速,取两者的平均值以在一定程度上抵消风和流的影响,从而得到更精确的结果。然后对计算的速度进行修正,考虑与合同吃水、纵倾和环境条件的偏差。虽然尚不清楚在舾装期间水下船体上附着了多少海洋生物,但这艘船的航速达到了非常可观的29.21节;仅比合同航速低0.14节,合同航速试验将在船东试航时再次进行。届时,水下船体会是重新油漆过的,非常洁净。

在第一次试验中也进行了回转和"Z"字形操纵试验,以证明其满足有关国际规范,即国际海事组织A.751(1993)文件。该船先保持航向稳定两分钟,以便记录初始状态,如航向、航速和推进器转速。在给出转舵指令后,两个推进器转到指定的角度,并保持该角度直到船转过720°(两个完整的圆圈),然后将推进器转回直线角度,并一直保持到航线稳定,船开始沿着直线航行。该船的航迹由GPS确定,并记录所有的参数,随后绘制成图。

only 0.14 knots less than the contract speed. The contractual speed test would be repeated on the owners' trials with the underwater hull freshly painted and immaculate.

Turning circle and 'Z' manoeuvre tests were also performed during the first trials to demonstrate compliance with the relevant international regulations, namely IMO A.751 (1993). The ship was initially maintained on a steady course for two minutes in order for the starting conditions to be noted, such as course, speed and propulsion pod revolutions. On a given command the two steering pods were then actuated to the desired steering angle and held until the ship had turned through 720 (two complete revolutions), before the pods were returned to a straight course. This was held until the course stabilised and the ship began running on a straight course. The ship's position was mapped by GPS fixing and all parameters noted and subsequently plotted.

"玛丽女王2号"正在出港去进行第一次海试，2003年9月25日。

Initial ship speed, knots	Pod angle, degrees	Time for 360° rotation,	Time for 720 rotation,	Advance, metres	Transfer, metres	Tactical diameter, metres	Turning diameter, metres	Maximum heel angle,	Drift angle, degrees
26	28° port	529	1,072	1,259	664	1,517	1,444	5	7
26	28° starboard	508	1,046	1,168	613	1,413	1,319	7.5	9
15	28° port	746	1,486	1,134	616	1,490	1,455	2	13
15	28° starboard	728	1,445	1,085	575	1,375	1,302	2.5	5

Key:

Advance: the distance that the QM2 moved in the direction of her original line of advance, measured from the point where the pods were put over.

Transfer: the distance that the QM2 moved at right angles to her original line of advance, measured from the point where the pods were put over.

Tactical diameter: the amount that the QM2 moved at right angles to her original line of advance when she turned through 180 . That is to say, that it is the transfer for an alteration of course of 180 .

Turning diameter: the diameter of the QM2's turning circle.

Maximum heel angle: the angle at which the QM2 heeled over during the turn.

Drift angle: the angle that the QM2's centreline was offset from the tangent of the turning circle.

An example of one of the turning circle tests: 26 knots, 28 starboard.

初始航速 / 节	推进器角 度 / 度	360° 回转时 间 / 秒	720° 回转 时间 / 秒	纵距 / 米	正横距 / 米	战 术 直 径 / 米	回 转 直 径 / 米	最大横倾 角 / 度	漂角 / 度
26	28 左舷	529	1 072	1 259	664	1 517	1 444	5	7
26	28 右舷	508	1 046	1 168	613	1 413	1 319	7.5	9
15	28 左舷	746	1 486	1 134	616	1 490	1 455	2	13
15	28 右舷	728	1 445	1 085	575	1 375	1 302	2.5	5

关键词：

正横距：当船沿前进方向移动时，船舶距初始直线航线的横向距离。

纵距：自转舵开始，船舶沿着初始直线航向移动的距离。

战术直径：当转艏 90° 时，船舶距初始直线航线的横向距离。也就是船舶转向 180° 的方式。

回转直径：船舶回转圆的直径。

最大横倾角：船舶在回转时的横倾角。

漂角：船舶的中心线与回转圆的切线偏移的角度。

例如一次回转试验：26 节，右舷 28° 。

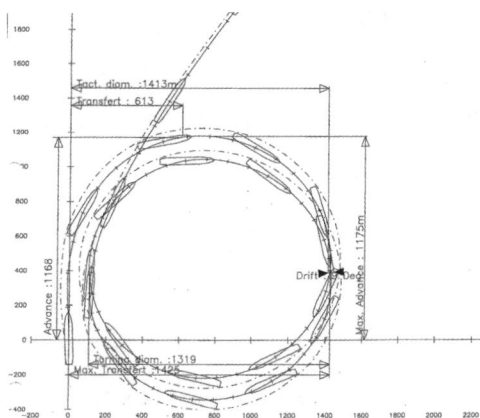

通过回转试验得到的回转轨迹图，显示了船舶的运动轨迹和姿态。

Tests were carried out for a range of ship speeds and steering pod angles according to the table above. These values were well within the stipulated requirements and Queen Mary 2 successfully completed the tests.

Another similar series of tests requires the ship to execute a series of zig-zags - the so-called 'Z' manoeuvre. This demonstrates the ship's ability to change course, the overshoot angle and the tendency for the ship to move sideways - sway. The evaluations are conducted at two helm angles, 20 /20 and 10 /10 at just over 25 knots and are somewhat more complicated than turning circles since the ship has to be steered with changes of course executed at precise moments according to the ship's track. GPS tracking is used to monitor the ship's position. As with the turning circles, Queen Mary 2 easily passed these tests.

Acceleration and deceleration appraisals are used to determine how long it takes for the ship to reach maximum speed from rest, and

根据上表对船舶航速和转向角进行了测试。这些数值完全符合要求，"玛丽女王2号"顺利完成了测试。

另一个类似的测试是要求船舶进行一系列的"Z"字形航行，即所谓的"Z"形操纵试验。通过测量超越角以及船向一侧移动–横荡的倾向来体现船改变航向的能力。试验采用了两组舵角，分别是20°／20°和10°／10°，航速采用略高于25节，这会比回转试验更复杂，因为船必须要根据她的精确运动轨迹进行操舵。GPS被用来定位船的位置。和回转试验一样，"玛丽女王2号"再次轻易地通过了这些测试。

加速试验用来确定船从静止到达到最高速度所需要的时间，反之，减速试验依靠推进系统的自动化控制系统，来确定减速到停止需要多长时间。在加速试验时，船舶处于静止状态，并位于一条笔直的航线上，驾驶室的推进杆从"停止"推到"全速前进"，

conversely how long it takes for it to slow down in a measured fashion to a stop using the automation system that controls the propulsion system. For the acceleration part of the test, the ship at rest is set on a straight course and the propulsion instruments on the bridge are moved from 'Stop' to 'Full Ahead' for 100% propulsive power. When a steady speed condition is reached the deceleration part of the test commences. The propulsion controls are moved successively back from 'Full Ahead', to 'Half Ahead', to 'Slow Ahead', to 'Dead Slow Ahead', to 'Stop', each step down being enacted after the ship speed remains at a nominally constant value for 20 seconds. On board Queen Mary 2 the propulsion controls are not annotated with the commands but with a power setting from 0 through to 10.

以获得 100% 的推力。当航速稳定后，测试的减速试验开始。推进控制器（车钟）依次从"全速前进""半全速前进""慢速前进""完全慢速前进"到"停止"，每当船舶航速保持稳定 20 秒后，再进行下一步降速。在"玛丽女王 2 号"上，推进杆上写的不是文字指令，而是标记的从 0 到 10 的功率设置。

Time, seconds	Speed, knots	Propeller revolutions
0	0	0
1,380	28.9	141
2,058	21.7	105
2,652	14.5	70
3,067	10.3	51
3,564	6.4	30
3,660	4.5	0

时间 / 秒	速度 / 节	螺旋桨 / 转
0	0	0
1 380	28.9	141
2 058	21.7	105
2 652	14.5	70
3 067	10.3	51
3 564	6.4	30
3 660	4.5	0

Note: 4.5 knots shown at zero revolutions is attributable to the ocean current.

注：推进器 0 转速时，显示航速为 4.5 节，是因为有洋流的作用。

A further test, coasting to a stop, is similar to the deceleration test but when the ship has reached maximum speed the propulsion controls are immediately set to 'Stop' or position'0'. The automation system gradually brings the propeller revolutions down from maximum to zero in a controlled manner so as not to put any undue stress on the sensitive generating plant and cause a 'trip'or 'blackout' where the engines automatically shut down. On this test Queen Mary 2 stopped after 2,734 seconds, having travelled a distance of 11,176 metres.

One of the most dramatic trials performed on a passenger ship is the testing of the fin stabilisers. In smooth weather the stabilisers are housed within the ship's hull to minimise drag. When rough weather is experienced the stabilisers are deployed by engaging powerful hydraulic rams that push the wing-shaped fins out from the hull. The fins are installed in pairs under the waterline, one on the port side and one to starboard, usually halfway along the length of the ship (midships). The fins are then activated by another set of hydraulic rams, changing their angle in relation to the water flow as the ship rolls to produce counterbalance forces to reduce the rolling. Gyroscopes were originally deployed to control the angles of the fins but modern equipment now uses solid-state electronics and accelerometers. Fin stabilisers are only effective against rolling and when properly dimensioned can reduce a very unpleasant 22 roll down to a barely noticeable 2 . Rolling is the most common motion associated with the onset of seasickness so it is worthwhile

接下来是进行惯性试验，类似于减速试验，当船达到最大速度后立即将推进控制器推到"停止"或"0功率"位置。自动化系统会以受控的方式逐渐将螺旋桨转速从最大值降低到0，以免给电站带来不必要的压力，避免发生由于引擎自动关闭导致的跳闸或失电现象。在这次测试中，"玛丽女王2号"前进了11 176米，于2 734秒后停船。

减摇鳍试验是客船试航中的另一个重大试验项目。在良好的天气状况下，减摇鳍收在船壳内以减小阻力。当天气恶劣时，强大的液压柱塞将机翼形的鳍叶推出船体而伸展开米。减摇鳍成对安装在水线下，左舷和右舷各一个，其通常布置在船舶长度的中点处（船中）。在船体横摇时，减摇鳍的另一套液压柱塞驱动鳍叶改变相对水流的角度以产生平衡力来减小横摇。早期依靠陀螺仪来控制鳍叶角度，但现代设备如今采用的是固体电子器件和加速度计。减摇鳍能有效地减小船舶横摇，尺寸适当的减摇鳍能将令人不适的22°横摇角减小到几乎察觉不到的2°。船舶横摇是最常见的使人晕船的原因，因此为了保证船上乘客的舒适性，应该尽量减小船舶的横摇，这样还可以减少打破瓷器的现象！

reducing it as much as possible for the comfort of those on board and minimising broken crockery!

Queen Mary 2 is unusual in having two pairs of stabilisers. Two pairs were specifically chosen because of the size of the ship and the extreme North Atlantic conditions that the ship was expected to experience in service. Two pairs also provide an increased level of redundancy so that if one or more should malfunction there is always sufficient capacity to provide a good level of roll reduction. Queen Mary 2's stabilisers may be individually deployed so that at any time there could be none, one, two, three or four fins deployed the number matched to the prevailing sea conditions. The least number of fins possible is always the maxim to reduce drag and lessen fuel consumption.

Stabilisers are tested by using them 'in reverse' to force the ship to roll, and then switching them to 'stabilise mode' to see how quickly they bring the rolling motion under control. This is usually performed manually with the fins controlled from the bridge or engine room console, the angle of the ship roll increasing each cycle. Since the motions can be quite violent, everything has to be carefully secured on board before the test, with all loose materials tied up, tools put away etc. Once the ship is rolling 10 or thereabouts, the stabilisers are engaged and the decaying roll motion is tracked as the fins bring the undulation under control. It is amazing to stand on the bridge wing during the tests to see the ship violently rolling before being brought to heel. Queen Mary 2's stabilisers were designed and manufactured by Brown Brothers of

"玛丽女王 2 号"不同常规地拥有 2 套减摇鳍。之所以特意采用 2 套减摇鳍是考虑到船舶尺寸和船舶运营所在的北大西洋极端海况的原因。采用 2 套减摇鳍提高了冗余度水平，这样当 1 个或者多个减摇鳍不能正常工作时，也会有足够能力保证降低横摇水平。"玛丽女王 2 号"的两套减摇鳍可以各自独立工作，因此有不同的工况组合以适应不同海况。为最大化地减小阻力和减少燃油消耗量，应尽量使用最少的减摇鳍个数。

减摇鳍测试时首先利用其"反向功能"强制产生船舶横摇，然后将减摇鳍切换到"减摇模式"来观察其从开始运作到消除横摇运动所用的时间。试验通常由驾驶室或机舱控制台人工控制减摇鳍，每个周期船舶的横摇角度都会增加。由于横摇可能会十分剧烈，因此在测试前船上所有物品都应该仔细固定住，包括绑扎好所有松散材料，收放好工具等。一旦船舶横摇 10° 左右时，使减摇鳍正常工作，鳍叶开始控制横摇的波动，记录下这期间横摇运动的衰减。在测试过程中，站在翼桥上看着船舶剧烈摇摆到稳定状态是一种很奇妙的体验。"玛丽女王 2 号"的减摇鳍由位于爱丁堡的布朗兄弟公司（现属于劳斯莱斯海事部

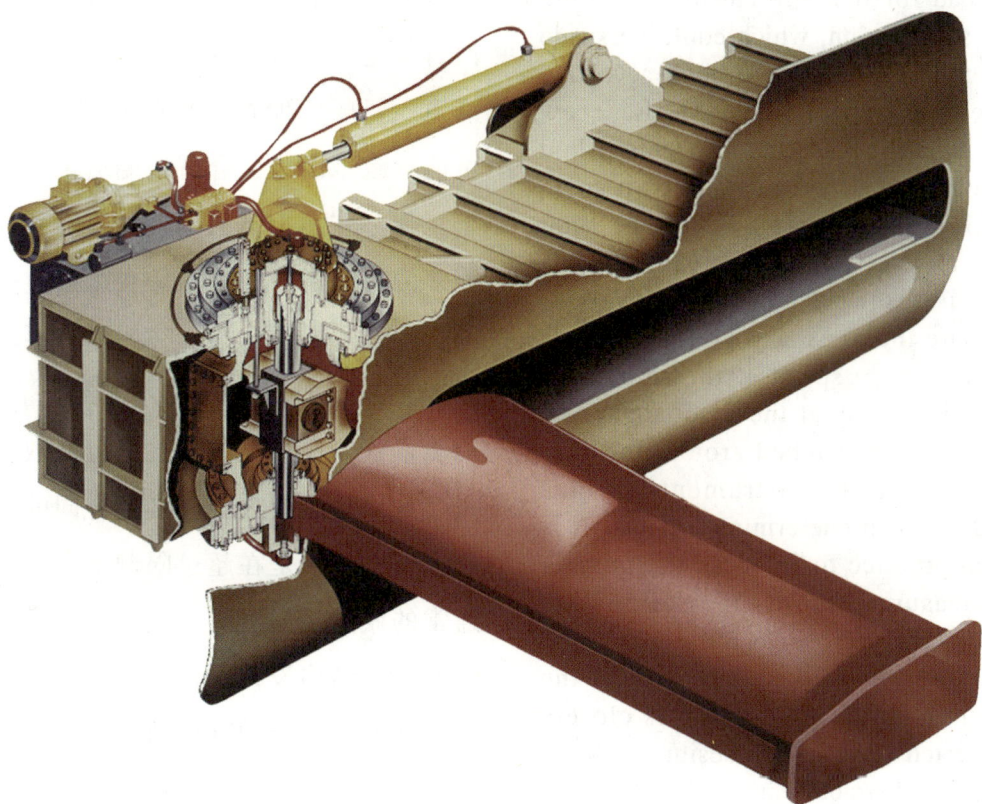

"玛丽女王 2 号"上有 4 个劳斯莱斯"海王星"减摇鳍。

Edinburgh (now part of Rolls-Royce Marine) and are very effective in their task. Force-rolling the ship for six cycles of increasing amplitude was damped out within just one cycle.

One of the most important aspects of any passenger ship is the comfort of all those on board, especially the passengers. Limiting levels of noise and vibration is a crucial factor that cannot be underestimated. If passengers have justifiable reasons to complain about noise and vibration it could result in the shipping line having to offer partial refunds or, in extreme cases, lead to legal claims. Such situations

门)设计和制造,其在任务中表现得非常高效。仅 1 个减摇周期就消阻了 6 个增放周期产生的船舶强制横摇。

客船的另一个重要方面就是保证船上所有人员的舒适性,特别是要保证乘客的舒适性。降低噪音和控制振动水平是一个不可忽视的关键因素。如果乘客有正当理由抱怨噪音和振动,可能会导致航运公司不得不提供部分退款,或在严重情况下引发法律索赔。这样的情况会对船舶和航运公

are bad for the ship and the shipping line's reputation, which could persuade potential passengers to book a voyage elsewhere. Similarly, if the crew are unhappy and the ship gets a bad reputation for crew habitability, it could result in difficulty attracting the right crew to work on the ship. Considerable time is reserved during sea trials to measure the noise and vibration levels at the service speed of the ship. With the ship sailing at the requisite speed, teams are dispatched around the ship with measuring instruments to take readings at predetermined points. It is usual practice to increase the number of measuring points if readings are consistently close to the contractual limits, especially if they exceed the requirements. As vibration is closely connected to structural design, with the ship's steel structure invariably complete at the time of the first sea trials, precise and reliable measurements can be taken. Any deficiencies can usually be dealt with through local reinforcement or other steps. Taking noise measurements on the first sea trials is not always possible, depending on the level of completion of the various areas. Invariably, ceilings, or deck heads as they are known, may not yet be installed as there is always a lot of cabling, ducting and pipework to be installed right up to the final weeks of construction. Ceilings, bulkheads and other outfitting have a big influence on noise levels and so it is usual for contractual noise levels to be performed on the final sea trials, with only indicative measurements being taken on the preliminary trials.

Vibration measurements obtained on the first Queen Mary 2 sea trial were

司的声誉不利，可能会迫使潜在乘客改订其他的航程。同样，如果船员不满意，船舶的船员宜居性声誉不好，可能导致难以吸引合适的船员来到船上工作。在海上试航期间，预留了相当多的时间用来测量船舶在服务航速下的噪音和振动水平。在船舶以要求的船速航行时，团队被分派到全船，用测量仪器在预定的点上进行读数测量。如果测量读数一直接近合同的限制要求，特别是在超过限制要求时，通常的做法是增加测量点的数量。由于振动与结构设计紧密相关，在船舶首次试航时，船舶钢质结构一般是已经完工的，因此可以进行精确和可靠的测量。振动缺陷通常可以采用局部加固或通过其他方式来解决。但并不一定能在首次试航时就进行噪音的测量，这需要依赖各个区域的完工程度。不可避免地总会存在直到最后一周还有大量电缆、通风管及管道需要安装的情况，这会造成天花板、或者说甲板反顶可能还没有安装妥当。天花板、舱壁和其他舾装件对噪音水平影响很大，因此通常在最后一次试航时才进行合同噪音水平测量，在初次试航时仅进行指示性质的测量。

尽管相较常规船舶，“玛丽女王2号”有更大的推进动力和更高的航

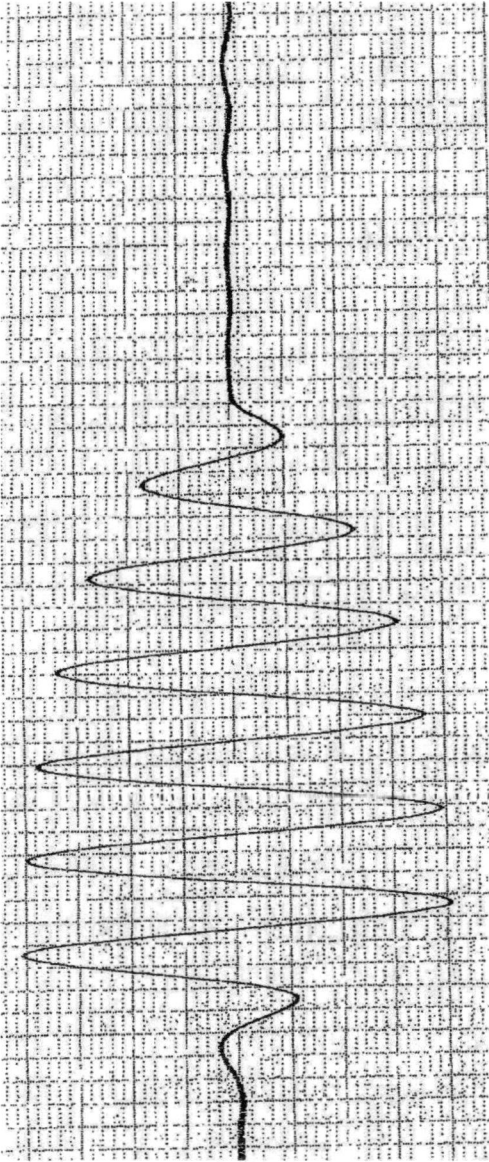

强制横摇稳定试验

"玛丽女王 2 号"上减摇试验的实际结果显示了减摇鳍从初始状态到强制产生横摇（6 个周期）和最后实现减摇稳定的高效减摇能力。（作者提供）

very low and well within the contractual limits, despite the much larger than normal propulsion power and high ship speed. This was largely attributable to the very high structural design and integrity as a result of the ship's transatlantic design pedigree.

Other tests conducted during Queen

速，但该船上的振动测量结果非常低并且较好地满足了合同的限制要求。这大部分归功于采用了在跨大西洋船舶设计谱系下非常高的结构强度设计和结构设计整体协调性。

"玛丽女王 2 号"首次试航期间

Mary 2's first sea trials included checking the launching procedure of the rescue boat; assessing the anchor windlasses by deploying and retrieving the anchors; evaluating the efficiency of the steering gear, which steers rotate the aft two steerable pods, and demonstrating that the freshwater evaporators were capable of each producing 630 tonnes over a 24-hour period.

Taken as a whole, Queen Mary 2's first sea trials were a tremendous success. The ship proved herself to be very manoeuvrable, quiet and vibration free, and there was the good prospect that with a clean hull she would exceed her contract speed requirement on the second trials.

As the vessel left the shipyard and headed out to sea on the first sea trials she was accompanied by a flotilla of small boats and helicopters. Much media interest was in evidence and many photographs and news reports were filed. Although the ship had her characteristic dark charcoal-grey hull, white upper works, red boot-topping and red and black funnel, several details were not yet done. These included the black stripes on the forward face of the Superstructure and aft quarter. However, to the casual observer the ship looked almost complete and Cunard were keen to capitalise on Queen Mary 2's first time at sea, and accordingly a helicopter was sent out to take pictures of her. Many excellent photographs resulted as the weather was fine, with sunshine and a bright blue sky. One image in particular captured the public's imagination. It was a powerfuI shot showing the bow head-on taken by the helicopter at a relatively low height. However, the picture was

进行的其他试验项目包括了救助艇下放程序检验、锚机抛锚及收锚试验、转向装置功效试验——此处为转动靠舰艉部的2台可转向吊舱推进器和淡水蒸发器24小时——630吨出水量验证试验。

从整体上看，"玛丽女王2号"的首次试航取得了巨大的成功。这艘船证实了具有良好的可操纵性，安静且低振动，也预示了在船体保持干净的状况下，在第2次试航时她将会超过合同航速要求。

当这艘船离开造船厂开始第一次试航时，她由一支包含小船和直升机组成的队伍陪同。这吸引了众多媒体的关注，拍摄了许多照片和播报了很多新闻报道。虽然这艘船已经涂装了她特有的炭黑色船体、白色的上层建筑、红色的船顶以及红色和黑色的烟囱，但是还有几个分工程没有完工，其中包括上层建筑正面和后部的黑色条纹。然而，在外行看来，这艘船已经是完美无缺的了。冠达邮轮公司利用"玛丽女王2号"第一次出海的机会，派了一架直升机去捕捉她的靓照。天气晴朗、阳光明媚、天空蔚蓝，其中一幅图片特别引人瞩目。这是一次强烈的视觉冲击，直升机在相对较低的高度上拍摄下她的弓形船首。然而，这张照片也存有一些争议，由于

also to prove to be a little controversial. As Queen Mary 2 was not fully loaded for the sea trials, she was at a relatively light draught and the bulbous bow that would normally have been fully immersed was breaking the surface. No harm in that you would have thought; after all, ships had been seen for years with their bulbous bows breaking the surface. However, whereas the original photograph was widely used within Europe for advance publicity in its unadulterated form, the North Americans insisted in air-brushing out the bulbous bow as it appeared to them to be quite obscene.

Upon returning to the shipyard Queen Mary 2 was dry-docked. The

"玛丽女王 2 号"没有进行满载海上试验,她处于相对较浅的吃水状态,而通常情况下,冲破海面的球鼻艏是完全浸没的。这并没有坏处,毕竟多年来人们都看到船只球鼻艏冲破了水面。然而,尽管这张原始照片在欧洲被广泛使用,以其原始的形式进行宣传,但美国人却坚持修改掉球鼻艏,因为在他们看来原图才像是明显被修改过了的。

"玛丽女王 2 号"返回船厂后,就进入了干船坞。水下船体首先进行压力清洗,然后重新涂上防污漆。在

海上试验,随着罗经的调整,"玛丽女王 2 号"缓慢地前进。目光敏锐的人可能注意到翼桥上正在工作的 4 名技术人员。(法国 STX 船厂提供)

underwater hull was first power-washed and then repainted with anti-fouling paint. Throughout October 2003 the hull and upper-works were rubbed down and given the final coats of paint. On 7 November 2003 the ship was ready for her formal owners' sea trials. The four most important sets of trials to be undertaken comprised the contractual speed runs, endurance test, noise measurements and crash stop. Other tests included adjustment and verification of the performance of the three bow thrusters with and without the aft pods in side thrusting mode, and adjustment for numerous systems for optimum performance. Queen Mary 2 once again brought the shipyard and the town of St-Nazaire to a halt as she made her stately Progress towards the open sea, many onlookers crowding every vantage point. She was looking much closer to how she would appear at delivery, since a lot of work had been completed both internally and externally in the intervening weeks. Expectations were running high that the ship would prove herself in every respect.

The official speed runs always considered one of the most important aspects of sea trials. The ship is run on a straight course, at as near to her design draught as possible, under the power settings stipulated in her construction contract and specification. Several runs are undertaken in opposite directions and averages noted. In the case of Queen Mary 2, the official speed trials were a repeat of those performed during the first sea trials, but with considerably more tension Severe penalties would have to be paid by the shipyard if there was a deficiency from 29.35 knots.

整个 2003 年 10 月份，船体和上层建筑锈迹被打磨，并进行面漆处理。2003 年 11 月 7 日，这艘船为船东做好了试航准备。将进行四项最重要的试验，其中包括合同航速测试、耐久性试验、噪音测量和紧急停车试验。其他试验包括调整和验证三个艏侧推在艉部吊舱启动和关闭侧推模式下的不同性能表现，以及众多系统的最佳参数设定。"玛丽女王 2 号"再次使船厂和圣·纳泽尔万人空巷，她驶向公海的时候，广大观众挤在每一个有利的观测位置上观看。她看起来离交付运行的状态更近了，因为在接下来的几周里，许多内部和外部的工作都将完工。人们对她的期望很高，她也将在各个方面证明自己。

正式测速一直被认为是海上试验中最重要的测试之一。根据建造合同和规格书规定的功率设置，该船在尽可能接近设计吃水状态下进行直线航行。在来回方向上进行多次测试，并计算出平均值。对于"玛丽女王 2 号"来说，正式的航速试验是第一次航行试验的重复，但紧张程度却大得多，因为如果航速低于 29.35 节，船厂将支付高额的罚款。

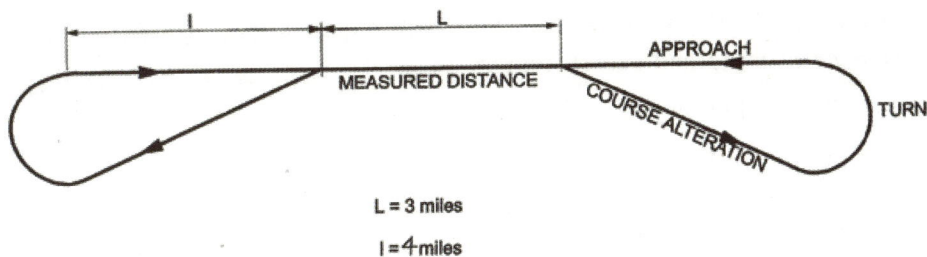

L = 3 miles

l = 4 miles

为了使航速测量数据能够准确，每次初始航行的距离接近4英里，通过全球定位系统在随后的3英里以上距离进行数据记录，然后逐渐转向，使船重新回到相反航向上，然后进行新的4英里初始跑。(作者收集)

The speed runs commenced just south of the island of Belle lIe near St-Nazaire on 9 November, between 18:00hrs and 19:30hrs. Three runs were performed with the ship displacing 74,635 tonnes, 9.86 metres draught aft and 9.80 metres forward. To enable the ship speed to stabilise, the approach to each run was four miles; the actual run was measured by GPS over three miles and a gradual turn made to bring the ship back on to a reciprocal heading with a new four-mile approach for the opposite run as shown below:

11月9日18：00至19：30之间，在贝尔利岛以南靠近圣纳泽尔的地方开始航速测试。该船共进行3次航行，排水量为74 635吨、船尾吃水9.86米、船首吃水9.80米。这张速度运行图显示了4英里的初始段，当速度稳定再进行3英里测量的测量段，以及随后的航向改变和转弯，使船在相反的方向返回相同的航线，以便进行正反向的测量，数据如下表所示。

Run	1	2	3
Power MW	86.885	86.706	86.669
Propeller rpm,average	143.5	143.7	144.0
Speed knots	29.539	29.188	29.797

测速航次	1	2	3
主机功率 / MW	86.885	86.706	86.669
螺旋桨平均转速 / (转/分钟)	143.5	143.7	144.0
航速 / 节	29.539	29.188	29.797

Using this raw data, corrections were first applied to compensate for the influence of wind and sea currents. These calculations gave a speed of 29.45 knots at 86.071 MW and 143.4rpm.

The sea swell was considered next. Readings taken during the trials are recorded below, with the calculated influence that the swell would have on the speed:

Run	1	2	3
Wave height, metres	2.0	2.0	2.0
Wave direction	270	270	270
influence on speed, knots	0.2	0.2	0.2

The effect of swell was finally calculated to slow the ship down by 0.17 knots. Therefore, the final 100% power speed test gave a speed of 29.62 knots, which was 0.27 above the contractual requirement - a very good result!

The endurance test is designed to test the ship's propulsion system and associated auxiliaries, such as the cooling system, to simulate as far as practicable the conditions that the ship will experience at sea on an extended voyage. The ship is run at maximum power for at least eight hours and all the propulsion parameters are carefully monitored to ensure that a steady state condition is reached with no increasing temperatures within the cooling systems,

利用这些原始数据，然后进行修正来补偿风和流的影响。计算结果表明，在主机功率为86.071 MW和转速为143.4转/分钟时，船舶航速为29.45节。

下一个考虑的影响因素是波浪，试验期间的数据记录如下。

测速航次	1	2	3
浪高/米	2.0	2.0	2.0
波浪角/度	270	270	270
航速影响值/节	0.2	0.2	0.2

最后计算出，波浪的影响使船速慢了0.17节。因此，最终100%功率航速测试的航速修正值为29.62节，比合同要求高出0.27节，非常好的结果！

耐久性试验旨在测试船舶的推进系统和相关辅助设备（如冷却系统），以尽可能模拟船舶在海上长航程时的情况。船舶以最大功率连续运行至少8小时，并仔细监测所有推进参数，以确保在冷却系统、轴承等温度不上升的情况下达到稳定状态。在柴油机和燃气轮机上，对海水和淡水冷却管路以及润滑油的温度进行了监测。在6台发电机上也进行了类似的测试，对

bearings etc. On the diesels and gas turbines, salt and freshwater cooling circuits were monitored, as well as the temperature of the lubricating oil. Similar measurements were taken on the six electrical generators, with windings, bearings and cooling air values being carefully watched. Finally, temperatures, pressures, voltages etc were monitored on the four propulsion pods. For the endurance test to be valid it has to run constantly without interruption at full power. If a pump should fail, or an engine or pod trip and come off-line, even momentarily, the test has to be repeated until perfection is reached. Queen Mary 2 successfully ran her endurance test during the night between 9 and 10 November, all systems proving to be satisfactory and stable.

The crash stop test is probably the most demanding test to be undertaken on sea trials. The ship is set on a straight course at service speed and then brought to a stop in the fastest achievable time by quickly reversing the propulsion. In normal operation acceleration and deceleration are enacted in a gentle controlled manner through the ship's automation system. In this way, the ship and her systems are put under the least stress possible. In the crash stop things are very different; all the niceties of a controlled stop are dispensed with and the whole ship is put under immense strain. Suddenly reversing the propulsion system causes the propellers to fight against themselves, thrusting violently against an inrush of water due to the vessel's initial significant speed

绕组、轴承和冷却空气进行仔细观察。最后，对4个推进吊舱的温度、压力、电压等进行监测。为了使耐久性测试有效，它必须在最大功率下不停地运行。如果一个泵发生故障，或者发动机或吊舱推进器脱离电网，即使是暂时的，测试也必须重新进行，直到达到完美效果为止。"玛丽女王2号"在11月9日至10日晚成功地进行了耐久性测试，所有系统都证明是令人满意和稳定的。

紧急停车试验可能是海上试验中最苛刻的试验。船舶以服务航速沿直线航行，然后在可达到的最快时间内通过快速反转推进器而停下来。在正常操作中，通过船舶的自动化系统以温和可控的方式实现加速和减速。以这种方式，船舶和她的系统被置于最小的应力下。在紧急停车时，情况却大不相同，控制停车的所有自动化程序细节都被取消了，整个船都承受着巨大的压力。突然反转的推进系统导致螺旋桨与其自身相抗衡。由于船自身的高航速和巨大动量，螺旋桨必须抗衡巨大的迎面水流。这个过程将会发出可怕的噪音，同时在船尾周围通常会涌现大量的水柱。更重要的是，推进系统本身承受着相当大的压力，因为它们拼命使螺旋桨逆流转动。对

and momentum. The noise can be truly horrific and it is not uncommon for huge plumes of water to be thrown up around the ship's stern. More importantly, the propulsion system itself is put under considerable pressure as it wrestles to keep the propellers turning against the backwash. In a diesel-electric ship where electric motors turn the propellers, it is the automation and control system that has to deal with this. There are many safeguards built into these systems to protect them should any anomaly be detected, such as a power surge or sudden fluctuation. The crash stop produces many such fluctuations and it is fundamentally crucial that it can cope with them without tripping and shutting down the whole propulsion system, or indeed the whole power system of the ship. This scenario is termed a 'blackout'. If, during the crash-stop test a blackout occurs, the systems have to be reset and adjusted to a less sensitive condition and the crash stop repeated. Only when the crash-stop manoeuvre is perfectly executed, with all systems remaining on line without a blackout, does the ship pass the assessment. Two crash-stop scenarios were tested with Queen Mary 2, one at her service speed (26.5 knots) and another at half speed (13.2 knots). Both tests were satisfactory and during the service speed test the ship came to a halt after 461 seconds, travelling 3, 115 metres.

After all other scheduled tests and trials were accomplished, including the contractual noise measurements Queen Mary 2 returned to the shipyard for final completion prior to delivery.

于柴油机－电力推进的船舶，自动化和控制系统需要处理这个问题。这些系统中内置了许多保护措施以便在发现异常情况时进行保护，如电网的突加负荷或瞬时波动。应急停车产生了许多这样的波动，而关键是它能在不切断和关闭整个推进系统，甚至是全船电力系统的情况下应对这些波动。这种情况被称为"失电"。如果在紧急停车测试期间发生停电，则系统必须复位并调整到较不敏感的状态，并且重复紧急停车试验。只有当紧急停车操作被完美地执行，并且所有系统都保持在线而没有停电时，船才能通过评估。"玛丽女王2号"测试了两种停车方案，一种是服务航速（26.5节），另一种是半速（13.2节）。这两次试验都令人满意，在服务航速下紧急停车试验中，船在461秒后停了下来，这期间行驶了3 115米。

在完成了所有其他预定的测试和试验包括合同约定的噪音测量之后，"玛丽女王2号"返回船厂，完成了交付前的收尾工作。

Delivery, naming and maiden voyages

交付、命名和处女航

Following the conclusion of successful sea trials, Queen Mary 2 was readied for delivery. Final outfitting was finished and as each part of the ship was finalised it was duly vetted by the inspection team before either being sealed off or protected with temporary coverings.

Sadly, on 15 November 2003 during the final stages of construction a fatal accident occurred, when an access gangway collapsed under a group of shipyard workers and their relatives who had been invited to visit the vessel. In total, 32 people were injured and 16 were killed, after the gangway fell 15 metres (49 feet) into the dry dock. The gangway was deemed to have given way due to overloading and although the tragic incident didn't impact on the delivery date, extensive celebrations and delivery parties were cancelled.

During the morning of 23 December, ownership of the Queen Mary 2 was transferred from Chantiers de l'Atlantique to the Cunard Line, and the shipping company accepted formal delivery of the vessel. The delivery protocol was unusually brief since the ship was almost fully finished in every respect and there were few comments made for adding to the list of outstanding works that required post-delivery completion. The ship had been

在成功完成海上试验后，"玛丽女王2号"准备交付。该船最终的舾装已经完成，当船的每个部件都完成后，在被封存或用临时覆盖物保护之前，检查组对每个部件进行了适当的审查。

令人悲伤的是，2003年11月15日，在建设的最后阶段，发生了一起事故。当时一条舷梯发生坍塌，上面载有众多船厂工人及其亲属，他们被邀请参观这艘船。舷梯坍塌后下落15米（49英尺）掉入干船坞，共有32人受伤，16人死亡。事故是由于舷梯超载造成的，虽然这起悲剧事件并没有影响到交船日期，但之后大量的庆祝活动和交船派对都被取消了。

12月23日上午，"玛丽女王2号"的所有权从大西洋造船厂移交给冠达邮轮公司，冠达邮轮公司接受了正式交船。由于本船几乎已全部完工，所以交船协议异常简短，而且几乎没有人对船交付完成的后续内容发表意见。这艘船已经按时交货，同时考虑到所有的额外费用和删减费用都控制在合同预算之内，这对所有相关人员来说都是一个了不起的成就。

handed over on time and after taking into account extras and deletions below the contract budget, which was a tremendous achievement for all involved.

After a delivery lunch with numerous invited guests, the Queen Mary 2 left the shipyard in mid-afternoon. As on the occasion of the two sea trials, crowds thronged the quayside and every vantage point to witness the departure of the new ship. As she moved down the River Loire towards the open sea, the French equivalent to Britain's national flying display team, Patrouille de France, flew over the ship in formation trailing red and blue smoke trails. A large banner had been prepared by Cunard that was unfurled over the starboard side of the ship, which proclaimed 'Merci! St-Nazaire'.

The ship then set course for Vigo in Spain where the large harbour was the ideal training place to practise harbour manoeuvres. Commodore Warwick and his bridge team spent many hours berthing and unberthing the ship before finally heading for Southampton. Christmas Day 2003 was spent at sea in transit, before a triumphant maiden arrival into Southampton on Boxing Day morning, 26 December 2003. Unfortunately the weather was absolutely dire, with heavy rain squalls and fog. But despite this, thousands of people turned out to see the ship for the first time, and in some sense the weather contributed to the dramatic entry as Queen Mary 2 loomed, massive

在与众多受邀客人共进午餐后，"玛丽女王2号"于下午3点左右离开了船厂。就像两次海上试航一样，人群占据了码头边的每一个有利位置，目送新船的离别。当她沿着卢瓦尔河向公海驶去时，与英国皇家飞行表演队齐名的法兰西"巡逻兵"飞行表演队以编队的形式飞过这艘船，机尾拉出红色和蓝色的烟带。冠达邮轮公司准备了一面大横幅，横在船的右舷，上面写着："谢谢！圣·纳泽尔"。

然后，这艘船在西班牙比戈进行训练，那里的大港口是进行港口操作的理想训练场所。在驶向南安普敦之前，沃里克船长和他的团队花了很长时间练习停泊和开泊这艘船。2003年圣诞节是在海上航行途中度过的，2003年12月26日，节礼日上午，"玛丽女王2号"顺利抵达南安普敦。不幸的是，当天天气非常糟糕，有大雨、狂风和大雾。尽管如此，成千上万的人第一次看到了这艘船，从某种意义上说，当"玛丽女王2号"从薄雾中出现时，天气因素也增强了登场演出的戏剧性。她沿着索伦特海峡，经过怀特岛到达南安普敦水域，越过她的最终泊位向南安普敦的集装箱码头继续航行，然后转弯回来并最终靠泊。

随后我们一直在为命名仪式做准

and regal, out of the mist. She sailed up the Solent past the Isle of Wight to Southampton Water, continuing beyond her eventual berth towards Southampton's container terminal before turning and finally docking.

Preparations were then made for the ship's naming ceremony by Her Majesty Queen Elizabeth II on 8 January 2004. In the intervening period the vessel left Southampton for a number of overnight trips with company staff and their families, to provide an opportunity for crew familiarisation and crew training. When back in port Queen Mary 2 hosted many civic functions as well as showcasing herself to the travel industry and the media. The naming ceremony was certainly a tremendous gala event with guests assembled in a huge temporary marquee, battered by ferocious wind and rain. One highlight of the ceremony was the artiste Heather Small singing 'Proud', and at the final note the back of the marquee dramatically dropped down to reveal the great bow of the ship, suitably floodlit, poised for her naming by Her Majesty the Queen. It was certainly a memorable occasion, which saw many of the ship's staff and Cunard officials being introduced to the Queen, including myself. The naming ceremony was followed by a gala dinner and overnight on board.

备，最终定于 2004 年 1 月 8 日由伊丽莎白女王二世陛下为该船命名。在此期间，该船驶离南安普敦，为公司员工及其家属提供一系列过夜旅行服务，以便为船员提供熟悉她和培训的机会。回到港口后，"玛丽女王 2 号"举办了许多公众活动，并向旅游界和媒体界展示。命名仪式无疑是一场盛大的庆祝活动，嘉宾们情愿忍受着狂风和暴雨，聚集在一个巨大的临时帐篷里。仪式的亮点之一是艺术家希瑟·斯莫尔演唱的《自豪》，在最后一个音符上，帷幕落下，露出了灯光映照下准备由女王陛下来进行命名的"玛丽女王 2 号"巨大的船首。船上的许多工作人员和冠达邮轮公司的官员被介绍给女王，包括我自己。这的确是一个难忘的时刻。命名仪式之后，船上举行了庆祝晚宴。

　　希瑟·斯莫尔献唱非常应景的和激情四溢的主题曲《自豪》将典礼推向高潮。（冠达邮轮提供）

　　伊丽莎白女王二世陛下偕菲利普王子抵达冠达邮轮公司新旗舰的命名典礼现场。（冠达邮轮提供）

何以为荣？黑色的帷幕落下，露出"玛丽女王2号"巨大的船首，一位风笛手独自一人站立其上。（冠达邮轮提供）

伊丽莎白女王二世陛下准备为"玛丽女王2号"命名。同时出席的还有罗恩·沃里克船长，冠达邮轮公司执行总裁帕米拉·科诺弗和嘉年华公司董事长兼首席执行官米奇·阿里森。（冠达邮轮提供）

命名仪式以盛大的焰火表演宣告结束。（冠达邮轮提供）

2004 年 4 月 25 日，"玛丽女王 2 号"和"伊丽莎白女王 2 号"组成历史性的编队，在横跨大西洋航行开始前，列队向自由女神像致意。（冠达邮轮提供）

2006 年 2 月 23 日，在加利福尼亚长滩，"玛丽女王 2 号"和"玛丽女王号"互相致敬。
（冠达邮轮提供）

2011 年 2 月 22 日，"伊丽莎白女王 2 号"和"玛丽女王 2 号"在悉尼港进行"皇室聚会"
的历史性一幕。（冠达邮轮提供）

Queen Mary 2 departed on her maiden voyage to Fort Lauderdale on the evening of 12 January 2004, the 14-day voyage calling at Funchal Madeira, Santa Cruz de Tenerife, Las Palmes de Grand Canaria, Barbados and St Thomas. After a season in the Caribbean Queen Mary 2 returned to Southampton on 16 April and departed for her maiden transatlantic crossing to New York. The six-day crossing was memorable for the ferocity of the weather, which was a real baptism of fire for the vessel. Despite mountainous seas and hurricane-force winds the ship arrived in New York on schedule to meet her fleet mate Queen Elizabeth 2 at the Hudson piers on the 22nd. After a three-day stay in port the ships departed together in tandem during the evening of 25 April 2004 for the transatlantic crossing back to Southampton. Stopping off at the Statue of Liberty for a fireworks display, the prophesy that the Atlantic ferry would be finally extinguished after Queen Elizabeth 2 was finally put to rest.

Since her introduction into service, Queen Mary 2 has criss-crossed the North Atlantic, and on 5 July 2013 she embarked on her 200th crossing, sailing from New York to Southampton. She has undertaken many Caribbean and European cruises (themed as 'voyage' by Cunard) and an extended around the world voyage is well established in her annual itinerary. On 23 February 2006 the ship met up with her namesake, Cunard's original Queen Mary, at

2004 年 1 月 12 日晚间，"玛丽女王 2 号"从劳德代尔堡出发，开始处女航。在随后 14 天的航行中，先后停靠了马德拉群岛的丰沙尔，加那利群岛的特内里费圣克鲁斯，大加那利岛的拉斯帕尔马斯、巴巴多斯和圣托马斯。在加勒比海度过了一个季度后，"玛丽女王 2 号"于 4 月 16 日返回南安普敦，从那里开始到纽约的横跨大西洋处女航。横跨大西洋的 6 天航行遭遇了罕见的恶劣天气，这是对船只的一次真正洗礼。尽管北大西洋海面风大浪急，飓风肆虐，但她还是如期抵达了纽约，并于当月 22 日在哈德逊码头与编队伙伴"伊丽莎白女王 2 号"会合。在港口短暂停留三天以后，两艘船于 2004 年 4 月 25 日傍晚编队启航，横渡大西洋返回南安普敦。编队一度在自由女神像前停泊，观看了盛大的焰火表演。而坊间之前所谓的跨洋航运将在"伊丽莎白女王 2 号"之后结束运营的传闻，也就此不攻自破。

自投入运营以来，"玛丽女王 2 号"多次往返横渡北大西洋。在 2013 年 7 月 5 日，她开始了自己的第 200 次跨大西洋航行，从纽约驶往南安普敦。在此期间，她还曾多次执行了在加勒比海和欧洲的邮轮巡航任务（冠达邮轮公司将主题命名为"航海"），并在其每年的行程中安排了一次环球航行。2006 年 2 月 23 日，"玛丽女王 2 号"在加利福尼亚的长滩与冠达邮轮

Long Beach, California. The two ships exchanged whistle salutes, which was made even the more poignant in that on of Queen Mary 2's whistles was originally from the middle funnel of Queen Mary.

When she entered service she was the largest passenger ship the world had ever seen by a sizeable margin, but in April 2006 she lost that title to Royal Carbbean's Freedom of the Seas. Since then several other even larger passenger ships have entered service, but Queen Mary 2 remains the only true liner, as opposed to cruise ship, in serive.

公司的"玛丽女王号"相遇。两艘船互相鸣笛致敬——"玛丽女王2号"的汽笛更响亮,因为"玛丽女王2号"的汽笛原本就是从"玛丽女王号"的中间烟囱上拆下来的。

在"玛丽女王2号"投入运营之初,她一度是世界上最大的客轮,但在2006年4月,随着皇家加勒比邮轮公司的"海洋自由号"投入运营,她失去了这一荣誉。虽然后来又有几艘更大的客轮已经投入运营,但"玛丽女王2号"仍然是唯一的真正的班轮,而不是邮轮。

（译者：陈大为、叶涛、邓志鹏）

第六章 "玛丽女王 2 号"解析
Chapter Six:Anatomy of Queen Mary 2

Queen Mary 2 is truly a destination in her own right. And as with any great destination a grand tour is the order of the day. So here is Queen Mary 2's grand tour - wear some comfortable shoes, as we'll be walking over four kilometres!

　　"玛丽女王 2 号"本身就是一个旅行目的地。一个著名的旅游景点肯定值得花上一天的时间来游览，我们今天就来好好参观一下"玛丽女王 2 号"。大家请穿上舒适的鞋子，因为我们要走上 4 公里！

注：除注明出处外，其他所有图片均由作者提供。

2011 年拍摄于汉堡的干船坞，"玛丽女王 2 号" 当时正在进行第一次改装。突出的前景是球鼻艏，这有助于改善船首波和减少船舶阻力。（国际油漆有限公司提供）

The grand tour

Welcome to the grand tour of Queen Mary 2 where I will describe the ship's layout, explain why the ship was designed this way and identify some of features that may not be readily apparent. We'll take in each deck in turn from top to bottom, working from forward to aft. You'll need some comfortable shoes as we'll be walking for several miles!

The public areas of Queen Mary 2 were decorated to the designs of two groups of marine interior architects. The lead architects were SMC Design of London and the associated Swedish firm of Tillberg SA. Several public spaces were shaped by the now defunct London-based company Design Team. These companies worked in close collaboration to ensure there was a harmonious and seamless transition between the various locations on board.

Deck 13

At the forward end of Deck 13 a sheltered 'Lookout' observation area is arranged across the end of the superstructure above the ship's bridge. This elevated platform has a windscreen and a partial glazed roof to provide some protection. The idea for the Lookout emanated from the open observation deck forward on board Queen Elizabeth 2. On that ship the observation area was frequently closed, to passengers1 angst, due to the danger of high winds. Crossing the North Atlantic often provides spectacular views of a tempestuous boiling sea, which some passengers prefer to experience outside,

盛大游览

欢迎参加"玛丽女王 2 号"的盛大游览，在这里我将描述这艘船的布局，解释为什么这艘船是这样设计的，并介绍一些可能不太明显的特征。我们将从上到下依次进入甲板，从前往后走。你需要一双舒适的鞋子，因为我们要走好几英里！

"玛丽女王 2 号"公共区域的装饰是由两个船舶室内设计师团队完成的。主要的设计师来自伦敦的 SMC 设计公司和瑞典的提尔伯格联合公司。其他一些公共空间是由总部位于伦敦、现已停业的"设计团队"公司设计的。这些公司密切合作，以确保在不同处所之间也能顺畅地过渡。

13 甲板

13 甲板的最前端，在驾驶室上方设置有一个遮蔽的瞭望观景区。这个架高的平台有挡风玻璃和部分玻璃屋顶提供一定的遮蔽保护。设立瞭望观景区的想法来自"伊丽莎白女王 2 号"的露天观景区。在那艘船上，由于风太大会产生潜在的危险，观景台经常对乘客关闭。穿越北大西洋通常能看到大海汹涌澎湃的壮观景象，有些乘客宁愿在外面体验，也不愿坐在舒适的休息室里欣赏。我想在"玛丽女王 2 号"上设计一个瞭望观景区来满足这

rather than from the comfort of a lounge. I attempted to design Queen Mary 2's Lookout to meet this expectation, but it did not work out as well as I had hoped. To provide the bridge with sufficient air-conditioning, an air-conditioning plant room is placed immediately above it under a helmet-type shield. Although the Lookout peers out over the top of the shield, it is not possible to see the bow of the ship so there is no forward point of reference. When asked what I would have done differently had there been a second ship, I often remark that reconfiguring the Lookout to provide a better view was one priority! Sadly, the Lookout also suffers from high-wind closure as access requires traversing the open deck, which at times can be restricted when the wind is strong.

On the centreline of the Lookout,

一愿望，但其效果并没有我希望的那么好。为了给驾驶室提供足够的空调，在驾驶室的正上方设置了一个空调机房，并在其上安装了一个头盔式的防护罩。尽管乘客是从防护罩的顶部向外张望，但由于看不到船头，所以没有前进的参考点。当被问及如果有第二艘船的话，我会有什么不同的做法时，我经常说，要重新设计瞭望观景区以提供更好的视野，这是一项应该首先考虑的事！不幸的是，瞭望区也经常会因大风而关闭，因为乘客需要穿过开敞的甲板才能到达这里。当风很大时，这里会被限制通行。

在瞭望观景区的中央，甲板室舱

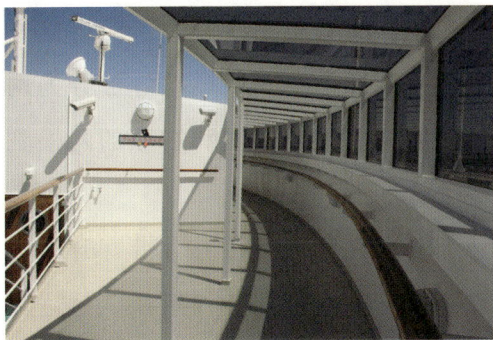

瞭望室里陈列着"玛丽女王 2 号"的船钟。最初打算展出一套皇家铸币局的钱币，但其在运输途中遗失。

a small display case is inset into the deckhouse bulkhead and it was originally intended that a set of British Mint coins from 2004, commemorating the year the ship entered service, would be displayed. The coins would have also been a nice link to the traditional 'Mast Stepping Ceremony' that took place on 16 March 2004 when coins were set in place at the base of the mast to give the ship good luck. Unfortunately, the specially commissioned coin display was lost in transit to the ship and was never replaced. One of the ship's bells is now exhibited in the recess.

The signal mast is located forward on top of the deckhouse and supports various radars and other navigation systems. I wanted the mast to replicate as far as possible the design of the mast of Queen Elizabeth 2, which was very distinctive and became an iconic feature on that ship. As explained elsewhere, the air draught restriction of 62 metres necessitated that the mast, at 17 metres' freestanding height, had to be somewhat shorter than Queen Elizabeth 2's. For good all-round visibility some of the navigation lights are duplicated and positioned on two poles offset to port and starboard from the mast.

The mast itself is equipped with a pair of angled yardarms with halyards for allowing various flags to be flown. The Cunard house flag is usually flown on the port side yardarm, while national courtesy flags and signal flags, such as the 'pilot on board' flag, are flown to starboard. A gaff (short angled yardarm) is placed aft at the centreline, angled slightly upwards for the nationality of registration flag. When Queen Mary

壁上嵌有一个小陈列柜，原本打算展出一套英国铸币局2004年的钱币，以纪念该船服役的年份。这些钱币也与2004年3月16日举行的传统"立桅仪式"有很好的渊源。当时，我们在桅杆底部安放了硬币，用来给船带来好运。不幸的是，特别订造的陈列钱币在运送到船上的途中丢失了，并且再没补换。现在在陈列处展示的是一个船钟。

信号桅杆位于甲板室顶部的前方，其中安装了各种雷达和其他导航系统。我希望桅杆尽可能地复制"伊丽莎白女王2号"的桅杆设计，它非常独特，并成为船上的标志性特征。正如前文所述，由于62米空气净高的限制，桅杆只有17米的高度，比"伊丽莎白女王2号"的要矮一些。为了保持良好的环照能见度，一些导航灯被分为两组并从桅杆移到左舷和右舷的两根副灯桅上。

桅杆本身装备了一对带有升降索的斜桁，用来悬挂各种旗帜。冠达邮轮公司的旗帜通常悬挂在左舷的斜桁上，而国旗和信号旗（如"引航员在船上"旗）则挂在右舷。一个斜桁（短斜桁）被放置在船尾的中心线上，悬挂着稍微向上倾斜的登记国的国旗。"玛丽女王2号"交船时，她注册在英国的南安普敦港，因此便悬挂了英联邦

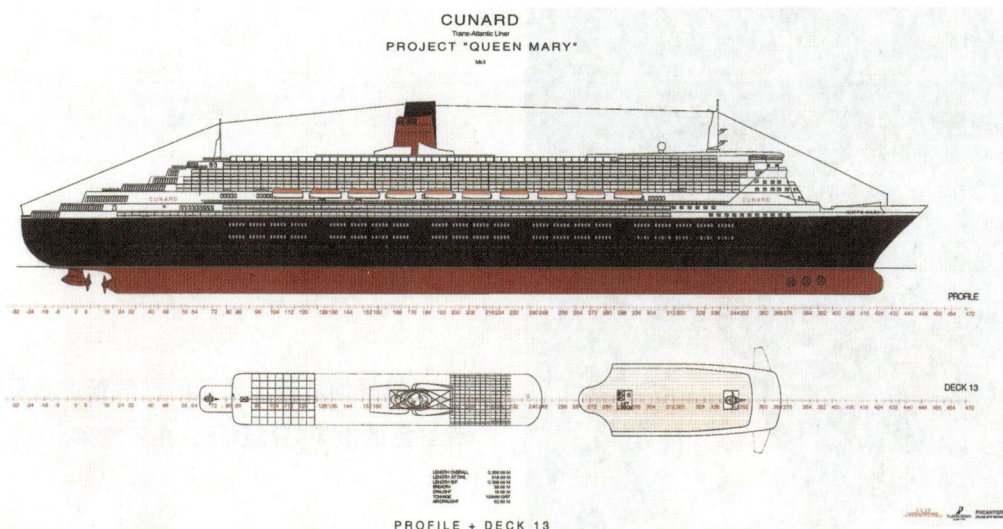

CUNARD
Trans-Atlantic Liner
PROJECT "QUEEN MARY"

PROFILE

DECK 13

PROFILE + DECK 13

初始概念设计图：13 甲板和侧视图

2 was delivered she was registered in the United Kingdom at the port of Southampton and therefore flew the red ensign. In December 2011 the ship was reflagged and registered in Bermuda at the port of Hamilton. As such Queen Mary 2 now flies the Bermuda version of the red ensign, which incorporates the coat of arms of Bermuda. The mast conceals a neat secret, a trick that I copied from Queen Elizabeth 2. With the ship at anchor or berthed quayside during daylight in a foreign port, it is usual to fly the Cunard house flag, the national courtesy flag and any other signal flags. In zero wind conditions the house flag and courtesy flag will lie limp and forlorn ... but the ensign will be proudly and defiantly fluttering as if in a moderate breeze - which in reality it will be, as an air-conditioning exhaust vents neatly and continuously beneath it!

红船旗。2011 年 12 月，这艘船在百慕大汉密尔顿港重新注册。正因为如此，"玛丽女王 2 号"现在悬挂的是百慕大的红船旗，它融合了百慕大的盾徽。桅杆上隐藏着一个巧妙的秘密，这是我从"伊丽莎白女王 2 号"那里学来的。由于船舶在白天抛锚或停泊在外国港口的码头，通常会悬挂冠达邮轮公司旗、到达港国旗和其他信号旗。在无风的情况下，公司旗和到达港国旗都会显得软弱无力，孤独无助……但旗帜应该骄傲地飘扬着，就像在和风中一样——事实上，它就是这样的，是因为有空调排气孔整齐而连续地排在它下面！

桅杆的后视图显示的排气管，总是确保红色的旗帜高高飘扬、永不垂落。

漂浮的温布尔登：位于 13 甲板右舷前部的网球场。

在炎热的晴天，赛船会酒吧是一个很受欢迎的地方，乘客可以在露天甲板上休息。

"赛船会"酒吧旁的漩涡泳池和喷水池可以为日光浴降温。

Below the mast, the forward 'A' staircase and three forward passenger lifts exit into a lobby with access to the open deck to port and starboard. The lifts are each rated for 21 persons while the stair is arranged in a single enclosure. This stair tower and associated lifts run from Deck 13 down to Deck 2. The open decks to the side of the deckhouse are equipped with sports courts - deck basketball and golf driving to port, and deck tennis to starboard.

Moving aft there is an open-air bar, called the Regatta Bar. This was intended to be used when the ship was cruising, rather than when sailing transatlantic as the weather conditions would invariably make the forward open decks untenable. A very shallow splash pool with two raised whirlpool baths is located aft of the bar to allow sunbathers to refresh and cool off. The deck is laid with teak throughout, with glass windscreens along the sides and at strategic locations across the deck.

Further aft a small deckhouse supports two large satellite communication domes,

在桅杆下面，艏部的梯道A和3个乘客电梯通向一个大厅，大厅通向左舷和右舷的露天甲板。电梯每台可容纳21人，而楼梯则被布置在独立的梯道环围内。这个梯道和旁边的电梯从13层一直延伸到2层。甲板室一侧的开敞甲板上设有运动场地——篮球场和高尔夫球场在左舷，网球场在右舷。

在船尾有一个露天酒吧，叫作"赛船会"酒吧。这个酒吧只在船作为邮轮巡游时使用，而不是在横渡大西洋时使用，因为天气原因，艏部开敞甲板总是让人难以站立。酒吧后部有一个非常浅的造波泳池，有两个抬高的漩涡泳池，可以带给日光浴者放松和凉爽的体验。整个甲板铺设了柚木，船舷两侧和甲板中间的关键位置有玻璃挡风墙。

and provides separated toilet facilities and the lift machinery room for two service lifts, which terminate at Deck 12 below. Beyond this deckhouse a large expanse of open deck is offered for games and sunbathing. Originally a large yellow capital 'H' and circles were painted on the deck indicating an area for helicopter operations. It was never intended that this would be a landing area for helicopters as an extensive firefighting and technical installation would have been required, along with specialist crew - instead, helicopters are meant to hover above the deck and not actually land.

Approaching midships the deck ends with sets of stairs leading down to Deck 12. An observation platform is located on the centreline, this being the lift machinery house for the six 'B'staircase passenger lifts. This area is a good vantage point to look aft towards the single funnel, which is 19.5 metres high. As with the mast, and as described in detail elsewhere, design inspiration

船尾是一个小型甲板室，里面布置了一个洗手间和两个通往12甲板的服务电梯的机房，顶部布置着两个大型卫星通信天线。在这个甲板室之外，有一大片开阔的露天甲板供人们活动和日光浴。最初，甲板上画着一个巨大的黄色大写字母"H"和圆圈，用来表示直升机作业区域。我们从来没打算把这里作为直升机的降落区，因为这需要大量的消防和技术设施，以及专业的机组人员，因此直升机只是在甲板上悬停，而不是降落。

这层甲板只延伸到船的中部，并在船中部连接了一组楼梯，直通12甲板。在船的中心线上有一个瞭望平台，这是梯道"B"的6个乘客电梯的机房。

主烟囱几乎位于船的中部，前面有一个平台，可以俯瞰周围。

烟囱和汽笛的细节。右舷的汽笛（向烟囱看去是在左手边的那个）来自最初的"玛丽女王号"（1936年）中间的烟囱的设计。

在甲板环境舒适性方面，允许部分空气通过穿孔挡风屏比采用实心挡风屏效果更好。

came from Queen Elizabeth 2. The funnel is in three parts: a tall black-painted structure supporting the exhaust pipes; a shorter red-painted cowling with two black stripes; and a wind scoop. The exaggerated red-painted wind scoop adds a dramatic aspect to the forward face of the funnel. In order to make the funnel appear taller than it actually is, the front section projects further forward and drops down to the deck below. The funnel combines the exhausts from the four diesel engines and two gas turbines, and numerous vents.

Two special Tyfon whistles are mounted near the top of the funnel. The starboard side whistle is an original from the Queen Mary of 1936 that was first attached to the second of the three funnels. The Swedish firm of Kockums manufactured the whistle in 1935 for the ship, along with a further two that remain set on the forward funnel. Originally activated by high-pressure steam direct from the liner's boilers, the whistles have a unique deep bass 'A' note that can be heard over ten miles away under favourable conditions. Since Queen Mary 2 doesn't generate high-pressure steam, the donated whistle required modification for sounding with 30-bar compressed air taken from the diesel starting air

从这个区域向船尾看，能够很清楚地看到19.5米高的烟囱。和桅杆一样，其设计灵感来自"伊丽莎白女王2号"。烟囱由三部分组成：一个高大的黑色支撑烟管的结构；较短的红色导流罩，其上面有两条黑色条纹；还有一个导风勺。夸张的红色导风勺使烟囱的前脸更加醒目。为了让烟囱看起来比实际尺寸更高，其前面的部分向前突出，并向下延伸到下层甲板。这个烟囱将4个柴油发动机和2个燃气轮机的排气口以及其他许多通风口结合在一起。

在烟囱顶部附近安装了两个特别的汽笛。其中右舷的汽笛是安装在1936年"玛丽女王号"上的原件，它被安装在3个烟囱中间的一个上。1935年，瑞典科肯姆公司为这艘船制造了汽笛，还有另外两个汽笛安装在前方的烟囱上。汽笛最初是由锅炉的高压蒸汽直接启动的，它有一种独特的低音"a"音，在适宜的条件下，10

system. It was agreed with the shipyard that this work, including a thorough reconditioning, should be undertaken by Kockums and that a replica should be manufactured so as to allow two whistles to be mounted. I was disappointed that although we would have the authentic 'voice' of the original Queen Mary on the new ship, we wouldn't enjoy the spectacle of steam erupting around the whistles as they sounded, as would have been the case on Queen Mary, which gave notice to all in the vicinity that it was that ship and not another that was sailing. I wanted to find a way of replicating this and the solution was to run a low-pressure steam line into the Tyfon horn and eject steam from it whenever the whistle was sounded. This I must add was much to the chagrin of my marine engineering colleagues!

The design and placement of all wind screens and side screens on this and the other decks was carefully optimised using wind-tunnel model tests. At first glance it may appear odd that the screens have gaps between the sections. This is deliberate and provides a degree of perforation that allows some of the wind flow to percolate through the screen to partially fill in the low-pressure area that develops behind such screens. Without this 'fill in' wind screens are invariably much less effective.

Deck 12 (staterooms 12.001-12.081)

The bridge is located at the forward end of the deck and at 45 metres wide spans the entire width of the ship. As with the mast and the funnel, I wanted the bridge to have some family resemblance with Queen Elizabeth 2 but there is a

英里以外的人都能听到它。由于"玛丽女王2号"不会产生高压蒸汽，因此原有的汽笛需要改装，使用由柴油机驱动的压缩空气机组以提供30巴[①]的压缩空气来发声。造船厂同意将包括彻底整修在内的所有工作交由科肯姆公司来做，并应再制造一个汽笛复制品，以安装两支汽笛。尽管我们能在新船上听到原版"玛丽女王号"的声音，但我还是有点失望，因为无法再欣赏到汽笛吹响时蒸汽在汽笛周围喷涌的景象了，而这可以提醒周围的船，这是伟大的"玛丽女王号"启航了，而非是别的什么小杂船。为了再现这一情景，我提议将一条低压蒸汽管线引入汽笛，并在鸣笛时喷出蒸汽，但可悲的是这么好的方案居然被我的工程师同行给否定了。

利用风洞模型试验，该甲板和其他甲板上所有挡风屏和玻璃挡风幕墙的设计和布置得到了详细的优化。乍一看，挡风屏在高度中部形成空隙似乎很奇怪。但这样设计是经过深思熟虑的，它提供了一定程度的空隙从而允许一些风流通过空隙渗透并填充在这些空隙后方形成的低压区域。如果没有这种"填充"，挡风屏的效果是会差很多的。

① 1巴=10⁵帕

fundamental difference between the two: Queen Elizabeth 2 has open bridge wings, while Queen Mary 2's bridge is fully enclosed. Although some navigating officers prefer open bridge wings so that they can 'feel' the prevailing weather conditions - especially when manoeuvring the ship - the preponderance of delicate electronic navigation equipment on modern ships really does require an enclosed environment. Queen Mary 2 was delivered with a bridge wing overhang of 2 metres on each side beyond the waterline beam, but in November 2006 this was extended to 4 metres each side to improve visibility further. The bridge is laid out with a number of equipment consoles that are set back from the bridge windows.

The central steering console provides access to the propulsion and manoeuvring controls, with numerous dials and displays conveying the status of the various systems. Most of the equipment is replicated within two bridge wing consoles, one each to port and starboard, where command is transferred as the ship manoeuvres in close quarters and finally docks. Glass panels are set into the floor of each bridge wing so that the ship's relative position to the quayside can be clearly seen. Originally, Queen Mary 2 was built with one such panel on each side, but with the extended bridge wings she is unique in now having two on each side. Some visitors to the bridge are wary of standing on the glass panels but the thickness has been carefully chosen to enable them to be used as part of the normal flooring. Unlike on most modern cruise ships, Queen Mary 2's bridge windows are of considerably smaller section in deference to transatlantic

12甲板（12.001~12.081 客舱）

桥楼位于甲板的前端，其横跨船身宽度达到了 45 米。就像桅杆和烟囱一样，我希望桥楼与"伊丽莎白女王 2 号"也有一些相似之处，但两者之间有一个根本的区别："伊丽莎白女王 2 号"有开敞的桥楼侧翼，而"玛丽女王 2 号"的桥楼是完全封闭的。尽管一些海员喜欢开敞的桥楼，以便"感觉"当时的天气状况，特别是在操纵船只时。但布置在现代船只上的高精度电子导航设备却是需要一个封闭的环境。"玛丽女王 2 号"水线上两侧各伸出两米长的桥翼，但在 2006 年 11 月，为了进一步提高能见度，这艘船的桥翼延长至每侧 4 米。桥楼布置有许多设备控制台，这些设备控制台布置在桥楼窗户后面。

中央驾驶控制台用于控制推进和转向，其上面带有许多用于传达各系统状态的表盘和显示器。大多数设备都设有两套，位于两个舰桥侧翼控制台内，左舷一个，右舷一个，以便船舶靠港时操作的。桥翼的地板都装有玻璃板，这样就可以清楚地看到船相对于码头的位置。最初，"玛丽女王 2 号"每边都只有一个这样的玻璃镶板，但是由于桥楼加长，现在每边都做了两个这样的镶板。一些参观者站在玻

crossings and possible wave impact loadings.

The aft bulkhead of the bridge incorporates a glass window, which allows passengers toobserve the workings of the bridge at selected times from a viewing gallery. To port a small office is arranged as the ship's safety centre. From here all the safety systems can be monitored and controlled. The systems include fire detection and suppression, ventilation systems, fire doors, watertight ship side doors (known as 'shell' doors), pumping and ballast. A bespoke computerised system monitors all these functions and enables the ship operators to instantly react to any situation that may arise.

On the starboard side a chartroom is arranged with space for route planning and the storage of charts. The usefulness of this facility has diminished somewhat in recent years with the steady progression away from paper charts and the increasing reliance on computerisation and electronic charts.

The bridge equipment has been constantly upgraded since the ship's entry into service and is described in chapter 8.

The master's cabin is located adjacent to the bridge on the starboard side, while the chief engineer's cabin is in

璃板上时会很紧张，但实际上我们已经仔细地计算了玻璃板的厚度，完全可将它们作为普通地板来使用。与大多数现代邮轮相比，"玛丽女王2号"的桥楼窗户的透光面积要小得多，这是为适应跨大西洋航行中可能受到的波浪冲击载荷。

桥楼的后舱壁上装有玻璃窗，允许乘客在选定的时间从观光廊参观桥楼内的工作。桥楼左舷处的一个小房间是安全中心。从这里可对所有的安全系统进行监视和控制。安全中心包括火灾探测和灭火系统、通风系统、防火门、船侧水密门（称为"舷"）、泵和压载水系统。定制化的计算机系统实时监控所有这些系统的功能，并使得船舶驾驶员能够对可能出现的任何情况立即做出反应。

在右舷有一间航海室，该室用于规划航线和储存海图。近年来，随着纸质海图的使用频率越来越低，以及计算机和电子海图的使用频率越来越

桥楼是"玛丽女王2号"的神经中枢，用于指挥船只。（冠达邮轮提供）

每个延伸的桥楼侧翼上都设有操纵控制台，用于操纵进出港口。图中显示的是左舷。

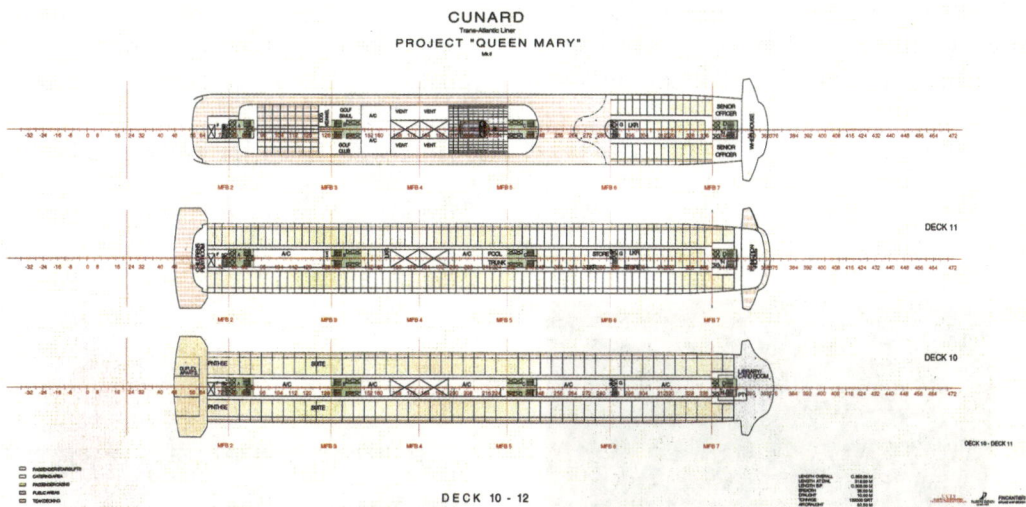

甲板 10–12 原始概念图

the same location on the port side. These cabins have a bedroom section complete with an en-suite bathroom, a sitting area and a working area. They are the largest crew cabins on the ship but have been criticised for not having sufficient space for entertaining and for not having a separate office area that can be made private from the rest of the cabin.

The forward 'A' passenger staircase, lobby and lifts are located inboard of the senior officer cabins. Moving aft, passenger staterooms 12.001 to 12.081 occupy the majority of the space. It should be noted here that Cunard call their passenger accommodations 'staterooms', rather than 'cabins' as part of their marketing differentiation. The outboard cabins are of the standard balcony type with glass bulwark, offering two berths, several being fitted with connecting doors for families and friends, while the inboard inside cabins have Pullman-style upper berths fitted. Towards the end of the cabin run, the passenger 'B' stair tower, lobby and six passenger lifts is accessed, with each lift being rated for 12 persons.

高，这种设施的用途越来越少。

自船舶投入使用以来，桥楼内的设备不断升级，详细情况将在第八章中加以描述。

船长室在右舷，与桥楼相邻，而轮机长室在左舷的相同位置。这些客舱有卧室、浴室、起居区和工作区。它们是船上最大的船员舱，但是因为没有足够的娱乐空间和单独的办公区域而备受诟病。

前方梯道"A"、门厅和电梯位于高级工作人员舱室的内侧。再往后，客舱12.001号至12.081号占据了大部分空间。应该注意到，冠达邮轮公司称他们的客房为"包房"，而不是"客舱"，这是他们差异化市场运营的一部分。外侧为标准阳台房，有玻璃栏杆，提供两个铺位，有几间房还为家人和朋友提供了来往才装设的家庭房联通门，而内舱装有下拉翻床。快到客舱房末端为乘客使用的梯道"B"、门厅和六部乘客电梯，每部电梯定员为12人。

梯道"A"和电梯门厅。这是贯穿甲板的最重要的乘客通道。

泳池外的露天游步长廊

Moving aft, the passenger cabin corridors open out into the Pavilion Lido. This area has a swimming pool, two whirlpool baths, a bar area and table tennis games area, and is covered with a sliding glass roof that can be deployed when the weather is inclement. The deck surface is composition and a small entertainment bandstand is provided. Behind the pool, changing rooms are arranged as well as two computerized golf simulators where participants can 'Play' at many major world golf courses.

Glass doors from the Pavilion lead out on to open promenades that are shielded with full-height windscreens. Moving aft along the promenades and looking up, the funnel dominates

走向艉部，客舱走廊直接通向露天泳池区，该区域包括一个泳池，两个漩涡泳池，一个吧台区以及乒乓竞赛区，浴场顶部采用滑移式玻璃顶结构，可以在天气不佳时展开。甲板表面为树脂材料，这里还有一个小型的看台。泳池后方设有更衣室，以及两套高尔夫模拟赛场区，玩家们在此可以模拟体验全球的一些著名高尔夫球场。

从浴场的玻璃门可以通往导风穴掩映下的开放式游步长廊。当漫步至长廊尾部向上仰望时，耸立云霄的烟囱清晰可见。之后是甲板室，其上的船名

the skyline, while beyond lies a large deckhouse with ship's name, 'Queen Mary 2', splet out on each side in large stainless steel letters with dark Lexan faces. These names extend for 22 meters and are 2.4 meters high.

The name is illuminated at night by an extensive fibre-optic system. We specified the type of installation based on our experience with similar names that were fitted to Statendam Class of Holland America line ships built by Fincantieri in Italy. However, the French shipyard lacked any experience with such an installation and we were concerned that we might be presented with an inferior representation.

是采用黑色的不锈钢字母拼出"Queen Mary 2"，船名长 22 米，高 2.4 米。

一套大规模光纤系统会在夜色下点亮船名。根据荷美邮轮在意大利芬坎蒂尼船厂建造史特丹级邮轮的经验，我们决定也采用这套系统。但考虑到法国船厂缺乏类似项目经验，我们担心实物效果可能难达预期。因此我们建议船厂制作一个字母的样品来演示。与此同时我们也要求我方的照明顾问——科尔切斯特国际项目公司，为我们准备一个方案和样品。船厂的

"玛丽女王2号"的船名，采用了前所未有的光纤照明。这是同船厂紧密协商的成果。

We therefore requested the shipyard to prepare a mock-up of one letter that would be displayed for our consideration. At the same time we asked our lighting consultants, Project international of Colchester, to propose a system and prepare a mock-up. The shipyard arranged for the demonstration test to take place early one moring while it was still dark at the yard, with the mock-up letter fixed on one of the upper decks of the half completed ship. We were bussed out to a suitable vantage point to observe the test and the fire optics were switched on. Pathetical! The illumination was so feeble that the letter was barely distinguishable from the surrounding temporary deck lights ranged on board.

Unperturbed, the shipyard announced that they had a second mock-up from an alternative contractor alongside the first that they would switch on for us to review. Although somewhat brighter, the second letter was not really a significant improvement over the first. Anticipating that we would be confronted with such a situation, we arranged for our mock-up to be placed in our office at a position that overlooked the shipbuilding dry dock where we were standing for the shipyard demonstration. We asked the shipyard representatives to turn around towards our office and at a given signal we had 'Our' letter turned on. Wow! What a difference! I explained that as Queen Mary 2 was to be the greatest passenger ship in the world, neither Gunard nor the shipyard would wish the ship's name to be outshone by any other ship that was berthed nearby and that we simply had to have the

演示安排在一个漆黑的清晨,演示样品被安装在处于半完工状态的上层甲板上。当我们乘车到达合适观察点后,演示开始了。不过太可怜了,灯光太弱了,以致这几个字母根本无法从周围的临时照明中区分出来。

泰然自若地,船厂表示他们有来自另外一个供货商的第二预案,并且也向我们做了演示。虽然其亮度有所增加,然而对比第一个方案,并没有足够的改善。我们把自己准备的样品布置在办公室内俯瞰船坞的位置,然后邀请船厂代表们转向我们办公室方向后,打开了照明。哇!差别太大了!"玛丽女王2号"即将成为世界上最伟大的客轮,不论冠达邮轮公司或船厂都不会希望她的名字在将来被她身旁的其他船掩盖,这就是我们需要更好的系统的理由。我创造性地提出一个口号,"我们希望可以在太空中看见她的名字",在所有参与者中间广为流传。船厂评估了我们倾向的系统和他们推荐的系统之间的差价,大约是 500 000 美元。

关于这项费用的变更讨论会议持续了数周,我意识到嘉年华管理层不会轻易接受,我们必须精心策划一个解决方案。往常我们的月度例会都在船厂召开,但偶尔船厂团队也会到伦敦参加会议,不过位于泰晤士河南岸

better system. I coined the phrase that, 'we wanted to see the ship's name from space', which was since entered popular folklore with those who were associated with the building of the ship. The shipyard evaluated the cost difference between our preferred system and their proposal and it was of the order of US dollar 500,000.

Discussions over this cost dragged on for several weeks and I was conscious that Carnival's management would not accept it, so a more elaborate solution had to be found to fund the fibre-optic system. It was usual for our monthly shipyard meetings to take place in the shipyard itself, but on a few occasions the French team joined us in London, For these meetings we had to hire rooms, as our offices in the Shad Thames area of London on the south bank of the River Thames near Tower Bridge did not have sufficient space. The illuminated sign issue was due to be finalized during one of the rare London meetings and we hired the Admiral's cabin on the preserved British Second World War cruiser HMS Belfast as our venue.

The French contingent were due to stay with us over a three-day period and I decided to have a party at my house at Grove park some 30 minutes' train ride from London Bridge station not far from HMS Belfast, I had pre-prepared the food, a selection of curries and tagines, which was kept ready for our arrival in several slow cookers. Our French friends were very appreciative and remarked that they had not been entertained like this by the owners' team before. With copious amounts of British beer and Scotch whisky adding to the merriment, we all

边的塔桥附近的办公室空间有限，我们不得不为这些会议租用场所。鉴于船名照明的事宜需要在一次为数不多的伦敦会议上定稿，我们租用了英国政府保留的二战巡洋舰"贝尔法斯特号"上的舰队司令房间作为会议室。

因为法国团队需要和我们共处约3天，我决定在家中举办一场家庭宴会，地址位于树林公园，距离"贝尔法斯特"号附近伦敦桥车站大约有30分钟火车路程。我事先为我们几位即将姗姗来迟的友人准备好了精心挑选的咖喱和陶锅。这让法国朋友们十分感激，他们表示从未获得过船东们的如此款待。在大量英国啤酒和苏格兰威士忌的助兴下，我们共度了一段愉快时光。次日上午在"贝尔法斯特号"上双方再次会面时，法国朋友们看起来略有疲惫，不过奇怪的是，团队和我都感觉良好。我们继续商讨了升级照明如何付款这一棘手问题，然而令人意外的是谈判进行得非常顺利，我们达成了一致共识，即双方共同努力，通过削减其他开支来补充此项费用。"玛丽女王2号"收获到了有史以来最耀眼（也是最大）的船名照明系统。可想而知昨晚的宴会为增进双方的友好关系做出了多大贡献。

光纤船名所在的甲板室是燃气轮

had a marvelous time. The following morning we met again on HMS Belfast and while our Gallic friends looked rather the worse for wear, strangely my team and I felt fine. We then had to discuss the thorny issue of how we were to pay for the upgraded illuminated sign. Miraculously negotiations were much simplified and we agreed mutual cooperation in working together to find equivalent savings elsewhere. In consequence, Queen Mary 2 received the brightest (and Largest) illuminated name in maritime history. How the previous night's party had contributed to the entente cordiale is open to conjecture!

The deckhouse on which the fibre-optic names attached is the gas turbine engine room. Two general electric LM2500+ gas turbines are installed within acoustic hoods, each connected to an attendant electrical generator. Combustion air for the turbines is drawing from behind the large baffles at the base of each side of the funnel. An engineers' lift connects the gas turbine engine room with Deck 2 where Engine Control Room (ECR) and engineering offices are located.

Moving past the turbine deckhouse there is a large expanse of open deck. A passenger entrance is set into the middle of the deckhouse, which leads down to the passenger 'C' staircase and lifts. The aft slightly curved bulkhead and of the deckhouse is arranged so that the area can be used as an open-air cinema with projection from across the deck from the aftermost deckhouse. During the model tests to optimize the funnel it was found that this section of deck was particularly

机舱。两台安装在隔音罩内的通用电气LM2500+燃气轮机各自连接到一台辅助发电机上。燃气轮机的进气口位于烟囱底部挡风板后侧。一部轮机员电梯直接连接着燃气轮机舱和2甲板，即集控室与轮机员办公室所在的甲板。

经过甲板室，是一片开阔甲板区。中间位置是一个乘客入口，通向乘客梯道"C"和电梯。艉部舱壁和甲板室都采用了略微弯曲的设计，以便该区域可被用作露天电影院，投影仪分别

安装在燃气轮机舱顶部的这套不起眼的栏杆神奇地改变了周围气体流向，阻止烟气向艉部甲板蔓延。

prone to contamination from smuts. The problem was that the bulk of the funnel produced a partial vacuum behind it under certain wind conditions that literally sucked the smoke plume down once it had emerged from the top of the funnel. Although raising the height of the funnel worked admirably, it was not an option as we wouldn't be able to sail under the Verrazano Bridge at the entrance to New York Harbour. Raising the wind scoop further didn't show any advantage so we had to think again. We decided we had to modify the air flow at the aft end of the deckhouse top. We tested the addition of some exaggerated deck-edge railings using large diameter pipes. These produced a remarkable effect and altered the air flow sufficiently to alleviate the problem.

The aftermost deckhouse contains the top lobby of the aft passenger stair tower 'D' and its attendant three 21-person lifts with two exits to the open deck. On the port side, opening out on to the large open deck, is a deck pantry that provides limited food service. This is called the boardwalks café. The starboard side of the deckhouse provides space for a unique shipboard facility – the kennels. As with Queen Elizabeth 2 previously, Queen Mary 2 is fitted with a comprehensive kennel facility, with the open deck at the side used as a dog-walking area. When the design of the ship was under consideration, Cunard's new executives from Carnival doubted the efficiency of providing a kenneling service. Cunard's old hands argued that there were a number of wealthy passengers who regularly travelled transatlantic only because they were able to bring their dogs.

安装在甲板对面最后的甲板室上。在优化烟囱的模型试验中我们发现，本层甲板易受烟气的污染。因为烟囱主体结构在一定风力作用下会在后方形成部分负压区，从而把烟囱排出的尾气反吸下来。提升烟囱高度的效果虽然不错，但由于本客轮将会航行通过纽约港入口处的韦拉扎诺大桥，这个方案显然不可行。进一步抬升导风穴的试验结果显示毫无益处，因而我们不得不另寻他法。我们试验了附加大直径管甲板栏杆的方法。试验获得令人意外的结果，这个方案充分地改变了气体流向，有效地解决了这个问题。

甲板室的末端是乘客"D"梯道顶部过渡区，包括荷载 21 人的电梯和两个通向露天甲板的出口。在左舷位置，进入一片开放式的露天甲板，是一个提供限类食品服务的甲板餐饮区，也称其为休闲咖啡馆。甲板房右舷区域，是一项特色船上空间——宠物区。和之前的"伊丽莎白女王 2 号"一样，"玛丽女王 2 号"也提供有综合性宠物设施和一个位于露天甲板侧的遛狗区。在设计筹划阶段，来自嘉年华集团的冠达邮轮公司的经理们都质疑提供宠物服务的效用。不过冠达的老手们都坚称有很多富人之所以经常选择跨大西洋的旅行，就是因为他们可以

It was decided to retain the service and 12 deluxe kennels are available for dogs and other pets. Space is normally booked over a year in advance and consideration has been given to increasing the size of facility.

A large air-conditioning room is located at the aft end of the deckhouse. The structure supports two large stylized uptakes and a final satellite communications dome. These are the main galley exhausts from Deck 2 and the exhausts from the ship's incinerating plant down on deck 1. The roof of the deckhouse is designated a crew area. During the development of the design at one of the meeting with senior Carnival management, it was suggested, maybe directed, that the deck should revert to passenger user as an observation deck. When challenged as to where the crew could relax, it was volunteered that they could use forecastle, ahead of the breakwater. This was obviously a complete nonsense as with a flush deck, and with the speed of ship, there would be a real danger of anybody on the deck being simply blown overboard. I certainly let my feelings be known and stated that this was a 'bloody stupid idea' in consequence, the notation was dropped, but I had certainly sailed very close to the wind.

The very aft end of deck 12 looks down on to the tiered decks at the back of the ship to the ensign staff at the very stern.

带上宠物狗。这项服务最终得以保留，包括 12 套寄养狗或者其他宠物的豪华狗舍。由于这项服务提前一年就被预定一空，大家已经开始考虑宠物设施的扩建计划了。

甲板室末端位置坐落着一个巨大的空调机房，两个风格特征明显的烟囱和卫星天线球安装在其上方。这些是 2 甲板主厨房和 1 甲板底部焚烧炉间的排气管。甲板房的顶部区域是船员专用区。在设计过程中，一次同嘉年华高层经理的会议中这个区域被建议取消——或者说是被要求改为乘客游览甲板。当被反问船员们去哪儿休息时，他们提出可以使用防浪区前部的艏楼甲板。这显然是胡说八道，航行时待在光滑的甲板上任何人都有被吹出船外的风险。我明确地表达了我的意见，而且坚持认为这是一个"冷血且愚蠢的想法"。最后，这个方案被否决了，不过我也确实冒了很大的风险。

在 12 甲板最末端可以俯瞰到船尾层叠的甲板和艉部旗杆。

休闲咖啡馆是一个露天活动区，在天气允许情况下可提供快餐服务。

"玛丽女王2号"继承冠达传统，提供了跨大西洋航行旅途中的宠物服务，图示为宠物甲板溜狗道。

主厨房和两台焚烧炉的尾气通过两个艉部的烟囱排出。

船尾甲板沿艉部方向布置得错落有致。这种兼顾重量分布考虑的美学设计产生了令人愉悦的效果,让乘客们在远洋航行时得以放松压力。

Deck 11(staterooms 11.001-11.153)

The forward end of Deck 11 is arranged as a passenger observation deck. The intention was to faithfully mimic the forward observation area on board Queen Elizabeth 2. The deck provides commanding views forward across the breakwater, and side extensions allow good views aft – something not possible on Queen Elizabeth 2. Accessibility is restricted to calm wind conditions. The deck is sheathed in teak-effect composition, which is brown in colour with fake black caulking lines marked on

11甲板(11.001~11.153客舱)

乘客观景平台布置在11甲板首部的尽头,其目的是模仿"伊丽莎白女王2号"船上的艏部观景区。在露天平台上可以居高临下地俯瞰到艏部的防浪板,同时两侧延伸的挑台也提供了船尾方向上的良好视野——这在"伊丽莎白女王2号"上是做不到的。这个区域只有在风平浪静的情况下乘客才能够进入。露天平台被带有柚木效果的材料覆盖着,在棕色背景上刻印

it to represent a teak deck. Access to the deck is arranged through two doors that are shielded by windscreens and which enter into passageways that connect with the passenger cabin corridors on the deck. Access is also arranged to two scenic lifts, one each to port and starboard, that run from this deck down to Deck 7. These lifts are glass fronted and run inside protective tubes tucked in behind the forward part of the superstructure. The lifts were added to provide easy local connection between all the public spaces laid one above the other in the forward superstructure face.

The Atlantic Room is a semi-circular room that looks out on to the

黑色条纹来伪装成拼缝，以此来实现柚木甲板的效果。露天平台入口是两扇通向乘客住舱走廊的由挡风屏保护的门。此外，在左舷、右舷分别设有一部观光电梯，从本层可运行最低至 7 甲板。这些电梯正面是玻璃的，并运行在坐落于艏部上层建筑后方的保护围井之中。增设电梯是为了方便连接艏部上层建筑中所有叠层式的公共空间。

大西洋厅是一个半圆形的房间，可以看到整个观景台，并作为"玛丽女王 2 号"的主卡牌室。卡牌游戏，特

左舷观景平台

observation deck and is used as Queen Mary 2's principal card room. Card games, particularly bridge, are played here most of the day, although the area is sometimes utilised for private parties and gatherings when not in use for cards. On longer sea journeys, especially the annual world voyage, the Atlantic Room is used as a concierge and meeting room for those guests participating in the complete voyage.

Behind the Atlantic Room, several officer cabins are located, while port and starboard passenger corridors extend the full length of the superstructure. Although these corridors are not the longest on the ship - this was attributed to those within

别是桥牌，大部分时间都在这里进行，不过在不进行卡牌游戏的情况下，这个区域有时会被用于私人聚会。在较长的海上旅行中，特别是每年的环球航行中，大西洋厅则作为参加整个旅程客人的观礼厅和会议室。

在大西洋厅后面，是几个高级船员的房间，而左舷和右舷的乘客走廊贯穿了整个上建区域。尽管这些走廊并不是船上最长的，但由于它们在船体内部，使得它们看起来遥无边际。在以前的"玛丽女王号"上，与其同时期

走廊向舱室甲板的远处延伸。

观景平台提供了俯瞰全船的景观。

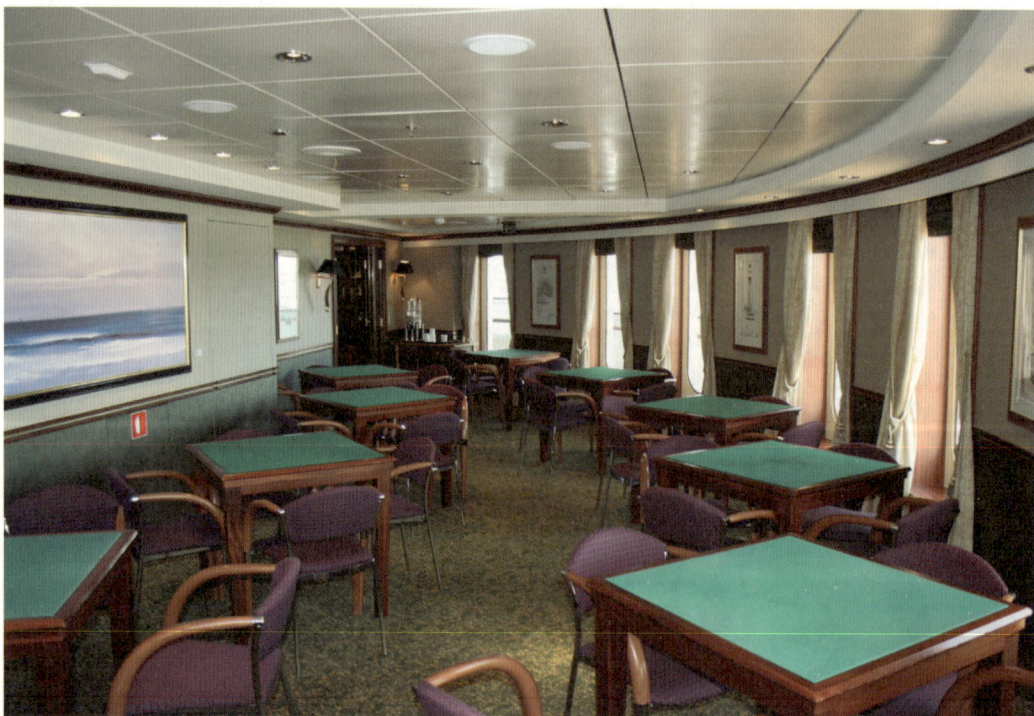

大西洋厅作为进行桥牌和其他流行的卡牌游戏的主卡牌室。

the hull itself - they seem to stretch into infinity. On the old Queen Mary, in common with most ships of the period, deck would be built with an Incline towards the bow and stem, so-called 'sheer'. This created the illusion that the corridors extended into a distant vanishing point, and it was often joked that although Queen Mary 2's corridors were perfectly flat, they appeared very similar to those on the original ship by virtue of the fact that they really did point to Infinity! Staterooms 11.001 to 11.153 are arranged on the deck, with a disposition of insides and standard balcony with glass bulwark staterooms and four Queens Grill suites.

Air-conditioning rooms are located inboard and at the end of the deck. At the stern a section of deck is arranged with side screens and excellent views aft over the back of the ship. This deck is nominated for the exclusive use of Queens Grill and Princess Grill passengers and includes a single raised whirlpool bath on the centreline. The deck edge protrudes slightly beyond the deckhouse below to afford some privacy to passengers occupying the duplex suites when using their balconies.

Two very long access staircases are provided, linking this deck with Deck 8. The stairs are enclosed within 'caverns' isolating them from the adjacent accommodation, and for safety they have an intermediate landing. The six 12-person 'C' lifts terminate on Deck 9 with their machinery room being located within the gas-turbine house.

的大多数船一样，甲板将沿艏艉方向倾斜，形成所谓的"脊弧"。这就造成了这样一种错觉：走廊消失在远处的尽头。人们经常开玩笑道，虽然"玛丽女王2号"的走廊非常平坦，但它们看起来确实如原来船上的走廊一般一望无垠！客舱11.001~11.153位于本层甲板，设有内舱房、配有玻璃舷窗的标准阳台房和4间"女王"餐厅对应的套房。

空调间位于本层内部的中间区域。在本层艉部，一部分区域放置了玻璃幕墙，并且有很好的视野可以观看到船的后侧。这层专供"女王"餐厅和"公主"餐厅对应舱房的乘客使用，并包括 个在中线上突出甲板的漩涡泳池。甲板边缘稍微突出，超出了下层甲板的舱室边缘，从而为下层复式套房的阳台提供了一些隐私遮蔽。

通过两个非常长的楼梯，连接本层甲板与8甲板。楼梯被封闭在一个"洞穴"内，将他们与相邻的住舱隔离开来，为安全起见，长楼梯设置了中间平台。6部载荷12人的"C"电梯组最远可达9甲板，电梯机房位于燃气轮机舱内。

“女王”餐厅和“公主”餐厅对应舱房的活动区设置了一个专属的日光浴平台。

长通道楼梯穿过复式住舱与下层甲板相连。

在11甲板上的"C"电梯大厅

Deck 10(staterooms 10.001-10.133)

This deck is utilised for stateroom accommodation (10.001 to 10.133) from bow to stern. Most of the ship's Princess Grill suites are located along its length, but the inventory includes inside staterooms, penthouse suites, Queens Grill suites, Royal suites and the upper levels of the duplex apartments. The Royal suites, four large sets of rooms at the forward end of the superstructure, are named Queen Anne, Queen Victoria, Queen Mary and Queen Elizabeth. The latter two suites have commanding views forward, to the

10甲板（10.001~10.133客舱）

该甲板从船头到船尾都用于客舱住宿（10.001~10.133）。船上的"公主"餐厅对应的套房大多位于本层，但也包括内舱房、顶楼套房、"女王"餐厅对应的套房、皇家套房和复式套房的上层。4套皇家套房位于上层建筑的最前端，分别命名为"安妮女王""维多利亚女王""玛丽女王"和"伊丽莎白女王"。后两间套房（"玛丽女王"和"伊丽莎白女王"）向艏部、舷侧

side and to the rear, and incorporate a large private balcony. These spectacular apartments have two sitting/dining areas, a master bedroom with full en-suite facilities including whirlpool bath, wardrobe dressing room and a second bathroom and shower. A novel feature means the occupants of these suites can summon the scenic lifts to stop at this level to allow private embarkation; similarly the room keys can be used to direct the lifts to halt for disembarkation into the suites.

All very good - but sometimes things can go wrong. While sailing on one transatlantic crossing with a party of friends I was informed that the Queen Elizabeth suite had been paid for but the occupants had failed to turn up. I was invited to upgrade from my Britannia balcony cabin to the suite in recognition for having designed the ship. Each evening my friends would join me in the suite for pre-dinner drinks and on one occasion I suggested that we should try the lift. I duly summoned it using my cabin key and as the lift door opened some passengers who were already in the lift tried to exit into the cabin. With great difficulty I explained that this was not a regular stop and that the passengers would not be able to exit. My party then squeezed into the lift and we pressed the button to close the door and resume the descent but nothing happened. Vainly we tried sending the lift both up and down, but to no avail. It had become stuck at the suite level and would not budge. There was nothing for it but for us all to disembark the lift through the suite, including the lift's original occupants who were very perplexed by the whole episode.

（一侧）和艉部都有居高临下的视角，并设有一个私人的大阳台。这些奢华的套间有两个用餐区，一个主卧室配有全套双人起居设施，包括漩涡浴缸、更衣室、第二盥洗室和淋浴。这些套房还带有一个新颖的功能，即居住者可以召唤观光电梯停在这层，并允许私人乘坐；同样，房间钥匙也可以用来指挥电梯直达套房所在的楼层。

一切都很不错——但有时也可能会出问题。在我与一群朋友进行跨大西洋旅行时，我被告知，"伊丽莎白女王"套房的居住者虽然已经付款但并没有登船。我被邀请从"布列塔尼亚"阳台房升级到套房，以表彰我对本船的设计做出的贡献。每天晚上我和我的朋友们都会在套房里享用餐前饮料，有一次我建议试试电梯。我用我的房卡召唤了它，当电梯门打开时，一些乘客已经在电梯里并试图走下电梯进入我们的房间。我十分尴尬地解释说，这不是一个常规的停靠，他们不可以在此处下电梯。随后，我和我的小伙伴们挤进了电梯，按下按钮关上电梯门，让电梯继续下降，但电梯并没有反应。我们徒劳地尝试控制电梯上升或下降，但电梯仍没有反应。它已经卡在了套房这一层，动不了了。我们所有人除了从套房这层下电梯以外，别无他法。

The Queen Anne and Queen Victoria suites only face forward and in consequence are not fitted with a private balcony. Nonetheless, they have commanding views across the bow. In fact the original plan for the ship didn't include the four Royal suites at all. The proposal was to incorporate a lounge to enable business people access to all the latest technology to enable them to keep their businesses running remotely. The idea for the lounge came from a schoolfriend who worked for a major telecommunications company. Unbeknown to me the company had a large facility that conducted research into a wide range of technologies well beyond mere telecommunications. Many consumer products started development there, the company licensing the technology to other manufacturers. It was suggested that there could be a role for such a group to operate the business lounge, showcasing new technologies under development and using passengers to evaluate the usefulness of some of the equipment. After a series of meetings a preliminary agreement was reached and all looked set for the provision of a unique cutting-edge space on board the ship. Sadly, it was not to be as the company sold off the relevant division before the final agreement was signed and the remaining sectors of the business didn't really know what to do with this idea so the whole project was dropped. Faced with a now empty space, it was decided to use it for the installation of the four forward Royal suites.

当然也包括那些之前就在电梯里面的人，他们在整个小插曲中一直都表现得不知所措。

"安妮女王"套房和"维多利亚女王"套房仅朝向艉部，因此没有配置私人阳台。尽管如此，他们享有船首方向居高临下的视野。事实上，本船最初的规划根本不包括这4个皇家套房，而是设立一个休息室，使商人们在其中能够通过最新技术远程控制企业的运营。休息室的想法来自我的一位在一家大型电信公司工作的同学。我所不知道的是，这家公司有一个大型设施，可以对各种技术进行广泛地研究，并不局限于通信技术。许多技术都是在那家公司进行开发，公司然后再将技术授权给其他生产厂家。有人建议，可以聘请这个小组来运营商务休息室，展示他们发展的最新技术，并证明其产品的有效性。经过一系列会议，我们达成了初步协议，并且都期待着这块拥有着前沿科技的区域能正式装备上船。遗憾的是，该项目并未达成，因为这家公司在最终协议签署前就被出售给了相关部门，而其他部门也不知道该如何将项目进行下去，所以整个项目都被放弃了。我们决定利用这个空间来构建四个艉部的皇家套房。

Deck 9 (staterooms 9.001-9.082)

The layout of this deck is very similar to that of Deck 10 although instead of Princess suites, the majority of staterooms are larger Queens suites. There was considerable debate as to whether these higher-priced staterooms should be located on this deck or elsewhere in the superstructure. It wasn't appropriate to site them on Deck 8 as the view from their balconies would have been blocked by the lifeboats and tenders, and there wasn't sufficient room to accommodate the numbers that we required on Deck 12, so the choice was between Decks 11 10 and 9. In the end Deck 9 was chosen as it was deemed more convenient for the Queens Grill restaurant and bar on Deck 7.

In place of the four Royal suites forward, an observation lounge is provided. The Commodore Club is a beautiful room with slightly raised seating areas to port and starboard and a large bar. As a backdrop the largest ship model on board Queen Mary 2 is displayed - this model is highly detailed and even includes passenger figures and was made by Dutch modelmaker Henk Brandwijk.

Discrete windows are fitted forward, aft and at the sides rather than continuous glazing, again in deference to the North Atlantic. On ships, forward-facing windows are usually fitted either externally or internally with fixtures to install 'deadlights'. These are steel covers to close off the window apertures in bad weather to mitigate any breakages and flooding in severe conditions. While the fixtures are somewhat ugly and detract from the

9甲板（9.001~9.082客舱）

这个甲板的布局与10号甲板非常相似，大多数客舱使用了更大的"女王"套房，而不是"公主"套房。对于这些价格较高的客舱是否应该位于这层甲板上还是上层建筑的其他地方，存在着相当大的争议。将它们放在8甲板上是不合适的，因为从阳台上看到的景色会被救生艇和标志挡住，而且没有足够的空间容纳我们在12甲板上需要的舱室数量，所以是在11、10和9甲板之间选择。最后选择了9甲板，因为它可以更方便地去往位于7甲板的"女王"餐厅和酒吧。

在原来10甲板4个皇家套房的位置，布置了一个观景休息室即"准将"俱乐部，它是一个漂亮的房间，在左舷和右舷有略微升高的座位区和一个大酒吧。作为背景，"玛丽女王2号"上最大的船舶模型在这里展示——这个模型非常详细，甚至包括乘客的模型，它是由荷兰模型制造商Henk Brandwijk制造的。

间断而不连续的玻璃窗安装在前面、后部和侧面，这也是为了适应北大西洋恶劣的环境。在船上，前置窗户通常安装外部或内部的风暴盖。这些钢盖，可以在恶劣天气时遮蔽窗户的开口，以减少航行时的任何破损和

decor, the covers - or shutters as they are known - are heavy and can be difficult to install correctly. There is also the problem of storage when they are not in use. We opened a discussion with the UK Maritime Coastguard Agency to determine whether they would accept a compromise agreement based upon providing an 'equivalent degree of safety'. This basically meant installing laminated glass of suitable thickness to provide the same level as security as if the storm shutters were permanently fitted. Agreement was forthcoming and, as a consequence, most of Queen Mary 2's public room windows follow this principle.

The Commodore Club is a popular quiet venue during the day and acts as

进水影响。虽然风暴盖有些难看,与装饰目的相背离,而且盖子(或人们所知的百叶窗)很重,很难安装。当不使用时,还存在收纳它们的问题。我们与英国海岸警卫队展开讨论,以确定他们是否会接受一项基于提供"等效安全程度"折中方案的协议。这基本上意味着要安装合适厚度的夹胶玻璃,以提供与安装风暴盖同等的安全等级。协议即将达成,因此,"玛丽女王2号"的大部分公共房间窗户都将遵循这一做法。

"准将"俱乐部提供了完美的设施——可以在白天放松和在晚上享受鸡尾酒会。(冠达邮轮提供)

a cocktail lounge in the evening. Jazz is predominantly played here, although during the cocktail hours a singer pianist entertains in a variety of styles.

The structural arrangement of the forward part of the ship is quite complex to provide sufficient height in the public rooms, including the Commodore Club, located there. The problem lies in that cabin decks only require a' tween deck height of 2.8 metres, but this is too low for most public spaces especially if they are wide. By locating the gymnasium forward on the 3.5-metre-high Deck 7 the deck head (ceiling) could be lowered to provide height for the public rooms above. The only negative to this is that ramps and steps needed to be incorporated to connect the forward public rooms with the cabin corridors on the same decks.

Either accessed directly from the aft end of the Commodore Club, or directly

"准将"俱乐部在白天是一个受欢迎的安静的场所，而在晚上则成为鸡尾酒吧。这里主要演奏爵士乐，不过在鸡尾酒会上，钢琴家演奏家会以各种不同的风格演奏。

船舶前部的结构设计相当复杂，无法在公共场所提供足够的高度，包括位于那里的"准将"俱乐部。问题在于机舱甲板仅需要介于2.8米之间的甲板高度，但这对于大多数公共空间来说太低了，尤其是在空间很宽的情况下。通过将健身房布置在层高为3.5米的7甲板上，甲板顶部（天花板）可以降低，从而为上部的公共空间留出更多的高度。这里唯一的负面影响是，需要设置坡道和台阶来连接前面的公

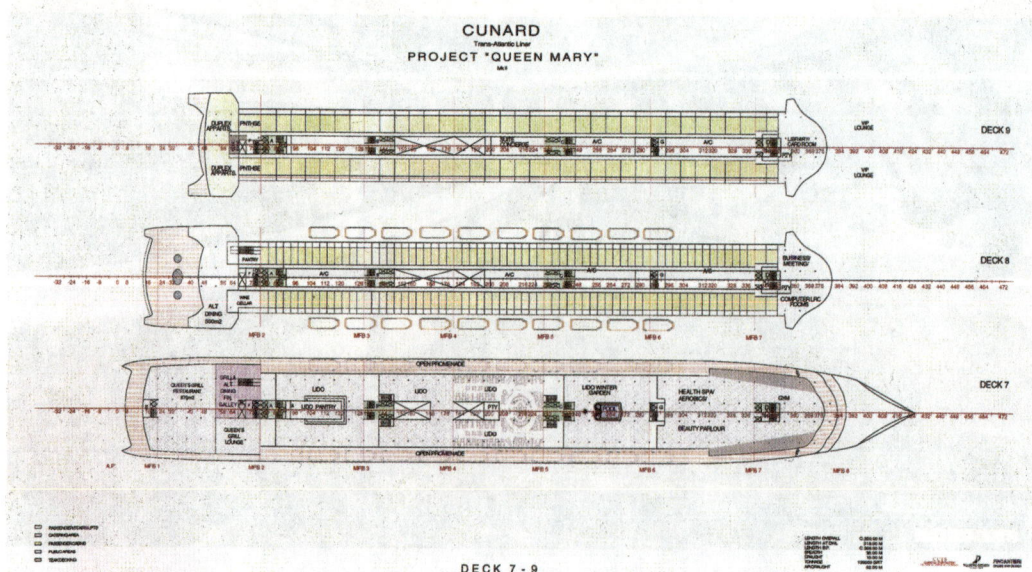

最初的概念设计图：7至9层。

会议室是多功能的，可以用于私人活动或小组活动。（冠达邮轮提供）

"丘吉尔"雪茄休息室是船上专设的吸烟室。空调排气被隔离起来，这样船的其他地方就不会被烟雾污染。（冠达邮轮提供）

贵宾休息室作为资讯中心和社交场所，为"女王"餐厅和"公主"餐厅对应的套房乘客提供便利的服务。（冠达邮轮提供）

from the passenger corridors are two small lounges one on each side of the ship. Churchill's Cigar Lounge on the starboard side is the ship's dedicated smoking room, with seating for 14 guests. Fitted with a special cigar humidor cabinet, this is now the only inside area where cigars may be smoked on board. The air-conditioning extraction is separately routed so that smoke-filled air doesn't contaminate other areas of the ship. The equivalent space on the port side is called the Boardroom and is used as a meeting room and a venue for private parties and special events for up to 15 guests.

A concierge lounge is conveniently located a short distance aft from the 'B' stair tower midships. This is a private staffed lounge available to Grill-room

共房间和后面甲板上的客舱走廊。

无论是直接从"准将"俱乐部的尾端进入，还是直接从乘客走廊进入，首先进入的都是两个小型休息室，每舷一个。右舷的"丘吉尔"雪茄休息室是该船的专用吸烟室，配有特殊的雪茄盒防潮橱柜，可容纳14位客人。这里的空调抽风系统是独立布置的，因此充满烟雾的空气不会污染船舶的其他区域。左舷同等的空间称为"董事会议室"，可用作会议室、私人聚会场所或者特别活动间，最多可容纳15位客人。

一个贵宾休息室位于离梯道"B"

passengers and is designed as a meeting point and a convenient place for making enquiries, service requests etc instead of having to go to the Front Desk on Deck 2. Tea and coffee facilities are available and snacks are on offer.

At the aft end of the deck are ranged the lower level of five duplex apartments. The outboard duplexes have oversized balconies, although the other three are also generously provided. The 'ground floors' of the duplexes are arranged as the living and dining areas with an internal staircase up to the bedroom level on Deck 10. As these are the most expensive apartments on the ship it was essential that they provided the best degrees of comfort in terms of the least noise and vibration. In consequence, these cabins are lined with heavy lead sheathing that acts as a dampening medium.

Large side-glazed windscreens are fitted outboard on each side of the ship at the aft end, in a style very reminiscent of those fitted to the aft deck of Queen Elizabeth 2. These are characterised by their angular glazing elements and their shape determined to provide the side elevation with an attractive tiered appearance aft.

不远的船尾方向附近。这是一间私密的服务间，可供"女王"餐厅和"公主"餐厅对应的套房的旅客使用，休息室设计成会面地，并可以方便地进行咨询、提出服务需求，而无需前往二楼的前台。休息室提供茶、咖啡并有小吃供应。

甲板的尾部排列着五套复式公寓的底楼。靠舷侧的复式公寓有全视野的超大阳台，当然其他三个套房也慷慨地配有了阳台。复式公寓的"底楼"被安排为起居和用餐区，内部楼梯通往10甲板的卧室。因为这是船上最贵的公寓，所以他们必须提供最好的舒适性，最小的噪音和震动。因此，这些小屋内衬着沉重的铅皮，铅皮作为一种抑振介质。

在船尾端，船的每一侧都安装了巨大的玻璃挡墙，这种风格很像"伊丽莎白女王2号"的后甲板。它们的特征是方正的玻璃构件，它们的形状决定了甲板侧立面那引人注目的外观。

船上最大的房间是五套复式公寓。这是巴尔莫洛复式阳台和玻璃挡墙。

QUEEN MARY 2-FACTS AND FIGURES

At 1,132 feet long, QM2 is:
m Five times longer than Cunard's first ship, Britannia (230 feet).
• 22 feet longer than the original Queen Mary (1,109 feet).
• Four football fields in length.
• Half as long again as the Canary Wharf tower is high.
• Three times as long as St Paul's Cathedral is high (366 feet).
• Three and a half times as long as the tower of Big Ben is high (310 feet).
• Longer than 36 London buses (31.5 feet each).
• Twice as long as the Washington Monument is high (555 feet).
• 147 feet longer than the Eiffel Tower is high (984 feet).
• Only 117 feet shorter than the Empire State Building is high (1,248 feet).
• Over two-and a half times longer than the height of the London Eye.
• She measures 237 feet (72 metres) from keel to funnel top, towering over 200 feet above her waterline.
• With her stern against the Empire State Building, QM2 would reach along Fifth Avenue to beyond 38th Street (over four city blocks).
• She covers an area of 3.5 acres.
• The total plant is capable of producing nearly 118MW of electricity, which is about twice the power of a 100,000-ton conventional cruise ship. This is equal to the power of 1,600 cars.
• QM2 would not fit into the Millennium Dome (now the home of the O2 arena). Her funnel would extend above the top and her length is 82 feet longer than its diameter. (The Dome is 1,050 feet wide and 164 feet high.)
• In the course of the flagship's 200 transatlantic crossings, Cunard estimates that passengers have consumed:
8.4 million cups of tea;
980,000 scones;
481,000 bottles of champagne;
644,000 eggs;
960,000 litres of milk.
• In total, Queen Mary 2 has served 22.4 million meals and sailed over 600,000 nautical miles during her first 200 crossings. These figures do not take into account her annual world cruise or her sailing to the Canaries, fjords, Iceland, Belgium, the Netherlands, Luxembourg, around Britain, up to Montreal and Quebec in Canada, or among the Caribbean islands.
• Of Cunard's previous Queens, Queen Mary (1936-67) crossed the Atlantic 1,001 times; Queen Elizabeth (1940-68) 896 times; and Queen Elizabeth 2 (1969-2008) 812 times.
• Her power plant can produce sufficient electricity to light a city the size of Southampton (population 200,000).
• Her engines can produce 157,000 horsepower-the equivalent of 1,570 family cars (of 100hp each).
• Her whistle, which is from the original Queen Mary, is audible for ten miles.

"玛丽女王2号"——事实和数据

长度为1 132英尺的"玛丽女王2号":

- 是冠达第一艘"布列塔尼亚号"Britannia(230英尺)的5倍长。
- 比"玛丽女王号"(1 109英尺)长22英尺。
- 相当于4个足球场的长度。
- 比金丝雀码头塔的高度长一半。
- 是圣保罗大教堂St Paul's高度(366英尺)的3倍。
- 是大本钟塔高度(311英尺)的3.5倍。
- 相当于36辆伦敦巴士(每辆31.5英尺)的长度。
- 是华盛顿纪念塔高度(555英尺)的2倍。
- 比埃菲尔铁塔的高度(984英尺)高147英尺。
- 只比帝国大厦的高度(1 248英尺)低117英尺。
- 比伦敦眼高度的2倍还多。
- 从龙骨到烟囱顶是237英尺(72米),水线以上的高度超过200英尺。
- 如果把船尾靠近帝国大厦的话,"玛丽女王2号"将沿着第五大道直达第38街(跨越四个街区以上)。
- 占地3.5英亩。
- 全船设备的功率将近118兆瓦,大约是10万吨级常规邮轮的两倍。相当于1 600辆小汽车的功率。
- "玛丽女王2号"将不能进入伦敦的千禧穹顶(现在是O2竞技场的主场)。她的烟囱比穹顶还高,其长度比其直径长82英尺。(穹顶的宽度是1 050英尺,高度是164英尺)
- 冠达估计,在其200次横渡大西洋的过程中,乘客总共消耗了:

840万杯茶;

98万份烤饼;

48.1万瓶香槟;

64.4万个鸡蛋;

96万升牛奶。

- 在她200次横渡大西洋的过程中,"玛丽女王2号"总共提供了2 240万顿饭和航行了60多万海里。而这些数字还没有考虑她每年的环球航行,以及航行至加那利群岛、北欧峡湾、冰岛、比利时、荷兰、卢森堡、英国周围、加拿大的蒙特利尔和魁北克或加勒比群岛之间。
- 冠达之前的"女王号"横渡大西洋的次数分别是,"玛丽女王号"(1936—1967)1 001次;"伊丽莎白女王号"(1940—1968)896次;"伊丽莎白女王2号"(1969—2008)812次。
- 她的发电机能够产生足够的电力来照亮一个像南安普敦那样大的城市(人口20万)。
- 她的引擎能产生157 000马力——相当于1 570辆家用汽车(每辆100马力)。

她那传承于"玛丽女王号"的汽笛声,10英里外都能听到。

Deck 8 (staterooms 8.001-8.0130)

The majority of standard-balcony staterooms on this deck have their balcony views obscured by the lifeboats and boats. Many cabins have a sofa bed for a third berth and few cabins have connecting doors. Four cabins are specially adapted for wheelchair access.

At the forward end of the superstructure, ranged across two-thirds of the ship with a bias to the starboard side, is the library and bookshop. The library is the largest facility of its type at sea with over 8,000 hardback books, 500 paperbacks, 200 audio books, 100 CD-ROMs and other media. Reading areas are arranged at the front end and to the starboard side. Free-standing lockable bookcases predominate and racks are provided for magazines and other periodicals. Several writing desks are arranged, following the curve of the superstructure and these were originally fitted with computer terminals but these have now been removed. The bookshop incorporates a sales counter, which is also used for library service, and is located at the entrance to the library with access via the starboard side cabin passageway. The bookshop is self-contained and can be completely closed off from the library so that the latter can remain accessible to passengers at all times. This is a requirement, as the library forms the secondary escape route from the adjacent beauty salon on the port side.

Originally the library was destined to occupy all the forward area but, as the layouts of health spa and gymnasium were being developed, it was thought

8 甲板（客舱 8.001~8.0130）

这层甲板上大多数标准阳台房的阳台景观被救生艇遮住了。许多舱室都有一张沙发床作为第三个床位，有些舱室之间有家庭连通门。还有 4 个舱室专门为无障碍通道做了特别的改装。

在上层建筑的前端偏右舷，横跨三分之二船宽的，是图书馆和书店。该图书馆是最大的海上图书馆，拥有 8 000 多本精装书、500 本平装本、200 本有声读物、100 张光盘和其他媒体。阅读区域布置在前部和右舷。杂志和其他期刊有独立的、可锁的书柜和架子。依照上层建筑的线型排列了几张写字台，这些写字台上面最初安装了电脑，但现在这些电脑已被移除。图书馆可通过右侧船舱走廊进入，书店位于图书馆的入口处，且设有用于图书馆服务的销售柜台。书店是自成一体的，可以与图书馆完全分开，这样图书馆就可以随时向乘客开放。这是有必要的，它可以把图书馆当成左舷相邻美容院的第二条逃生路线。

起初，图书馆注定是要占据所有的前部区域，但随着健康休闲中心的布局和健身房的开发，有人认为美容沙龙的空间将不足，于是决定占据图书馆空间的三分之一，并将其放置在那里。因此，图书馆的空间就比较紧张。

图书馆布置了许多座位，供游客安静地阅读和沉思。这一区域的右舷有良好的向前视野，右舷和船尾也是一个特别受欢迎的位置。（冠达邮轮提供）

by some that there would be insufficient room for the beauty salon and it was decided to take one-third of the library space and place it there. In consequence, the library is the poorer for it. The bookshop and library are operated as a concession through Ocean Books of Romsey. The bookshop sells a large, varied selection of books, prints, puzzles and games and is always well patronized. The aforementioned hair and beauty salon is operated by Canyon Ranch as part of their concession, as described in the Deck 7 tour. Services for both men and women are offered, including hair

书店和图书馆是由罗姆塞海洋书店特许经营的。书店出售各种各样的书籍、印刷品、拼图和游戏，而且非常受欢迎。上面提到的美发沙龙是由"峡谷"农场经营的，这是他们特许经营的一部分，就像 7 甲板导览中所描述的那样。为男性和女性提供服务，包括发型设计、指甲护理治疗、美甲、修脚、化妆咨询和美容。

在甲板的尾部有一家名叫托德·英吉利的收费餐厅。现代风格的餐厅包

design, nail care treatments, manicures, pedicures, make-up consultations and makeovers.

At the aft end of the deck there is an extra tariff restaurant called Todd English. The modern-styled restaurant incorporates a dramatic entrance foyer, waiting area and bar and looks out on to the open deck and swimming pool beyond. The room incorporates intimate alcoves and architectural features and Mediterranean-themed cuisine is offered. The restaurant seats 156 guests and is serviced from a dedicated galley

括一个醒目的入口门厅、等候区和酒吧，并可以向外眺望外面的露天甲板和游泳池。这间餐厅将壁龛作为建筑特色，并提供地中海主题的菜肴。餐厅可容纳156名客人，并由左舷的一个专用厨房提供服务，该厨房与2甲板上的主厨房有服务电梯连接。在"托德·英吉利"餐厅被选为特许经营餐厅之前，伦敦的Rule餐厅*也在考虑范围之内。Rule餐厅是伦敦最古老的餐厅，也是包括皇室在内的许多社会

乘客正在"托德·英吉利"餐厅享受烤肉。这家餐厅是船上主要的收费餐厅之一，其为所有乘客提供午餐和晚餐服务。（冠达邮轮提供）

*Rule餐厅在1798年由Thomas Rule创建，是伦敦历史最悠久的餐厅——译者注。

"托德·英吉利"餐厅外有露台和甲板酒吧

on the port side, which has service lift connection with the main galley on deck 2. Before Todd English was chosen as the concession to operate the restaurant, Rules of London was actively under consideration. Rules is the oldest restaurant in London and is frequented by many of the social elite, including royalty. Rules sources its produce from its own Scottish estate and there was the possibility of offering passengers pre- and post-cruise excursions to the estate. In the event Cunard's management ultimately selected Todd English, a restaurateur and celebrity chef from Boston, Massachusetts, in the United States to operate the restaurant. Originally offered without surcharge, the

精英经常光顾的地方。Rule 餐厅的食材源自于苏格兰地区自家的庄园,并为乘客提供登游轮前后游览庄园的机会。结果,冠达的管理层最终选择托德·英吉利——来自美国马萨诸塞州波士顿的餐厅老板和名厨经营这家餐厅。餐厅最初是提供免费的服务,但随着餐厅声望的增长和提高收入的压力增大,很快就变为固定的费用。自那以后,又改为量贩收费的方式。

"托德·英吉利"餐厅延伸出来的露天甲板(露台酒吧)和一个栏杆区能提供一个供56人使用的用餐平台。主乘客游泳池在甲板尽头处,配备有

popularity of the restaurant and pressure to increase revenues soon led to a fixed cover charge being levied. This has since been amended to per item charge.

The Todd English bar extends out on to the open deck (Terrace Bar) and a railed-off area provides an al fresco dining terrace for 56 guests. Towards the end of the deck the main passenger swimming pool is located, complete with two whirlpool baths and shower cubicles. The deck is sheathed in teak.

Sometime after the contract had been signed, but before fabrication had advanced too far, I sailed on a cruise with the Cunard liner Caronia. At the aft end of one of her decks, small observation platforms projected from each side of the ship just like aft 'docking bridges' of ships of the past. I asked the shipyard if they would agree to incorporate a similar feature on Queen Mary 2 at no additional cost and happily they conceded to my request.

两个按摩浴缸和淋浴间。甲板上面铺着柚木。

在合同签订之后，在船舶建造工作还没完全展开之前，我上了冠达邮轮公司的"卡洛尼亚号"邮轮航行。在船上其中一层甲板的尾端，从船的每一边挑出来一个小观察平台，就像过去船只的尾桥台一样。我问造船厂是否愿意在"玛丽女王 2 号"上加入类似的特征，而不需要额外的费用，令人高兴的是他们接受了我的要求。

Deck 7

Deck 7 is the transition between the superstructure above and the hull below. A wide wraparound promenade is provided, with the forward end shielded from the weather by the superstructure front. The inspiration for this arrangement came from experience with sailing on the former Holland America Line flagship, SS Rotterdam (1959) - now serving as a museum ship in the city of her name. The forwardmost part of the deck is the V-shaped top of the massive breakwater, described later. The ship's spare 23-tonne anchor is positioned at the tip of the V section, with a mechanised hatch that provides access to the ship's forward stores areas. A steel bulwark separates the forward area from the passenger observation deck behind.

Two things dominate the view from the passenger deck. The first is the massive curved forward superstructure front, or face, which rises up before the observer and is crowned with the navigation bridge. The second, on a somewhat smaller but nonetheless impressive scale, are eight large stainless steel sculptures, set on mountings on the deck amid strategic safety railings. The sculptures are well rounded and have a very complex compound curve form. Each has a perfect hole running through the section roughly two-thirds up from the base.These are, of course, not sculptures – although many passengers think they are - but the ship's spare

7 甲板

7 甲板连接了上层建筑和下层的船体。这一层有一个宽敞的漫步步道,步道的前端被船首的上层建筑遮蔽起来。这种设计的灵感来自荷美邮轮公司的旗舰,"鹿特丹号"(1959)——现在在鹿特丹作为博物馆使用。甲板的最前部是大型防浪犁的 V 形顶部,后文再详细叙述。邮轮的 23 吨重的备锚固定在 V 形区域的顶部,船员可以经由机械操作的舱盖进入前部的储存区域。一道钢制舷墙将艏部区域和后方的乘客观景甲板隔开。

乘客甲板有两个显著的特点:首先,上建的止面形成一个巨大的弧面,高高耸立在乘客面前和桥楼一起构成了一个皇冠的造型;其次,8 个不锈钢"雕塑"放置在环形的安全护栏内,这 8 个"雕塑"虽然尺寸较小,但是令人印象深刻。每个"雕塑"有着圆润的外形,具有非常复杂的复合曲线面。每一个"雕塑"的底部都有一个固定用的开孔,高度大致是基底部分的三分之二。当然,这些不是雕塑——虽然每个乘客都这么认为——它们其实是备用桨叶。"玛丽女王 2 号"有 4 个螺旋桨,靠前的一对螺旋桨和靠后的一对设计不同。每一个螺旋桨根据旋转方向,分为左旋和右旋,所以 4 个螺旋桨都是不同的。

艏部甲板布置有备桨和一个备锚

propeller blades! Queen Mary 2 has four propellers, with the forward pair being a different design to the aft pair. Each propeller is either left-handed or right-handed depending on the direction of rotation, so in effect each of the four propellers is different. Ranged on the observation deck are two spare blades for each of the four-bladed propellers. The deck sheathing in this location was originally to have been teak, but as this was determined to be a non-critical area it was agreed with the shipyard that fake teak-effect composition could be substituted against a credit offer that could be used elsewhere within the ship.

Two other prominent features in this

每个螺旋桨都有两片备用叶片布置在观景甲板上。这一区域的甲板覆盖物本来是柚木，但由于被认定为非关键区域，所以我们同意船厂在此区域使用仿柚木材料，而根据信用要约，原本用于此处的真柚木将被应用在该船的其他区域。

另外两个显著的特点是，两台起重机和它们后方的短桅杆。每台起重机的安全工作载荷是 4 吨，用于将物品吊到备锚后面的舱口上方。事实上，桅杆是为了制造一种错觉，即起重机是那种吊臂的升降是通过桅杆底部的

location are the two cranes and the two short masts set immediately behind them. The cranes have a safe working load (SWL) capacity of 4 tonnes each and are used to hoist items aboard and into the hatch set behind the spare anchor. In fact the masts are there to create the illusion that the cranes are of the old-fashioned type with their jibs raised and lowered by pulleys and wires from the top of the masts. Modern ships' cranes are very utilitarian with just a jib mounted on a pedestal, raising and lowering being enacted by a hydraulic ram. I didn't relish the idea of such industrial units marring the forward part of the ship so I convinced the shipyard to install the masts immediately behind the crane pedestals to give a much more aesthetic appearance. The starboard side mast supports the ship's foghorn, which is sounded when sailing in fog.

The superstructure front is the most complicated structural shape on board the ship. The shape is an idealised representation of the superstructure front of the original Queen Mary. On that ship deckhouses were arranged in tiered fashion one on top of the other, the fronts being of reducing semi-circular section moving upwards. Gallery walkways were installed, but considering the speed at which the ship travelled and the transatlantic routing, these would have only been useful while entering or departing a port. The lowest level acted as a screen for the enclosed promenade, with large observation windows, while

经常被游客误认为不锈钢雕塑的备用桨叶。

缆绳和滑轮控制的传统样式。现代船舶的起重机非常实用，只用在底座上方安装一个吊臂，升降由液压油缸控制。笔者不希望机械装置破坏艏部的视觉效果，所以说服船厂在起重机底座后面安装桅杆，使起重机外观更漂亮。右舷的桅杆上安装了雾笛，它在雾中航行时就会鸣笛。

上建前部是全船最复杂的结构，是从"玛丽女王号"的结构形式演变来的。旧船的房间布置得层层叠叠，上建前部的形状是向上逐渐缩小的半

甲板起重机和短桅杆

on higher levels smaller windows were fitted for the cabins located behind. Queen Mary 2's superstructure front is even more massive and provides space for various public rooms, as described earlier, the only walkway being at Deck 11 level with an arrangement more akin to Queen Elizabeth 2 than Queen Mary. In essence Queen Mary 2's superstructure front is a fully plated-in version of Queen Mary with a Queen Elizabeth 2 top. The resulting front shape is something like a landslip on a steep earth mound, with the curved surface blending into flat sides. However the shape is described, it was immensely difficult to design properly and the draftsmen at the shipyard spent

圆形。考虑到航速和海况,画廊只在进出港时开放。最底层的封闭走廊设有大型观景窗,上面的舱室设有较小的窗户。如前所述,"玛丽女王 2 号"的上建更宽敞,设有各种公共空间,唯一的步道设在 11 甲板,这种布置相对"玛丽女王号"而言,更像"伊丽莎白女王 2 号"。本质上,"玛丽女王 2 号"的上建前部是在复制"玛丽女王号"的基础上,加上了"伊丽莎白女王 2 号"的顶部。由此产生的效果是,其前部看起来像雪崩后的雪山绝壁,通过曲面过渡到平坦的侧面。

many hours perfecting the form before they were happy to present it to me for my approval. The next challenge was converting it into a number of sections that could be prefabricated so that when they were assembled together they presented a smooth contour. The shipyard admirably fulfilled all our expectations and the resulting shape is simply superb. To break up the huge expanse of frontage on what would otherwise be all white punctuated with windows, three black bands are painted at each side to represent the gallery walkways that were on the original Queen Mary. Faux, yes, but justified I am convinced.

Behind the superstructure front lies the forward part of the wraparound

无论何种语言描述这一形状，都很难准确地设计出这种效果，船厂的制图员用了很多工时来完善这个造壁，并提交给我审批。下一个挑战是将其分割成若干方便预制的部件，以便当它们组装在一起时，呈现出平滑的轮廓。造船厂出色地完成了这个任务，最终的外形简直是一流的。上建正面一般全是白色的，布置有很多窗户。为了改变这种风格，"玛丽女王 2 号"在每舷喷绘了三条黑色带，用以模仿"玛丽女王号"的画廊走道。笔者认为其具有以假乱真的效果。

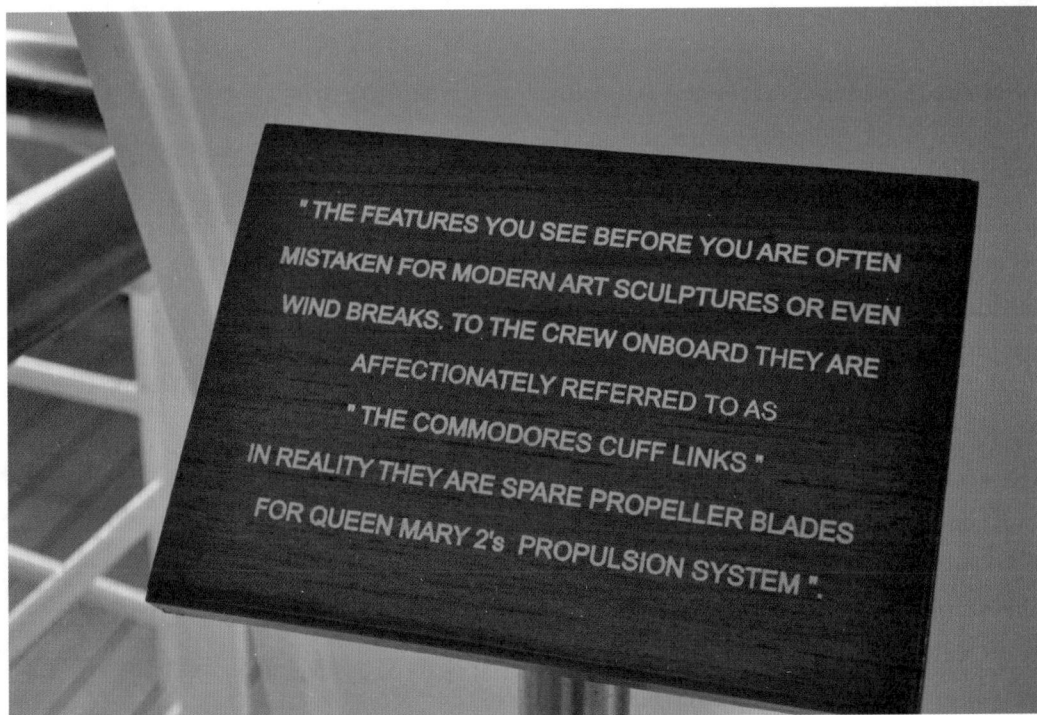

一块不言自明的告示牌

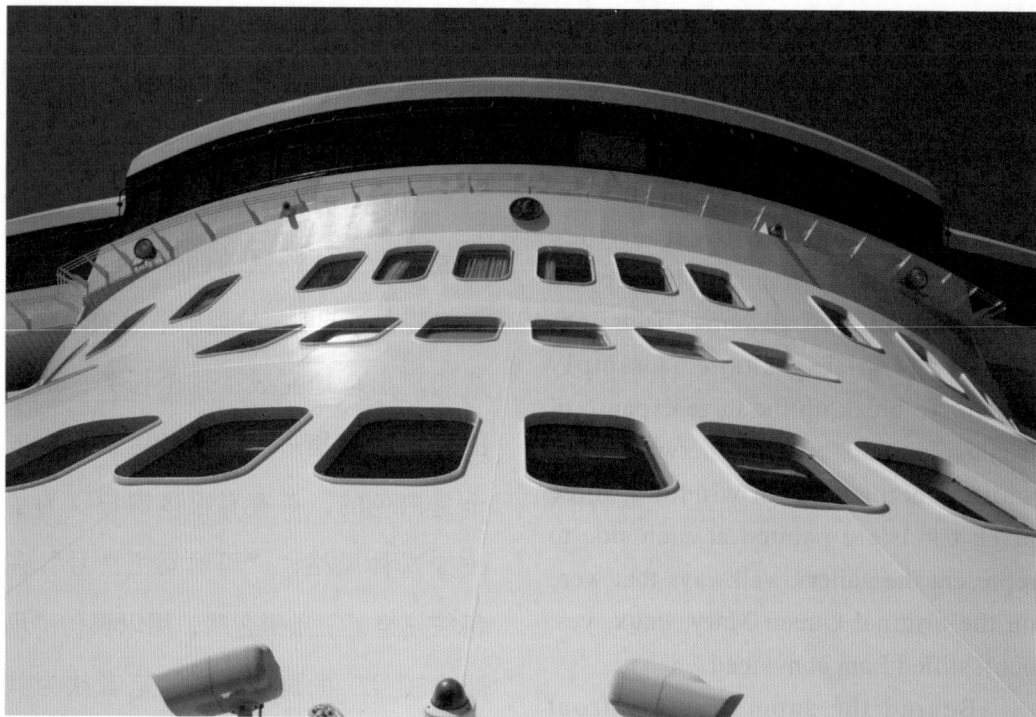

上层建筑前端壁是"玛丽女王2号"的标志性外观特征之一，也是设计和建造中最复杂的部分。

promenade with two screened doors to the open deck. During construction of the ship with the superstructure front in place, shipyard representatives asked me to accompany them on board to look at a 'situation' that had arisen. We walked up to the forward part of the promenade and on the steel deck were chalked two lines. The outermost one represented the eventual positioning of the forward bulkhead to the gymnasium complex that lay behind the promenade. But what was the second line? I was advised that an over-zealous individual was attempting to maximize the area inside the gymnasium by squeezing the space available in the promenade. All very laudable, but

环形步道的前部位于上建前端壁的后面，有两扇门通向露天甲板。在上建前端壁的建造过程中，船厂代表让笔者陪他们上船看看发生了什么"情况"。我们走到步道的前部，在甲板上画了两条线。最外面的一条代表了位于长廊后面的健身中心前舱壁的最终位置。但是第二条是什么呢？有人告诉我，一个过分热心的人试图通过缩小步道来扩大健身中心的面积。所有这些努力都是值得称赞的，但是这样做会导致步道宽度只满足一个人通行！人们没有意识到的是，有两根由

in doing so the individual would have completely blocked off the promenade! What hadn't been appreciated was that there were two immense girders fashioned from 38mm steel plate - the thickest steel used on board - that were the main structural support for the entire superstructure front. These jutted out into the promenade, and the gymnasium dividing wall had been carefully positioned to preserve an adequate passage. The shipyard requested that I clarify the owners' position, which I did in no uncertain terms, and the wraparound promenade was instantly reinstated.

The gymnasium is wrapped around the forward 'A' staircase on three sides, providing three distinct areas for various activities within the space. Over 50 pieces of cardio and weight training equipment is installed, including 14 treadmills, 10 elliptical gliders, 4 upright bikes, 4 steppers, 4 recumbent bikes and 2 rowing machines. On the port side there is a separate connecting stair to the beauty salon above, all nicely decorated with plants and a waterfall feature. To port there is a side passage that allows access aft that opens into the reception area of the spa and health complex. This area comprises individual male and female changing rooms with lockers, a relaxation area with views out to the starboard side of the promenade, a large hydrotherapy pool with whirlpool bath, and various steam rooms and saunas. The pool measures 30 feet by 15 feet and its thalassotherapy attractions comprise air-

"玛丽女王号"（1936年）的上层建筑前端壁被复制到"玛丽女王2号"上。

38毫米钢板——船上使用的最厚的钢板——制成的加强筋是整个上建前端壁的主要支撑结构。突出到步道范围内的健身房的前端壁被仔细布置好，确保步道的宽度。船厂要求我澄清船东的立场，我毫不含糊地马上要求将步道恢复原样。

健身房三面被"A"梯道环围，其为各种活动提供了3块独立的空间。健身房内安装了50多台心肺和体重训练设备，其中包括14台跑步机、10台摆动式跑步机、4辆动感单车、4台踏板机、4辆卧式脚踏车和2台划船机。左舷有一个专门的楼梯通向上面的美容沙龙，它用植物装饰出瀑布的效果。左舷有走廊通至艉部的SPA和综合健身馆。这个区域包括独立的男女更衣室，休息区可以看到右舷的步道，一个大型的漩涡水疗池以及各种蒸汽室

bed recliner lounges, neck fountains, a deluge waterfall, air tub and body massage jet benches. The thermal suite features a herbal sauna, Finnish sauna, reflexology basins and an aromatic steam room. Some 24 treatment rooms are also conveniently arranged, and the whole complex along with the gymnasium and beauty parlour requires a staff of about 50 beauticians and health experts. Spa treatments offered include massages and therapeutic bodywork, mud, aromatherapy, Ayuvedic and seaweed remedies, facials, masks, conditioning body scrubs and body cocoons.After the ship contract had been signed it was decided to appoint Canyon Ranch Resorts, Hotel and SpaClub, as the concession to operate the spa complex. As a result of their requested modifications to the original layout, the shipyard asked for a significant extra cost, which we were able to mitigate against the cancellation of a specified auxiliary steering rudder that was deemed unnecessary when we agreed to adopt electric rather than hydraulic

和桑拿房。游泳池尺寸为30英尺×15英尺，配套的海滨理疗设备包括气垫躺椅、颈部按摩喷泉、大瀑布、气泡浴缸和冲气按摩长凳。桑拿房有草药桑拿房、芬兰桑拿房、足疗室和芳香蒸汽室。24个理疗室、健身房和美容院需要大约50名美容师和健康专家。温泉疗法包括按摩和纤体、泥浆浴、芳香疗法、瑜伽和海藻疗法、美容、面膜、身体清洁和身体除死皮。船舶的建造合同签署后，决定指定"峡谷牧场"酒店集团的宾馆和水疗俱乐部事业部来特许经营船上的水疗中心。

受"鹿特丹号"的启发，前端步道的后面是健身房。

steering actuation.

Moving further aft down the port side, the Winter Garden is accessed. This space is decorated to represent a tropical hothouse with parts of the deck-head painted to represent the window panes of hothouses. British artist Ian Cairnle decorated the painted trompe I'oeil ceiling panels. Wicker furniture and a waterfall add to the effect. A bar is provided and the lounge serves as a cocktail venue, meeting space and as an overflow to the informal restaurant areas located further aft. Depending on demand, afternoon tea is sometimes served in this venue as well as the Queens Room on Deck 3. The original intention was to diffuse botanical scents through the air-conditioning system into the Winter Garden, but concerns that these might trigger an asthmatic or other allergic reaction with some guests prevented this being realised. The passenger 'B' staircase and lift lobby is located behind the Winter Garden. The single staircase flight splits into two and these move slightly aft as they descend down into the hull. This is to allow safe egress for the larger number of people accommodated within the hull compared to the superstructure. With the exaggerated deck height of 3.5 metres on this level the staircase lobby and the thresholds to the stairs themselves are certainly imposing spaces compared to most cruise ship equivalents, invoking the spirit of the great 'ships of state' of the 1930s.

Moving further aft beyond the 'B'

由于需要修改原有的设计布置，造船厂要求非常多的加账，我们用取消辅助转舵装置省下的钱来补偿该加账部分。当我们同意采用电动吊舱推进时，就不再需要用这种液压驱动的舵机了。

在左舷往艉部走，可以进入冬季花园。这个空间装饰成热带温室的样子，部分天花板涂装成热带温室的玻璃面板。英国艺术家伊恩·凯恩斯设计了具有视觉幻象效果的天花板。藤编家具和瀑布增强了其效果。其间设有的吧台使休息室可用作鸡尾酒会会场、会议空间，并可作为更远船尾端的非正式餐厅区在客满后的备选场地。根据需要，此区域有时还和3甲板女士大厅一样提供下午茶点。最初曾设想将植物的芬芳气息通过空调系统散布到冬季花园，由于担心这些气味可能会引发某些客人哮喘或其他过敏反应，这一设想最终没有实现。位于冬季花园后面是乘客"B"梯道和电梯间。单个梯道的台阶分成两部分，下降进入船体的那部分向艉部稍微延伸。这保证了船体住舱内人员的安全进出，而这些人员的数量比在上层建筑内的人员数量要多得多。由于这一层甲板层高为3.5米，相对较高，与大多数同类邮轮相比，楼梯厅和楼梯梯道本身空间就已相当宏大，从而唤起了20世纪30年代伟大"国

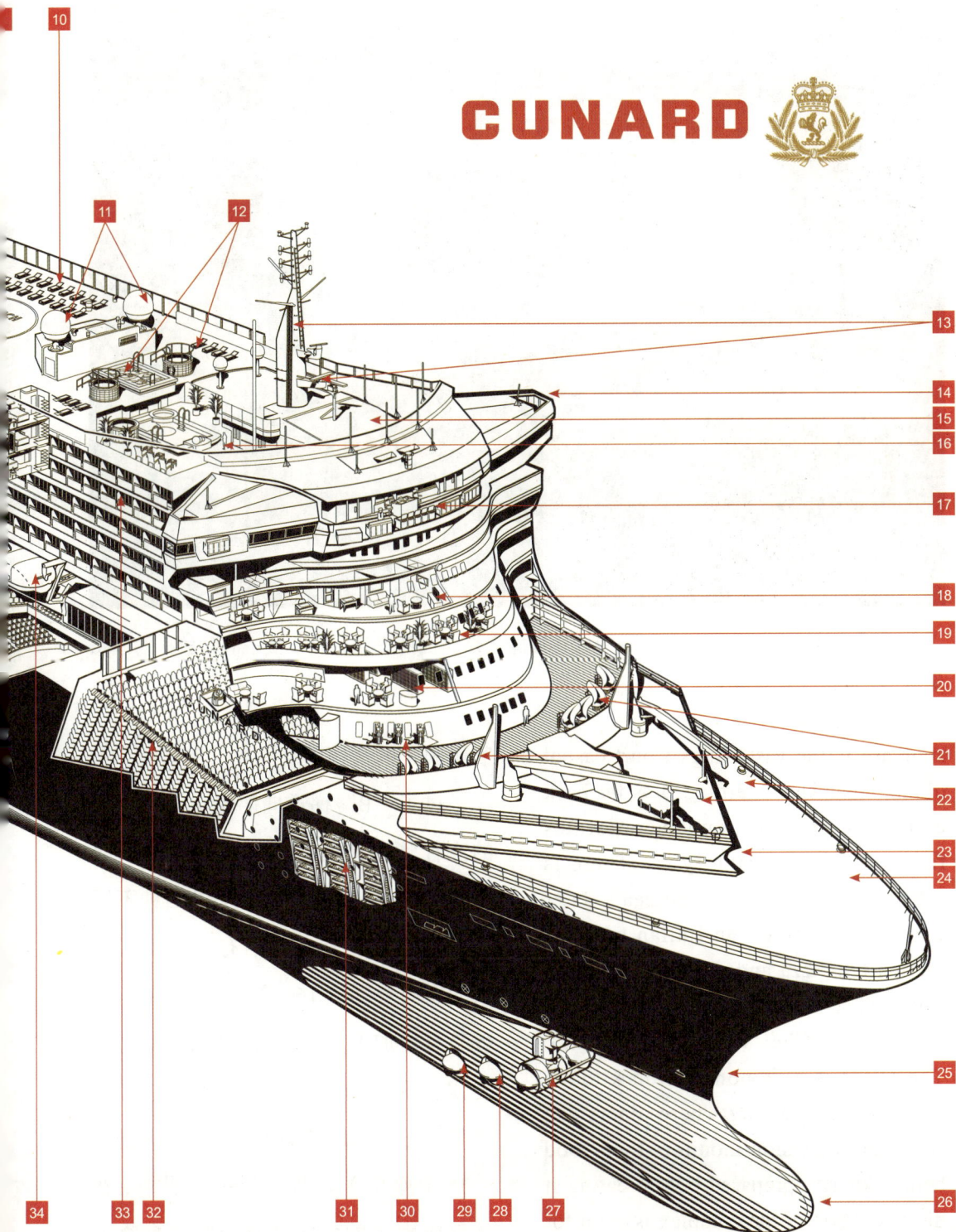

"峡谷牧场"水疗中心拥有迄今冠达班轮上最全面的设施，是享受宁静和放松的理想场所。（冠达邮轮提供）

staircase is the vast Kings Court casual dining area. This is arranged as far back as the 'D' staircase and incorporates four different catering types. There is a British-style carvery (164 seats, later increased slightly), an Italian trattoria section for pizza and pasta (66 seats), a Lotus Thai-Asian restaurant area (212 seats) and a Chef's Galley (36 seats). The latter is a demonstration kitchen with adjacent seating where diners can watch on television monitors their food being expertly prepared before eating it directly. Most of the complex is open for breakfast and lunch on an open-sitting, self-service basis. At dinner part of the area is screened off and operates with

家旗舰"的情怀。

过了"B"梯道向船尾走就是巨大的杰仕华庭休闲用餐区。此区域一直布置到"D"梯道背部，提供四种不同的餐饮类型。其中包括有一个英式风格的烤肉餐厅（164个座位，后来座位数略有增加），提供比萨和面食的意大利饮食区（66个座位），莲花亚洲泰式餐饮区（212个座位）和主厨餐厅（36个座位）。后者是一个明档，在相邻座席里的食客在直接吃掉食物前可以在监控屏幕上观看他们餐点经专人准备的过程。其中的大部分区域采

waiter service, while self-service dining is also available from another section. Tea and coffee stations are located within each space and limited 24-hour availability of some items is operated, mostly in the Italian domain. Many guests prefer the informal dining option for breakfast and lunch, while maintaining their fixed main restaurant sitting for dinner. For those who do not want to adopt evening dress code, especially on formal nights, the Kings Court is a viable option. Two observation lifts run from the main lobby on Deck 2 up into the forward section of the Kings Court. The floor in this area originally included three large glass inserts but these were

用开放和自助的方式供应早餐和午餐。晚餐时,部分区域由屏风隔开,并有服务员服务,在其他区域仍提供自助餐饮服务。每个区域内都设有茶和咖啡服务台,在意大利餐区24小时提供有限食品。许多客人喜欢在早餐和午餐时选择非正式用餐方式,而在晚餐时选择在主餐厅固定的座位用餐。对于那些不愿在正式晚宴上依从严格着装标准的客人,杰仕华庭餐厅是一个较好的选择。两台观景电梯从2甲板的主进厅上升到杰仕华庭餐厅的前部。这个区域的地板最初布置有三个大的玻璃镶

冬季花园明亮通风的休息室,让人联想起大型温房。(冠达邮轮提供)

杰仕华庭休闲餐厅中的卡弗里主题区域（冠达邮轮提供）

soon plated over so that extra seating could be accommodated when demand for seating in the Kings Court exceeded expectations. Serveries are a mix of self-contained islands and sections abutting galley and pantry spaces. Much of the food for Kings Court is pre-prepared in the main galley on Deck 2 before being transported by service lifts to the Kings Court preparation facility. Seating with tables for 2-6 persons is arranged throughout the restaurant areas, including a number of bay windows that look out on to the wraparound promenade.

The aft end of the Deck 7 deckhouse accommodates the two premium Grill rooms: the Princess Grill and the

嵌，但很快就被移除平整了，以便当杰仕华庭餐厅的座位需求超出预期时，用来容纳额外的座位。服务台兼有独立取餐台及邻接厨房和配餐区服务的功能。杰仕华庭餐厅的大部分食物在通过服务电梯运送到备餐设施之前，都是在2甲板的主厨房里预先准备的。整个餐厅区设有服务于2~6人的桌椅，拥有许多可以眺望游步长廊的挑窗。

7甲板的甲板室后端布置了两个高级餐厅："公主"餐厅和"女王"餐厅。这些点菜餐厅的座位与相关的套房住宿等级对应。菜单的选择更多，食物准

Queens Grill. Seating in these a la carte restaurants is paired with the relevant suite accommodation grades. Menus are extensive and extra special care and attention is placed on the food preparation and table service. The Queens Grill is located on the starboard side with seating for 200, while the Princess Grill is to port with 178 seats. A large dedicated galley space separates the two restaurants, which have similar styling to their decor, with the Queens Grill accentuated with gold and the Princess silver. Seating allocation to these two restaurants allows access to the Queens Grill lounge, which is located forward of the Queens Grill and has a cocktail bar. The lounge and the two Grill rooms have spectacular views out through numerous windows that look across the wraparound promenade. An early design proposal saw the Deck 8 swimming pool tank on the deck above having either a

备和餐桌服务也更为细致和用心。"女王"餐厅位于右舷,拥有200个座位,而位于左舷的"公主"餐厅则有178个座位。这两个餐厅由一个大型的专用厨房隔开,它们的内装风格相似,"女王"餐厅突显金色而"公主"餐厅突显银色。在两家餐馆内就餐的乘客可以进入"女王"餐厅休息室。"女王"餐厅休息室位于餐厅的前部,其间设有一个鸡尾酒酒吧。休息室和两个餐厅有大量的窗户,乘客可以透过窗户望向周围长廊之外的壮观海景。早期设计方案能看到上一层8甲板的游泳池,池体设置在烧烤室范围内,采用玻璃底或玻璃侧面,从而使游泳池的光线可以透入餐馆。尽管当时设想了采用磨砂玻璃等方案,但这

在主厨餐厅里,客人在用餐之前可观看到由高级厨师准备美味餐点的过程。(冠达邮轮提供)

"玛丽女王2号"船上的顶级餐厅——"女王"餐厅

glass bottom or glass sides and setting the tank within the confines of the Grill rooms, thus allowing light from the pool to filter through into the restaurants. Even though frosted glass was envisaged, the idea was too avant-garde for Cunard and the idea was dropped.

Adjacent to the entrance of the Princess Grill there is a small lobby with a staircase up to the pool deck on Deck 8. A wooden model of a steamboat called Swan is set within a glass case at the foot of the stairs. The model was a gift to the ship from the shipyard.

个想法对冠达来说太前卫了，所以最后还是放弃了这个想法。

"公主"餐厅的入口旁边布置了一个小型厅，通过大厅内的楼梯可以直达位于8甲板的泳池。楼梯入口处的玻璃橱窗里摆放着一个船厂送给"玛丽女王2号"的礼物："天鹅号"蒸汽船模型。

宽大的环绕式休闲步道是"玛丽王后2号"的一张靓丽名片。正如前面描述的那样，尽管"伊丽莎白女王2

The wide wraparound promenade is a particular feature on board Queen Mary 2. As previously described, although Queen Elizabeth 2 offered a wraparound promenade it was open and elevated by one deck at its forward end. This made it untenable in all but the most benign conditions. Queen Mary 2's promenade is protected by the forward superstructure screen and is maintained throughout on Deck 7. The deck is sheathed in teak and fitted with side railings beyond the forward screen and solid bulwark/screens aft. The promenade circuit is 580 yards long, making one lap equivalent to just over a third of a mile. It is used extensively for observation, casual promenading, walking exercise, sunbathing or lounging on traditional wooden steamer chairs, and under emergency conditions for the embarkation of lifeboats, tenders and liferafts. Side doors provide access from the deck to the main staircase lobbies and some public areas. Teak boxes are arranged each side as ready lockers along the length of the promenades for the stowage of additional lifejackets; these also act as large seat benches. The lifeboat and tender davits are structurally tied into the superstructure deck house sides and do not impede promenading.

On each side of the ship located above the promenade are:

• 7 partially enclosed lifeboats for 150 persons, fitted with a single diesel engine;

① 1 米 =1.0936 码

号"也配备有一条环绕式休闲步道，但是这条长廊的前段位于开敞的升高甲板上，这就导致了在大多情况下人们很难在上面立足，除非是风和日丽的情况下。相比较而言，"玛丽女王2号"上的休闲步道有艏部上层建筑的结构遮蔽，且在7甲板整个游步甲板区域都有遮蔽保护。整个步道采用将柚木铺设在钢制甲板上的工艺，除了艏部挡风墙结构区域及艉部舷墙区域，其他位置都在舷侧布置了扶手及栏杆。休闲步道一圈长580码①，相当于三分之一英里，游客可以在上面远眺、散步、健走、晒日光浴或者躺在木制躺椅上。在紧急情况下，休闲步道可用做救生艇、交通艇和救生筏的登乘等待区。通过紧挨步道的各个侧门，可以便捷地到达主梯道大厅和其他公共区域。布置在步道一侧的许多柚木箱用来储存备用救生衣，这些箱子也兼做大的长条凳。救生艇和交通艇的艇架同上层建筑结构连接在一起，而且其布置并不影响休闲步道的空间。

每舷的休闲步道上方布置有：

• 7艘半封闭救生艇。每艘可容纳150人，配备一台柴油机。

• 4艘半封闭双体式救生兼交通艇。每艘可容纳150人，配备两台柴油机。

• 4 partially enclosed catamaran-type tender/ lifeboats for 150 persons, fitted with twin diesels;

• 1 fast rescue boat.

On each side of the ship sited on the deck aft of the lifeboats and tender/ lifeboats:

• 4 liferaft davit cranes for 37-man liferafts; liferafts are stowed for davit launching and float free.

All arrangements of this equipment are in accordance with International Maritime Organisation 'Safety of Life at Sea' regulations. The working deck for the boats is a grating platform deck accessed from the promenade by vertical ladders.

• 1 艘快速救助艇。

在船舷两侧，沿着救生艇／交通艇向后靠船尾方向布置有 4 台用于救生筏下放的吊机。每个吊离式救生筏可容纳 37 人，配有静水压力释放器。

所有救生设备的布置均满足国际海事组织《国际海上人命安全公约》。各类艇筏的操作平台为钢制格栅平台，位于游步甲板上方，可以从游步甲板通过直梯到达。

"公主"餐厅为高端客人提供亲密的用餐氛围。（冠达邮轮公司提供）

　　环绕着上层建筑的游步甲板。这一区域是最佳赏景地，可以躺在舒适的木制躺椅上欣赏大海永无止境的壮丽景象。

　　夜色中的游步甲板，木制躺椅已被收起，呈现出一副完全不同的美丽景象。

　　右舷的高速救助艇是两艘快速反应艇之一，它可以快速下放以应对可能遇到的他船事故。

巨大的救生艇架上存放着救生艇和交通艇，在撤离时负责将它们降放到海面。

存储在左舷的救生筏，这些筏是船员的首选撤离方式。

Deck 6 (staterooms 6.001-6.304)

Staterooms 6.001 to 6.304 are ranged along this deck. There are standard balcony cabins with a solid, rather than glass, bulwark due to the proximity with the waterline, outside window cabins and inside cabins. Some cabins have interconnecting doors, while others have one or two extra Pullman-type beds. A few have a third berth in the form of a sofa bed. Six inside cabins have windows that look out into the atrium.

At the forward end of the deck the huge V-shaped 'snow plough' breakwater is set defiantly on the forecastle deck. The breakwater was inspired by a similar fixture on board the former French Line flagship Normandie (1935) and is used as a store room. Elsewhere on the deck are several air-conditioning plant rooms, a large computer room, a computer workshop and equipment for ensuring an uninterrupted power supply to essential electronic equipment.

At the aft end of the deck the children's facilities are organised. These consist of a nursery where passengers may leave their young babies under supervision, and separate areas for toddlers up to the age of seven (the Play Zone: 27 places) and older children aged eight to twelve (the Kids' Zone: 27 places). Integral toilet facilities are on hand and all is managed by a team of specially trained nannies and junior assistants. These spaces are conveniently

6 甲板（6.001~6.304 舱室）

舱室 6.001~6.304 布置在 6 甲板。这层甲板布置有标准的阳台房、带窗户的海景房和内舱房。阳台房因为离水线很近，所以用钢质舷墙取代了玻璃护栏。有些舱室配有相互联通的门，另外一些舱室配有一个或两个下拉式翻床。有些舱室则是配有第三张沙发床。有 6 间内舱房设有可以看向中庭的窗户。

在这层甲板的前端，设计师大胆地设计了一个巨大的 V 形"雪犁"挡浪板。其灵感来源于 1935 年投入运营的前法国班轮"诺曼底号"旗舰的一个类似结构物，当时这个结构物被用来作为储物间。在甲板的其他区域，设有几个空调机间、一个大型计算机处理中心、一个计算机机房和向船上重要电气设备提供不间断电源的设备间。

在这层甲板的后端，儿童游乐设施布置得井然有序。其中包括一个托儿所，游客可以将他们的小孩留在这里，而且这些小孩随时都处于监护之下；还有单独的游乐区：即 7 岁以下的幼儿专区（含有 27 个游乐设施）和 8~12 岁的儿童专区（含有 27 个玩乐设施）；整体式厕所设施随处可见，而且全部由经过专门培训的保育员和初

arranged close to a special children-friendly open deck. The deck is not covered with teak but with a visco-elastic composition, which is much softer than teak and acts a cushion should there be trips or falls. A gated shallow swimming pool in the centre of the deck has a separate circular splash pool, and two pedestal-mounted water pistols are positioned on a dais for water play. The side railings beyond the windscreens are fitted with special canvas covers to prevent children being able to climb up the railings, and a chess board and a hopscotch frame are marked out on the deck.

级护理工来打理。这些儿童游乐设施位置便利，临近儿童专用的开敞甲板。开敞甲板没有采用柚木，取而代之的是敷设缓冲垫，垫子由具有弹性的复合材料组成，当有儿童绊倒或者摔倒的时候，可以很好地起到缓冲作用。在中央地带，设置了一个浅水游泳池。游泳池配有门禁设施，一个独立的圆形嬉水池和两把水枪，水枪固定在高台上，儿童用它们来打水仗。同时在缓冲垫上还刻画有一个棋盘和跳格子游戏框架。玻璃挡墙布置在开敞甲板外侧，其上配有扶手栏杆，上方配有经过特殊设计的帆布遮阳蓬，以防止儿童爬上栏杆产生危险。

Deck 5 (staterooms 5.001-5.269)

Staterooms 5.001 to 5.269 are distributed on this deck. Standard balcony cabins with solid bulwark, outside window cabins and inside cabins are available, some featuring connecting doors, extra Pullman berths and sofa beds. Six inside cabins have windows that look out into the atrium.

At the forward end of the deck a number of stores and workshops are arranged. These include a large paint store, a carpet store and separate workshops for upholstery and deck

5 甲板（5.001~5.269 舱室）

舱室 5.001~5.269 布置在 5 甲板。这层甲板布置有带钢质舷墙的标准阳台房、海景房和内舱房。有些舱室配有相互联通的门、下拉式翻床或沙发床；有 6 间内舱房设有可以看向中庭的窗户。

在这层甲板前端布置了很多储物间和工作间，其中包括一个大型油漆储存间、一个地毯储存间以及独立的软装用品车间和甲板属具车间。在艉

fittings. Elsewhere, there are several air-conditioning plant rooms, electronic equipment rooms and a food service pantry for room service for staterooms within the hull.

Two emergency diesel-driven generators are located at the stern of the ship and their exhausts are led horizontally aft to discharge overboard through openings in the shell plating. One of the generators can provide enough power to maintain the statutory 'Safety of Life at Sea' systems (such as emergency lighting, radio transmission and navigation lights), while the extra generator is available to provide limited additional services. These generators are usually only required if the ship loses power from the main diesels/gas turbines, although they can be used for limited periods at dry-dockings or for other special circumstances.

Deck 4 (staterooms 4.001-4.225)

Passenger staterooms 4.001 to 4.225 are located on this deck with a similar distribution to those on Deck 5.

At the forward end of the ship the two Rolls-Royce Marine anchor windlasses are installed. These deploy and recover the two 23-tonne side anchors and chain used for anchoring. The size of the anchors and chain is calculated by Classification Society Rules (Lloyd's Register) according to the side profile of the ship. The calculation produces an 'Equipment

部其他区域，设有几个空调机间、电气设备间以及一个食品配餐间。配餐间为舱室的乘客提供客房服务。

两个应急柴油发电机布置在船的尾部，排气管水平向后布置并通过船体外壳板的开口排到船外。其中一台应急发电机为船上维持"海上人命安全"法规规定的系统（如应急照明、无线电传输和信号灯）提供充足的电力；另外一台应急发电机则提供有限的额外服务。当船在干船坞内或在其他特殊情况下可以用两台应急发电机提供一段时间的临时动力，但是应急发电机通常只有在船舶主动力失电时才投入使用。

4甲板（4.001~4.225舱室）

乘客舱室4.001~4.225分布在这层甲板，其基本布局同5甲板相似。

在船的前端，安装着两台由罗尔斯－罗伊斯公司制造的锚绞机。当船舶需要锚泊时，锚以及其附带的锚链就通过锚绞机来下放和回收。锚以及锚链的选型按照劳氏船级社的规范要求，参照经验公式、根据船舶的侧投影面积等相关参数计算得出舾装数，然后采用插值法从舾装数分级表中确

Numeral', which is based on previous experience and good practice, and this is used to interpolate a table to determine the size required. The U3 anchor chains are 385 metres long and are of 114mm section; they collectively weigh 273 tonnes and have a breaking strain of 9,300kN. Unusually, Queen Mary 2's forward mooring deck is not integral with the capstan deck, but is one deck lower, on Deck 3. The separation of the two functions was deemed necessary to provide an optimum run for the anchor cables to self-stow within the attendant chain lockers, while providing an optimal run for mooring lines to the quayside. As part of the shipbuilding contract the shipyard was required to build a model of the bow of the ship with mooring lines and hawse pipes/anchors to demonstrate that the proposed arrangements would work well in practice.

At the bow of the ship a deck store is provided. Elsewhere there are

定舾装数所处档位。最终本船选取了直径为114毫米的锚链,锚链等级为U3、单舷锚链的总长为385米、总重约273吨,破断负荷为9 300千牛。和通常布置不一样的是,"玛丽女王2号"艏部系泊甲板和绞盘甲板不是同一层甲板,而是将系泊甲板降低了一层布置在3甲板。两个功能区域被分开是很有必要的,这样既可以方便锚链的存储,又优化了系泊缆绳同码头系柱缆桩之间的的系泊缆绳的布局。作为造船合同的一部分,船厂要制作一个涵盖艏部系泊设备的等比例模型,来模拟锚以及锚链的收放动作,以验证设计方案在以后的实际使用中切实可行。

在船的首部布置了一个甲板储物间。艏部其他区域则布置了大量的空调机间、变电站以及几个属于下层公

庞大的锚绞机,可以回收重达23吨的锚。(汉普顿·迪克森提供)

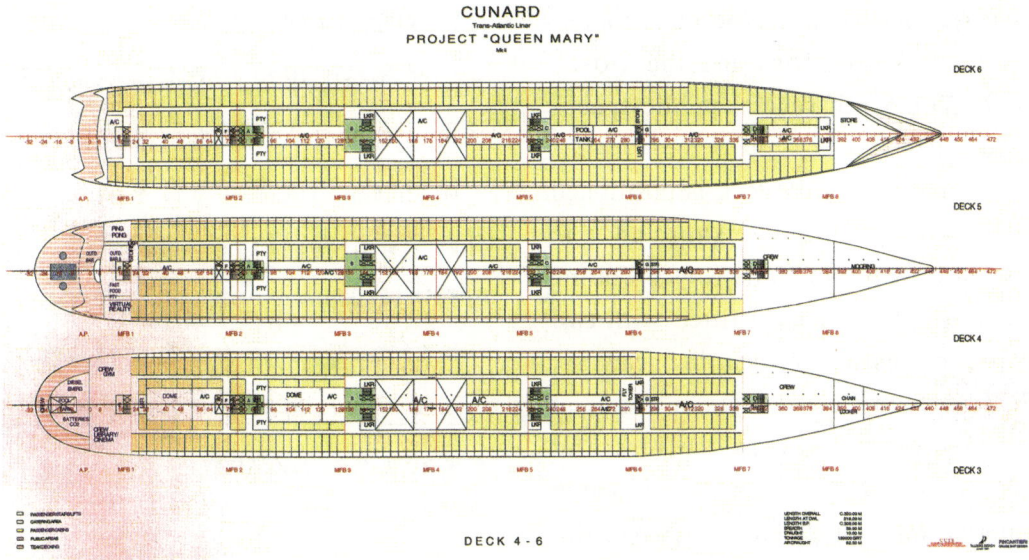

CUNARD
Trans-Atlantic Liner
PROJECT "QUEEN MARY"
Mk II

DECK 4 - 6

初始的概念方案：4 甲板到 6 甲板。

艏部的一台系泊绞车，当船靠泊码头的时候用来收绞系泊缆绳。（汉普顿·迪克森提供）

numerous air- conditioning plant rooms, electrical substations and the closed wells (domes) of several public spaces located below.

The aft mooring deck is positioned at the very stern of the ship and it is equipped with four Rolls-Royce Marine mooring winches, each fitted with two hawser drums and one warping head. Six Panama double chocks, seven universal rollers, eight pedestal rollers and eight double bollards are fitted. Three mooring-line storage bins are provided.

共区域的升高的穹顶。

艉部系泊甲板处于本层甲板的最艉部，安装有4台罗尔斯－罗伊斯公司制造的系泊绞车。每台系泊绞车配有两个系泊卷筒以及一个副卷筒。甲板系泊属包括6个巴拿马双式导缆孔、7个滚柱导缆器、8个羊角滚轮导缆器以及8个双柱带缆桩。同时甲板上还布置有3个缆绳存储箱。

艉部的一个系泊观察平台。当放出平台后，船员可以站在平台上直接观察系泊过程状态以方便工作。（汉普顿·迪克森提供）

艉部系泊设备的就地控制柜。从面板左侧的示意图可以知道每个绞车的具体位置。（汉普顿·迪克森提供）

Deck 3

The forward mooring deck is arranged at the bow of the ship. Four mooring winches, each with two hawser drums and one warping head are provided. Deck fittings include seven Panama double chocks, eight universal rollers, nine pedestal guide rollers, eight double bollards and four mooring-line storage bins.

The forward 'A' passenger stair tower and lift lobby expand out at each side to two long passageways that are angled downwards along the ship's side. Decoration within the passageways takes the form of large prints of famous movie stars that were frequent passengers on previous Cunard liners. Each passage opens out to a magnificent foyer entrance to Illuminations, Queen Mary 2's spectacular planetarium, movie theatre and lecture hall.

Upon entering this space, guests are usually struck by its size and total lack of any clue that it is on board a ship. Seating 493 guests, sight lines are excellent as the space is completely devoid of pillars through careful structural design. The side entrances lead to a cross passage at the back of the room that looks down at the tiered seating level. A control booth is positioned behind the cross passage, while above the central section of seating is ranged a huge retractable dome. The diameter of the dome is only marginally less than the 18-metre-diameter dome of the former London Planetariumin Marylebone. The dome is deployed using a pulley mechanism,

3 甲板

位于船首的是艏部系泊甲板。该甲板共有4台系泊绞车,每台系泊绞车配两个主卷筒和一个副卷筒。甲板上有7具巴拿马双式导缆孔,8具滚柱导缆器,9具羊角滚轮导缆器,8具双柱带缆桩和4个系泊缆绳储存箱。

船首的"A"梯道和电梯门厅向两侧展开,构成两条向船舷延伸的长廊。长廊内装饰着著名电影明星的巨幅海报,这些明星都曾是冠达邮轮的常客。每一条长廊都通过一个宏伟的门厅来到"光耀"大厅——"玛丽女王2号"壮观的天文馆厅,其也可兼作电影院和报告厅。

来到"光耀"大厅后,客人们都会被它巨大的尺度和齐备的设备震撼,以至于忘记此刻还身在船上。经过精心设计,这个空间完全不需要任何的支撑结构,493个客位的视线非常好。侧方的入口通向一条位于大厅后面的横向通道,这里可以俯瞰阶梯坐席。控制室位于横向通道的后面,而中间座位的上方有一个巨大的可升降穹顶。穹顶的直径仅仅略小于前伦敦马里奥利天文台圆顶18米的直径。穹顶通过一套滑轮装置展开,前端下降3.5米的同时后端仅下降1.5米——造成这一差异的原因是由于阶梯坐席的倾斜角度。

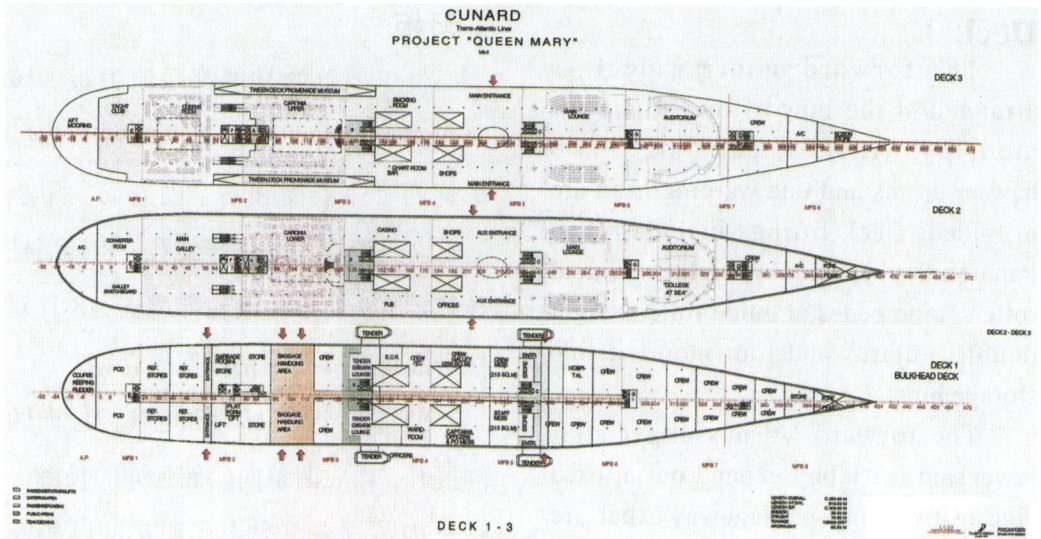

初始概念设计图：1 甲板至 3 甲板。

the whole lowering about 3.5 meters at the front and 1.5 meters at the back from the stowed position – the difference due to the rake of the seating.Some 150 seats, identified by their red colour (the others being gold) are placed below the dome and have a special mechanism allowing them to tilt back for the optimum viewing experience. A raised stage is located at the end of the room with access from the seating at each side. Illuminations is fully equipped as a movie theatre with various screens and back-curtains. Planetarium shows are produced by four projectors set in clear domes at the end of seating rows.

The side passageways continue aft from the planetarium; chairs are positioned in pairs with views looking out though large picture windows. These seats are perfect for watching the endless pattern of the sea and spending a few

设置在穹顶正下方的约 150 个座位进行了特殊的红色标志（其他座位为金色），通过特殊的装置可以使这些座位向后倾斜，以便获得最佳的观看体验。一个抬高的舞台设置在大厅的后部，可以从各个方向登上舞台。作为一个设备齐全的剧院，“光耀”大厅配有各种背景和幕布。天文展演通过 4 架投影仪完成。

侧向通道越过天文馆后继续前行。椅子成对布置，通过大窗可以看到外面的风景。乘客们可以在这些座位上尽赏海洋的美景，并且还可以花上一些时间去沉思。轮椅升降机保证了残疾人士也能轻易通行。这些楼梯通向皇家宫廷剧场二楼包厢的入口。皇家

"光耀"大厅——壮观的天文馆、电影院和演讲厅。

quiet moments of contemplation. At the aft end of the passages short flights of access stairs connect with rest of Deck 3 at the 'B' stair tower cross-passage. Wheelchair lifts are also available for disable access. These stairs lead to the entrances to the balcony-level of the Royal Court Theatre. This is the main entertainment venue on board and seats 1,094.The theatre has a 'thrust' stage at Deck 2 level in which the seating is arranged in front and at each side. The stage incorporates a turntable and within the rotating area five hydraulic lifting sections are fitted for stage acts. At the forward end of the stage a lifting orchestra pit is installed, with

宫廷剧场是船上的主要娱乐场所,配备有 1 094 个坐席。皇家宫廷剧场在 2 甲板有一个伸出式舞台,在其前方和两侧都布置有座席。这个舞台由转台和驱动转台工作的 5 台液压机组成。在舞台的前端,设置有一个可升降的乐池,升降台的进出口在下面的 1 甲板。剧场配有一整套完善的灯光音响组合系统以及一套舞台背景和幕布娱乐系统,这些系统由位于二层中线处的中控台统一控制。皇家宫廷剧场被用来进行具有伦敦西区风格的表演、娱乐

穿过"光耀"大厅后，走廊里陈设有许多座位，可供乘客们玩桌游、猜谜或者安静地享受海景。

access from Deck 1 below. The room is equipped with a comprehensive outfit of light and sound systems, a scenery loft and curtain/scenery screens. The entertainment systems are controlled from a large booth set on the balcony on the centerline. The Royal Court Theatre is used for full-stage West End-

活动、音乐和戏剧表演、讲座和教堂服务。在剧院内展出的众多艺术品中，就有荷兰艺术家帕特拉·伯姆那件令人印象深刻的栩栩如生的玻璃连衣裙。剧院外陈列的艺术品中，就包含有一副塞缪尔·丘纳德爵士引人注目的肖

从远处看，塞缪尔·丘纳德爵士肖像并无二样。（作者提供）

style production shows, entertainment acts, musical events, plays, lectures, and church services. Among the artworks on display within the theatre are impressive glass lifesize dresses by Dutch artlist Patula Berm. Decoration outside the theatre includes a striking portrait of

像。从远处看，它与别的肖像并无二样，但是仔细观察，就能发现它其实是由许多印有冠达邮轮的小图片组成，这些小图片通过巧妙的组合构成了巨幅肖像。

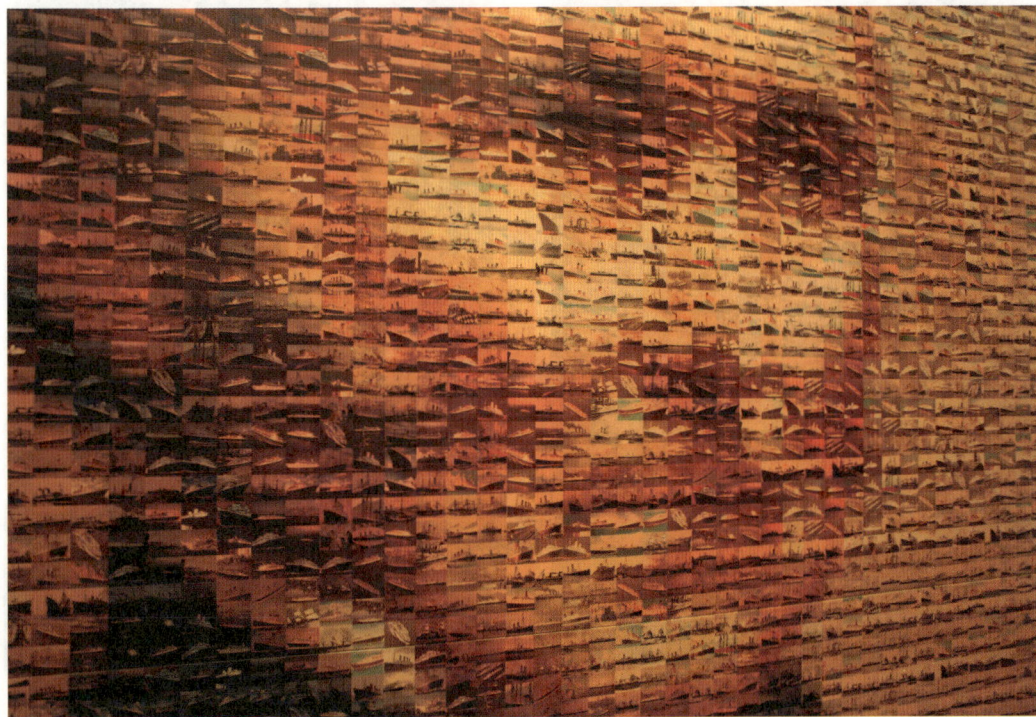

近距离特写，塞缪尔爵士透露了他的秘密：其实是由很多印着冠达邮轮公司旗下客轮的小图片组成的。

乘客们登船后的第一印象便是专门为展示奢华印象而设计的巨大中庭。

Sir Samuel Cunard.Form a distance the portrait does not appear anything more than a normal portrait, but on closer inspection it is clear that it is made up entirely of small pictures of Cunard

皇家宫廷剧场有三条通道通向船尾。最中间的一条位于有着6部电梯的"B"梯道中间，而左右侧的通道则穿过梅费尔购物区来到大堂中庭的中

约翰·麦凯纳创作的史诗般的青铜浮雕作品《大西洋上的"玛丽女王2号"》被安装在大堂中庭的天井高处。

从中庭的这个视角，正好可以充分展示出"玛丽女王2号"的庞大体量。

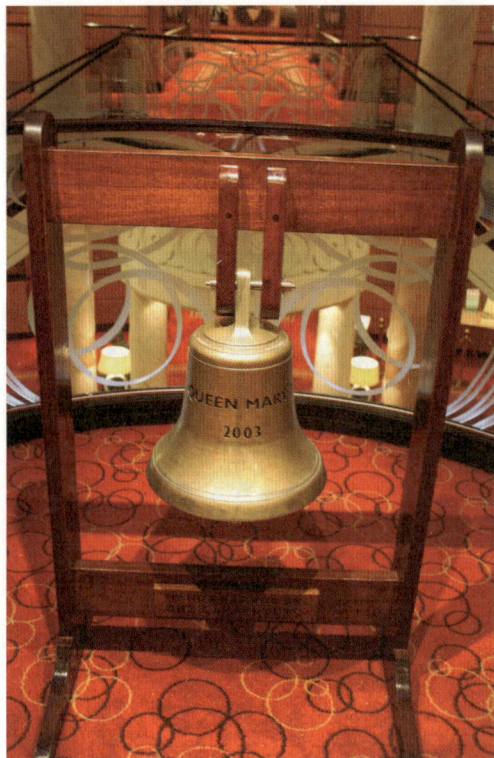

大堂中庭。船钟被安放在3甲板的两部观光电梯中间。

liners, skillfully manipulated to form the large image.

Three access routes move aft from the Royal Court Theatre. The central one is located between the six passenger 'B' lifts, while those to port and starboard pass by retail outlets forming part of the Mayfair shopping arcade before emerging at the mezzanine of the Grand Lobby atrium. Sweeping curved stairs lead down to the base of the lobby on Deck 2 where the Front Desk is situated. The Grand Lobby is a spectacular space rising up from Deck 2 to the underside of Deck 7 where the original glass-floor inserts were once positioned.On the centerline at the forward end of the mezzanine there is a short thrust section that juts out into the atrium opening.

层。弧形楼梯通到2甲板,那里是中庭的底部,设有前台接待区。大堂中庭有着宏伟的空间,从2甲板一直到7甲板,7甲板的地面之前曾设想采用玻璃地面,在大堂中庭的中层有一个短平台突出到中庭内。在平台的尾部,有两部观光电梯分别在7甲板和2、3甲板之间运行。在两部观光电梯之间,一口巨大的船钟装在木框架结构内。由英国艺术家约翰·麦凯纳创作的,面积达42平方米的铜质浮雕《大西洋上的"玛丽女王2号"》安装在大堂中庭顶部的前壁上。

在中庭的右边是有着69个座位的

凯歌香槟酒吧是一个有着奢华氛围的精致场所。（冠达邮轮提供）

At the aft end of the opening the tracks of the two scenic lifts run between Deck 7 and Deck 2 and 3. One of the ship's bells, set in a wooden frame, sits between the lifts. A huge bronze bas-relief of Queen Mary 2 on the Atlantic by British artist John McKenna, measuring 42 square meters, is located on the forward bulkhead at the top of the atrium.

On the starboard side of the lobby an attractive 69-seat Veuve Clicquot champagne bar is arranged, with access through to the Chart Room. The bar is very stylish with portraits of famous film stars gracing the bulkheads.

The Chart Room has a circular bar and originally catered for only 87 guests, but as one of the most popular pre-dinner cocktail venues, seating has been greatly

凯歌香槟酒吧，酒吧内有通往"海图室"酒吧的通道。整个酒吧的陈设非常时尚，四周舱壁上有著名影星的画像作为装饰。

"海图室"酒吧是一个最初被设计为接待87名客人的圆形酒吧，但是作为最受欢迎的餐前鸡尾酒吧，座位通过更紧凑的家具布置方案而大大增加。这个酒吧的设计灵感来自于"伊丽莎白女王2号"的海图室，同时受到"玛丽女王号"头等餐厅里设置巨幅跨大西洋航线海图的启发。"海图室"酒吧的墙壁上装饰有三块大型海蓝色的玻璃板，上面分别刻有索伦特海峡、

expanded by a more dense furniture plan, Inspiration for the decor in this room came from the Chart Room on board Queen Elizabeth 2, which in turn was inspired by the large transatlantic route map found in the First-class dining room on board the original Queen Mary. The bulkheads are adorned with three large aquamarine glass panels with etching depicting the nautical charts of the Solent, the transatlantic crossing and the Eastern seaboard approaches.

The equivalent space on the starboard side forms the main logo shop on board where branded items depicting Queen Mary 2 and Cunard are sold. On the maiden voyage in January 2004 this

跨大西洋航线和美国东海岸的海图。

　　船的右舷，在中庭的前方设有船上的纪念品商店，出售带有"玛丽女王2号"和冠达邮轮公司标记的纪念品。在2004年1月份的处女航中，这家商店顾客爆满，所有的纪念品几乎售罄！这就要求必须尽快空运更多的纪念品，并在马德拉补给到船上。纪念品商店的生意始终火爆，经常是在开门营业前店外的顾客就已经排成了长龙。一般而言，商店和商品总是格外受到顾客青睐。另外一个鸡尾酒吧，即隔着

　　"海图室"酒吧是一个倍受欢迎的场所。在午餐和晚餐前，客人们可以在这里进行各种社交活动。

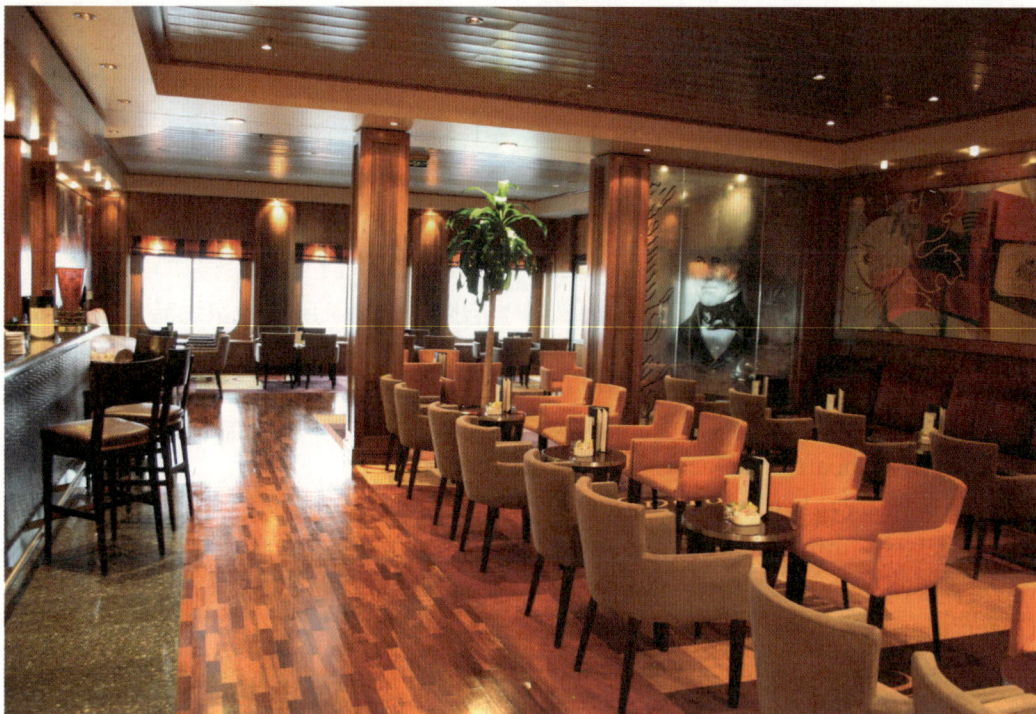

"海图室"酒吧在船交付时的布局，随后因为这个酒吧很受欢迎，需要增加额外的座位。

shop was besieged by guests purchasing souvenirs and almost the entire stock inventory was sold on the first day!Such was demand that additional items had to be flown out to meet the ship at Madeira. Business continued to be brisk and queues constantly developed outside the shop before opening time. In normal service, the shop and its wares is always popular with guests. Another cocktail/wine bar, Sir Samuel's, seating 66 lies beyond the shop and runs towards the centreline passage. The bar serves a selection of wines and other drinks, as well as tea and coffee; pastries are also available. Bar food was not originally served at Sir Samuel's but

中央走廊与"海图室"酒吧相对的"塞缪尔爵士"酒吧，设有66个坐席。酒吧提供葡萄酒及其他饮料，同时也提供茶、咖啡以及糕点服务。最初"塞缪尔爵士"酒吧并不提供食品，但为了分担"杰仕豪庭"餐厅拥挤的用餐人群，"塞缪尔爵士"酒吧也开始提供午餐服务。

一条宽阔的中央通道将中庭与"C"乘客电梯和梯道连接起来。通过将机舱棚分成两个，分别设置在左舷和右舷，就可以分割出三块区域，使得同

was introduced as an alternative dining option for lunch to alleviate crowding in the ever-popular Kings Court.

A wide central passageway connects the atrium with the passenger 'C' lifts and stairs beyond. The three-way split of the Chart Room, central passageway and logo shop was made possible by dividing the engine casing into two, one each to port and starboard. My intention was to replicate as far as possible the placement on the French Line Normandie (1935), where her bisected casing allowed for a different disposition to the normal centerline scenario. (Normandie's arrangement was in fact preceded by Hamburg America Line's Vaterland

时设置"海图室"酒吧、中央通道和纪念品商店成为可能。我的想法是尽可能地复制法国邮轮"诺曼底号"（1935）的布置，她的机舱棚一分为二，允许对中心线情景采取不同的处理。（实际上，汉堡美国邮轮公司旗下1914年的"祖国号"采用类似的布置更早于"诺曼底号"。）中央通道的舱壁装饰有丰富的艺术品。该区域内的防火门高3米，宽4.6米，是船舶建造时最大的铰链式船用防火门，由芬兰Parmarine工厂制造。从塞缪尔·丘

通过宏伟的中央通道可到达主要公共区域，比如上图为位于3甲板的中央通道，在"海图室"酒吧，可以远远地看见塞缪尔爵士的肖像。

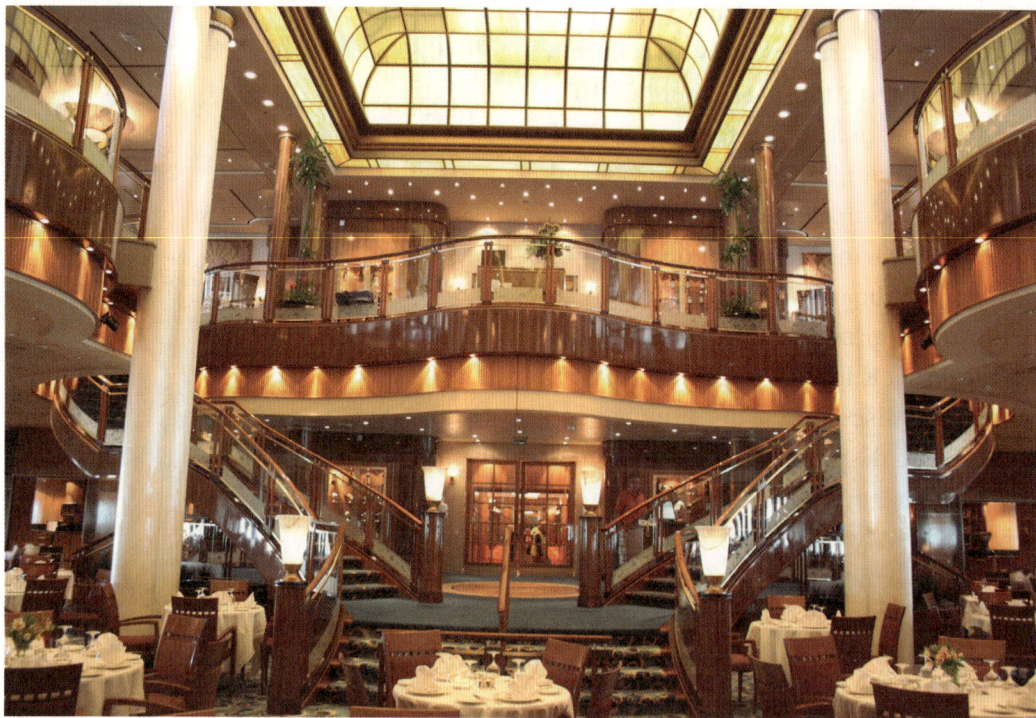

"布列塔尼亚"餐厅是海上最壮观的餐厅之一，能够与20世纪30年代黄金一代的"国之旗舰"的内装水平相比肩。（作者提供）

(1914)). The bulkheads of the central passageway are richly decorated with artwork panels. The fire doors within this area, measuring 3 metres high and 4.6 metres wide, were the largest hinged shipboard fire doors at the time of the ship's construction and were made at the Parmarine factory in Finland. The central passage provides a spectacular perspective, from the Sir Samuel Cunard portrait forward right up to the entrance of the Britannia restaurant beyond the 'C' lifts.

In the 'C' staircase lobby between the Chart Room and the upper entrance

纳德爵士的肖像向前一直到"C"电梯旁边的"布列塔尼亚"餐厅入口的中央通道，提供了一路令人惊叹的装饰场景。

"海图室"酒吧和"布列塔尼亚"餐厅上层入口之间的"C"梯道大厅内，放着一座体现冠达邮轮历史的独一无二的奖杯，象征着"玛丽女王2号"的旗舰船地位。这是颁发给冠达邮轮的"布列塔尼亚"奖杯，庆祝冠达邮轮的第一艘船——"布列塔尼亚号"

to the Britannia restaurant is placed a unique piece of Cunard history that possession of which has come to symbolise flagship status. This is the Britannia cup given to Cunard to celebrate the maiden arrival in Boston of Cunard's first ship Britannia (1840). It was paid for and made on behalf of the city merchants and presented to Samuel Cunard. It was displayed on board Queen Elizabeth 2 until 2004 when it was transferred to Queen Mary 2 to symbolise her flagship status.

The Britannia restaurant is one of the truly epic rooms on board Queen Mary 2. In scale and execution it was inspired by the grand dining rooms of the golden era of great 'ships of state'

（1840）抵达波士顿的处女航。她是以城市商人的名义出资制造的，并赠送给塞缪尔·丘纳德爵士。这座奖杯一直在"伊丽莎白女王 2 号"邮轮上展览直至 2004 年，后被转移到"玛丽女王 2 号"邮轮上展览以象征其旗舰船地位。

"布列塔尼亚"餐厅是"玛丽女王 2 号"上真正史诗级的场所之一。在规模和运营方面，它的灵感来自 20 世纪 30 年代那些黄金岁月的"国之旗舰"，包括"不莱梅号""雷克斯号""国王号""英国女皇号""诺曼底号"和"玛

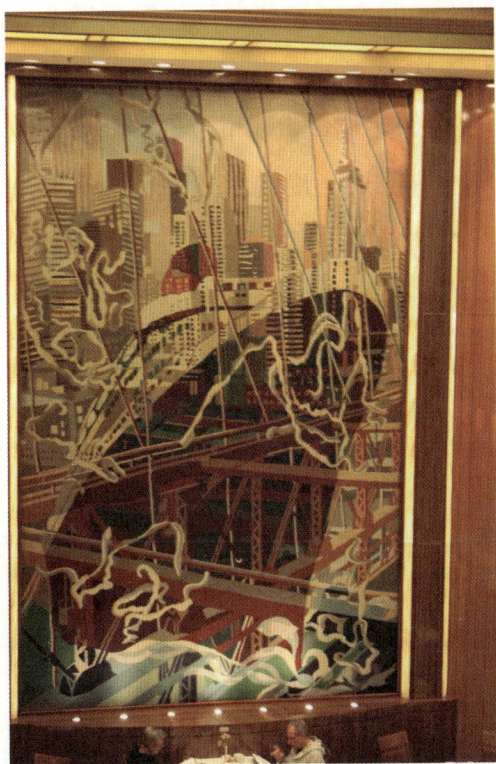

Barbara Broekman 设计的壁毯为"布列塔尼亚"餐厅的照壁提供装饰。（作者提供）

服务员满怀期许等待乘客进入"布列塔尼亚"餐厅享受美食体验。（作者提供）

of the 1930s: Bremen, Rex, Empress of Britain, Normandie and Queen Mary. The restaurant operates on a two-sitting basis and spans two decks, with seating for 1,347. The mezzanine floor accessed from Deck 3 is split over several levels, providing a commanding vista across the whole room. Tables for 2-8 persons are arranged and it is possible to sit among the baronial splendour of the central lower section, or more discretely on one of the levels.

A large glass skylight is placed above the central well opening. The lighting behind the skylight can be varied according to the time of day, with white or dark blue effects. On the original Queen Mary and the other great 'ships of state', only passengers

丽女王号"的宏伟餐厅。餐厅运营以双餐次为基础，跨越两层甲板，包含1 347个座位。由3甲板进出的餐厅中层上有数层高度递增的平台，从那里可以总览餐厅的风貌。餐厅设置了2~8人的餐桌，乘客可以选择坐在贵族般华丽的餐厅底部中央，或者分散坐在其中某一层上。

中央天井上方设置大型玻璃天窗。天窗下部的灯光可以随一天中的时间而变化，呈现白色或深蓝色效果。在原先的"玛丽女王号"和其他伟大的"国之旗舰"上，只有乘坐头等舱的乘客才能进入最宏伟的公共场所。在许多

travelling in First class were allowed access to the grandest public spaces. In many cases the First-class contingent amounted to less than 30% of the ships'complements. Queen Mary 2 is different. She offers numerous grand spaces to all her passengers and nothing exemplifies this more than Britannia, which is the restaurant allocated to even the entry grade of accommodation.

The main artwork is a hand-woven goblin wall carpet of 6.4 4.5 metres (20 15 feet), featuring the Queen Mary 2 interwoven with the skyline of New York and the Brooklyn Bridge, which hangs on the aft bulkhead under the dome within the well opening. The Dutch artist Barbara Broekman designed the

情况下，头等舱乘客的数量可能不到船舶总乘客量的30%。"玛丽女王2号"与众不同。她为所有乘客提供了许多宏伟的空间，并且没有什么比"布列塔尼亚"餐厅更能体现这一点——"布列塔尼亚"餐厅对入门级乘客也开放。

餐厅的主要艺术品是一块6.4米×4.5米（20英尺×15英尺）的手工编织壁毯，表现"玛丽女王2号"与纽约的天际线以及布鲁克林大桥交相辉映的场景，悬挂在天井下近船尾的舱壁上。荷兰艺术家 Barbara Broekman 设计了该场景，随后在波兰进行编织。

位于 3 甲板的 "D" 梯道和电梯大厅

冠达邮轮的典型风格，"女王"厅是船上的舞厅，举办各种鸡尾酒会、下午茶和其他社交活动。（冠达邮轮提供）

scene that was then woven in Poland. Due to fire safety demands, the tapestry was executed in wool combined with Trevira CS on a Trevira CS background. The tapestry was duly delivered to the shipyard during the latter half of 2003 for installation on board the ship. However, in the confusion of the shipyard where there were no less than five passenger ships under construction at the same time, the tapestry was lost. With such a huge gap to fill, frantic efforts were made to trace it. Eventually, with just a few weeks to spare, it was located

根据防火安全要求，壁毯是基于特雷维拉阻燃涤纶纺线采用混合羊毛的方式进行编织。按期壁毯应于 2003 年下半年正式交付给造船厂，以便安装在船上。然而，在船厂同期有不少于 5 艘客船正在建造之中，在这样的混乱局面下，壁毯居然丢失了。面对如此巨大的纰漏，人们疯狂地努力去寻找它。最终，在交付日期只剩下几个星期时，暴露在户外几个月的壁毯终于

rolled up and soaked through, having lain out in the open and been exposed to the elements for several months. It was in a terrible state but, fortunately, after a thorough steam cleaning was as good as new. Although the tapestry is supposed to represent Queen Mary 2, to my mind the vessel depicted appears more like the North German Lloyd Bremen (1929).

The aft sections of Britannia on Deck 2, although integral, are more secluded and may be considered as annexes to the main space. On the port side the area has been rebranded as the Britannia Club restaurant. This now operates on a single-sitting basis with an extended menu and is paired with former twin-sitting Britannia deluxe balcony cabins at a premium fare, reflecting the enhanced dining option.

At the stern end of Britannia the

被人们找到，它已经卷起并被淋透了。壁毯的状态很糟糕，但幸运的是，经过一次彻底的蒸汽清洗后崭新如初。虽然壁毯描绘的是"玛丽女王2号"，但在我看来，壁毯所描绘的这艘船更像是北德劳氏航运的"不莱梅号"（1929）。

"布列塔尼亚"餐厅的尾部更加私密，可以认为是餐厅的附属空间。左舷区域已更名为"布列塔尼亚俱乐部"餐厅。现在以单餐次模式运营，配合扩充了的菜单，与之前"布列塔尼亚"豪华阳台客房提供的价格适中的双人套餐搭配，增加了乘客的用餐选择。

在"布列塔尼亚"餐厅的尾部，

G32 夜总会的名字来源于该船的船厂合同号。（冠达邮轮提供）

aft-most passenger 'D' staircase and lift is accessed. Beyond this, approached via side passages, is the 562-seat Queens Room. This is Queen Mary 2's grand ballroom and as befitting the ship has the largest dance floor afloat, measuring 7.5 metres by 13 metres. A stage is set at the aft end under a Hollywood Bowl-style arch and is the venue for solos and small groups. Decoration within the room includes two huge chandeliers mounted in an arch and is the venue for solos and small groups. The lounge is the principal dance venue and is also used daily at 3.30pm for afternoon tea, cocktail receptions, gala balls and some private parties. Decoration within the room includes two huge chandeliers mounted in arched dome above the dance floor.

The final public room on this deck is the G32 nightclub, which is accessed via the Queens Room. The name of the room, G32, was the shipyard's contract number for the ship before the name Queen Mary 2 was chosen and assigned. The room seats 251 and is arranged on two levels; the Deck 3 mezzanine is reached by two staircases from the Deck 2 level. The mezzanine overlooks the dance floor on the port side, while a bar is located to starboard. This room is primarily used as a nightclub and disco late at night but it is also used for private parties and other functions during the day.

可以进入最尾部的乘客"D"梯道和电梯。除此之外，通过侧面通道可到达拥有562个座位的"女王"厅。这个大厅拥有海上最大的舞池，面积为长7.5米乘以宽13米，这使"玛丽女王2号"成为拥有海上最大舞池的船。舞台设置在好莱坞露天音乐厅式拱门的后方，可进行独奏和小型合奏。大厅是主要的跳舞场所，同时每天下午3点半提供下午茶、鸡尾酒会、庆典舞会和一些私人派对服务。房间内的装饰包括安装在舞池上方拱形穹顶中的两盏巨型吊灯。

这个甲板上的最后一个公共区域为G32夜总会，可通过女王宴会厅进入。房间的名称，G32，是船舶被命名为"玛丽女王2号"之前的船厂合同号。夜总会共有251个座位，分布在两层；位于3甲板的挑层可通过2甲板的两个楼梯抵达。挑层俯瞰着左舷的舞池，而酒吧位于右舷。该区域主要用作夜晚的夜总会和迪斯科舞厅，但白天也用于私人聚会和其他活动。

Deck 2

The passenger 'A' staircase opens out into two passageways that lead aft. These are richly decorated with commemorative plaques given to the ship on the occasion of her inaugural call at each of the ports, while interactive terminals for the ship's heritage trail are provided en route for guests to explore Cunard's rich history. A museum-quality audio 'Maritime Quest' tour is also accessible, describing this and other display areas on board. The passages lead past seven classrooms that are used for lectures and the Connexions

2 甲板

乘客 "A" 梯道通向两条连接船尾的通道。这些通道上装饰着形式多样的纪念铭牌，纪念铭牌是在船舶首次拜访某港口时，港口当局赠送给她的，而交互终端也给乘客提供了探索冠达邮轮悠久历史，从而成为了解其丰厚历史积淀的途径。也可以通过一段讲解音频 "海上探索之旅"，来了解船上的这些铭牌和其他展品背后的故事。这些通道贯穿了 7 个用于演讲的教室

在 "帝国" 赌场小赌怡情一下对很多客人来说是一种流行的娱乐方式。(冠达邮轮提供)

金狮酒吧

computer room where passengers may use the internet and send/receive emails etc. Cunard's College at Sea programme includes classes for computing, seamanship and navigation, art wine appreciation, languages and photography. A lobby area is available, with seating and light refreshment stations on hand.

Passage continues further aft along side corridors that are fitted with tables and chairs for playing board games. These tables and chairs are always popular with guests and as with Deck 3 above, large side windows look out across the ocean. When conditions are

和一个互联网电脑室，乘客们可以在那里使用互联网发送/接收电子邮件等。还有冠达邮轮的海洋学院课程，包括计算类、航海和导航类、艺术品鉴赏类、语言类和摄影技术类。电脑室还带有一个门厅，里面提供座位和点心站。

通道继续向船尾延伸形成舷侧走廊，走廊里设置有可以进行棋盘游戏的桌子和椅子。这些桌子和椅子总是大受乘客欢迎，因为这里可以透过宽阔的舷窗看海景。当海况恶劣时，海

4个交通艇登乘休息室之一。

rough, the sea frequently washes past the windows and at first it can appear quite alarming to see huge waves rearing up in front of them. However, after a few such encounters with no ill effects, confidence is normally gained and guests relish the experience. It certainly focuses the mind during a game of Scrabble and leads to some choice words!

At the end of the passageway on the starboard side is the Future Sales office. This was originally a video games room for teenagers but its function changed during an early reorganisation of spaces following operating experience with the ship. Further aft past the 'B' stairs and lifts the Grand Lobby atrium is reached. On the starboard side the Front Desk is ranged, with various support offices behind Offset to starboard, an office for the sale of shore excursions opens out into the atrium. On the port side the casino and bar is located, with table games in the forward section and various slot machines and games aft. Some 24 staff operate the Empire Casino, which features 115 slot machines and 11 custom-designed gaming tables, including blackjack, roulette and three-card poker. The forward painted curved bulkhead by British artist lan Cairnie represents a scene from a classic Mediterranean casino setting.

As on Deck 3 there is a central passageway that runs along Deck 2. On the starboard side immediately before the 'C' lifts are reached is the Golden

水会频繁地冲刷窗口。起初人们在看到巨浪高耸在他们面前时会非常惊慌。然而,在见多了这种场面并发现船舶没有出现问题后,乘客通常会信心倍增,并对这种场面不屑一顾了。当然人们就会更沉浸于Scrabble*并取得更棒的拼字成绩!

在右舷通道的尽头是期货交易室。这原本是一个青少年电子游戏室,但在早期根据船的运营经验重组了空间后,其功能就改变了。再往后通过"B"梯道和电梯,就到达了大厅。在右侧是宽大的前台,后侧有各种服务办公室、一个向中庭开门的岸上旅游售票办公室。在左舷一侧是赌场和酒吧,前部是桌牌游戏,后部是各种老虎机和其他游戏项目。"帝国"赌场共有24名员工,拥有115台老虎机和11张定制的游戏桌,提供包括二十一点、轮盘赌和三张扑克的博彩游戏。前方由英国艺术家兰恩·卡尔尼绘制的弧形舱壁再现了一个经典的地中海赌场的场景。

与3甲板相同,2甲板也有一个前后贯通的中央通道。"C"电梯出口右侧即是金狮酒吧。这家酒吧的名字取自冠达的徽章,上面是一只金色的狮

*一种拼字游戏——译者注

Lion pub. The name of this hostelry is taken from Cunard's emblem which is a golden rampant lion. This emblem is set in the floor with mosaic tiles at the entrance. The pub serves traditional British-style draught beers as well as other varieties, as any normal land-based pub does Traditional pub food is served at lunchtime, including fish and chips. In 2011 the pub was refitted and a number of banquettes were installed, replicating those found ashore.

The 'C' passenger staircase lobby runs across the ship, terminating each side in a staircase linking it with Deck 3 above. Half-height landings connect with two long 'hidden' passageways that are concealed within the Britannia restaurant below the mezzanine levels. These passageways have large circular windows looking out to sea and connect with the 'D' staircase lobby and the Queens Room on Deck 3 beyond. Crucially therefore, guests don't have to pass through the Britannia restaurant to access the Queens Room or G32. Wheelchair lifts are installed to provide access for these users. The port side passageway is outfitted as the photo gallery and shop for photographs taken by the ship's photographers, while the starboard side is utilised as an art gallery. A large Queen Mary 2 model can be found in the port side photo gallery. At the end of the passageways the 'D' passenger staircase lobby provides access to the aft part of the lower Britannia restaurant.

子。这标志设置在入口处的地板上由马赛克砖铺成。酒吧供应传统的英式生啤酒和其他品种，就像任何普通的陆上酒吧一样，传统的酒吧食物在午餐时间提供,包括鱼和薯条。在2011年,酒吧进行了改装，并安装了许多软垫长椅，这些都参考了那些岸上的酒吧。

"C"梯道的门厅横跨整船，每一侧的楼梯连接到上面的3甲板。梯道半当中的平台连接着两条隐藏的通道，它们位于"布列塔尼亚"餐厅内的夹层下面。这些通道有大的圆形窗户，可以眺望大海，并通过"D"梯道的门厅与"女王"套房相连。至关重要的是，客人不必穿过"布列塔尼亚"餐厅进入"女王"厅或G32俱乐部。安装的轮椅升降机为特殊用户提供了便利。左舷通道装修成照相馆和店铺，供船上的摄影师拍照，而右舷通道则用作美术馆。可以在左侧照相馆中找到一个大型的"玛丽女王2号"船模。在通道的尽头，"D"梯道的门厅提供了"布列塔尼亚"餐厅下层的后部通道。

Deck1

Deck 1 is the main artery of the ship as far as the crew is concerned. It is the highway where the crew move along the ship to access the best stair tower to reach their work station. The forward compartments are fitted out with crew, officer and staff cabins. A large area on the port side is devoted to the medical facility. There are separate entrances for passengers and crew, with the passenger access via the 'B' staircase/lifts, which terminate at this level. The medical facility has a nursing station, a bathroom, stores, two consulting rooms with adjacent waiting rooms (passenger and crew), an emergency operating ward, a dentistry surgery, physiotherapy room, an isolation ward, two crew wards, two passenger wards and a high dependency ward. Outboard of the 'B' stairway enclosure are two passenger tender embarkation lounges, Belgravia to port and Kensington to starboard. The latter is positioned immediately forward of the Officers' Wardroom with access between the two to enable the officers, should they wish, to extend hospitality on a more generous scale than just the Wardroom would allow.

When the ship is at anchor and tendering is in progress using the ship's tender boats, the lounges allow passengers to be conveniently held in groups before being directed to embarkation gangways. At cruise ports the lounges allow passengers and their carry-on baggage to be security screened using security arches and X-ray machines. Stairs at each lounge

1 甲板

对于船员来说，1甲板是船舶的主动脉。这是一条高速公路，船员们通过它穿梭于船舱间，到达最合适的楼梯，以进入他们的工作站。前部舱室配备了船员、官员和职员的住舱。左舷一侧的一个大区域被用作医院。乘客和船员有单独的医院出入口，乘客通过"B"梯道/电梯进出，该梯道在这一层终止。医疗设施包括一个护理站、一个浴室、商店、两个咨询室，相邻的是候诊室（乘客和船员）、一个急诊手术室、牙科诊疗室、理疗室、隔离病房、两个船员病房、两个乘客病房和一个重护病房。在"B"梯道间围墙外面，有两个旅客登乘交通艇的休息室，"贝尔格莱维亚"在左侧，"肯辛顿"在右侧。后者直接位于官员餐厅的前面，两者之间有出入口，如果官员们愿意，他们可以去"肯辛顿"休息室用餐，从而获得比官员餐厅所能提供的更贴心的服务。

当船位于锚地，正在用交通艇进行转运时，休息室使乘客可以被很容易组织起来，从而有序地前往登艇跳板。在邮轮港口，进入休息室时要求对乘客及其随身行李使用安全门和X光机进行安全检查。每个休息室的楼梯都向下通向舷侧平台，当这些平台

船员酒吧

lead down to side platforms that when deployed allow easy access to the tender boats when this facility is in operation for shore transfers. Provision is also made for wheelchair access. At sea, the lounges can be used for various crew or passenger activities, including recording the daily early morning television show.

Aft of the 'B' its the central passageway flanks the main crew galley/mess to port and the officers' and staff mess to starboard. The main crew bar, called the Pig and Whistle is also located to starboard. As with the 'B' lifts, the six 'C' its terminate at this level and provide passenger access, with the 'C' stair tower leading to two aft tendering

展开时，可以使乘客方便地进入交通艇，开展对岸转运操作。此外，还提供了轮椅通道。在海上，休息室可用于各种船员或乘客的活动，包括录制每天清晨的电视节目。

在"B"梯道的后面，中央通道将主要船员与官员和工作人员的厨房／食堂分别隔开到左右两舷。主船员酒吧，被称为"Pig and Whistle"*，也位于右舷。与"B"电梯一样，6部"C"电梯也在这一层终止，与相连的"C"梯道通向两个后部休息室，分别被称为"骑

* 一家著名的坐落在好莱坞的餐厅，始创于 1927 年——译者注

lounges called Knightsbridge (port) and Chelsea (starboard). Beyond these lounges the corridor opens out into a wide open space utilised as a luggage handing area for all the baggage brought on board at the embarkation terminals before being distributed throughout the ship to the cabins. Similarly, at the end of the voyage, luggage collected from the cabins overnight on the last day of the voyage is held in carts ready for disembarkation and sorting ashore for passenger retrieval. This area was also designed to act as an exhibition space on long voyages but it has yet to be used in capacity. A crane beam is installed overhead across the handling area for moving heavy items in and out of the ship, and a platform lifts provides access down to the machinery areas on Deck B. On the port side at the at end of the luggage space, parking and charging

士桥"(左舷)和"切尔西"(右舷)。除这些休息室之外，走廊通向一个宽敞的开放空间，乘客在登船时携带的行李在此临时存放，然后被分发到各个船舱。类似地，在航行结束时，在航行最后一天从客舱收集的行李被临时存放在这里并准备向岸分拣，以便靠岸后转运到接送乘客的大巴上。这个区域也被设计成在远航时可以作为展览空间，但是它还没有被充分利用。在装卸区上方安装有吊车，用于将重物吊运进出船舱，平台电梯提供通往B甲板机舱区域的通道。在行李间的末端左侧，有供叉车停靠和充电的设施。这些叉车用于搬运行李车和商店用品。

在行李间的后面，主走廊移到右

船员食堂和食堂设施

facilities are available for the forklift trucks that are used for moving around the luggage carts and provision stores.

Aft of the luggage space the main corridor is displaced over to the starboard side, To starboard is the ship's garbage handling and processing plant. This consists of a room with two incinerators, a refrigerated refuse store used to hold rubbish before processing, sorting stations glass crushers, drinks can crusher and so on. Food waste throughout the ship is transported by a vacuum transfer system; following water extraction the waste is burnt. To port, the Engine Control Room(ECR) is conveniently located, with a large hotel and technical office nearby. In the ECR all the machinery functions can be monitored and controlled from the propulsion plant, as well as all the hotel services such as air-conditioning, water production and distrbution, etc. The control room is situated close to the main machinery spaces and is manned 24 hours a day. The watchkeepers work a rotation of four hours on and eight hours off.

Beyond these areas various food preparation rooms are laid out with associated stores and thawing rooms nearby Freezer rooms are provided for meat, poultry and fish at-25C while the slow thaw rooms are held at +2C. Four service lifts link these areas with the main and other galleys. At the stern of the ship the steering-gear rooms for the aftermost steerable pods are located. Actuation for steering the pods is electric rather than hydraulic: Queen Mary 2 pioneered this type of installation.

舷，通往右舷的垃圾处理和加工厂。这间舱室有两个焚烧炉、一个用来存放待处理垃圾的冷藏垃圾库、一个分拣站、一个玻璃压碎机和饮料瓶压碎机等。整个船上的厨余废物通过真空传输系统传送；在水分被抽干之后，残渣被焚烧掉。左舷是机舱集控室，设置在便利的位置，其旁边是一个大的住舱和技术办公室。在集控室中，可以监控推进机组的机械状态，同样还包括所有酒店服务功能，如空调、淡水制备和供给等。控制室靠近主要机器处所，每天 24 小时有人值班。值班人员每工作 4 小时轮休 8 小时。

在这些区域的后面，布置了各种食品预处理室，并配备储藏间和解冻室，旁边是为肉、禽类和鱼提供的冷冻室，其温度控制在 –25℃，而化冻室维持在 +2℃。四部服务电梯将这些区域与主厨房和其他厨房连接起来。船尾是舵机室，用于操纵最尾部的可转向吊舱进行转向。驱动吊舱转向的舵机是电动驱动的而不是液压驱动的——"玛丽女王 2 号"首创了这类舵机驱动模式。

Deck A

Deck A is almost entirely devoted to crew cabin accommodation. Two-berth cabins each with private facilities are arranged within each watertight compartment, with access between compartments being possible through watertight doors. The bow thruster room is located forward, each of the three thrusters being driven by a 3.2MW electric motor. The thrusters are fitted with butterfly-valve-type side doors that seal off the thruster tunnels once the ship is under way above close manoeuvring speed to reduce the frictional resistance of the tunnels. The bakery is located at the aft end of the deck with fruit and vegetable refrigerated storage at + 7 C as well as ice cream and frozen food at -25 C.

Deck B

Aft of the bow thruster room, which extends down to this level, two ballast tanks and four potable freshwater tanks are sited. Further aft the main linen store and laundry are arranged in separate compartments. The laundry employs industrial-sized machines with optimal usage of water. It includes folding machines and a dry-cleaning facility with special extraction resources. The laundry supplies a service for the ship's hotel (bed linens, towels, table cloths, napkins, etc) and officers and crew. Passengers may also utilise this service for an additional charge. Launderettes are also available to passengers and crew, with several being located within

A 甲板

A 甲板几乎完全用于船员住宿。每个水密隔舱内都设有带独立卫生间的双人间,各隔舱之间通过水密门相连通。艏侧推室位于船首,有 3 台推进器,每一台都由 3.2 兆瓦的电机驱动。推进器管隧的两端装有蝶阀式侧盖,一旦船舶以正常航速航行,蝶阀式侧盖将封闭推进器管隧,以减少管隧两端开口产生的摩擦阻力。面包房位于甲板的尾部,水果和蔬菜库内保证温度为 +7℃,冰淇淋和冷冻食品库内温度保证为 −25℃。

B 甲板

艏侧推室的尾部向下延伸到 B 甲板,设置了 2 个压载水舱和 4 个饮用水舱。继续往船尾是位于独立围壁处所内的主被服间和洗衣间。洗衣间内配备了工业型洗衣机以节约用水,还配备有折叠机和干洗设备。洗衣间为船舶酒店以及官员和船员提供服务(床单、毛巾、桌布、餐巾等)。乘客也可以利用这项服务,但需支付额外费用。自助洗衣店遍布住舱区域内,可供乘客和工作人员使用。两个服务电梯用于向上方各甲板传送布草。洗衣

3 台右舷的艏侧推,其蝶阀式侧门处于关闭状态。

the cabin areas. Two service lifts provide distribution to the upper decks. Aft of the laundry, four heavy fuel tanks are positioned in pairs on the centreline, with various stores outboard to the ship sides. These stores include areas for uniforms, bedding and cruise staff. On the starboard side is located the ship's print press shop and photo lab. The print shop uses the latest digital printing techniques to produce the ship's glossy-colour daily programme and newspapers, as well as marketing material for the shops and shore excursions.

间的后面,4 个重燃油舱成对地沿中心线对称布置,舱外两侧布置多间储藏室。这些储藏室存储制服、床品和酒店用品等。位于右舷的是印刷间和照相室。印刷间使用最新的数字技术来印刷船上多彩的节目海报和报纸,以及商店和岸上游览的营销材料。

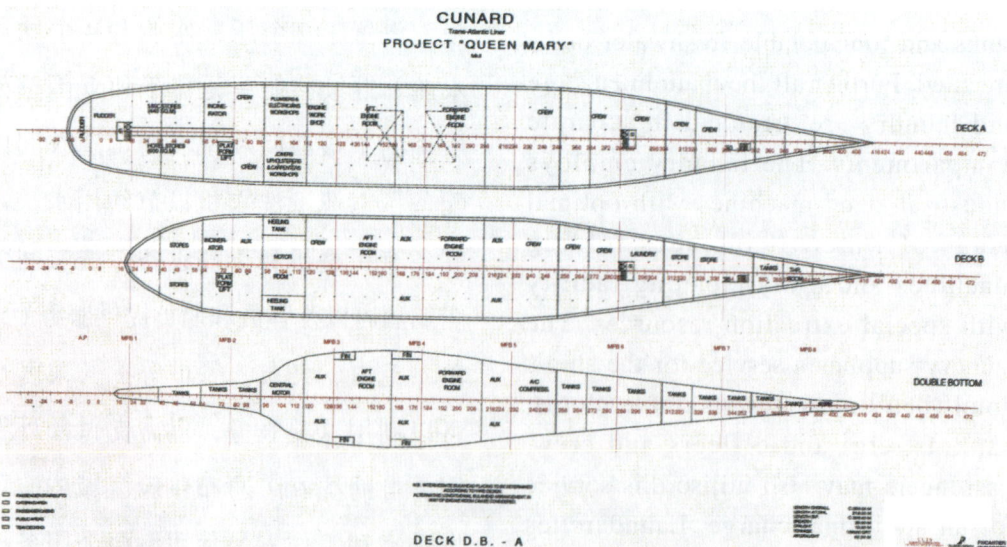

初始概念设计图:双底层、B 甲板和 A 甲板

大堂装饰的艺术品

皇家宫廷剧院展出的玻璃礼服

ARTWORKS ON BOARD

More than 5,000 separate works of art are displayed on board Queen Mary2, many of them being specially commissioned for the ship as part of the 3.5 million art budget. Some 128 artists from 16 countries were responsible for 565 original commissioned works, 190 works of graphic art and 3,500 limited edition prints for display within the staterooms. Art on display includes free-standing bronze and glass sculptures, expansive murals, oil

船上展出的艺术品

"玛丽女王2号"上展出了5 000多件不同的艺术品，其中许多是专门为这艘船定制的，这些也是350万英镑艺术预算的一部分。来自16个国家的128名艺术家负责565件原创作品、190件平面艺术作品和3 500件限量版印刷品装饰在客舱内。展出的艺术品包括青铜和玻璃雕塑、宽广的壁画、油画、水彩画、镶嵌画和其他作品。2、3号甲板上的乘客

paintings, watercolours, mosaics and other works. The main central passenger passageways on Decks 2 and 3 are decorated with relief panels by British artists Gonzalez and Harms, and DKT, while the verre églomisé glass panels are by American artists Christianson Lee and Bolae.

中央通道装饰着英国艺术家冈萨雷斯、哈姆斯和DKT设计的立体挂屏，而彩镶玻璃则由美国艺术家克里斯蒂安松·李和博拉设计。

Further aft, one watertight compartment is outfitted with a crew gymnasium, crew library, crew shop, crew training and a crew cinema/bar. Numerous stores, workshops, technical spaces and a large central technical store are distributed further aft, while at the stern end of the deck refrigerated and dry stores are located.

再往后，一个水密隔舱内设有船员健身房、船员图书馆、船员商店、船员培训室和船员电影院/酒吧，众多储藏室、工作间、技术空间和大型中央信息数据储藏室分布在其后，而甲板的艉部则布置为冷库和干粮库。

Double bottom

The Queen Mary2's double bottom forms an inner skin along most of the ship's length and is 2 metres high. Tanks built into the bottom void are used for water ballast, grey water (from showers and baths) and technical fresh (for deck wash but not potable), while others remain as dry spaces. Ranged on the double bottom are the various machinery installations. These include the diesel generating room with the four Wartsila ZA40S 16-cylinder diesels and their attendant generators, four Rolls-Royce stabilisers, freshwater generating

双层底

"玛丽女王2号"的双层底结构沿船长形成一个高2米的内层空间。双层底结构内的水舱用于存放压载水、灰水（来自淋浴和盥洗）和技术水（用于甲板清洗，但不用于饮用），而其他的则保留为空舱。各种轮机机组被安置在双层底上面。这些设备包括位于柴油发电机间的和4台瓦锡兰公司ZA40S 16缸柴油主机及其附带发电机、4台罗尔斯－罗伊斯公司的减摇鳍、淡水制备站、空调冷凝器、污水处理厂、

plant, air-conditioning chillers, sewage plant, toilet vacuum collecting system and fuel plant.

黑水真空收集系统和燃油供给机组。

3 甲板中央走廊装饰的艺术作品

FIRST REFIT – NOVEMBER-DECEMBER 2011

The Queen Mary 2's first refit took place at the Blohm+Voss Shipyard in Hamburg, Germany, from 24 November to 7 December 2011. Major soft furnishings renewals included all staterooms, Canyon Ranch SpaClub, the Queens Grill and princess Grill restaurants, the commodore club, the veuve clicquot champagne bar, sir samuel's wine bar, the play zone/kid's zone, and a complete redesign of the golden lion pub.

Peter shanks, President of the cunard line remarked, 'Queen Mary 2 is an iconic leader in the world of luxury ocean travel and continues to receive high ratings by guests and the cruise industry. A ship that still turns heads everywhere she goes, she is unquestionably the pride of our fleet. We are committed to maintaining that impeccable reputation, and this significant refurbishment is an important investment on behalf of our guests.'

The 14-day refit required a team of thousands of workers replacing the equivalent of almost 10 football pitches of carpet and manufacturing about 18 square miles of fabric into over 6,000 individual items.Staterooms. All 1,310 staterooms aboard Queen Mary 2 received a new look, with replacement carpeting, curtains and beddings, some also acquiring new furniture.Golden lion pub. With its increasingly popular traditional British pub lunch menus, busy bar, exciting sports events and nightly music offerings the pub benefited from a complete refurbishment and redesign to enhance its endearing appeal. The new design retained the British pub atmosphere while evoking an American country club feel. Upgraded television screens were also installed. Canyon Ranch SpaClub. An extensive refurbishment of the first Canyon Ranch SpaClub at sea included the teak surrounds of the hydrotherapy pool and adjacent wet areas, and a general upgrade of all the facilities. In addition, new exercise machines in the fitness centre and new and improved features in the beauty salon were installed.

Queens Grill and Princess Grill restaurants. A new, lighter carpet design for both Grill restaurants was designed to enhance the existing ambience, maintaining the reputation of these fine dining venues as among the best at sea or on land.

Commodore Club. One of the most visited public rooms aboard Queen Mary 2, this breathtaking lounge overlooking her bow was refreshed with a new carpet design and additions to the white leather furnishings of chairs, sofas and bar stools.

Veuve Clicquot champagne bar. A popular space especially on transatiantic crossings, this venue featuring the exquisite Veuve Clicquot brand of champagne saw a new carpet and soft furnishings design.

Sir Samuel's wine bar. This busy venue promoting speciality coffees during the day and an impressive menu of wines at night, received a new complement of carpeting and furniture coverings.

The Play Zone/Kids' Zone. Facilities for younger guests underwent a complete refurbishment, including new soft play areas, plus upgrades to the very latest in electronic gaming technology and entertainment. Throughout the ship there are 280,000 square yards (250,000 square metres) of fitted carpets, 144,000 square yards (120,000 square metres) of insulating material and 3,800 square yards (3,200 square metres) of galley space.

第一次改装——2011年11月~12月

2011年11月24日至12月7日,"玛丽女王2号"在德国汉堡的布卢姆·沃斯船厂进行了首次改装。软装更换的主要区域包括所有客房、"峡谷牧场"水疗俱乐部、"女王"和"公主"餐厅、"船长"俱乐部、凯歌香槟酒吧、"塞缪尔爵士"酒吧、游戏区/儿童活动中心以及金狮酒吧的完整重新设计。

冠达航运公司总裁彼得·尚克斯说:"'玛丽女王2号'是世界豪华海洋旅游的标志性领导者,她一直受到游客和邮轮业的好评。这艘船无论走到哪里都会引起人们的注意,毫无疑问,她是我们船队的骄傲。我们致力于维护这一无可挑剔的声誉,这次重大翻新是以我们乘客的名义所进行的一项重要投资。"

这项为期14天的改装工程需要一个由数千名工人组成的团队,将相当于10个足球场大小的地毯替换掉,并将大约18平方英里的织物加工成6 000多个小块。

客房:"玛丽女王2号"上所有1 310个客房都焕然一新,更换了地毯、窗帘和床上用品,有些客房还添置了新家具。

金狮酒吧:除了日益流行的传统英国酒吧午餐菜单之外,繁忙的酒吧、令人兴奋的体育赛事和夜间音乐节目,这些都通过酒吧的完整翻新和重新设计得以实现,从而增强了吸引力。新设计保留了英国酒吧的氛围,同时还融入了美国乡村俱乐部的感觉,还安装了升级的电视屏幕。

"峡谷牧场"水疗俱乐部:对第一个"峡谷牧场"水疗俱乐部进行了大规模的翻新,包括水疗池和邻近的潮湿区的柚木以及对所有设施的全面升级。此外,健身中心安装了新的健身器,美容院也安装了新的和改进的设备。

"女王"餐厅和"公主"餐厅:两个餐厅都采用了一种新的、更明快的地毯设计,以增强现有的氛围,保持这些美食场所在海上或陆地上的最佳声誉。

"准将"俱乐部:"玛丽女王2号"上最受欢迎的公共房间之一,通过这个令人惊叹的休息室可以俯瞰她的船头。新的地毯设计和白色皮革家具的椅子、沙发和酒吧凳子使房间焕然一新。

凯歌香槟酒吧:这是一个很受欢迎的空间,尤其是在横跨大西洋航行时,这个场地以精致的凯歌香槟品牌为特色,配以新地毯和软家具。

塞缪尔爵士酒吧:这个繁忙的场所在白天推广特色咖啡,在晚上提供令人印象深刻的葡萄酒菜单,翻新时新铺设了地毯和家具饰面。

游戏区/儿童活动中心:为年轻客人的设施进行了完整的翻新,增加了一个爱婴世界,采用最新的电子游戏技术对娱乐项目进行升级。船上有28万平方码(25万平方米)的固定地毯,14.4万平方码(12万平方米)的绝缘材料和3 800平方码(3 200平方米)的厨房空间。

Passenger cabins

True to her ocean-liner lineage, Queen Mary 2 provides a range of and preferences from the merely ample to the spectacularly opulent.

There are 1,310 passenger staterooms, of which 77.6% are outside. Features include king-size beds (convertible to twin), a computer dataport for personal laptops, direct-dial telephone, refrigerator, individual thermostat control, hair dryer, 110-/220-volt outlets and bathroom with bath and/ or shower. Originally email access was available from every passenger cabin via an interactive television set using a wireless keyboard. However, this was notoriously slow and led to many frustrated users. In the meantime, wireless technology great evolved and it was therefore decided to discontinue the interactive system and offer the possibility of connecting to the ship's email and internet system wirelessly from any wireless-enabled personal laptop from within the cabins and elsewhere throughout the passenger accommodation. Sadly, other interactive features of the system, such as the film and music channels, were lost, being replaced by standard non-interactive channels accessed through the television. The televisions were originally cathode-ray models but these have now all been replaced with flat-screen variants Outside staterooms also feature a sitting area with sofa and all Queens Grill accommodation offers a butler service.

• 955 (73%) of staterooms feature

乘客舱室

她是纯正的远洋班轮，从经济实惠到奢侈享受，“玛丽女王 2 号”提供了一系列选择。

船上有 1 310 个乘客舱室，其中 77.6% 是外舱房。设有特大床（可拆为 2 个单人床），一个服务于个人便携式电脑的计算机数据端口、直拨电话、冰箱、独立恒温控制器、吹风机、110/220V 插座和带有浴缸和 / 或淋浴的卫生间。最初每个客舱通过一个配有无线键盘的交互式电视机可以使用电子邮件功能，然而因为网速过于缓慢而致使很多用户感到不满。与此同时，无线技术有了巨大的改变，因此我们决定停止使用交互系统，改为向客舱内和乘客居住区其他地方的个人笔记本电脑提供无线连接，从而使其可以连接到船舶电子邮件和互联网系统。遗憾的是，系统的其他交互功能，例如电影和娱乐频道被取消了，最终通过用电视机的非交互式频道作为替代。电视最初采用 CRT 形式，但现在这些都已经用平板屏幕替代了。外部也设有一个带有沙发的休息区。所有的“女王”级客舱都可享受管家服务。

• 77.6% 的客舱为外舱房。

• 955（73%）个客舱是阳台房，这多于英国邮轮市场的任何其他船舶。

balconies-more than any other ship serving the British cruise market. All of the balconies are very large-approximately 2.5 metres (8 feet) deep.

• 77.6% of staterooms are outside.

• At 194 square feet (18 square metres), queen Mary 2 offers among the largest standard staterooms of any passenger ship

• 30 disabled staterooms (in various category grades) have been specially designed to be fully accessible to disabled persons, with wheelchair access, wider doors and disabled toilets. Facilities for blind guests include braille signs and tactile room signage

• 36 staterooms have been designed to accommodate deaf or hearing-impaired passengers with public room resources including headsets in the theatre and planetarium and closed-caption television.

所有的阳台都非常大,进深大约有2.5米(8英尺)。

• 标准客房为194平方英尺(18平方米)的尺寸,"玛丽女王2号"的标准客舱相比于其他客船是最大的。

• 30个残疾人房间分布于多个等级,通过特殊设计使这些舱室对残疾人来说是完全无障碍的。房间内有轮椅通道、更宽的门和残疾人卫生间。为失明客人提供的设施有盲文标记和可触觉感知的房间标牌。

• 36个为聋人或有听觉障碍的乘客设计的舱室,配置有为在公共区域活动所需的设备,包括用于剧院和天文馆的耳机、CC字幕电视[*]。

Total number of stateroom	客舱总数	1 310
Outside doubles	外舱双人间	1 017(77%)
Inside doubles	内舱双人间	293(23%)
Balconies	阳台房	955(73%)
Staterooms equipped for disabled passengers	残疾人客舱	30

*CC字幕即close-caption字幕,主要是为了方便有听力障碍的残障人士,里面除了对白之外,还有现时场景的声音和配乐等信息——译者注。

Combinations

• The four forward suites can be combined to create one suite of 3,980 square feet (including balcony) or 3,744 square feet (excluding balcony).

• Grand duplex apartments can be joined at the lower level to the adjacent penthouse making each 2,185 square feet (203 square metres) in total, excluding the balcony.

• Duplexes may be combined with the grand duplexes and two penthouses for a living space measuring an unprecendented 8,288 square feet (770 square metres), excluding balconies.

The passenger cabins were jointly designed by the associated companies of SMC Design (London) and Tillberg Design (Sweden).The interior architects

组合

• 4 个套房可以组合成 1 个 3 980 平方英尺（包括阳台）或者 3 744 平方英尺（不包括阳台）的套房。

• 超豪华复式套房的底层可同相邻的套房组合，使每一个豪华复式房除阳台以外的面积达到 2 185 平方英尺（203 平方米）。

• 复式套房可以和豪华复式套房以及两个套房组合成一个居住空间，除阳台外的总面积达到惊人的 8 288 平方英尺（770 平方米）。

乘客舱室的设计是由 SMC 设计公

建造舱室样板间以固化装饰方案，并在生产前和船东敲定室内布置的最终方案。

presented mood boards to Cunard representing how they envisaged the cabins should look. Following some discussion agreement was reached and the architects prepared detailed design drawings for the shipyard, including a specification of the materials and colours that would be required. As part of the shipbuilding contract, the shipyard had to construct a mock-up cabin block comprising a standard cabin, a Princess suite and a Queens suite and a section of cabin corridor complete with handrails, pillars, technical lockers, etc. The corridor grid cabins had to be fully outfitted with all lighting and cabin furnishings so that Carnival and Cunard's senior managements could make any changes and sign off on the design before the production of the real cabins commenced. The mock-ups were required to be maintained as a reference throughout the ship construction in case of disputes between the owners and shipyard of the production cabins. A two-berth crew cabin was also required.

The original passenger staterooms had a preponderance of dark wood-effect panelling in line with traditional transatlantic practice. During the owners' inspection of the mock-ups it was decided that this was rather oppressive and would not be appropriate for when the ship was cruising in warm climes. Accordingly, it was requested to change to a much lighter wood effect and the mock-ups were rebuilt by the shipyard and presented for approval to the owners, which was subsequently granted in full.

司（伦敦）和蒂尔伯格设计公司（瑞典）共同完成的。室内设计师通过情绪板向冠达展示舱室样式的设想。在一些讨论达成一致意见后，建筑师为船厂准备详细的设计图纸，包括所需的材料和色彩规格书。作为船舶建造合同的一部分，船厂需要建造一系列的舱室样板间，包括标准舱房、"公主级"套房和"女王级"套房，以及包含扶手、立柱、技术储藏室等的局部舱室走廊。走廊和舱室需要完全舾装到位，带有所有的灯光和舱室家具陈设，这样嘉年华和冠达的高级管理者可以在真正的舱室生产前对设计修改进行评估并签发设计图。舱室样板间要求在船舶建造期间，作为标准和参照妥善留存，以备在船东和船厂针对舱室制造期间发生争执时，可以有实物依据。此外一个双人的船员舱室也要求留存。

起初乘客舱室大量使用深色木纹板，这符合传统的跨大西洋航线的风格。在船东检查样板间的过程中他们认为这种设计很压抑，不适合温暖气候中航行的船舶。因此，他们要求更换为浅色的木质效果方案，船厂重新建造样板间并呈交船东批准，随后全部获得了认可。

Type of staterooms

There are ten different types of stateroom: grand duplex apartments, duplex apartments, Royal suites, penthouses, suites, junior suites, deluxe and premium balcony, standard outside, atrium and standard inside.

The breakdown is as follows:

舱室类型

一共有10种不同类型的舱室：豪华复式套房、复式套房、皇家套房、顶楼套房、普通套房、迷你套房、豪华复式阳台房、标准海景房、中庭内景房和标准内舱房。

其分类如下：

Type	类型	Number 数量	Square metres 平方米
Grand duplex apartments	豪华复式套房	2	209
Duplex apartments	复式套房	3	120
Royal suites	皇家套房	4	145/174
Penthouses	顶楼套房	6	70
Suites	普通套房	82	47
Junior suites	迷你套房	76	35
Deluxe and premium balcony	豪华复式阳台房	782	23/25
Standard outside	标准海景房	62	18
Atrium	中庭内景房	12	18
Standard inside	标准内舱房	281	18
Total	总数	1310	

Grand duplex

The 2,249-square-foot Balmoral and Sandringham duplexes are the most lavish and magnificent suites afloat. The sweeping living quarters with extensive balcony and spectacular views over the stem include a fully stocked bar, dining area for eight, dressing room, interactive plasma screen TV and home office corner. Upstairs, the master bedroom has private exercise equipment, a second TV,

豪华复式套房

2 249平方英尺的"巴尔莫洛"和"桑德林汉姆"复式套房是最豪华的套房。其生活区外环绕着宽敞的阳台，可以看到船首的美丽景色。其中包括一个塞得满当当的酒吧、8人用餐区域、更衣室、交互式等离子电视和家庭办公区。楼上配备有私人健身器材的主卧室、第二个电视，两间大理石装饰

two marble 'his and hers' dressing rooms with connecting bathrooms and separate whirlpool bath and shower. (Guest bathroom with shower is downstairs.)

的男女更衣室和浴室、独立式漩涡浴池和淋浴区相连（客人的盆浴和淋浴间在楼下）。

5 个大复式套房之一的"巴尔莫洛"复式套房，客厅布置在底层。

豪华复式套房有宽敞的浴室，就像"巴尔莫洛"复式套房中的这个一样。

豪华复式套房的卧室

复式套房（冠达邮轮公司提供）

Duplex apartments

The 1,471-square-foot Windsor and Buckingham duplexes and the 1,566-square-foot Holyrood duplex are similar to the above but feature slightly smaller staterooms and balconies. These two-storey apartments with panoramic views over the stem also feature a fully stocked bar, dining area for eight, dressing room, plasma screen TV system and home office comer. The open stairway leads to the vaulted ceiling bedroom area with private exercise equipment and two connecting baths with whirlpool bath and shower with body jets.

复式套房

1 471 平方英尺的"温莎"和"白金汉"复式套房和 1 566 平方英尺的"霍利鲁德"复式套房与豪华复式套房很相似，只是房间和阳台稍微小了一些。这种复式套房在船首有全景视野，同样也有一个塞得满当当的酒吧、8 人用餐区域、更衣室、等离子电视系统和家庭办公区。开敞楼梯通向带有拱形天花板的卧室区域，卧室区域内有私人健身设备、两个相邻的漩涡浴和带喷水按摩的淋浴。

Royal suites-Queens Grill

A glass lift with private access on Deck 10 opens into the 1,194-square-foot Queen Mary and Queen Elizabeth suites. Located all the way forward with commanding ocean views, the luxuriously furnished living quarters feature a marble floor entrance, fully stocked bar and dining area for eight. A secondary living area offers a guest bath and interactive TV system. There is also a second TV in the master bedroom. The master bathroom features a shower and separate whirlpool bath.

The 796-square-foot Queen Anne and Queen Victoria suites offer commanding views over the bow of the ship and are the same as the Queen Mary and Queen Elizabeth suites but with no balcony. Apart from a living and dining area, there is a guest bath, marble entryway, Frette linens, fully stocked bar, two TVs in both the living room and master bedroom, a dining area for four and walk-in wardrobes. The master bathroom has a shower and separate whirlpool bath.

皇家套房－"女王"餐厅

一台玻璃电梯在10甲板有一个私人停层，可以通向1 194平方英尺的"玛丽女王"和"伊丽莎白女王"套房。那里位于通道的前方，可以观赏秀丽的海景。装饰豪华的起居区域设有敷设大理石地面的入口，塞得满当当的酒吧和8人用餐区域。第二个起居区可为客人提供洗浴和互动电视系统。主卧室还有第二台电视机。主浴室设有淋浴区和独立式漩涡浴池。

796平方英尺的"安妮女王"和"维多利亚女王"套房有和"玛丽女王"套房、"伊丽莎白女王"套房一样拥有较高的船首视野，但并没有阳台。除了起居和餐饮区，还有一个乘客浴室、大理石铺砌的入口、弗莱丹浴衣、塞得满当当的酒吧、分别位于起居室和主卧室的2个电视、4人用餐区域以及步入式衣帽间。主卧有一个淋浴和独立式漩涡浴池。

　　"玛丽女王"皇家套房位于船的左舷，是一个宽敞的房间，有一个由几个相互连接空间组成的阳台。有很好的艏部、艉部和左舷视野。

女王级套房提供了极为舒适的空间

Penthouses-Queens Grill

At 758 square feet, penthouses feature a living and dining area with large balcony. Other provisions include Frette linens and a full dressing room. The entrance and dining areas accommodate seating for four and there is a fully stocked bar and guest bath. Both the bedroom and living rooms connect to a teak balcony.

顶楼套房 - "女王"餐厅

758 平方英尺的顶楼套房有一个起居室和带有大阳台的用餐区。此外还提供弗莱丹浴衣和一个齐备的更衣室。入口和用餐区设有可容纳四个人的座位,并有塞得满当当的酒吧和客人浴室。卧室和起居室都与柚木地面的阳台相连。

Suits-Queens Grill

Each 506-square-foot suite boasts a large balcony, spacious living area, dressing room and bathroom with separate shower and whirlpool bath. Original art graces the walls. The sitting area incorporates a sofa and dual-height coffee table that can be extended to a dining table. The bedroom area features a king-size bed and a separate dressing area with walk-in wardrobes.

普通套房 - "女王"餐厅

每间 506 平方英尺的普通套房都拥有一个大阳台,宽敞的起居区、更衣室、带有独立的淋浴和漩涡浴池的浴室。原始风格艺术品使墙壁增色不少。起居区包括沙发和可以延伸到餐桌的两档调高咖啡桌。卧室里有一张特大床,另外还有一个配有步入式衣帽间的更衣区。

Junior suites-Princess Grill

Each 381 -square-foot junior suite has a sitting area with full-size sofa and interactive TV, a large balcony furnished with loungers and tables and a full bathroom with bath and shower. There are also separate glass cabinets and a walk-in wardrobe.

迷你套房 - "公主"餐厅

每间 381 平方英尺的迷你套房都设有一个休息区,配有全尺寸的沙发和交互式电视,一个配有躺椅和桌子的大阳台,以及一个带浴缸和淋浴的完整浴室。还有独立式的玻璃柜和步入式衣帽间。

公主级迷你套房比"布列塔尼亚"级舱室提供了舒适的空间和更好的用餐体验。

豪华阳台房根据它们在船上的位置，采用如图所示的钢质或玻璃阳台舷墙。（冠达邮轮提供）

Deluxe and premium balcony-Britannia restaurant

Deluxe balcony cabins offer 248 square feet and premium balcony cabins offer 269 square feet including a panoramic hull balcony with loungers and tables. King-size beds may be converted to twins and a dual-height coffee table may be used for in-room dining. The sitting area features a sofa and there is ample wardrobe space and bathroom with shower.

Standard outside-Britannia restaurant

At 194 square feet these staterooms provide spacious comfort with king-size or twin beds. Other features include a dual-height coffee table for in-room dining.

豪华复式阳台房 - "布列塔尼亚"餐厅

豪华复式阳台房有 248 平方英尺，更优质的阳台房有 269 平方英尺，含有带有躺椅和桌子的全景阳台。特大床可以换成双人床，两档调高咖啡桌也可以用于室内用餐。休息区配有沙发、空间充足的衣柜和带淋浴的浴室。

标准海景房 - "布列塔尼亚"餐厅

194 平方英尺的客房提供宽敞舒适的特大床或双人床。此外还有一个两档调高咖啡桌用于室内用餐。

带有一个画框大小的方窗或超大舷窗的标准海景房。（冠达邮轮提供）

Atrium

These 194-square-foot staterooms provide spacious comfort with king-size or twin beds. Each of these 12 cabins have views into the atrium below. A dual-height coffee table is provided for in-room dining.

中庭内景房

这些 194 平方英尺的客房配有特大床或双人床，非常宽敞舒适。这 12 个舱室都可以看到下方的中庭，提供一个可以两档调高的咖啡桌用于室内用餐。

中庭内景房是内舱房，但带有一个面向中庭的窗户。

Standard inside

At 194 square feet these staterooms provide spacious comfort with king-size or twin beds. Other features include a dual-height coffee table for in-room dining.

Since entering service 28 staterooms have been redesignated as Britannia Club and these afford a single-sitting enhanced Britannia alternative to the two-sitting Britannia restaurant offering.

标准内舱房

在 194 平方英尺的客房内设置有特大床或双人床，非常宽敞舒适。此外还有一个两档调高的咖啡桌用于室内用餐。

自运营以来，28 个客房被重新指定为"布列塔尼亚"俱乐部级，从而可以享受到单餐次用餐安排以取代"布列塔尼亚"餐厅的双餐次用餐安排。

（译者：陈大为、韩鑫、邰洋、丁悦、贺明鸣、高金军、鲁鼎、谢旭晨）

标准内舱房提供了一个只需少许花费就可以体验高标准的住宿环境的机会。（冠达邮轮公司提供）

第七章 船上生活
Chapter Seven:Life on Board

With over 3,800 souls on board at any given time, Queen Mary 2 is like a small town with every aspect of life played out within her steel shell. Within this town a bakery and numerous restaurants operate around the clock, bands play, actors act, nurses nurse and sea water is converted into fresh from the waste heat of her engines. This town rocks! – and moves from place to place.

　　无论何时，"玛丽女王 2 号"上都承载着超过 3 800 个人，她就像裹在钢铁外壳内的一座小镇，上演着形形色色的各类生活。在这个小镇里，面包房和众多餐馆全天候营业，乐队在演奏，演员在表演，护士在护理，与此同时，利用她引擎中的废热，海水被转换成淡水。举镇欢腾！并不断从一个地方航行到另一个地方。

20世纪30年代的"国之旗舰"的荣耀已经演变进入21世纪："玛丽女王2号"上的"布列塔尼亚"餐厅。（作者提供）

在一个正常的周转日内，"玛丽女王2号"停靠在南安普敦的新港口内。（乔纳森·福尔克纳提供）

客人通常通过3甲板上的舷侧门，由一个倾斜的曲折的舷梯登船。注意，叉车是用来沿着码头运送货物的。（乔纳森·福尔克纳提供）

大厅起始于2甲板，通过金碧辉煌的马蹄形楼梯一直延伸到上层。（作者提供）

欢迎登船！为"玛丽女王2号"的新客人提供基本配置——一套甲板平面图以及邮轮特色指南。（作者提供）

一项引以为荣的传统被保留下来：乘客在登船后会受到热情问候，当需要的时候，甚至还会被护送至他们的客房。（冠达邮轮提供）

3甲板上的中央大道是连接"B""C"电梯和梯道之间公共空间的主要通道。（作者提供）

Welcome aboard

After passing through security, guests usually board Queen Mary 2 via the side shell doors on Deck 3 that open out into the Grand Lobby. The first impression is of spaciousness with restrained luxury. There is no glitz or the myriad of flashing lights that feature on many other ships.

Although Queen Mary 2 was designed primarily with the transatlantic crossing between Southampton and New York in mind, she is equally at home as a holiday cruise ship. Her unique design provides a wide range of public rooms that can be used to after a diverse array of activities and entertainments.

Passengers accommodated in staterooms tied to the Britannia restaurant will have either requested or been designated late or early dinner sittings, all

欢迎登船

通过安检后，宾客通常从3甲板的舷门登上"玛丽女王2号"，这扇门通往大厅。其给人的第一印象是宽敞而又内敛的奢华。这艘船没有其他船上显著的炫目的灯光和无数的闪光灯。

尽管"玛丽女王2号"的设计初衷是作为往返于南安普敦和纽约的跨大西洋班轮，但她也同样是一艘度假邮轮。她独特的设计提供了宽敞的公共空间，可以用于各种活动和娱乐。

住在与"布列塔尼亚"餐厅相配套的客舱里的乘客，会被指定或要求在该餐厅的早场时段或晚场时段进场用餐，餐厅里的所有其他餐点都是开

Captain Kevin Oprey

Phil Aldridge　　　*Dariusz Gozdzik*　　　*John E. Duffy*
Chief Engineer　　　*Deputy Captain*　　　*Hotel Manager*

Cordially request the pleasure of your company to join them for cocktails on Friday 23 March 2012 at 7.45pm in Queens Room

Dress Code: Formal
Kindly present this invitation at the entrance.

一次令人垂涎的工作人员私人鸡尾酒会的邀请函。这种老式的聚会最初是在工作人员自己的小木屋里举行的，但这种做法在嘉年华接手管理冠达邮轮时就结束了。客人需要被精挑细选出来，饮料费用全免。因此，酒会只能持续45分钟。（作者提供）

QUEEN MARY 2
CUNARD

Voyage Routine
Southampton-New York
16th-23rd October 2011

Day/Date Sunrise Sunset	Navigation	Pier/Gangway	Guest Events	Crew Events	Dress Code
0 Sunday – 16th October Southampton Security Level 1 07:29/18:12	Clocks Retarded 1 Hour – GMT +1 SBB: 0330 Pilot on: 0345 Arrive: 0630 Depart: 1630 Pilot off:1900 Distance to New York: 3084 Nautical miles speed required: 19.5kts	Ocean terminal stbd side alongside guests – air bridge dock 3 fwd crew & contractors – 1 Dock fwd	0800 disembarkation 1200 commence embarkation 1600 guest emergency drill 1600 all aboard. All visitors ashore	1300 induction 1 – odeon bar 1400 SWG and muster personnel training – odeon bar 1600 guest emergency drill 1600 all aboard, all visitors ashore	Blues 1800 informal (guests elegant casual)
1 Monday – 17th October 06:52/17:53	Clocks retarded 1 hour – GMT	At sea	1715 captain's cocktail reception – Britannia early sitting – queens room 1945 captain's cocktail reception – Britannia late	0930 watertight doors tested under power from Bridge 1000 FRC muster 1100 liferaft training davit team 2 1530 – 1630 PEASI Testing	Blues 1700 formal
2 Tuesday – 18th October 06:37/17:38	Clocks retarded 1 hour – GMT -1	At sea 0800 PAW MEETING	1830 captain's cocktail reception – grills – queens room 2045 & 2230 "viva italia" 2145 – 0000 big band ball	0900 & 1600 lifeboat hook & engine training – deck 4 forward anchor deck 1000 full crew drill	Blues 1800 formal
3 Wednesday – 19th October 06:20/17:23	Clocks retarded 1 hour – GMT -2	At sea 0930 scattering of ashes		Time TBA crew bottle sales 1000 induction 2 – royal court theare 1100 liferaft training davit team 3 1600 white star committee meeting – connexions	Blues informal (guests semi-formal)
4 Thursday – 20th October 06:59/18:04		At sea 0900 SMT MEETING 1700 ROV	1130 senior officers cocktail party – Winter garden	1000 security drill 1030 crew cabin inspection Inspection – supervisors only	Blues 1800 formal 2030 DINNER
5 Friday – 21st October 07:36/18:46	FLU JABS	At sea 1030 BOOK SIGNING 1130 star of month In Britannia annex 1730 ROV	1930 cunard world club cocktail party – queens room 2145 masked ball 2045 & 2230 "apassionata"	Unannounced galley rounds 1000 induction 3 – royal court theatre 1115 liferaft training davit team 4	Blues 1800 formal 2030 DINNER
6 Saturday – 22nd October 07:22/18:45	Clocks retartded 1 hour – GMT -3	At sea 1700 ROV		1100 liferaft training davit team 5	Blues 1800 informal (guests elegant casual)
7 Sunday – 23rd October New york Security level 1 07:18/18:02	Clocks retarded 1 hour – GMT -4 SBB: 0330 Pilot on: 0345 Arrive: 0630 Depart: 1700 Pilot off:1900 Distance to Southampton: 3084 nautical miles speed required: 19.5kts	Brooklyn cruise terminal Pier 12 Port side alongside Passengers -2 & 3 fwd. Crew -1 dock fwd	0800 disembarkation 1200 commence embarkation 1600 guest emergency drill 1800 all aboard. All visitors ashore	1300 induction 1 – odean bar 1400 SWG and muster personnel training – odeon bar 1600 guest emergency drill 1600 all aboard. All visitors ashore	Blues 1800 informal (pax elegant casual)

QUEEN MARY 2
CUNARD

航行日程：
南安普敦—纽约
2011 年 10 月 16 日至 23 日

航行日 / 日期 日出、日落	航行	码头 / 舷梯	乘客活动	船员活动	着装要求
0 星期日 –10 月 16 日 南安普敦 安全等级 1 07:29/18:12	时钟拨慢 1 小时 时区 +1 SBB：0330 引航员：0345 到达：0630 出发：1630 引航员离船：1900 距离约 3 084 海里 航速要求：19.5 节	右舷停靠码头 乘客 –3 号舢部廊桥 船员和服务商 –1 号码头前	0800 离船 1200 开始登船 1600 乘客紧急演习 1600 所有乘客上船，所有访客上岸	1300 培训 1– 剧院酒吧 1400SWG 和人员集合训练 – 剧院酒吧 1600 乘客紧急演习 1600 所有访客上岸	蓝色 1800 非正装（乘客得体的便装）
1 星期一 –10 月 17 日 06:52/17:53	时钟拨慢 1 小时 时区	海上航行	1715 船长欢迎鸡尾酒会 – 布列塔尼亚餐厅头场 1945 船长欢迎酒会 – 布列塔尼亚餐厅晚场	0930 驾驶室控制水密门测试 1000 消防控制中心集合 1100 第 2 组救生筏训练 1530–1630 PEASI 测试	蓝色 1700 正装
2 星期二 –10 月 18 日 06:37/17:38	时钟拨慢 1 小时 时区 –1	海上航行 0800 联席会议	1830 船长欢迎酒会 – 女王餐厅 2045&2230"意大利万岁"演艺 2415–0000 大乐队舞会	0900&1600 救生艇钩和引擎训练 – 第 4 甲板舢部锚系泊甲板 1000 全体船员演习	蓝色 1800 正装
3 星期三 –10 月 19 日 06:20/17:23	时钟拨慢 1 小时 时区 –2	海上航行 0930 排放固体垃圾		时间待定，船员推销酒水 1000 培训 2– 皇家剧院 1100 第 3 组救生筏训练 1600 白星委员会会议 – 联络	蓝色 1800 非正装（乘客半正装）
4 星期四 –10 月 20 日 06:59/18:04		海上航行 0900 高管任务会议 1700 航海报告	1130 高级船员酒会 – 冬季花园	1000 安全演习 1030 船员舱室检查 检查 – 仅限主管	蓝色 1800 正装 2030 晚宴
5 星期五 –10 月 21 日 07:36/18:46	流感预防	海上航行 1030 书籍签名 1130 每月之星在布列塔尼亚附属房间 1730 航海报告	1930 冠达全球俱乐部酒会 – 女王套房 2145 面具舞会 2045&2230 阿佩苏纳塔演艺	无预告厨房巡查 1000 培训 3– 皇家剧院 1115 第 4 组救生筏训练	蓝色 1800 正装 2030 晚宴
6 星期六 –10 月 22 日 07:22/18:45	时钟拨慢 1 小时 时区 –3	海上航行 1700 航海报告		1100 第 5 组救生筏训练	蓝色 1800 非正装（乘客得体的便装）
7 星期日 –10 月 23 日 纽约 安全等级 1 07:18/18:02	时钟拨慢 1 小时 时区 –4 SBB：0330 引航员：0345 到达：0630 出发：1700 引航员离船：1900 距离南安普顿：3 084 海里 航速要求：19.5 节	布鲁克林邮轮码头 泊位 12 左舷靠岸 乘客 –2 和 3 号舢部 船员 –1 号舢部	0800 离船 1200 开始登船 1600 乘客紧急演习 1800 所有访客上岸	1300 培训 1– 剧院酒吧 1400 SWG 和人员集合训练 – 剧院酒吧 1600 乘客紧急演习 1600 所有访客上岸	蓝色 1800 非正装（乘客得体的便装）

other meals in the restaurant being on an open basis. The Britannia Club restaurant and Grill Rooms operate on a single sitting basis, although with assigned seating.

Early on in the cruise the ship's master hosts several 'welcome aboard' cocktail parties for each of the restaurant sittings where he introduces his senior staff. Many other parties are usually scheduled throughout each voyage to commemorate frequent travelers and special events .

Each day several 40-minute 'Enrichment' lectures are given in the Illuminations area by a myriad of guest speakers who usually follow up with a book signing if they have had a relevant

放的。"布列塔尼亚俱乐部"餐厅和烤肉房都是以单餐次模式来运营的，但是以指定座位的方式。

在航行的早期，船长会为每个餐次的客人举办几场"欢迎登船"鸡尾酒会，在酒会上他会介绍他的高级职员。许多其他的聚会通常被分开安排在每个航海日中，以纪念经常旅行的人和特殊的事件。

每天都会进行几场40分钟的"干货"讲座，已经来过无数的客座演讲者，如果他们出版过相关的书籍，他们通常会进行签名售书。如果需要的

在奢华的环境中，"玛丽女王2号"的客人在船上享受了一个美好的夜晚。（冠达邮轮公司提供）

在船上，舒适的夜晚为乘客提供许多拍照机会。（冠达邮轮提供）

板球只是在船上消遣的一种方式。（冠达邮轮提供）

在 SPA 区的放松提供了另一个机会来体验航行的美妙，哪怕只是在那聊聊天。（冠达邮轮提供）

准备好迎接朝阳的朝拜者们，经典的木制躺椅上铺满了绿色的垫子。（作者提供）

一种流行于海上航行的消遣活动——
在广阔的游步甲板上慢跑。（作者提供）

游步甲板上的里程标志。（作者提供）

2012 年 3 月 16 日，在前往大阪的途
中船上的节目表。（作者提供）

BRITANNIA RESTAURANT

Make a grand descent into
the Britannia Restaurant.
This magnificent two-tiered salon soars three
stories to an overhead light well. Classic
columns accent the vertical grandeur.
Her message is clear –
Britannia does indeed rule the waves.

QUEEN MARY 2
MAY 22ND - 28TH 2005

00487029

船长的餐桌。能被邀请至这张神圣的餐桌，被视为航行中最大的奖赏之一。（作者提供）

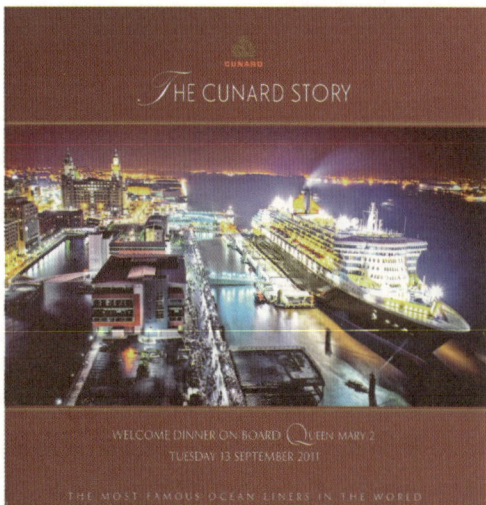

THE CUNARD STORY

WELCOME DINNER ON BOARD QUEEN MARY 2
TUESDAY 13 SEPTEMBER 2011

THE MOST FAMOUS OCEAN LINERS IN THE WORLD

菜单封面（作者提供）

跨大西洋处女航已经结束了。"玛丽女王2号"在纽约泊位中。（冠达邮轮提供）

"玛丽女王2号"从纽约著名的自由女神像出发，开始她的第200次跨越北大西洋的旅途。2013年7月6日。（冠达邮轮提供）

book published . Where demand exists, these are sometimes switched to the Royal Court theatre. Computer lessons, acting classes, bridge lessons, craft works, dance lessons and a host of other activities are programmed each day when the ship is at sea.

　　The full range of activities can be gleaned from the excerpts from the daily programme opposite, and one of the highlights of any voyage is the dining experience.

　　All too quickly the voyage is over and it's time to start planning the next one!

话，这些讲座有时会转到"宫廷"剧院。当船在海上时，计算机课、表演课、桥牌课、工艺课、舞蹈课和许多其他活动都被编入每天的计划当中。

　　完整的活动安排可以在每日节目单上看到，在任何航程中用餐体验一定是一个亮点。

　　旅程很快就结束了，是时候开始计划下一个了！

'This is your captain speaking'

船长之声

Captain Kevin Oprey on the responsibilities of being master of Queen Mary 2

凯文·奥波雷船长肩负着管理"玛丽女王 2 号"的重任

As master of Cunard's flagship, Queen Mary 2, my principal responsibility is for the safe and efficient navigation and operation of the ship and the well-being of all her passengers and crew. In many ways the role of captain is similar to that of a CEO. As the ship's most senior officer I am both its figurehead and its lead, accountable and responsible for overseeing the daily operations of the ship and encouraging and supporting the officers and crew in their duties.

In the effective discharge of there responsibilities I head a senior management team made up of the deck, Hotel and Technical departmental heads, supported by a larger operations team consisting of officers from all departmental divisions.

The diverse and varied nature of shipboard operations demand decisive leadership. Our operating conditions can be challenging and the welfare of the ship, her passengers and company are paramount. A complex regulatory environment requires the ship's management team to achieve and maintain the highest health, safety, environmental

作为冠达邮轮公司旗舰"玛丽女王 2 号"的船长，我的主要职责是确保船舶安全、高效地航行和运作，以及兼顾所有乘客和船员的身心健康。在许多方面，船长类似于首席执行官的角色。作为这艘船的最高指挥官，我既是她的形象担当，也是她的领导，负责监督船舶的日常运作，鼓励和支持官员及船员们履行好职责。

为有效分摊任务，我领导了一个由甲板、酒店和技术部门主管组成的高级管理小组，并由一个规模较大的来自各部门的干事组成的业务小组提供支持。

船舶操作的多样性需要果断的领

凯文·奥波雷船长在"玛丽女王 2 号"的驾驶室。（作者提供）

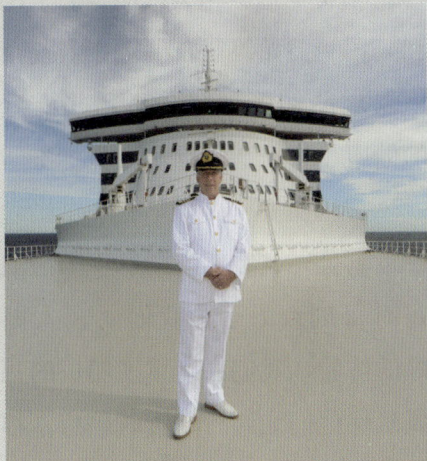

奥波雷船长站在大防浪犁前面的前部甲板上，他总揽全局。（冠达邮轮提供）

Captain Kevin Oprey grew up on the edge of Southampton Water in England, coming from a long line of seafarers.

As a boy, he spent most of his time in sailing boats on the Solent, which is one of the world's great sailing waters. He was fascinated by the grand liners as they gracefully transited the Solent and Southampton Waters and it was this attraction that inspired Kevin to choose a life at sea.

Kevin began his career as a navigating cadet on ships of the Pacific Steam Navigation Company, trading from the UK to the North and South Americas and Caribbean. Throughout his career he has sailed worldwide on a range of ships including cruise ships, cargo ships, supertankers and high-speed catamarans. His keen interest in sailing also led him to serve for two years as mate aboard the Sail Training Association's three-masted topsail schooners Sir Winston Churchill and Malcolm Miller.

Kevin joined Carnival UK in 2007 as staff captain on the Oriana and later sailed as captain on the Arcadia. He recently transferred to the Cunard Line and is very proud to be part of such a historic company and to be in command of the Queen Mary 2.

凯文·奥波雷船长是在英格兰的南安普敦海边长大的，具有丰富的航海经验。

小时候，他大部分时间都驾帆船航行于索伦特海峡，这是世界上最著名的航道之一。当那些伟大的船优雅地穿越索伦特和南安普敦航道时，他被迷住了，正是这种吸引力激发了凯文选择成为一名水手。

凯文的航海生涯开始于太平洋汽船公司的一名航海实习生，该公司从事从英国到南北美洲和加勒比的贸易。在他的整个航海生涯中，他乘坐了包括邮轮、货船、超级油轮和高速双体船在内的各种船只航行于世界各地。他对航海的浓厚兴趣也使他作为助手在帆船训练协会的三桅帆船"温斯顿·丘吉尔爵士号"和"马尔科姆·米勒爵士号"上服役两年。

凯文于2007年加入嘉年华英国公司，担任"奥丽安娜号"的安全官，后来又在"阿卡迪亚号"上担任船长。近期他又被调到冠达邮轮公司，他为可以成为这样一个历史悠久的公司的一员以及指挥"玛丽女王2号"而感到非常自豪。

and security standards.

Queen Mary 2 has a hard-working ship's company, dedicated to providing the finest possible experience for our guests in every area of the ship, every moment of their day. A high regard is given to the crew's welfare to ensure the crew are happy as they go about their duties.

As captain I recognise the importance of being seen and visiting various working areas of the ship whenever the ship is at sea: this allows me the opportunity to take an interest in the crew's concerns. This affords me the chance to address issues early, while identifying areas needing support and focus, so essential to the continued improvement of the function of the ship.

Likewise, as well as regular informative announcements, a varied range of social activities and engagements mean that I remain visible to our guests and offer the chance for guest interaction. Cocktail parties, formal dinners at the captain's table and speeches, together with weddings, renewal of vows and book signings, allow me to contribute to our guests' experience, helping to encourage them back to Queen Mary 2 again and again.

导。我们的操作条件非常具有挑战性，与船舶安全息息相关，但是船上的乘客和公司利益始终是首要因素。复杂的环境要求船舶管理团队达到并维持最高的健康、安全、环保和安保标准。

"玛丽女王 2 号"有一个勤勉的船舶运营公司，在船上的每一个区域以及每时每刻致力于为我们的客人提供最好的体验。我们高度重视船员的福利，以确保他们在履行职责时倍感幸福。

我认识到每当船舶在海上航行时，作为船长而言，保持存在感，并造访船舶各个工作区域的重要性：这不仅使我有机会对船员的关切感兴趣，还使我有机会尽早解决问题，同时确定船员需要支持和关注的领域，这对于持续改进船舶的效能至关重要。

同样地，除了定期发布信息外，各种各样的社交活动和聚会也意味着我能让我们的客人看到我，并提供与客人互动的机会。鸡尾酒会、船长餐桌上的正式晚宴和演讲，以及婚礼、续期誓言和签名售书仪式，让我为提升客人们的体验做出贡献，鼓励他们一次又一次地回到"玛丽女王 2 号"上来。

A day in the life of the master of Queen Mary 2

There is not really a typical day at sea for the captain; every day presents a different challenge due to the ever-changing position of the ship and the associated change in environmental and weather conditions. This is an exciting aspect of the job, every day is different and I have to be prepared to deal with those challenges.

Dependent upon the ship's itinerary, I often spend long periods on the bridge, particularly when we are in near proximity to the land, experiencing reduced visibility or encountering heavy traffic conditions.

I also have the responsibility for manocuvring thc ship in and out of port; this is the most technical aspect of the role, and handling the controls of Queen Mary 2 is one of the most rewarding parts of my position as master.

The diverse and varied nature of the ship's operational functions, together with the multi-cultural make-up of her crew, mean that the challenges each day brings vary, but nonetheless make the working experience hugely rewarding.

It is impossible to be captain without enjoying the many social functions. All our guests have the opportunity to meet me at the 'welcome aboard' cocktail parties. The captain's table is an enjoyable end to the day, with many different and interesting guests invited on formal evenings, whenever navigational duties allow.

"玛丽女王2号"船长一天的生活

对船长来说，在海上并没有什么典型的一天；由于船舶位置不断地变化以及相关的环境和天气条件变化，每天都会遇到不同的挑战。这是工作中令人兴奋的一个方面，每天都是不同的，我必须准备好应对这些挑战。

根据船舶的行程，我通常在驾驶室度过很长时间，特别是当我们遇到靠近陆地、能见度降低或遇到交通繁忙的情况。

我还负责操纵船舶进出港口，这是最具技术性的工作，操控"玛丽女王2号"是我作为船长的最具成就感的工作之一。

船舶操作的多样性，再加上船员的多元化文化构成，意味着每天的挑战都是不同的，但工作经历却让人受益匪浅。

作为船长必须要参加许多社交活动。我们所有的客人都有机会在"欢迎登船"的鸡尾酒会上与我见面。船长的餐桌是一天愉快活动的终点，只要航行日程允许，许多形形色色有趣的客人会受邀穿着晚礼服出席。

Captain Oprey describes what makes Queen Mary 2 so special

Queen Mary 2 is very different to the normal cruise ship. She is an iconic and thoroughly British ocean liner, which maintains the tradition of the great and historic ocean liners of the past. Designed and constructed specifically as an ocean liner, she has all the liner design properties including a streamlined hull, fine lines, a deep draught and long bow to ensure she is capable of handling the severest of Atlantic weather conditions. In heavy weather, when proceeding at a suitable speed, her ability to remain extremely comfortable and stable makes her stand out from other cruise ships and resort ships that would struggle in similar conditions.

A transatlantic crossing on Queen Mary 2 is far more than just elegant transportation. With a length of 345 metres and beam of 41 metres, there is a feeling of space and luxury throughout, with many spectacular and spacious areas for guests to enjoy and interior

奥波雷船长阐述"玛丽女王2号"的特别之处

"玛丽女王2号"与常规的邮轮不同。她是一艘标志性的英国远洋班轮，她保持了过去伟大而具有历史意义的远洋班轮的传统。她专门设计和建造成一艘远洋班轮，具备所有班轮的设计特性，包括流线型船体、尖瘦型线、深吃水和长船首，以确保她能够应对大西洋最恶劣的天气条件。在恶劣的天气里，当以合适的速度行驶时，她具有保持舒适性和稳定性的能力，使她从在类似条件下只能苦苦挣扎的其他邮轮和度假船中脱颖而出。

乘坐"玛丽女王2号"进行跨洋航行，得到的不仅仅是优雅的体验。邮轮全长345米，宽41米，充满空间感和奢华感，拥有许多壮观而宽敞的区域供客人欣赏，室内装饰展现了过去海洋旅行时代的辉煌、优雅和宏伟。在"光耀"剧院，乘客们可以体验海上第一座天文

位于宏伟的中央通道的艺术品。Arnvid Brandal 创作的壁画。（作者提供）

宏伟的"波士顿"杯。（作者提供）

features showcasing the splendour, elegance and grandeur of a bygone era of ocean travel. In Illuminations, guests can experience the wonders of space in the first planetarium at sea, attend one of the many lectures offered by the Cunard Insights programme, or spend time watching a movie in the cinema, which when available offers 3D films. The Royal Academy of Dramatic Art presents workshops, lectures and performances, allowing the guests not only to watch the stars of tomorrow in person, but actually study the skills of acting with them, and the West End stage is bought to full effect in the two-tier Royal Court Theatre with dynamic musicals and celebrity entertainers. One of the amazing features of our ship is the

馆的太空奇观，参加冠达邮轮公司科学探索项目提供的众多讲座，或者在可播放 3D 电影的电影院看电影。皇家戏剧艺术学院提供研讨会、讲座和表演，让乘客不仅可以亲眼目睹明日新星，还可以学习与他们一起演出的技巧，并且这座两层皇家"宫廷"剧院完全呈现出伦敦西区的剧院本尊的风貌，包括其动感的音乐剧和演艺明星。本船另一个惊艳的区域为"女王"舞厅。它是海上最大的舞池，在整个航行过程中提供大型爵士乐舞蹈活动。

这艘船上满是纪念品，展示过去

Queens Room ballroom. It is the largest dance floor at sea and provides big-band dancing throughout the voyage.

The ship is filled with memorabilia depicting past great liners and the famous that have travelled on board former Cunard Line ships, and our guests can follow the 'Maritime Quest' tour, which relates in audio the history of the company from Samuel Cunard's first transatlantic with Britannia in 1840, through to the present day.

的优质班轮和冠达邮轮公司曾经的著名船只，我们的乘客可以跟随"海洋探索"之旅，从音频讲解中体验冠达邮轮公司的历史——从1840年塞缪尔·丘纳德爵士搭乘"布列塔尼亚号"的第一次跨大西洋之旅，直到今天。

"光耀"剧院在演出中。"玛丽女王2号"上的独一无二的天文馆。（冠达邮轮提供）

"光耀"剧院前方是历史展区，陈列了曾经光顾过冠达邮轮公司的著名乘客的照片。

每一个拐角处都装饰有艺术品，如图所示为"光耀"剧院的大厅入口。（作者提供）

The floating hotel

The ship's officers

Queen Mary 2 is a vast floating hotel that has the ability to move from one place to another across the oceans of the world. With 1,310 guest bedrooms and up to 2,800 guests, a huge organisation ashore and on board is required to ensure everything runs smoothly and guests receive the service, care and attention that is expected from the renowned brand that is the Cunard Line.

On board Queen Mary 2 there are four main departments, each presided over by a departmental head and all reporting to, and overseen by, the ship's master, the captain. The four departments are termed Deck, Medical, Technical and Hotel.

The deputy captain is responsible for crew discipline and the management of the Deck Department. This involves ensuring that the ship is well maintained externally through painting the hull and superstructure and varnishing wooden handrails, wood doors and benches. Open decks need to be kept in good condition ,with any necessary re-caulking/sanding of wood decks, repairing decks laid with composition and repainting painted decks, being periodically undertaken. The deputy captain makes certain that the ship is loaded and trimmed correctly to ensure the requisite margin of stability and is in

漂浮酒店

高级船员

"玛丽女王2号"是一座巨大的漂浮式酒店,能够跨越海洋从一个地方移动到另一个地方。她拥有1 310间客房,可承载多达2 800名客人。为确保一切顺利进行,乘客能够得到服务和照顾,冠达品牌能够保持一贯的品质,公司需要一个庞大的岸上和船上团队。

在"玛丽女王2号"船上有4大部门,每个部门由一个部门长主持工作并向船长报告,接受船长监管。4个部门分别称为甲板部、医务部、技术部和酒店部。

副船长负责船员纪律和甲板部的管理,这包括油漆船体和上层建筑以及给木扶手、木门和长凳上漆,以确保船只的外部得到良好的维护。开敞区域的甲板必须保持良好状态,需要定期对木质甲板进行任何必要的再填缝/砂光、用复合材料修补甲板和油漆甲板。副船长负责本船装载适度和保持正确的浮态,以确保必要的稳定性裕度,并负责桥楼值班人员的管理——包括航海员、大副、二副、三副和四副。

甲板部还包括一名安全官、一名

NAUTICAL TERMS

ABEAM Off the side of a ship, at a right angle to its length

AFT Near or toward the rear of a ship

AHEAD Something that is ahead of a ship's bow

ALLEYWAY A passageway or corridor

ALONGSIDE Side of a ship, when it is beside a pier or another vessel

AMIDSHIPS In or toward the middle of the ship; the longitudinal centre portion of the ship

ASSEMBLY STATIONS Allotted place for each person during a lifeboat drill or an emergency. The number of your station can be found on the rear of your cabin door together with all safety instructions

ASTERN At or toward the stern (back) of the ship

BACKWASH Motion in the water caused by the propeller(s) moving in reverse (astern) direction

BELOW Anything beneath the main deck

BERTH Space for anchoring or mooring a ship, a built-in bunk for sleeping

BLAST The sound made by a ship's horn or whistle

BOAT DECK The deck on which lifeboats and other lifesaving gear are stowed

BOW The forward-most part of the vessel

BRIDGE Navigational command control centre in the forward part of the ship

COLOURS Refers to the national flag or emblem flown by the ship

CABLE LENGTH A measured length equalling 100 fathoms or 600 feet

CHART A nautical map used to navigate a ship

DRAFT Depth of water measured from the surface of the water to a ship's keel

DOCK Berth, pier, quay or wharf

FATHOM Measurement of distance equal to six feet

GALLEY The ship's kitchen

GANGWAY The stairway or ramp link between ship and shore

HOLD Store area for cargo and provisions

KNOT One nautical mile per hour

LEEWARD The direction away from the wind

NAUTICAL MILE One sixtieth of a degree of the earth's circumference, equal to 6,080.2 ft. (land mile = 5280 feet)

PITCH The alternate rise and fall of a ship's bow, which may occur when the ship is under way

PILOT A person licensed to navigate ships through difficult waters, and to advise the Captain on handling the ship during these procedures

PODS Designed to provide both propulsion and manoeuvrability, they are large motors within a formed steel casing, suspended from the ship's hull at the stern, each with a propeller at its forward end.

STARBOARD The right side of a ship when facing forward

STERN The aft-most part of a ship which is opposite the bow

SWELL A large wave that moves without breaking

TENDER A smaller vessel, often a lifeboat, used to transport passengers between the ship and shore when the vessel is at anchor

WAKE The track of agitated water left behind a ship when in motion

WATERLINE The line along the side of the ship's hull corresponding to the surface of the water

WINDWARD Direction from which the wind is blowing. The opposite is leeward

A GUIDE TO EPAULETTES

DECK
- 3+1 DOUBLE GOLD STRIPE — Master
- 4 GOLD — Deputy Captain
- 3 GOLD — Chief Officer, First Officer
- 2.5 GOLD — Second Officer
- 2.5 GOLD W/S — Security Officer
- 2 GOLD — Second Officer
- 1.5 GOLD — Third Officer
- 2 GOLD — Marine Supervisor
- 1 GOLD — Captain's Secretary

DECK
- 3 GOLD/W GREEN — Environmental Officer
- 3.5 GOLD/W RED — Senior Doctor
- 2.5 GOLD/W RED — Senior Nurse

HOTEL
- 4 GOLD W/WHITE — Hotel Manager
- 3.5 GOLD W/WHITE — Food & Beverage Manager
- 3 GOLD W/WHITE — Executive Housekeeper, Chief Purser, Executive Chef, Entertainment Director

HOTEL
- 2.5 GOLD W/WHITE — Crew Purser, Senior Maitre D'Hotel, Public Rooms Manager, Crew Housekeeper, Chef de Cuisine, Cashier, Food & Beverage Controller, Asst Food & Beverage Manager, Provisions Master
- 2 GOLD W/WHITE — Night Purser
- 1.5 GOLD W/WHITE — Assistant Crew Purser, Assistant Provisions Manager, Assistant Public Room Manager
- 1 GOLD W/WHITE — Hotel Manager's Personal Assistant, Sous Chef, Assistant Housekeepers, Assistant Maitre D'Hotel, Assistant Purser Reception

TECHNICAL
- 4 GOLD W/PURPLE — Chief Engineer, Staff Chief Engineer
- 3.5 GOLD W/PURPLE — Ship's Services Engineer, Chief Electrical Officer
- 3 GOLD W/PURPLE — First Electro Technical Officer, First Engineer
- 2.5 GOLD W/PURPLE — Ventilation Officer, Second Engineer, Second Electro Technical Officer
- 2 GOLD W/PURPLE — Technical Storekeeper, Hotel Service Engineer, Third Engineer, Third Electro Technical Officer
- 1.5 GOLD W/PURPLE — Fourth Engineer
- 1 GOLD W/PURPLE — Technical Secretary

冠达的船只等级制度在 1840 年形成，船员是伟大海事服务的代表。（冠达邮轮提供）

charge of the bridge watchkeepers. The latter group includes the navigator, the chief officer, and first, second and third officers.

The Deck Department also includes a safety officer, a security officer and an environmental officer. The latter is becoming more and more important as the rules and regulations pertaining to the accidental, or otherwise, discharge of any fluid or disposal of any solid material overboard become more and more onerous, with penalties to match. Deck officers wear epaulettes with gold stripes set on a plain black background with a diamond on the first stripe. The environmental officer is an exception to this in having two green bands set

安保官和一名环保官。随着有关的规章和条例（如在事故或其他情况下，液体或固体物质排放）变得越来越繁杂，相应的惩罚条款随之加重，后一职务也显得越来越重要。甲板上的高级船员戴着肩章，上面镶有金色条纹，底色是纯黑色，在第一条纹上绣有钻石花纹。特别的，环保员肩章在三条金色条纹之间设置了两条绿色条纹。理论上还会任命一位船长秘书，尽管这个角色通常由轮机长兼任。

为了确保船舶的机器（例如空调、黑水系统、海水淡化等）得到维护，

甲板部	人员	甲板部	人员	酒店部	人员	技术部	人员
3 细+1 粗金色条纹	船长	3 金色条纹配绿色间纹	环保官员	2.5 金色条纹配白色间纹	船员管事、酒店高级主管、公共场所经理、船员管家、厨师长、收银员、食品和酒水管理员、食品和酒水经理助理、供应主管	4 金色条纹配紫色间纹	轮机长、行政轮机长
4 金色条纹	副船长	3.5 金色条纹配红色间纹	高级医师	2 金色条纹配白色间纹	夜间管事	3.5 金色条纹配紫色间纹	船舶服务工程师、首席电气主管
3 金色条纹	总干事、大副	2.5 金色条纹配红色间纹	高级护士	1.5 金色条纹配白色间纹	船员管事助理、供应经理助理、公共场所经理助理	3 金色条纹配紫色间纹	第一电气技术主管、二管
2.5 金色条纹	二副			1 金色条纹配白色间纹	酒店经理私人助理、副厨师长、管事助理、酒店主管助理、接待管事助理	2.5 金色条纹配紫色间纹	通风主管、三管、第二电气技术主管
2.5 金色条纹配 S 标志	安保官员	酒店部				2 金色条纹配紫色间纹	技术仓储员、酒店服务工程师、四管、第三电气技术主管
2 金色条纹	二副	4 金色条纹配白色间纹	酒店经理			1.5 金色条纹配紫色间纹	五管
1.5 金色条纹	三副	3.5 金色条纹配白色间纹	食品和酒水经理			1 金色条纹配紫色间纹	技术秘书
2 金色条纹	海事监察员	3 金色条纹配白色间纹	客房部经理、首席管事、行政主厨、娱乐项目主管				
1 金色条纹	船长秘书						

"玛丽女王 2 号"的酒店部各种岗位上的工作人员合影。（冠达邮轮提供）

between three gold stripes. A captain's secretary is also appointed, although this role is shared with the chief engineer.

To make sure that the ship's machinery is maintained and available to propel the ship and that all the hotel services are available - such as air-conditioning, toilet systems, fresh water production etc - a large engineering staff is required within the Technical Department. Presided over by the chief engineer, the department maintains the following key positions:

Staff chief engineer, ship's services engineer, chief electrical officer, first electro technical officer, first engineer, ventilation officer, second engineer, second electro technical officer, technical storekeeper,

以便船舶的航行和所有酒店功能正常进行，技术部需要大量的工程人员。由轮机长负责，该部门设置下列关键职位：

行政轮机长、船舶服务工程师、首席电气主管、第一电气技术主管、二管、通风主管、三管、第二电气技术主管、技术仓储员、酒店服务工程师、四管、第三电气技术主管和五管。技术秘书协助完成轮机官员的工作。技术工程船员佩戴金色条纹伴以紫色间纹的肩章。这是为了表彰在白星班轮公司的"泰坦尼克号"上展现出英勇奉献精神的船舶工程师们，英国国王

客房服务人员在铺好的床铺上做最后的整理。（冠达邮轮提供）

hotel service engineer and fourth engineer. A technical secretary completes the engineering officer complement. Engineering officer wear epaulettes with purple set between gold stripes. This colour was specially granted to all marine engineers by HM King George V in recognition of the valiant and heroic service the marine engineers displayed on board White Star Line's Titanic in Keeping the pumps running and the lights on as the ship sank beneath them to enable as many passengers and crew to escape. None of the Titanic's marine engineering officers survived.

By far the largest department on board Queen Mary 2 is the Hotel Department. As the name implies, this

乔治五世特别授予了所有的船舶工程师这种配色，他们在船下沉时保证了水泵运转，船灯通明，从而使尽可能多的乘客和船员逃生。"泰坦尼克号"的轮机工程师最终无一人生还。

酒店部是"玛丽女王2号"上面迄今为止最大的部门。顾名思义，该团队包括了为保障酒店高效运营所需的所有工作人员，包括客房服务人员、餐饮服务人员、公共区域服务人员、餐饮部门员工、娱乐工作人员以及前台接待人员。整个团队的运营由酒店经理来管理。传统客船上的酒店部管事通常领导酒店部员工，在诸如娱乐

group covers all the staff necessary for the efficient operation of the hotel services and includes stateroom and dining room stewards, service staff in public areas, the catering department, entertainment staff and the personnel who look after passenger queries at the purser's office Front Desk. The whole operation is underpinned by the hotel manager. Historically, a passenger ship's purser would have led the team, with areas such as entertainment being additional to the primary role of managing the ship's day to day finances. Up until the 1970s, entertainments, especially on line voyages as distinct from holiday cruises, were rather sparse, with the highlights consisting of a 'race night' or perhaps a film shown in a hastily configured lounge.

Holland America Line is widely attributed to redefining the roles of staff within the hotel section of a passenger ship to align them to the requirements of modern-day cruising. The process saw the introduction of the hotel manager as the overall head of the department and appointment of a dedicated entertainment staff led by an experienced professional termed the cruise director. This allowed the purser to concentrate on financial and back of house issues, such as managing immigration formalities at ports of call. In recent years, Cunard has renamed the cruise director as the entertainment director in order to eliminate the term 'cruise'- in Cunard marketing parlance their ships undertake 'voyages' and not

场所等地方为乘客提供服务，从而作为船舶日常盈收的辅助性收益。这种模式一直持续到 20 世纪 70 年代，不同于假日邮轮丰富多彩的娱乐活动安排，尤其是在班轮航线上的娱乐活动特别稀少，仅包括一些比如"竞赛之夜"或者一场在临时休息室中播放的电影等亮点。

荷美邮轮公司是公认的最适应现代巡游的邮轮公司，因为她重新定义了客船的酒店部门定位。通过宣传介绍可以看出酒店经理为总负责人，而且配备有由经验丰富的邮轮总监带领的专业娱乐团队。这一安排可以使酒店主管更加专注于财务和客房服务方面的工作，例如停靠港口的签证手续办理等问题。近年来，为了在市场营销中，强调冠达的船是在"航海"而不是"巡航"，冠达邮轮将邮轮总监

侍应生正在女王餐厅的阳台精心准备晚间甜点和酒水。（冠达邮轮提供）

'cruises'.

The second most senior member of the hotel staff is the food and beverage manager, with overall responsibility for the massive catering and beverage operation on board, including the ship's 14 bars. The next level of accountability comprises the executive housekeeper, with responsibility for cleanliness throughout the ship, especially within passenger areas, chief purser, executive chef and the entertainment director. The executive chef is in charge of the menus and food production throughout the ship, including liaison with any relevant celebrity associations such as Todd English for the alternative restaurant menus within his affiliated on-board facility.

At the next level the appointments are crew purser, senior maitre d'hotel, public room manager, crew housekeeper, chef de cuisine, cashier, food and beverage controller, assistant food and beverage manager and provisions master.

The remaining hotel officers are night purser, assistant crew purser, assistant provisions manager, assistant public room manager, hotel manager's personal assistant, sous- chef, assistant housekeepers, assistant maitre d'hotels and assistant purser reception.

重新命名为娱乐总监。

食品和酒水经理是酒店员工中排第二位的高级经理，全面负责船上庞杂的餐饮和酒水运营管理，包括船上的14个酒吧。下一层级岗位包括负责全船客房清洁特别是乘客舱室清洁的客房部经理、财务经理、行政总厨和娱乐经理。行政总厨负责全船的菜单制定和食品烹饪，包括同相关的著名烹饪协会如"托德·英吉利"餐厅沟通并利用其在船上配备的厨具制定灵活多样的菜单。

再下一个层级的员工包括船员事务长、酒店高级领班、大堂经理、船员客房部经理、厨师长、收银员、食品和酒水侍应生、食品和酒水经理助理以及库房主管。

其余的酒店部员工还有：夜班值班人员、船员事务长助理、库房主管助理、酒店经理生活助理、副厨师长、客房部经理助理、酒店领班和接待员。

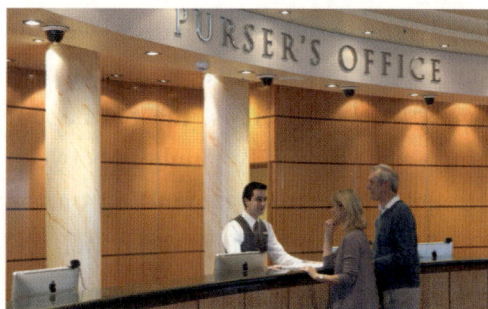

前台接待，接待乘客任何咨询。（冠达邮轮提供）

The entertainment staff

The entertainment director is the most visible of the ship's officers to guests. The incumbent will be present at most social events on board such as the 'welcome aboard' cocktail parties held in the Queens Room (there are three of these - one for each Britannia restaurant main and late sittings, and a combined one for the Queens Grill and Princess Grill guests), and will also introduce entertainment shows and acts and guest lecturers, as well as appearing each morning on the ship's televised breakfast show detailing the highlights of the day's activities.The entertainment director has a deputy and a large permanent staff of entertainers such as social hostesses, sports organisers, dance professionals, gentlemen hosts (dancing partners for single women), computer centre staff and the 16-strong troupe of 'Cunard Royal Singers and Dancers' who perform at various showtime events. In addition, celebrity acts, bridge-class (cards) instructors and lecturers constantly come and go, providing variety in the entertainments offered. A large show band is carried, as well as smaller groups, pianists and a harpist. Apart from musicians, the permanent cruise staff normally numbers between 16 and 22 persons, depending on the requirements of a particular voyage.

娱乐部职员

娱乐总监是最容易被乘客认出的船舶管理人员。在工作时间中他将参加船上的大多数社交活动，例如出现在"女王"餐厅举办的"欢迎登船"鸡尾酒派对（船上共有三个派对地点，另外两个派对一个是在"布列塔尼亚"餐厅的主餐厅和晚餐厅举办，一个是由"女王"餐厅和"公主"餐厅联合举办）。他还将介绍船上的娱乐节目安排和乘客告知，以及在每天的早餐秀当中出镜推介当天船上的活动亮点。娱乐总监的团队由一名副手以及大量的固定演职人员组成。如礼仪小姐、健身教练、舞蹈老师、男性伴舞（给单身女性伴舞）、电脑中心工作人员和一个 16 人的"冠达"皇家歌舞团，在各个表演活动中都可以看到这个剧团的高水准演艺。此外，娱乐部门还定期举办一些如明星演出、桥牌培训班等丰富多彩的娱乐活动。同时船上常驻有一个大型的表演乐队，以及小乐队、钢琴家和竖琴师。除了娱乐活动需要外，根据航次需要，固定职员通常在 16 人至 22 人之间。

"宫廷"剧院惊艳的舞蹈表演。（冠达邮轮公司提供）

The catering department

One of the highlights of any voyage on board Queen Mary 2 is undoubtedly the epicurean experience. The quality of the catering on board is exemplary, as would be expected at any premium-class hotel.

The Britannia restaurant is the largest catering facility on board. This operates on an open-sitting basis for breakfast and lunch, and on a two-sitting basis for dinner, termed Main (6.00pm) and Late (8.30pm). Britannia Club, Princess Grill and Queens Grill are all one-sitting venues with a more personalised service level than Britannia. Twenty-four hour informal dining is available at the various Kings Court

餐饮部

享乐主义的体验无疑是"玛丽女王2号"上任何一次航行的亮点之一。像在任何高档酒店都可以预期的那样，船上餐饮的质量是一个典型的代表。

"布列塔尼亚"餐厅是船上最大的餐厅。早餐和午餐采用了随时入座的形式，晚餐采用双餐次的运营模式，分别为主餐（下午6点）和晚餐（晚上8点30分）。"布列塔尼亚"餐厅、"公主"餐厅和"女王"餐厅全都只有一个餐次，提供了比"布列塔尼亚"餐厅更高水平的个性化服务。24小时的非正式用餐可以在不同的"国王"小餐厅进

宏伟的"布列塔尼亚"餐厅（冠达邮轮公司提供）

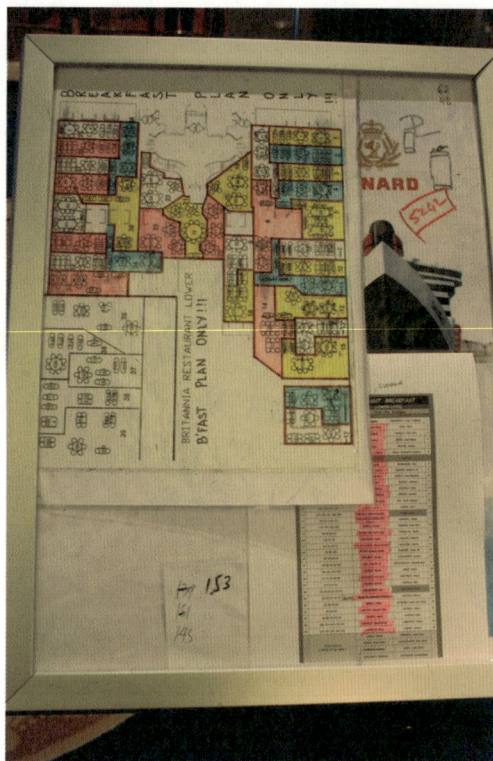

每个人负责哪块？"布列塔尼亚"餐厅早餐服务区规划图，贴在领班的台柱上。（作者提供）

eateries, predominantly self-service but with a full service option at dinner; Todd English provides a premium alternative dining experience; and food service is also available at Sir Samuel's and the Golden Lion pub at lunchtime. Afternoon tea is served at 3.30pm at various venues, predominantly in the Queens Room and the Queens Grill lounge, sometimes at the Winter Garden. The open-air Boardwalk Cafe operates when conditions allow, providing a casual fast- food option on deck. Room service with an extensive hot and cold selection is available day and night.

To provide all these catering services Queen Mary 2 is equipped with the following galleys:

• Britannia galley serving the Britannia

行，其主要是自助形式，但晚餐会提供全套服务；"托德·英吉利"餐厅提供了另一种丰富的用餐体验；午餐时间，"塞缪尔爵士"酒吧和"金狮"酒吧也提供餐饮服务。下午 3 点 30 分乘客们可以在不同地方享用下午茶，地点主要是在"女王"大厅和"女王"餐厅休息厅，有时也在冬季花园。在条件允许的情况下露天咖啡厅会营业，提供休闲食品。客房服务可以通宵提供多种热食和冷食。

为提供所有这些餐饮服务，"玛

"布列塔尼亚"餐厅的领班办公室（作者提供）

下午茶：神圣的冠达传统（冠达邮轮公司提供）

restaurant, with meals served on a two-sitting basis with over 1,200 meals per sitting. Central bakery and pastry sections make products used throughout the ship.
• Queens Grill and Princess Grill galley serving both grills, with 400 covers per meal.
• Todd English galley - speciality restaurant.
• La Piazza galley - Italian-themed cuisine.
• Chef's galley - interactive cooking demonstration.

丽女王 2 号"配备了以下厨房：

• "布列塔尼亚"厨房为"布列塔尼亚"餐厅供应了基于两餐次的膳食，每餐次超过 1 200 座。中央面包房和糕点房提供了全船所需的糕点。

• "女王餐厅"和"公主"餐厅的厨房同时供应两个餐厅，每餐 400 位。

• "托德·英吉利"厨房——特供餐厅。

• "广场"厨房——意大利主题餐厅。

• "主厨"厨房——互动式烹饪演

厨师们在厨房中为提供日常的上千种菜肴而辛苦地工作着。

万事俱备：开胃菜已经在主厨房内备好。

• Lotus - Asian cuisine.
• The Carvery - traditional English roasts.
• Room service galley, Deck 10.
• Boardwalk Cafe galley - open-air dining.
• Crew galley - catering for officers, crew and ship staff.

Some 160 chefs work within the various galleys under the supervision of an executive chef and an assistant, an executive sous-chef. A dedicated chef de cuisine is appointed to lead each main galley.

The whole galley and dining operation is supported by a team of 05 dishwashers, pot-washers and galley cleaners working on a 24-hour basis, supervised by two specialist sanitation offers who are ultimately responsible for cleanliness. Queen Mary 2 loads dry and frozen stores every 12-14 days, depending on the ship's schedule, while perishable foodstuffs such as dairy products, fresh fish and seafood are brought in every week. The food and beverage department submits requisitions up to 3 months in advance for longer voyages, but typically these are submitted 3-4 weeks in advance of transatlantic crossings.

Queen Mary 2 employs a permanent provisions team of 13 persons who load all the stores when the ship is berthed at major ports of call and distribute them to the galleys when needed by the catering staff on each voyage. The storerooms are located on Decks 1. A and B and consist of 21 refrigerated rooms for all food and beverage items.

示厅。

• "莲花"厨房——亚洲风味餐厅。
• 烧烤厨房——传统英式烧烤餐厅。
• 客房服务厨房，10 甲板。
• 漫步道咖啡馆餐厅——露天餐厅。
• 船员厨房——为官员、船员和船舶职员提供饮食。

大约 160 名厨师在一名行政主厨、一名主厨助理和副主厨的督导下在各个厨房内工作。每一个主要的厨房都有一位指定的厨师指导工作。

整个厨房和餐饮服务都离不开保洁团队的支持，他们配备有 5 台洗碗机、几台洗锅机。保洁员采用三班倒 24 小时不停工作，有两位卫生专职官员负责督导团队的工作。"玛丽女王 2 号"依照船期计划，每隔 12~14 天对冷库和干货库进行补给，而易腐坏的食品如乳制品、鲜鱼和海鲜每周都会进货。食品和饮料部门会提前 3 个月提交申请，以备更长时间的航行，但通常都是在跨大西洋航行开始前的 3~4 周提交。

"玛丽女王 2 号"雇用了一个由 13 人组成的常务库管团队，当船停泊在主要停靠港时，他们负责补给所有库房，并在每次航行中为餐厅配发餐饮工作人员所需的食材。库房位于 1 甲板、A 甲板和 B 甲板，由 21 个冷库构成，储存了全船所有的食材和酒水。

FOOD AFLOAT

Food consumption on Queen Mary 2 On a typical 7-day transatlantic crossing the following quantities of food are consumed:

· 58 tons of fresh fruits and fresh vegetables.

· 14 tons of red meat.

· 9 tons of chicken, duck and turkey.

· 15 tons of fish and seafood.

· 2.5 tons of dairy and cheese products.

· 2.5 tons of sugar.

· 24,000 litres of fresh milk.

· 37,800 eggs.

· 5 tons of flour.

· 2.5 tons of rice.

Queen Mary 2 food facts

· 120 pizzas are consumed every day.

· 700 English scones are served during afternoon tea every day.

· 9,500 canapes are consumed during the captain's cocktail parties.

· Daily, almost 16,000 meals are served on board.

· 87,000 pieces of china and glassware are used daily on board (and washed afterwards!).

· Over 8,000 linen napkins are used and laundered every day.

· 6,000 cups of tea are served every day.

· Almost 610 miles of cling film is used on board every year (that's 1.7 miles daily!).

船上食物

以一个传统的7天跨大西洋航行为例，"玛丽女王2号"会消耗掉以下食物量：

·58吨新鲜水果和蔬菜；

·14吨牛羊肉；

·9吨鸡肉、鸭肉和火鸡；

·15吨鱼肉和海鲜；

·2.5吨奶和芝士制品；

·2.5吨糖；

·24 000升鲜牛奶；

·37 800个鸡蛋；

·5吨面粉；

·2.5吨大米。

"玛丽女王2号"食物数据细节：

·每天消耗120个披萨。

·每天下午茶时供应700份英式烤饼。

·在船长的鸡尾酒会上消耗了9 500份开胃菜。

·每天大约要在船上供应16 000顿饭。

·每天在船上使用87 000件瓷器和玻璃器皿（然后洗完！）。

·每天使用并洗涤8 000多个亚麻餐巾。

·每天提供6 000杯茶。

·几乎每年都有610英里长的保鲜膜在船上使用（每天1.7英里！）

热处理线，每天处理700份家禽食材。（作者提供）

专注于完美的展现。这就是"女王"餐厅厨房。（冠达邮轮公司提供）

The Crew

A passenger ship is only as good as her crew. If the crew are happy with their home and their work, a ship especially a passenger ship has a strong chance, with effective management, of being a successful ship.

There are nominally about 1,250 permanent crew members on board Queen Mary 2, which with supernumeries such as lecturers, entertainers, office staff, etc, can reach nearly 1,300. This is a sizeable community. Regular transatlantic crossings leave little opportunity for shore leave and so to keep the staff happy and loyal to the ship it was essential to provide them with good facilities.

On the 2012 world voyage, two crew members who are husband and wife approached me and told me how proud they were to work on Queen Mary 2. They shared many of the crew's belief that there is simply no other passenger ship in the world to match Queen Mary 2. There is a consistent view that the crew facilities and conditions on board are excellent.

船员

客船想要好，必须她的船员要好才行。当船员对自己的家庭和工作感到惬意时，那么一艘船——尤其是一艘客轮，就可以通过有效的管理，并且有很大机会成为一艘成功的船。

在名册上，"玛丽女王 2 号"共有 1 250 名在编船员，若再加上讲师、演员、其他职员等额外人员，船上总人数最高可达 1 300 余人。这是一个庞大的社群。跨大西洋的定期航程使得他们几乎没有离船休假的时间，因此，为了让他们能够开心并且踏实地投入工作，就必须为他们提供良好的环境。

在 2012 年的环球航行中，船员中有两对夫妻档。他们告诉我，他们以能够为"玛丽女王 2 号"服务而骄傲。和其他船员一样，他们坚信世界上没有比"玛丽皇后 2 号"更好的的班轮。船员们有一个共识，那就是"玛丽女王 2 号"提供的设施和条件都非常棒！

（译者：陈大为、陈霖、孙哲、杨勇、高茜、陈熙）

没有快乐的船员，一艘客船就不可能伟大："玛丽女王 2 号"上的夫妇档。他们赞美在最伟大班轮上的工作——这是他们原话，非作者臆造！

"能把球丢回给我吗？"——甲板部官员。

高级船员餐厅

船员餐厅

众多船员酒吧的一角

客舱清洁和服务推车是服务人员必备的工具器材。

行李搬运区拥有巨大的空间，以确保在几个小时内可以转运数以千计的行李。

不常见的一幕：透过一扇门，看到的 5 甲板船员楼梯。

综合垃圾处理站能够有效地处理船上产生的所有垃圾。

第八章　成功之道

Chapter Eight:Power behind the throne

Queen Mary 2 is the embodiment of state-of-the-art maritime technology. From the navigating bridge on the top deck to the machinery systems laid out on the double-bottom, the ship is a marvel of efficiency and efficacy.

　　"玛丽女王 2 号"是最先进的海事技术的化身。从上层甲板的驾驶台到双层底上的机械系统，这艘船是效率和效能的奇迹。

2011年，"玛丽女王2号"在汉堡的干船坞进行首次整修。（国际涂料有限公司提供）

The technical face of a Queen

One hundred and eighteen Megawatts could power 118,000 single-element 1 kW electric fires - or it could power Queen Mary 2, providing lighting, heating, services, and propulsion for nearly 30kts. It's enough power to satisfy the energy needs of a city the size of Southampton with 240,000 inhabitants. Not that all this power is needed all the time; but when the Atlantic kicks up rough, Queen Mary 2 has the reserves of power necessary in combination with a true liner hull to make the grade. But power is not the only prerequisite. With a multitude of systems and services at her disposal including sewerage, air-conditioning, cooking, stabilisation and fresh water production, Queen Mary 2 is well-equipped to provide a luxurious environment for her passengers and crew. The bridge personnel ensure the safe navigation of the ship on the world's oceans, keeping constant watch and vigilance. Down below, engineers monitor the ship's systems, ensuring the most efficient mode of operation is maintained under all conditions. Keeping Queen Mary 2 in good condition requires constant maintenance, most of which is undertaken with the ship in service. However, periodically (up to five years) the ship is taken out of service for dry-docking for an extended two-week maintenance period.

"女王号"的技术面板数据

118 兆瓦可以为 118 000 个单丝 1 千瓦电炉提供电力——或者它可以为"玛丽女王 2 号"提供照明、供暖、服务和近 30 节的推进速度。这足以满足南安普敦这样一个人口为 24 万的城市的能源需求。并不是说随时需要提供所有这些能量，而是当大西洋开始变得狂暴时，"玛丽女王 2 号"拥有必要的能量储备。再加上真正的班轮船体，才能取得成功。但能量不是唯一的先决条件。"玛丽女王 2 号"拥有众多系统和保障设备，包括污水收集系统、空调系统、烹饪系统、稳定系统和淡水制备系统，她的配置能为乘客和船员提供奢华的环境。桥楼人员确保船舶在全球的航行安全，时刻保持观测和警戒。在下面，工程师监控船舶的系统，确保船可以在任何条件下保持最有效的操作状态。"玛丽女王 2 号"的良好状态需要持续的维护，大部分的维护工作都是在船处于营运状态下进行的。然而，定期（最多 5 年）维护将使该船停止运营，进行为期两周的维修。

Engine power

The powering calculation

Once the basic design of the ship has been established and the propulsion powering requirement estimated, it is necessary to determine what engines to install. A diesel-electric power plant works somewhat differently to a normal installation where both main and auxiliary engines are fitted. With a diesel-electric plant the engines are just used to produce electricity, the amount required determining how many of the engines are brought into use to supply the propulsion needs and the hotel load.

Various factors have to be taken into consideration:
• Medium-speed diesel engines are normally operated up to 85% of their rated capacity, in continuous use to minimise maintenance.
• Medium-speed diesel engines are most efficient when running above 55% of their rated capacity.
• Electrical generators and the control system incurs approximately a 7% power loss in the conversion of mechanical energy into electrical energy, which has to be deducted from the available energy.
• Other losses, generally shaft losses, account for a further 3%.

引擎动力

动力的计算

一旦确定了船舶的基本设计并评估了推进功率需求，接下来就必须确定要安装什么发动机。柴油发电机组的工作原理与那种主机加辅机的常规配置有些不同。使用柴油发电机组，柴油机仅仅用于产生电能，就可以通过总需求来决定多少台柴油机投入运行，用于满足推进系统的需要和酒店运营的负载。

必须考虑以下各种因素：
• 中速柴油机通常运行在 85% 的额定负荷，以便在持续使用过程中减少维修。
• 中速柴油机的最高效运行点是在额定容量的 55% 以上。
• 机械能转化为电能的过程中，发电机和控制系统大约会有 7% 的能量损失，这些需要从有效能量中扣除。
• 其他损失，主要是轴系损失，按照 3% 计算。

FIRST REFIT – NOVEMBER-DECEMBER 2011
首次修整：2011 年 11 月至 12 月

Length 船长	345m（1,132ft） 345 米（1 132 英尺）
Beam 船宽	41/45m（135/147ft）（waterline/bridge wing） 41/45 米（135/147 英尺）（水线处 / 驾驶台桥翼处）
Draught 吃水	10m（32ft） 10 米（32 英尺）
Air Draught 水上净高	62m（203ft）from design waterline 62 米（203 英尺）从设计水线开始测量
Displacement 排水量	c. 76,000 tonnes 76 000 修正总吨
Deadweight 载重量	c. 16,000 tonnes 16 000 修正总吨
Machinery 机械	4 × 16–cylinder medium speed diesels 4 台 16 缸中速柴油机 2 × gas turbines 2 台燃气轮机
Speed 航速	29.62kts maximum on sea trials 海试最大航速 29.62 节
Propulsion power 推进功率	85MW 4 × Mermaid Pods 85 兆瓦总功率 4 台美人鱼吊舱推进器
Hotel load 酒店负荷	15MW 15 兆瓦
Passengers 乘客人数	2 800
Passenger cabins 乘客舱室	1 310
Crew 船员人数	1 250
Cost 成本	US $780 million, c. US$1 billion with owner's supply and costs 七亿八千万美元，外加 10 亿美元的船东供品和花销

"玛丽女王 2 号"安装有 4 台瓦锡兰公司的 16 缸 V46C 中速柴油机，它们安装在烟囱下面船底的机舱里。每台发动机额定功率超过 11.5 MW。（瓦锡兰公司提供）

With Queen Mary 2 the situation was further complicated in that it was decided to limit the number of diesels to four, the maximum that could be comfortably fitted across the ship in one compartment, so that only one vertical uptake casing would be required - although this was split in two to provide a central passageway through the public room decks on Decks 2 and 3. The power shortfall was made up through the installation of two gas turbines; due to their light weight these could be installed at the top of the ship, thus negating the need for additional intake and exhaust casings to be put in, which would have taken up valuable space.

对于"玛丽女王 2 号"而言情况更加复杂，因为柴油机的数量必须控制在 4 台以内，并尽可能安装在一个隔舱内，这样就可以只需要一个垂直的烟囱——尽管这个烟囱被连接 2 甲板和 3 甲板的公共空间的走廊一分为二。通过两台燃气轮机来弥补电力不足；由于重量轻，它们可以安装在船的顶部，因此不需要额外的送风管和抽风管，而这些管道往往会占用宝贵的空间。

根据以往的经验来估算酒店的电

From past experience it was estimated that the hotel load - that is, the power needed for lighting, heating, cooking, lifts etc throughout the ship - would be in the order of 16MW. The propulsion power estimate was 86MW. On this, the calculations could proceed.

Adding 3% losses to the propulsion estimate meant that $86 \times 1.03 = 88.58$MW. Adding the 16MW hotel load signified that $88.58 + 16 = 104.58$MW of electrical power was required. Remembering that we had to account for 7% of losses denoted that $104.58 \times 1.07 = 111.90$MW mechanical power was required in total. Assuming the gas turbines could run up to 100% without concern, and with a combined rating of 50MW, the four diesels needed to produce a total of $111.9 - 50 = 61.9$MW. However, this had to be produced at only 85% of their capacity, so we required diesels with a combined rating of $61.9/0.85 = 72.82$MW. Therefore, it was essential that each of the four diesels was rated for 18.2MW at 100% capacity.

Power generation

The diesels on board Queen Mary 2 are Wartsila 16-cylinder V46C medium-speed diesels, running at 514 revolutions per minute. These are rated at 16.8MW, slightly less than the calculated 18.2MW. However, with podded propulsion the 3% shaft loss figure is questionable; the 16MW hotel load is likely to be less under most

力负荷,即全船的照明、供暖、烹饪、升降机等所需的电力为 16 MW。推进功率估计为 86 MW。必须依据这些要素进行计算。

考虑增加 3% 的功率损失,推进的电力负荷估计为 $86 \times 1.03 = 88.58$ MW。再加上 16 MW 的酒店电力负荷,意味着需要 88.58+16=104.58 MW 的电力。再考虑 7% 的功率损失,意味着总共需要 $104.58 \times 1.07=111.90$ MW 的机械功率。假设燃气轮机可以一直在 100% 的负荷下运行,并且并机功率为 50 MW,那么这四台柴油机的总发电量为 111.9–50=61.9 MW。然而,还需考虑 85% 的效率,所以柴油机的综合发电量为 61.9/0.85=72.82 MW。因此,每台柴油机在 100% 的负荷下的额定功率必须不小于 18.2 MW。

发电机

"玛丽女王2号"的柴油机是瓦锡兰的 16 缸中速柴油机 V46C,转速为 514 转 / 每分钟。这是运行在输出功率为 16.8 MW 时测得的数值,略低于 18.2 MW。然而,吊舱推进器的轴功率损失不一定为 3 %;大多数情况下,酒店的电力负荷可能小于 16MW;船

circumstances; the ship will rarely be called upon to travel at maximum speed; and, finally, if circumstances really necessitate full power, the diesels can be run without concern for a limited period well above the 85% rating figure - about 92% rating being required if none of the previously described mitigations are available. When choosing this engine configuration, we were therefore confident that it would work well.

Each engine is resiliently mounted to the ship's structure using rubberised elements to minimise the transmission of engine vibrations. Similarly, elastic

很少以最高航速航行；最后，如果确实需要全功率运行，柴油机可以在有限时间内运行在远高于额定 85% 工况下——如果问题得不到缓解，那么柴油机还可以运行在大约 92% 的工况下。因此，我们相信这型柴油机能够很好地满足工作要求。

每台柴油机都弹性安装在船体结构上，通过橡胶元件，最大程度地降低柴油机震动的传播。同理，在柴油机和其附属的刚性安装的交流发电机

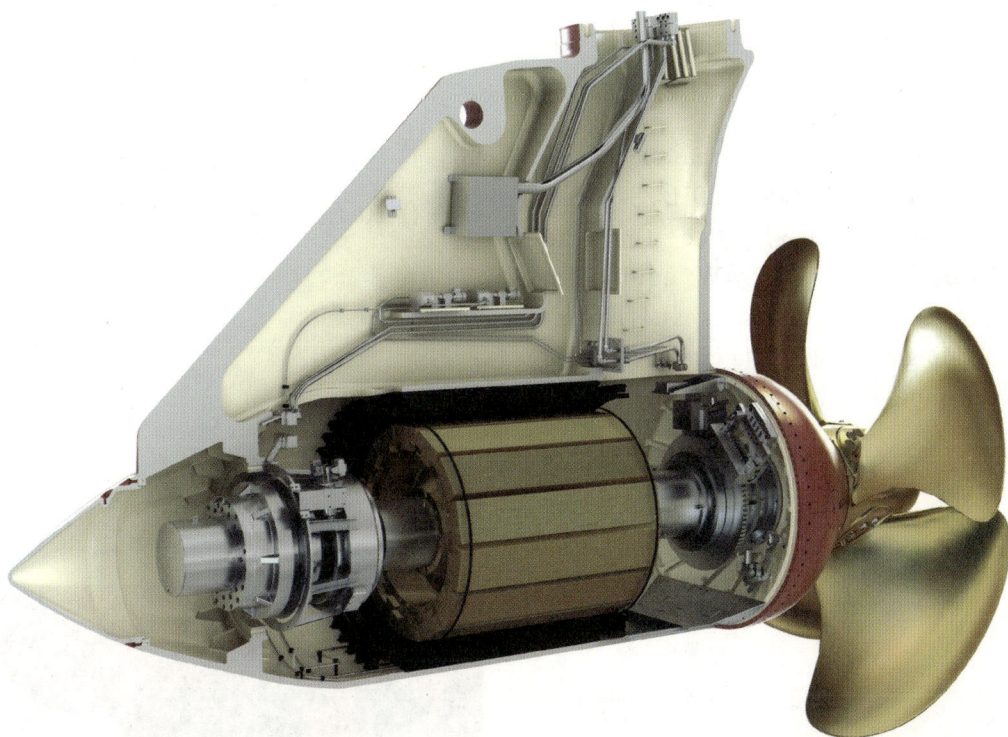

4 台美人鱼吊舱推进器安装在船尾下方，每台的额定功率为 21.5MW。前部两个是固定式的，只是提供向前或向后的推力，而后部的一对是全回转的。（罗尔斯 – 罗伊斯公司提供）

couplings are installed between the diesels and their attendant rigidly mounted alternators. The engines are equipped with a fuel system, a lubrication system, starting air system, cooling system, exhaust gas and charge air system, as well as various other control, alarm and instrumentation functions.

The two gas turbines are General Electric LM2500+ models running at 3,600 revolutions per minute, each being rated at 25MW. These turbines are packaged as a module within acoustic enclosures on a mounting skid and the alternators are positioned on the same skid. Whereas the diesels are started using compressed air, the turbines are commenced using a hydraulic reservoir fed by a variable delivery pump and driven by an electric motor.

The alternators generate electricity at high voltage: 11,000V, 60Hz, 3-phase. Therefore the total power that can be produced is 117.2MW, equivalent to 157,168HP. This is sufficient generating capacity for a city the size of Southampton with 200,000 inhabitants.

之间安装弹性联轴器。发电机配备有燃油系统、润滑系统、启动空气系统、冷却系统、废气和空气系统以及各种控制、报警和仪表功能。

两台燃气轮机是通用电气公司的LM2500+型，转速为3 600转/分钟，每台的额定功率为25 MW。这些燃气轮机被封装在降噪壳内，以模块化的形式和交流发电机安装在同一滑轨上。柴油发电机是使用压缩空气启动的，但是燃气轮机是通过液压系统启动的，液压系统通过变频输送电动泵运行。

交流发电机产生高压电：1 100V、60 Hz、三相。因此，其能够产生的总功率为117.2 MW，相当于157 168 hp。这些电能可以满足像南安普敦这样拥有20万居民的城市的需求。

左舷全回转美人鱼吊舱安装到位。不锈钢螺旋桨位于吊舱前部具有明显的优势；银色条是牺牲锌阳极，用于保护吊舱本体。（法国STX船厂/伯纳德比格提供）

Fuel consumption

• Diesel engines - 3.1 tonnes/hour each of Heavy Fuel Oil (HFO) at 100% load.
• Gas turbines - 6.0 tonnes/hour each of Marine Gas Oil (MGO) at 100% load.

Daily consumption at a speed of 29 knots, depending on the sea state and wind, is approximately 261 tonnes of HFO for the diesel engines and 237 tonnes of MGO for the gas turbines.

Fuel tank capacities:
HFO - 5,348.7m3 or 1,412,977 US gallons.
MGO - 3,658.8 m3 or 966,553 US gallons.

Podded propulsion

Four 21.5MW propulsion pods are installed on board Queen Mary 2, providing a total of 86MW propulsion power - equivalent to 11 5,328HP. These are called Mermaids and were developed jointly by Rolls-Royce and Alstom Power. The pods are mounted as pairs at the stern of the ship, the two aftermost pods are fully steerable over 3600 and provide steering and propulsion, while the forward pods are fixed and simply supply forward or aft propulsion. Podded propulsion has distinct advantages over conventional shaftline propulsion. Shaftlines and their 'A' bracket supports create turbulence and disruption of the orderly flow of water around the aft end of the ship, which feeds into the propeller causing vibration and a loss of

耗油量

• 柴油机：100% 工况下，每小时消耗 3.1 吨重柴油。

• 燃气轮机：100% 工况下，每小时消耗 3.1 吨轻柴油。

在一定的海况和风速下，保持 29 节的航速，柴油机每天消耗 261 吨重柴油，燃气轮机每天消耗 237 吨轻柴油。

油舱舱容：

重柴油舱：5 348.7 立方米（1 412 977 加仑）。

轻柴油：3 658.8 立方米（966 553 加仑）。

吊舱推进器

4 台 21.5 MW 的推进吊舱安装在"玛丽女王 2 号"上，总共提供 86 MW 的推力，相当于 115 328 Hp。这些吊舱的品牌为美人鱼，是由罗尔斯－罗伊斯公司和阿尔斯通电力公司联合开发的。吊舱成对地安装在船尾，后两个吊舱可以 360 度回转，提供转向和推进的动力，而前吊舱是固定的，仅提供向前或向后的推力。吊舱推进与传统轴系推进相比具有明显的优势。轴系和 "A" 形支架会产生紊流，扰乱船尾的水流，这些水流进入螺旋桨后，会造成振动和效率损失。具有前置螺旋桨的吊舱不会受到这种扰流的

efficiency. A pod with a forward-facing propeller suffers no such disruption of flow and in consequence experiences much less vibration and a hydrodynamic advantage of about 7% in propulsion power is achieved. The need for stern thrusters is also removed, leading to further economies in maintenance and first cost.

Queen Mary 2's pods are fitted with four- bladed stainless steel propellers of 6.0 metres in diameter. These are 'built-up' propellers, with the individual blades weighing 4.5 tonnes (9,900 1b) being bolted to a central hub. Stainless steel was chosen rather than nickel-aluminium bronze for the propellers as stainless steel maintains its smooth surface finish rather than degrading like the other material, thus maintaining efficiency. The steerable pods with their electric steering gear and attendant equipment weigh about 320 tonnes each, the fixed pods slightly less. This is roughly the equivalent of carrying four fully laden 747 Boeing jumbo jets beneath the stern!

Queen Mary 2 is the first four-propeller ocean liner built since the SS France in 1962 and, indicative of the tremendous extra power that is needed to maintain a timely and reliable North Atlantic service, is powered by over 150,000 horsepower. With such manoeuvrability, she is usually able to dock without the assistance of tugboats and is able to turn around within its own length.

干扰，因此振动被降低了，并且推进功率获得了约7%的水动力优势。尾侧推的取消降低了维护成本和前期投资的金额。

"玛丽女王2号"的吊舱装有直径6.0米的四叶不锈钢螺旋桨。这些螺旋桨是"组装"式的，单个叶片重4.5吨（9 900 lb）被螺栓固定在中心轮毂上。螺旋桨之所以选用不锈钢而不是镍铝青铜，是因为不锈钢能保持其表面的光洁度，而不会像其他材料那样退化，从而保持了效率。每台可回转吊舱及其电动转向装置和辅助设备的重量约为320吨，固定式吊舱略小。这大概相当于在船尾下方搭载四架满载的波音747大型喷气式客机！

自1962年的"法兰西号"以来，"玛丽女王2号"是第一艘四桨远洋班轮，其动力超过15万匹马力，足以满足在北大西洋航行的需求。有了这种机动性，她通常能够在没有拖船的帮助下实现靠泊，并能够在一个船长的距离内转弯。

一台美人鱼吊舱在安装前调整位置。
（法国 STX 船厂 / 伯纳德比格提供）

"玛丽女王 2 号"独特的艉部是科斯坦兹型巡洋舰艉部和悬垂式艉部（分别是圆形和平坦的）的混合体，旨在提供良好的稳性和水动力性能。也可以看到 4 个美人鱼推进吊舱。（法国 STX 船厂 / 伯纳德比格提供）

Stabilisers

Queen Mary 2 is fitted with four VM Series Brown Brothers Rolls-Royce stabilisers manufactured in Edinburgh. Each stabiliser weighs 70 tonnes and is an underwater wing (called a fin) that can be stowed inside the ship within its 'fin box' when not required and deployed to jut out from the side of the ship using hydraulic rams. Each stabiliser extends 6.25 metres and is 2.5 metres wide with an area of 15.63 square metres.

减摇鳍

"玛丽女王 2 号"装有 4 台 VM 型号减摇鳍，由位于爱丁堡的"布朗兄弟 / 罗尔斯－罗伊斯"公司制造。单个重达 70 吨的减摇鳍是水面下的机翼（称为鳍叶），当不使用时，鳍叶可以收储在船体内的"鳍穴"中，当使用时，靠液压柱塞驱动伸展出舷外。

The fins have an aerofoil section and produce an opposing force to the rolling motion of the ship when angled into the waterflow by another set of hydraulic rams. The fins are controlled by solid-state electronics, which senses the roll motion and computes the angle the fins have to make to cancel out the motion. The ship's stabilisers can reduce rolling by 90% and take only 30 seconds to deploy or rehouse. The fins may be used in any combination depending upon the severity of the prevailing conditions.

每个减摇鳍长 6.25 米，宽 2.5 米，面积为 15.63 平方米。鳍叶的截面为机翼型，靠另一套液压柱塞驱动鳍叶转动，从而与水流形成夹角以产生相对船舶横摇运动的反力作用。通过固体电子器件检测横摇运动，并计算出鳍叶的角度，进而控制鳍叶动作来抵消横摇。船上的减摇鳍可减少 90% 的横摇，只需 30 秒，鳍叶就可完全伸展或缩回。鳍叶可依据当前海况来灵活组合使用。

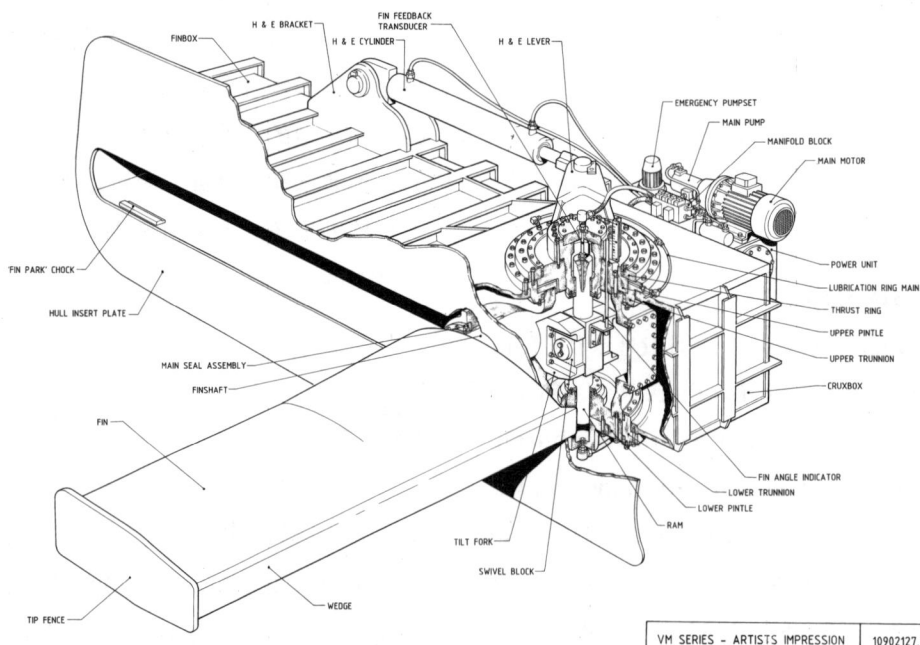

VM SERIES - ARTISTS IMPRESSION | 10902127.

罗尔斯－罗伊斯公司 VM 型减摇鳍组件。船舶有 4 个减摇鳍，每舷 2 个，能显著降低横摇运动的不利影响。（罗尔斯－罗伊斯公司提供）

位于船舶弧形舯部，处于收储状态的减摇鳍，共4个。（法国STX船厂／伯纳德比格提供）

等待安装的减摇鳍。翼型剖面的鳍叶，根据朝向产生向上或向下的力以抵消横摇运动。（作者提供）

工厂试验中，处于展开状态的减摇鳍。（作者提供）

QUEEN MARY 2 FACTS AND FIGURES

The ship has:
- 2,500 kilometres of electric cable.
- 310 miles (500 kilometres) of ducts, mains and pipes.
- 2,000 bathrooms.
- 80,000 lighting points.
- 3,000 telephones.
- 8,800 loudspeakers.
- 5,000 stairs.
- 5,000 fire detectors.
- 1,100 fire doors.
- 8,350 automatic water-mist extinguishers.

"玛丽女王2号" 实况和数据

船舶有：
- 2 500公里电缆。
- 310英里（500公里）各类通风管道、主干管线和管道。
- 2 000间浴室。
- 80 000个照明点。
- 3 000部电话。
- 8 800个扬声器。
- 5 000座梯道。
- 5 000个火灾探测器。
- 1 100道防火门。
- 8 350个自动水雾灭火点。

Bow thrusters

For manoeuvring, Queen Mary 2 is fitted with three bow thrusters. These are Rolls-Royce transverse thrusters each rated at 3.2MW, with the thrust provided by four-bladed variable- pitch propellers driven by electric motors. The diameter of the thrusters is 3.3 metres and each is fitted as a hull door on each side of the ship. These doors are like large butterfly valves and are opened for manoeuvring; they are closed at sea to create a smooth flow over the bow and reduce turbulence, thus giving the vessel true liner capabilities.

艏侧推

为了便于操纵，"玛丽女王 2 号"配备了 3 台艏侧推装置。罗尔斯－罗伊斯公司提供的每个侧推器额定功率为 3.2 MW，靠电动马达驱动四叶变螺距桨产生推力。侧推器直径达到 3.3 米，每个侧推器在两舷边都设有涵道盖门。这些盖门类似于蝶阀，侧推操纵时开启；平时航行时保持关闭，使船首来流平滑，减小紊流，以确保班轮的性能要求。

3 个开启状态的艏侧推整流盖门。每个涵道内均有一个 3.2 MW 可调螺距桨，为靠近和驶离码头提供侧向推力。（法国 STX 船厂／伯纳德比格提供）

处于关闭状态的蝶阀式艏侧推盖门。（作者提供）

Plant

Air-conditioning

Providing a habitual environment throughout the ship is a huge undertaking requiring a large plant. Central to the system are six Carrier chillers, five of which are in use at any one time, with the sixth on standby. The chillers produce cool water that is distributed throughout the ship to the numerous air-handling units that serve public areas and the cabin accommodation. Air is drawn into the ship from ducts arranged within a cofferdam space situated between Deck 7 and Deck 8. Fans are used to draw the air into the ship and distribute it to the air-handling units (AHUs) within each fire zone. The AHUs first filter the air, then either cool or heat it depending on the ambient conditions, and then distribute it to localised zone conditioning rooms. Cooling is achieved by chilled water circulating in coils, while heating is arranged through electric coils. In the zone units the air is further heated or cooled before being distributed to the consumers.

Different arrangements apply to each category space. For passenger and officer cabins, the treated air from the zone units is fed to each cabin where final heating or cooling takes place by individual fan coil units. The fan coil units are in reality miniature conditioning units as they have electric heating and chilled water-cooling coils and these are located within lockers

设备机组

空调装置。为整船提供一个舒适的环境是一项巨大的挑战，这需要一个大型空调机组。该系统的核心是6台开利公司的冷媒水机组，其中五台随时保持运转，第六台处于待命状态。冷媒水机组产生的冷水传输到整艘船上，分配给服务于公共区域和住舱的众多空调器。风机将外界空气从布置于7甲板至8甲板之间隔舱内的风管吸入船内，并将其分配给每个主竖区内的空调器(AHUS)。空调器首先进行空气过滤，然后根据环境条件进行冷却或加热，然后将其分配到每个区域自己的空调机间。冷却是通过盘管中的冷媒水循环来实现的，而加热则是通过电加热线圈。在各区域空调机间内，空气被进一步加热或冷却后，最终输送给旅客。

不同的空调配置适用于不同级别的舱室。对于乘客和官员住舱，处理后的空气从区域空调机间被分配到每个舱室，在那里通过风机盘管进行最后的加热或冷却。风机盘管实际上是微型空调器，它们有电加热线圈和冷媒水盘管，位于每个住舱之间的储藏室内。风机盘管中的风机通过布置在住舱卫生单元上方的风管将空气输送到住舱内。每个住舱都有自己的控制单元来控制风机盘管内的加热/制冷回

between each cabin. The fans in the fan-coil units distribute the air out through the ducts placed above the cabin bathrooms. Each cabin has its own control unit that controls the heating/cooling circuit within the fan-coil, and the air is exhausted from within the bathroom space.

Crew cabins are fitted with a variable air volume system (VAV). This takes air from zone handling units and temperature control is achieved by altering the flow rate of the air entering the individual cabins. As with passenger cabins, the exhaust from crew cabins is arranged through the bathroom spaces.

Public rooms are served directly from the central conditioning rooms via a single duct system employing low/medium flow rates for distribution through open ceilings or via diffusers. Systems are oversized using a 30% occupancy margin and an increased flow rate to provide boost capacity for a quick response when sudden changes occur.

In some instances a proportion of recirculated air is used to minimise energy usage, and heat recovery using enthalpy wheel heat exchangers is employed between the stale and fresh air components.

路，并从卫生单元内抽风。

船员住舱配置变风量空调系统（VAV），从区域空调器获取空气，通过改变进入各个住舱的空气流量来实现温度控制。与乘客住舱一样，船员住舱也是从卫生单元内抽风。

公共区域采用单风管空调系统直接通过中央空调器送风，并采用低/中速气流通过冲孔天花板或散流器分配。公共区域空调设计额外考虑30%余量以增加空调的送风风量，来提高应对突发状况时的快速反应能力。

7甲板上不锈钢椭圆形空调进风口。（作者提供）

Freshwater generation

Queen Mary 2 has a huge freshwater generating capacity that utilises waste heat from the diesel engines that would otherwise be lost. Potable drinking water production is from three Alfa Laval multi-effect plate evaporators, each producing 630 tonnes/day. Seawater is basically distilled within the evaporators and the resulting water is mineralised and finally treated with chlorine to ensure purity and potability.

The daily freshwater consumption on board Queen Mary 2 is approximately 1, 100 tonnes/day, which equates to approx 302 litres - or 79 US gallons - per person per day. This includes water used for cooking and washing the ship. Potable water-tank capacity is 3,830m3 or 1,011,779 us gallons. These tanks are kept clear of the side shell of the ship to ensure that no cross-contamination would occur if the hull was breached.

Steam production

Steam is produced by two Saacke oil-fired boilers. Steam is also produced by exhaust gas economisers (heat exchangers) by using waste heat from the four diesel engine and two gas turbine exhausts. The amount of waste heat that is extracted from the diesel exhausts for steam generation is carefully controlled, to prevent condensation within the exhausts themselves. This is also to stop sulphur, inherent within the heavy fuel oil, from producing sulphuric acid droplets, which would quickly rot the exhaust casing. This will be less of a

造水机

"玛丽女王2号"拥有巨大的淡水制备能力，其利用柴油发动机的废气余热来制备淡水。饮用水的生产是由三台阿尔法拉法公司的多效板式蒸发器，每台生产能力为630吨/天。海水在蒸发器内蒸馏，由此产生的水再被矿化，最后用氯进行处理，以确保水是纯净的和可饮用的。

"玛丽女王2号"每天的淡水消耗量约为1 100吨，相当于每人每天约302升（79加仑），这包括用于烹饪和清洗的水。饮用水舱容量为3 830立方米（1 011 779加仑）。这些水舱的位置应和船外板保持一定距离，以确保一旦船体受损，水源不会被污染。

蒸汽制备

蒸汽是由两个扎克公司的燃油锅炉制备的，也可以利用4台柴油机和两台燃气轮机排出的废气余热，通过废气回收器（热交换器）产生。从柴油机排气管中回收余热要小心控制，以防止排气管内产生冷凝水。因为在重燃料油中固有的硫元素形成的硫化物与水结合会产生硫酸液滴，将迅速锈蚀排气管。如果即将生效的法规对使用含硫量较高的燃料逐步进行限制，

problem when forthcoming legislation progressively inhibits the use of fuels with a high sulphur content, but at a significantly higher operating cost. Steam on board Queen Mary 2 is utilised for accommodation heating, laundry-wash water heating, fuel oil heating and for steaming food in the galleys.

The bridge

The bridge of Queen Mary 2 is located on deck 12 forward and acts as the navigation and safety hub of the vessel. Consists of a central navigation area, Chart Room, safety center, and two totally enclosed bridge wings, the bridge is manned 24 hours a day by two navigating officers. The officers operate on watches, with one senior officer (either a first or second officer) and one third officer on each of the watches.

The watches are organized as follows:

• The 12 to 4 watch, covers the period from 0:00hrs to 04:00hrs

这就不是什么大的问题了，但船舶运营成本却要高出很多。"玛丽女王2号"船上的蒸汽用于住宿供暖、洗衣用水加热、燃油加热以及在厨房里蒸食物。

驾驶室 *

"玛丽女王2号"的驾驶室在12甲板向前的位置，是全船航行和安全的中心。驾驶室包括中央操控区、海图室、安全中心和两个全封闭式的桥翼。驾驶室由两名高级船员督导，一天24小时有人值守。每个瞭望点都有一名高级船员（大副或二副）和一名三副值守。

瞭望值班制度安排如下：

• 12点至4点方向瞭望的值班时段，从凌晨0点到4点，以及中午12

驾驶室内的凯文·澳波雷船长，"玛丽女王2号"的主人。（作者提供）

驾驶室右舷的海图室。大多纸版海图已被电子海图取代。（作者提供）

* 船舶驾驶室也称桥楼，本书根据上下文可能会采用不同译法——译者注。

(12.00am to 4.00am) and from 12:00hrs to 16.00hrs (12.00pm to 4.00pm)

• The 4 to 8 watch, covers the period from 04:00hrs to 08:00hrs (4.00am to 8.00am) and from 16:00hrs to 20.00hrs (16.00pm to 20.00pm)

• The 8 to 12 watch, covers the period from 0:80hrs to 12:00hrs (8.00am to 12.00am) and from 20:00hrs to 24.00hrs (20.00pm to 24.00pm)

The primary duty of the bridge officer is the navigation of the ship, allowing for safe and timely arrival of the Queen Mary 2 at her destination. The involves knowing the ship's position and being aware of her surrounding at times (including the presence of other ships, fishing boats and yachts, hazards to navigation, currents, sea floor characteristics, etc), being well versed in all environmental regulations and knowing the meteorological conditions such as rain, fog, snow, and strong winds, and their effect upon the safety of the ship and comfort of the passengers. They also control the speed of the ship and coordinate with engineering officers in the engine control room to ensure the ship will arrive on time.

驾驶室左舷的安全中心。所有安全系统都可以在这里监测和控制，也可计算船舶的装载和稳性状态。（作者提供）

点到下午4点。

• 4点至8点方向瞭望的值班时段，从凌晨4点到上午8点，下午4点到晚上8点。

• 8点至12点方向瞭望的值班时段，从上午8点到12点，晚上8点到12点。

驾驶室高级船员的首要职责是操控船只，保证"玛丽女王2号"安全和准时到达目的地。其具体工作包括实时掌握船舶位置和她的周边情况（包括周围影响航行的其他船舶，如渔船和游艇、浪流、海面条件等），精通所有的环境保护法规，熟知雨、雾、雪、强风等气象条件及其对船舶安全和旅客舒适性的影响。同时与集控室轮机部的船员们协同进行船速控制，从而确保船舶按时抵达目的地。

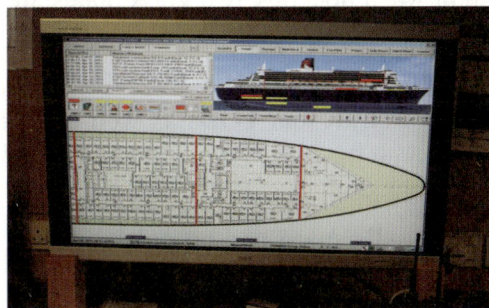

通过计算机数字化后的6甲板前部区域安全画面。红色线条表示主竖区的边界，采用被动式防火绝缘进行保护，确保火灾可以被限制在一个主竖区内。（作者提供）

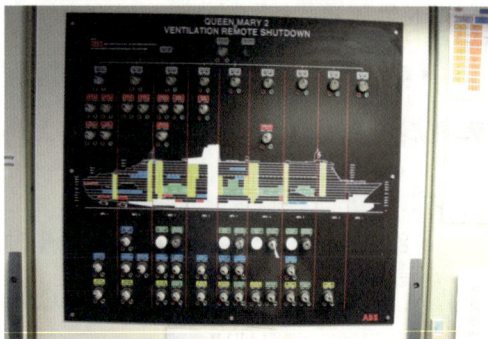

安全中心的风道切断控制板，显示出船船采用分区控制，每个区域都设有独立的控制开关和显示。（作者提供）

安全中心可以使用一份综合布置图，对船上发生的意外事故进行评估。（作者提供）

Bridge Wings

Spanning 148 feet and projecting out over the side of the hull, the enclosed bridge wings offer a dramatic, unobstructed view down the side of the ship. Necessary for docking, these allow the captain and senior officer to watch the ship's hull as it approaches a pier and to judge distances when manoeuvring in harbours. To further improve lines of sight when docking, two glass plates are cut into deck on each wing, allowing the officer to look directly beneath them. Control of all four PODs as well as the three bow thrusters can be taken on the bridge wings and displays concerning the vessel's speed and propulsion status are available here as well. Two screens incorporated with Manta system are available on each wing and allow the officers to select between radar and chart display, cameras from the closed-circuit TV system, and the vessel's "Harbour Approach" display, Also on the bridge wings are controls for the Dynamic

桥翼

全封闭式的桥翼跨度为 148 英尺，突出在船体两侧，从而提供了一个不受遮挡的沿船侧的下方视野。这是靠泊必需的，船长和高级船员可以在靠泊过程中观察船舶位置，评估船体和码头的间距。为了进一步改善靠泊的操作视野，每个桥翼甲板的地面上还嵌有一面玻璃观察板，船员可以直接从此观察下方的状况。在桥翼可以直接控制 4 台吊舱推进装置和 3 台侧推装置，以及观察船舶速度和推进器状态，等等。船员可以通过两翼"曼塔"系统的一体化显示屏切换显示雷达和海图界面、有线闭路电视系统系统的摄像头画面或者"靠泊方案"界面。当然两翼位置也可以操作动力定位系统。由于桥翼的观察点高 134 英尺，可以观察到 13.5 英里远的地方，

Positioning system. With a height of eye of 134 feet, the horizon is 13.5 miles away, although other vessels and land can often been seen from much further away due to their respective height above the water.

而且由于一些船只和陆地建筑相对水面比较高，它们可以在更远的距离被观察到。

左舷桥翼操纵台，可见艏侧推装置和吊舱推进装置的独立控制设备、集成电子海图的雷达屏幕。这个操纵台用于进出港控制，右舷有相同的一套装置。（作者提供）

左舷桥翼横向视图，一名船员正在操纵台上。左侧可见位于窗帘边的安全中心入口。窗帘用于夜间驾驶室的灯火管制。（作者提供）

右舷桥翼的操纵台，目前处于操船状态，因为吊舱推进装置的控制手柄有向前角度，进行前进控制，而停止时手柄应处于垂直位置。操纵台后方可见甲板观察窗的边缘。

Bridge equipment
Gyro and magnetic compasses

Queen Mary 2 has two fibre-optic gyro compasses, which are electronic compasses that align themselves with true north. The information they give is sent to various repeaters throughout the ship and is used by the helmsman when steering and as an input into the Automatic Radar Plotting Aids, the Electronic Chart Display Information System (ECDIS), and satellite communication equipment. The officers still check the accuracy of the gyro several times a day by taking bearings on stars and the sun and comparing the compass bearing versus the calculated bearing that the astronomical body should read. Queen Mary 2 also carries a magnetic compass, which reads slightly differently from true north due to variations in magnetic fields around the world, as well as the influence of the magnetic field surrounding the ship. This magnetic field is influence- by the ship's steel and electrical equipment and changes according to the ship's heading.

GPS

The GPS, or Global Positioning System, utilizes 24 satellites circling the Earth to pinpoint Queen Mary 2's position and give instant course and speed made good of the vessel. The information from the GPS is fed to various equipment on the bridge,

驾驶室设备
电罗经和磁罗经

"玛丽女王 2 号"配有两个电子罗盘指向真北的光纤罗经，并将航向信息发送到全船的各个复视器上，供舵手在操舵时使用，同时也为自动雷达助航装置、电子海图系统和卫星通信系统提供舵向信息。通过将恒星相对太阳的定位轴线与在罗盘上读取到天体的定位轴线进行比较的方法，船员每天对罗经的精度进行几次检查。"玛丽女王 2 号"还携带一个磁罗盘，由于世界各地磁场的变化，以及船体周围磁场的影响，它的读数与真北略有不同。这些磁场受到船体的钢铁结构和电气设备影响，并根据船舶航向而变化。

全球定位系统

全球定位系统（GPS），利用 24 颗环绕地球的卫星以确定"玛丽女王 2 号"的位置，并给出即时的路线和对地船速。GPS 提供的数据被输入到驾驶室的各种设备中，包括雷达和电子海图。

including the radars and ECDIS. The GPS also has the capability to receive differential signals from shore-based stations, which correct any error in the position and increase the accuracy of the GPS from less than 100 metres to fewer than 10 metres, Two sextants are still carried on board as a backup and all officers are thoroughly trained in celestial navigation.

全球定位系统还能够接收来自岸基的差分信号,来纠正错误的位置信息并将GPS的精度从小于100米提高到小于10米,两个六分仪仍作为备品安装在船上,所有的船员都接受过天体导航方面的全面训练。

Autopilot

Queen Mary 2 is often steered by an autopilot, which sends signals to the pods to keep the vessel on a set heading. A quartermaster is always on the bridge, however, and the ship is steered by hand through a conventional wheel when approaching ports, in times of heavy traffic, or during restricted visibility from fog or rough weather. Because Queen Mary 2 needs 1.7 miles to stop from 28 knots and her turning diameter is approximately 0.8 mile, the officers usually arrange to pass ships at a distance of at least 1 nautical mile.

自动航行

"玛丽女王2号"经常在自动舵模式下航行,通过向吊舱发送信号来保持船舶的航向。同时,一个舵手需要常驻在驾驶室并在临近港口、交通繁忙、雾或恶劣天气限制能见度的情况下,采用传统的舵轮进行操舵。由于"玛丽女王2号"在28节航速下需要继续航行1.7英里才能完全停下来,转弯直径约为0.8英里,因此船员们在超越别船时通常预留至少1海里的距离。

中央操纵控制台包括舵轮,当不使用自动舵时,舵手通过舵轮手动操舵。(作者提供)

Global Maritime Distress and Safety System

GMDSS is a worldwide system that allows vessels to quickly transmit distress messages to both shore-based rescue centres as well as nearby vessels. The system also provides for more routine uses, such as weather forecasts or navigational information and warnings. The equipment consists of medium and high frequency radios with telex transceivers, VHF radios and two INMARSAT-C satellite terminals and largely replaces the radio officer of past years.

全球海事遇险及安全系统（GMDSS）

GMDSS 是一个世界范围的系统，允许船舶迅速向岸基救援中心以及附近船只发送遇险信息。该系统还提供更多的常规应用，如天气预报或航行信息和报警。该设备包括配备电报收发器的中频和高频无线电、甚高频无线电和两个国际海事卫星组织的卫星终端 C 站，其在很大程度上取代了过去早年的无线电报务员。

Whistles

Queen Mary 2 has four whistles: two on the funnel, one on the mast, and one on the bow. Of the two whistles on the funnel, the starboard one is the original whistle from the Queen Mary, while the port whistle is an accurate but modern replica. The forward whistles can be heard for over ten miles and are used for manoeuvring signals to other vessels and during periods of reduced visibility. AM whistles are tested every day at noon when at sea.

汽笛

"玛丽女王 2 号"有 4 个汽笛：两个在烟囱上，一个在桅杆上，一个在船首。在烟囱上的两个汽笛中，右舷的就是"玛丽女王号"上原来的那个，而左舷的汽笛则是个高仿的复制品，但是已经是现代化的设备了。艏部的汽笛声响可以覆盖超过 10 英里的范围，并在能见度低的情况下将船舶的操作信号发送给其他船舶。上述汽笛每天中午都在海上接受测试。

Kelvin Hughes MANTA system

At the heart of the navigation equipment is the Manta system, which consists of the electronic charts, radars and Computer Safety System.

Five flat screens with interchangeable displays allow the officers to choose which of the radar and chart displays they want shown. With integration allowing different units to 'talk' to each other and share information, the deck officer is able to more easily assimilate and make use of the available navigational information.

Electronic Chart Display Information Systems

Queen Mary 2 has two independent Electronic Chart Display Information Systems (ECDIS) as well as a separate Route Planning Terminal. One of the advantages of electronic charts is the instant access to navigational information, including speed required, estimated time of arrival, distance to go, or how far off track the vessel is. The digital-format charts from the Admiralty Raster Chart Service (ARCS) are either scanned versions of standard paper British Admiralty charts, or are 'Vector'-style charts, which allow the operator to choose various information layers within the chart and individually tailor the display. With the ECDIS, Queen Mary 2 is able to reduce the number

凯文·休斯公司 MANTA 系统

导航设备的核心是由电子海图、雷达和计算机安全系统组成的 Manta 系统。

5 台显示界面可以互通的平面显示器，让船员可以选择他们想要显示的雷达和海图。由于集成系统允许不同的单元相互"交谈"和分享信息，甲板部船员能够更容易地接收和利用导航设备的信息。

电子海图信息显示系统（ECDIS）

"玛丽女王 2 号"有两套独立的电子海图信息显示系统以及一个独立的航线规划终端。电子海图的优点之一是可以获取实时的导航信息，包括所需的船速、预计到达时间、剩余距离，或船舶距离目的地有多远。光栅格式航海海图服务（ARCS）提供的数字格式海图表要么是英国标准的纸质海图的扫描版本，要么是矢量格式的海图，允许操作人员在海图中选择各种信息的菜单，并单独定制显示。有了电子海图系统，"玛丽女王 2 号"能够减少 80% 的纸质海图携带数量。鉴于"伊丽莎白女王 2 号"携带了 1 800 张纸质海图，而"玛

of paper charts carried by 80%, and whereas 1,800 paper charts are carried on the QE2, on Queen Mary 2 all the world's charts can now be stored on only 11 CD-ROMs. Updates and corrections to reflect new soundings, changes in buoyage or other pertinent navigational equipment, is supplied weekly, ensuring that the charts are safely up to date. Paper charts are used for critical areas, and a chart table is provided on the starboard side of the bridge. Traditional navigational practices can still be used on electronic charts, as visual and radar ranges and bearings to points of land can be plotted on to the ECDIS, thereby verifying the accuracy of the GPS position.

Radars

Queen Mary 2 has five radar scanners and four radar processors. Four of these antennae can easily be seen rotating on the main mast and allow for long-range, forward-facing detection and navigation, while a fifth antenna is located on the stern and gives complete, 360 coverage. The stern radar is not usually used when at sea as the main radars provide an adequate long-range view astern, but the aft radar might be employed in congested waterways or harbour manoeuvring.

Two of the radars operate on a wavelength of 3 centimetres (which gives good definition) and two operate on a wavelength of 10 centimetres

丽女王 2 号"上的所有的海图都存储在 11 张光盘上。每周提供更新和修正来保证海图得到安全的更新，用以体现最新的测深、浮标变化或升级其他相关的导航设备。纸质海图用于关键区域，并在驾驶室的右舷设置海图桌。传统的航行操作仍然可以在电子海图上进行，因为通过目测或雷达确定的陆地方位轴线可以绘制到电子海图上，从而验证 GPS 的准确性。

雷达

"玛丽女王 2 号"有 5 台雷达扫描天线和 4 个雷达处理器。可以很容易地看到其中 4 个雷达天线在主桅杆上，可以长距离的面向艏向进行扫描探测和导航，而第五个天线则位于船尾，从而提供完整的 360° 雷达覆盖。在航行中船尾雷达通常不使用，因为主雷达在船尾方向提供了足够的远距离覆盖，但船尾雷达可能被用于拥挤的水道或港口作业。

其中两个雷达的操作波长为 3 厘米（提供好的扫描效果），两个雷达的操作波长为 10 厘米（从而能更好地穿

(which gives better penetration of rain and snow etc). While the radars provide excellent long-range detection, a lookout with binoculars is still the primary means of locating targets, and at night the bridge Is kept dark and all forward-facing lights are curtained off so as not to hamper the night vision of the lookout.

With the built-in Automatic Radar Plotting Aid (ARPA), over 40 targets can be tracked simultaneously. Any target's true course and speed, as well as its closest pant of approach, the time of its closest point of approach, how far ahead of the vessel's bow the target will cross, and other collision avoidance information, is instantly accessible on the radar. The ARPA Is an important tool for collision avoidance and graphic depiction of the target's true motion as well as relative motion towards Queen Mary 2 can also be displayed. Should the officer of the watch wish to alter course, the ARPA can predict both numerically and visually the expected path of targets based upon Queen Mary 2's intended new course and speed. With the integration of the bridge equipment, the course line can be overlaid on to the radar screen and radar targets along with their predicted motion can be overlaid from the radar on to the ECDIS display. This is a tremendous aid to navigation and collision avoidance, especially in congested waterways where course changes are frequent.

透雨雪等）。尽管雷达提供了良好的远程探测。通过望远镜进行瞭望仍然是定位目标的主要手段，而在夜间，桥楼保持黑暗并且所有向前的灯光都被遮蔽／关闭，以免妨碍瞭望台的夜视。

借助内置的自动雷达绘图辅助装置（ARPA），控制系统可以同时跟踪40多个目标。任何目标的真实航向和速度，以及其最近的接近点、达到最接近点的时间、目标与船首之间的距离、其他避免碰撞的信息，都可以立即在雷达上显示。ARPA是一个重要的工具，可以避免碰撞，并用图形描绘目标的真实运动，以及相对"玛丽女王2号"的运动趋势也可以显示出来。如果值班船员希望改变航向，ARPA可以根据"玛丽女王2号"的航向和速度，用数字模式或图形模式显示预测的路径。通过驾驶室航行设备的集成，可以将航线显示在雷达屏幕上，雷达目标及其预测的运动轨迹可以从雷达显示到电子海图显示屏上。这对航行和避免碰撞是一个巨大的帮助，特别是在需要频繁改变航线的拥堵航道中。

Computer Safety System

The Computer Safety System (CSS) allows the officer to monitor all safety systems throughout the ship and, with the detailed deck plans covering the entire vessel, have a visual indication of any developing situation.

All watertight doors, fire-screen doors, ventilation, low-level lighting and other safety systems can be operated through this system on the bridge and in the safety centre. While not actually a part of the CSS, other equipment on the bridge permits the officers to monitor engine performance, adjust the level in the heeling tanks to keep the craft upright, calculate the ship's stability or empty and fill all the swimming pools.

计算机安全系统（CSS）

计算机安全系统使船员能够监测整个船舶的所有安全系统，并配备全船的详细布置图，从而可以对任何状况设置可视化的指示。

所有水密门、防火门、通风闸、低位照明和其他安全系统都可以通过该系统在驾驶室和安全中心进行操作。虽然实际上不是 CSS 的一部分，但驾驶室的其他设备允许船员监控主机性能、调整倾斜水舱的液位以保持船身直立、计算船舶的稳性，指示排空或注满所有的泳池。

（译者：陈大为、叶涛、邓志鹏、韩鑫、邰洋、陈霖、孙哲）

凯文·休斯公司的雷达显示带有海岸线和船舶轨迹的海图，自动显示雷达扫射到的周围目标并计算出目标与本船的最接近点的数据。（作者提供）

Computer Safety System 计算机安全系统

计程仪和减摇装置（作者提供）

计程仪分显，罗经复视器，回转速率指示器，吊舱舵角指示器，吊舱转速指示器。（作者提供）

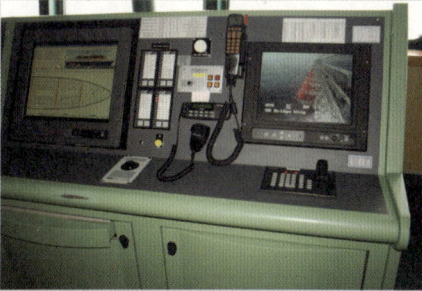

安全系统－摄像头监控台（作者提供）

广播和外部灯光控制台（作者提供）

对外通信控制台（作者提供）